MILTON
AND THE CHRISTIAN
TRADITION

Oxford University Press, Ely House, London W. 1

GLASGOW NEW YORK TORONTO MELBOURNE WELLINGTON
CAPE TOWN SALISBURY IBADAN NAIROBI LUSAKA ADDIS ABABA
BOMBAY CALCUTTA MADRAS KARACHI LAHORE DACCA
KUALA LUMPUR HONG KONG TOKYO

MILTON

AND THE CHRISTIAN

TRADITION

BY

C. A. PATRIDES

OXFORD
AT THE CLARENDON PRESS
1966

TO MY PARENTS

κρεῖττον γάρ που σμικρὸν εὖ ἢ πολὺ
μὴ ἱκανῶς περᾶναι

ACKNOWLEDGEMENTS

THE present study owes its completion to the two Fellowships I was awarded by the John Simon Guggenheim Memorial Foundation (1960–61 and 1963–4). In acknowledging my gratitude to the Foundation, I am particularly happy to express my thanks to Dr. Henry Allen Moe and Dr. Gordon N. Ray for their encouragement. In addition, I am indebted to the University of California at Berkeley and the University of York for a series of modest but annual grants, and to the American Council of Learned Societies for a substantial grant-in-aid that made the final phase of my research possible.

Of libraries where my investigations were pursued, two in particular should be named: the British Museum and the Bodleian Library. The manifold courtesies extended to me at both, and the extraordinary patience of their staffs, can never sufficiently be set forth by me. I do most gratefully acknowledge their services.

In some thirty-five studies published in various journals I have pursued matters that are here mentioned only in passing. Chapter VIII may be regarded as an exception, for there I give a shorter version of a monograph published in 1964. In a number of other cases I have undertaken drastic revisions with almost totally new documentation, while in the remaining instances I merely refer the reader to my separate articles. I am grateful to the University of California Press and the editors of the following publications for permission to adapt previously published material: *Franciscan Studies, Harvard Theological Review* (copyright by the President and Fellows of Harvard College), *Huntington Library Quarterly, Isis, Journal of English and Germanic Philology, Journal of the History of Ideas, Modern Language Notes, Modern Language Review, Neophilologus, Notes and Queries, Publications of the Modern Language Association of America, Philological Quarterly, Studia Neophilologica, Studies in English Literature, Studies in Philology, Studies in the Renaissance, Texas Studies in Literature and Language,* and *Theologische Zeitschrift.*

The expression of my indebtedness to individuals must begin with the late Charles M. Coffin, Professor of English at Kenyon College, who was the first to introduce me to Renaissance literature and to the subject of the present study. At Oxford University I was fortunate to have the patient and inspiring supervision of Dr. M. E. Seaton, of St. Hugh's College, and The Revd. I. T. Ramsey, the Nolloth Professor of Christian Philosophy. Since then, as the scope of my work was enlarged with the present study, my debts have multiplied accordingly. I wish to thank L. J. Ludovici, who has devoted his high professional skills as author and editor to my manuscript; J. P. Brockbank, who has improved these pages through a host of detailed suggestions; Douglas Bush, V. H. Galbraith, Merritt Y. Hughes, Marjorie H. Nicolson, and Joseph H. Summers, who have encouraged me precisely when their authoritative judgements were most needed; Roland M. Frye, William B. Hunter, and T. F. Torrance, who have liberally imparted to me of their knowledge of theology; Dorothee Finkelstein and Wayne Shumaker, who have patiently read and corrected endless pages; and J. F. de Freitas, who has contributed his unfailing interest and support.

I am also pleased to acknowledge the generous assistance of the following critics and scholars, for their encouragement at crucial moments or for their constructive observations on parts of the present study: J. H. Adamson, B. H. Bronson, John Carey, M. C. D'Arcy, S.J., Hugh G. Dick, C. S. Duthie, Wallace K. Ferguson, Willard Farnham, Helen Gardner, Myron P. Gilmore, T. Francis Glasson, James H. Hanford, Frank L. Huntley, Sears Jayne, Charles W. Jones, J. E. Kramer, William G. Madsen, E. L. Mascall, R. L. P. Milburn, Josephine Miles, A. D. Momigliano, G. F. Nuttall, William R. Parker, F. T. Prince, Marjorie Reeves, Irene Samuel, Mark Schorer, Henry Nash Smith, John M. Steadman, Arnold Stein, E. W. Strong, Kester Svendsen, Ernest L. Tuveson, Robert H. West, Arnold Williams, and Don M. Wolfe. To my profound regret, six scholars to whom I owe very much died recently: E. M. W. Tillyard and J. Milton French in 1962, F. P. Wilson, C. S. Lewis, and J. B. Leishman in 1963, and Rosemond Tuve in 1964.

C. A. P.

Langwith College
University of York
16 November 1965

CONTENTS

ABBREVIATIONS

THE place of publication is given only if it is other than London or New York.

Milton's poetry is quoted from *The Poetical Works of John Milton*, ed. Helen Darbishire (Oxford, 1952–55), 2 vols. Quotations from Milton's prose are from *The Works of John Milton*, gen. ed. Frank A. Patterson (1931–40), 20 vols., hereafter cited as *Works*.

Spenser and seventeenth-century poets are quoted from the Oxford English Texts; Shakespeare from the edition by W. A. Neilson and C. J. Hill (Cambridge, Mass., 1942). Biblical quotations are from the A.V.; the poetry is typographically distinguished from the prose in accordance with *The Reader's Bible* (1951).

The following abbreviations are used in the notes:

ACW	*Ancient Christian Writers*, ed. Johannes Quasten and J. C. Plumpe (Westminister, Md., 1946 ff.).
Ames	William Ames, *The Marrow of Sacred Divinity*, tr. Anon. (1642).
ANCL	*Ante-Nicene Christian Library* (Buffalo, 1884 ff.).
Angl.	*Anglicanism: The Thought and Practice of the Church of England, illustrated from the religious literature of the Seventeenth Century*, ed. P. E. More and F. L. Cross (1935).
Arminius	*The Works of James Arminius*, tr. James Nichols (1825–75), 3 vols.
Athanasius, *De Inc.*	*De Incarnatione Verbi Dei*, tr. James Ridgway (Oxford, 1880).
Augustine, *Conf.*	*Confessiones*, tr. William Watts (1631) [sometimes cited in the revised version by W. H. D. Rouse (1912)].
—— *De civ.*	*De civitate Dei*, tr. John Healey (1610) [compared with the revised version by R. V. G. Tasker (1945)].
AV	The King James ('Authorized') Version of the Bible (1611).
Baxter	Richard Baxter, *The Saints Everlasting Rest*, 2nd rev. ed. (1651).
Browne, *RM*	Sir Thomas Browne, *Religio Medici*, ed. J.-J. Denonain (Cambridge, 1955).
Bucanus	Gulielmus Bucanus, *Institutions of Christian Religion*, tr. Robert Hill (1606).
Bullinger	Heinrich Bullinger, *Common Places of Christian Religion*, tr. John Stockwood (1572).

Calvin, *Comm.*	*Commentaries*, ed. D. W. and T. F. Torrance (Edinburgh, 1959 ff.).
—— *Inst.*	*Institutio christianae religionis* (definitive edition: 1559), tr. Thomas Norton (1561) [compared with the revised version by Henry Beveridge (Edinburgh, 1845–6)].
Cassirer	Ernst Cassirer, *The Individual and the Cosmos in Renaissance Philosophy*, tr. Mario Domandi (1963).
CH	*Church History.*
CL	*Comparative Literature.*
Conf. Aug.	*Confessio Augustana*: The Confession of Augsburg (1530).
Copleston	Frederick Copleston, S. J., *A History of Philosophy*, ii (1950), and iii (1953).
Corcoran	Sister Mary Irma Corcoran, *Milton's Paradise with Reference to the Hexameral Background* (Washington, D.C., 1945).
CQR	*Church Quarterly Review.*
Dante, *Inf.*	*Inferno*, tr. J. A. Carlyle; *Purgatorio*, tr. Thomas Okey;
—— *Purg.*	*Paradiso*, tr. Philip H. Wicksteed (repr. 1941–6),
—— *Par.*	3 vols.
Denzinger	Heinrich Denzinger, *Enchiridion symbolorum*, tr. Roy J. Deferrari, *The Sources of Catholic Dogma* (St. Louis, 1957).
Donne, *Essays*	*Essays in Divinity*, ed. E. M. Simpson (Oxford, 1952).
—— *Sermons*	*The Sermons of John Donne*, ed. E. M. Simpson and G. R. Potter (Berkeley and Los Angeles, 1953–62), 10 vols.
DR	*The Downside Review.*
Du Bartas	Guillaume de Salluste du Bartas, *Deuine Weekes and Workes*, tr. Joshua Sylvester (1611).
ELH	*Journal of English Literary History.*
Erasmus, *Ep.*	*Epistles*, tr. F. M. Nichols (1901–18), 3 vols.
—— *De lib. arb.*	*De libero arbitrio* (1524), tr. Ernst F. Winter [with excerpts from Luther's *De serv. arb.*] (1961).
ES	*English Studies.*
ESEA	*Essays and Studies* by members of the English Association.
FC	*The Fathers of the Church*, ed. L. Schopp (1947 ff.).
Ficino, *Comm.*	Marsilio Ficino, *Commentarium in convivium Platonis*, ed. and tr. Sears Jayne, University of Missouri Studies, xix (1944), §1.
Frye	Roland M. Frye, *Shakespeare and Christian Doctrine* (Princeton, 1963).
FS	*Franciscan Studies.*
Gerhard	Johann Gerhard, *The Summe of Christian Doctrine*, tr. Ralph Winterton (Cambridge, 1640).
Ginzberg	Louis Ginzberg, *The Legends of the Jews*, tr. Henrietta Szold (Philadelphia, 1909–38), 7 vols.

Goulart	Simon Goulart, *A Learned Summary upon the famous Poeme of William of Saluste Lord of Bartas*, tr. Thomas Lodge (1621).
Harnack	Adolph Harnack, *History of Dogma*, tr. Neil Buchanan *et al.* (repr. 1958), 7 vols.
Heppe	Heinrich Heppe, *Reformed Dogmatics, set out and illustrated from the sources*, ed. Ernst Bizer, tr. G. T. Thomson (1950).
HLQ	*Huntington Library Quarterly*.
Hom. I	*Certayne Sermons, or Homelies, appoynted by the Kynges Maiestie* (1547).
Hom. II	*The Second Tome of Homelyes* (1563).
Hooker	Richard Hooker, *Of the Lawes of Ecclesiasticall Politie* (1617).
HR	*Bibliothèque d'humanisme et renaissance.*
HTR	*Harvard Theological Review.*
JEGP	*Journal of English and Germanic Philology.*
JHI	*Journal of the History of Ideas.*
JR	*Journal of Religion.*
JTS	*Journal of Theological Studies.*
JWCI	*Journal of the Warburg and Courtauld Institutes.*
Kelly	J. N. D. Kelly, *Early Christian Doctrines*, 2nd ed. (1960).
Kirkconnell	Watson Kirkconnell, ed., *The Celestial Cycle: The Theme of 'Paradise Lost' in World Literature* (Toronto, 1952).
KR	*Kenyon Review.*
LACT	*Library of Anglo-Catholic Theology* (Oxford, 1841 ff.).
LCC	*Library of Christian Classics*, ed. John Baillie *et al.* (1953 ff.).
LF	*A Library of Fathers of the Holy Catholic Church* (Oxford, 1838 ff.).
Luther, *De serv. arb.*	*De servo arbitrio* (1525), tr. J. I. Packer and O. R. Johnston (1957).
—— *Table-Talk*	*Tischreden*, tr. Henry Bell, *Colloquia mensalia* (1652).
—— *Works*	*Luther's Works*, ed. Jaroslav Pelikan and H. T. Lehman (St. Louis, 1959 ff.).
LXX	The Greek version of the OT: the Septuagint (third cent. B.C. ?).
McColley I	Grant McColley, '*Paradise Lost*', *HTR*, xxxii (1939), 181–235.
McColley II	Grant McColley, '*Paradise Lost*' : *An Account of its Growth and Major Origins* (Chicago, 1940).
Madsen	William G. Madsen, 'The Idea of Nature in Milton's Poetry', in *Three Studies in the Renaissance* (New Haven, 1958 [Yale Studies in English, cxxxviii]), pp. 181–283.
Melanchthon, *LC*	*Loci communes* [the 1521 ed.], tr. C. L. Hill (Boston, 1944).
Milton, *Comus*	*A Mask presented at Ludlow Castle* (publ. 1637).

Milton, *DDC*	*De doctrina christiana* (discovered 1823; publ. 1825).
—— *DDD*	*The Doctrine and Discipline of Divorce* (publ. 1643).
—— *Nativity Ode*	*On the Morning of Christ's Nativity* (publ. 1645).
—— *PL*	*Paradise Lost* (publ. 1667; 2nd rev. ed. 1674).
—— *PR*	*Paradise Regained* (publ. 1671).
—— *RCG*	*The Reason of Church Government urg'd against Prelaty* (publ. 1642).
—— *SA*	*Samson Agonistes* (publ. 1671).
MLN	*Modern Language Notes.*
MLQ	*Modern Language Quarterly.*
MLR	*Modern Language Review.*
MP	*Modern Philology.*
Musculus	Wolfgang Musculus, *Common Places of Christian Religion* tr. John Man (1563).
NPNF	*Nicene and Post-Nicene Fathers* (Buffalo: 1st Series, 1886 ff.; 2nd Series, 1890 ff.).
NQ	*Notes and Queries.*
NS	*New Scholasticism.*
NT	New Testament.
NT Apocr.	*The Apocryphal New Testament*, tr. Montagu R. James (Oxford, 1924; repr. 1953).
Origen, *C. Cels.*	*Contra Celsum*, tr. Henry Chadwick (Cambridge, 1953).
—— *De pr.*	*De principiis*, tr. G. W. Butterworth (1936).
OT	Old Testament.
OT Pseud.	*The Apocrypha and Pseudepigrapha of the Old Testament*, ed. R. H. Charles (Oxford, 1913; repr. 1963), vol. ii: *Pseudepigrapha.*
Pascal	*Pensées*, ed. Jacques Chevalier, *Œuvres complètes* (Paris, 1957), pp. 1081–1345; tr. J. M. Cohen (Harmondsworth, Middx., 1961).
Patr. g.	*Patrologia*, Series graeca, ed. J.-P. Migne (Paris, 1857 ff.).
Patr. l.	*Patrologia*, Series latina, ed. J.-P. Migne (Paris, 1844 ff.).
PBA	*Proceedings of the British Academy.*
Perkins	William Perkins, *An Exposition of the Symbole* (Cambridge, 1595).
PMLA	*Publications of the Modern Language Association of America.*
PQ	*Philological Quarterly.*
PR	*Philosophical Review.*
QQ	*Queen's Quarterly.*
Rajan	Balachandra Rajan, '*Paradise Lost*' *and the Seventeenth Century Reader* (1947).
Ralegh	Sir Walter Ralegh, *The History of the World* (1614).
RES	*Review of English Studies.*
Robb	Nesca A. Robb, *Neoplatonism of the Italian Renaissance* (1935).
RPM	*The Renaissance Philosophy of Man*, ed. Ernst Cassirer et al. (Chicago, 1948).
RR	*Review of Religion.*

RSR	*Recherches de science religieuse.*
Schaff	Philip Schaff, ed., *The Creeds of Christendom*, 4th ed. (1877), 3 vols.
Scholem	Gershom G. Scholem, *Major Trends in Jewish Mysticism*, 2nd rev. ed. (repr. 1961).
SEL	*Studies in English Literature.*
SJT	*Scottish Journal of Theology.*
SN	*Studia Neophilologica.*
SP	*Studies in Philology.*
SQ	*Shakespeare Quarterly.*
SR	*Studies in the Renaissance.*
SS	*Shakespeare Survey.*
Svendsen	Kester Svendsen, *Milton and Science* (Cambridge, Mass., 1956).
Talmud	*The Babylonian Talmud*, gen. ed. Isidore Epstein (1935–52), 35 vols.
Tappert	Theodore G. Tappert, ed. & tr., *The Book of Concord: The Confessions of the Evangelical Lutheran Church* (Philadelphia, 1959).
Thomas Aquinas, *S. th.*	*Summa theologica*, tr. by the English Dominican Fathers (1911–25), 22 vols.
—— *S. c. Gent.*	*Summa contra gentiles*, tr. as before (1924–9), 4 vols.
Tixeront	L. J. Tixeront, *History of Dogmas*, tr. H. L. B. (St. Louis, 1910–16), 3 vols.
TLS	*The Times Literary Supplement.*
Trelcatius	Lucas Trelcatius, *A Briefe Institution of Common Places of Sacred Divinitie*, tr. John Gaven (1610).
TS	*Theological Studies.*
TSLL	*Texas Studies in Literature and Language.*
TZ	*Theologische Zeitschrift.*
Ursinus	Zacharias Ursinus, *The Summe of Christian Religion*, tr Henry Parry (Oxford, 1595).
UTQ	*University of Toronto Quarterly.*
Vulg.	St. Jerome's Latin version of the Bible: the 'Vulgate' (*c.* 384–404).
West. Conf.	*The Confession of Faith, together with the Larger and Lesser Catechismes, composed by the Reverend Assembly of Divines sitting at Westminster* (1658).
Whale I	J. S. Whale, *Christian Doctrine* (Cambridge, 1952).
Whale II	J. S. Whale, *The Protestant Tradition* (Cambridge, 1955; repr. 1959).
Whiting	George W. Whiting, *Milton's Literary Milieu* (Chapel Hill, 1939).
Williams	Arnold Williams, *The Common Expositor: An Account of the Commentaries on Genesis 1527–1633* (Chapel Hill, 1948).
Wolleb	Johann Wolleb, *The Abridgment of Christian Divinitie*, tr. Alexander Ross (1650).

XXXIX Art. The Thirty-Nine Articles of the Church of England, cited from E. J. Bicknell's *Theological Introduction* etc., 2nd ed. (1925).

Zanchius Hieronymus Zanchius, *The Whole Body of Christian Religion*, tr. Ralph Winterton (1659).

TO THE READER

τὴν ἐξ ἀρχῆς παράδοσιν καὶ διδασκαλίαν καὶ πίστιν τῆς καθολικῆς Ἐκκλησίας, ἣν ὁ μὲν Κύριος ἔδωκεν, οἱ δὲ ἀπόστολοι ἐκήρυξαν, καὶ οἱ πατέρες ἐφύλαξαν.

ST. ATHANASIUS, *Epistola ad Serapionem*, I. 28

THE centre of the present study is Milton's conception and presentation of the principal themes of the Christian faith. Its circumference is the Christian tradition: in Donne's words, not so much the singularities of 'left-handed men' as the 'intirenesse that goes through the whole Church'.[1]

Yet 'tradition', it would seem, is hardly the appropriate term to use in connexion with Milton or indeed any Protestant of his age. After all, we are well aware of the persistent Protestant view that the Bible—'the head and Empress of all faculties and Arts', 'the Encyclopædia of all knowledge'—should be accorded absolute primacy as 'the ground of all, the touchstone to try all, and the Iudge to determine of all truth'.[2] From such sweeping assertions we are led to the rejection of *humanae traditiones*, categorically affirmed by Milton ('We are expressly forbidden to pay any regard to human traditions, whether written or unwritten') no less than by individuals who went on to denounce, with mounting hysteria, 'vnwritten traditions, Popes decretalls, Scholemens labyrinths, Iesuites Pamphlets, or Seminary Priests buzzing suggestions'.[3] Extreme statements of this nature, irresponsibly translated by Catholics, led to the wild impression that Protestants had reduced the accumulated wisdom of the Church to a position 'inferiour euerie way' to themselves.[4] In the heat of controversy there was a real danger that 'tradition' would

---

[1] *Sermons*, vii. 239; x. 113.

[2] Seriatim: Luther, *Table-Talk*, p. 4; Daniel Price, *The Marchant* (Oxford, 1608), p. 8; Griffith Williams, *The True Church* (1629), p. 123. Milton's statement ('the rule and canon of faith is Scripture alone' (*Works*, xvi. 267)) is a reaffirmation of the Protestant view that the Bible is 'the only rule and norm according to which all doctrines and teachers alike must be appraised and judged' (The Formula of Concord (1557), in Tappert, p. 464).

[3] Milton, *DDC*, *Works*, xvi. 281, and Robert Barrell, *The Spirituall Architecture* (1624), p. 12.

[4] Lawrence Anderton (?), *Epigrammes* (Rouen, c. 1630), p. 86.

B

be ostracized from the Protestant movement, inevitably creating a proliferation of fantastic extremes abhorrent even to the least reasonable partisan of the Reformation.

In certain cases, as at Münster, this is precisely what did happen. Fortunately for Protestantism, however, responsible thinkers soon intervened and in time devised the formula that to this day stands at the centre of the theology of all Protestant denominations. Lucidly stated by Calvin, this formula called for the adjustment of the decrees of Councils and the opinions of the Fathers to 'the standard of Scripture'; for thus, Calvin observed, 'Coũcels should haue the maiestie that they ought: but in the meane season the Scripture should be alone in the hier place, that there might be nothing that shold not be subiect to the rule therof.'[1] Thereafter, in express answer to Catholic misrepresentations, the note sounded by Andrew Willet in 1602 ('Traditions we absolutely condemne not') is heard repeatedly. 'We reuerence the Fathers', declared John White, 'and study their writings, and thereby attaine to great knowledge in things concerning our faith, & account their books as most excellent monuments of antiquitie; but we allow the Scripture onely to be judge, whereby we trie both the Fathers and our selues.'[2] The seeming censure of the Fathers continued none the less, as in Samuel Gibson's charge in 1616 that 'they agree not amongst themselves, but are one *opposite* to another in many things, and amongst many *Truths* haue some great Errors'—yet even in this statement, we observe, no attempt is made to deny the validity of the 'truths' expounded by the Fathers. This reasonable attitude of reasonable men was finally summed up in the moving plea of Anthony White in 1628: 'I onely call for so much modesty, and good manners, that when wee perceaue a doctrine to bee generally receaued, by holy and learned men, in our owne and elder Churches, we take them along

---

[1] *Inst.* IV. ix. 8. On the Protestant view of 'tradition' see further the full expositions by Martin Chemnitz, *Examinis Concilii Tridentini* (Frankfurt, 1596), i. 60 ff.; Lucas Osiander, *A Manuell . . . of Controuersies*, tr. Anon. (1606), ch. iv; Bullinger (below, p. 3, n. 2), chs. xxi–xxv; François de Croi, *The Three Conformities*, tr. W. Hart (1620), Bk. III, ch. x; Jean Daillé, *A Treatise concerning the Right Vse of the Fathers*, tr. Thomas Smith (1651); Robert Tynley, *Two Learned Sermons* (1609), pp. 32–43; Robert Mossom, *The Preacher's Tripartite* (1657), iii. 99–116. Melanchthon's attitude has been fully studied by Peter Fraenkel, *Testimonia Patrum* (Geneva, 1961). The Catholic position is stated by Edmund Lechmere, *A Disputation of the Church* (Douai, 1632), Bk. v, chs. i–ii; on the Tridentine decree on 'tradition' consult Maurice Bévenot, S.J., *The Heythrop Journal*, iv (1963), 333–43. Cf. J. Pelikan, *Obedient Rebels* (1964), Pt. i.

[2] Willet, *A Catholicon* (Cambridge, 1602), p. 54; White, *The Way to the True Church*, 4th impr. (1616), p. 325.

with vs in our inquiry after truth, and not hastily breake from them, to follow our owne way vpon a presumptuous conceit of our owne iudgements.'[1]

To such a presumption—common in the sixteenth century as it was to be in the seventeenth—Heinrich Bullinger had also addressed himself earlier, beginning with a severe attack on 'those wanton wits . . . which doe despise the catholike vnderstanding and consent of the Church, and al councels without difference', and ending with the astonishing declaration—perilously close to the Tridentine assertion—that 'the true vnderstanding or interpretation of the Scripture belongeth to the Church'.[2] On less passionate occasions, however, Bullinger reverted to the distinctly Protestant position, as in the Second Helvetic Confession of 1566 where he summarily observed that 'we do not despise the interpretations of the holy Greek and Latin Fathers, nor reject their disputations and treatises as far as they agree with the Scriptures; but we do modestly dissent from them when they are found to set down things differing from, or altogether contrary to, the Scriptures.'[3] This was to be the attitude of Milton as well, who unhesitatingly rejected human traditions if they happened to conflict with what he considered to be the sense of the Scriptures, yet readily invoked the Fathers if he found them supporting his individual—Protestant—interpretation of a particular idea.[4] In all, as I shall have occasion to demonstrate later, Milton accepted the Protestant view that the only substantial extra-Biblical exponents of the truth were the primitive Christians: not indeed Epiphanius, who had commended tradition as an independent authority (οὐ γὰρ πάντα ἀπὸ τῆς θείας Γραφῆς δύναται λαμβάνεσθαι), but such defenders of the faith as St. Athanasius, who had proclaimed the validity of the original tradition and teaching and faith of the universal Church as given by the Lord Jesus, taught by his apostles, and upheld by the Fathers.[5]

---

[1] Gibson, *The Only Rule* (1616), p. 11; White, *Truth and Error Discovered* (Oxford, 1628), p. 48. See further Whale II, pp. 129 ff.

[2] *The Woorthynesse . . . of the Holy Scripture*, tr. John Tomkys (1579), fol. 77ᵛ. On the Council of Trent see Schaff, ii. 83.

[3] *Confessio helvetica posterior*, II (Schaff, iii. 833).

[4] Thus in *DDC*, in connexion with his affirmation of traducianism, Milton invoked Tertullian, Apollinarius, Gregory of Nyssa, and Augustine (*Works*, xv. 42, 194).

[5] Epiphanius, *Adversus haereses*, LXI, 6; Athanasius [quoted at the outset, above]. On 'tradition' in the early Church see Tixeront, iii. 6 ff., 313 ff.; Harnack, iii. 191–239; G. L. Prestige, *Fathers and Heretics* (1940), Lect. I; Nicholas Arseniev, Louis Bouyer, *et al.*, in *Tradition and Scripture*, being the supplementary issue of *The Eastern Churches*

If nominally Protestants focused their attention on the early Church, in reality they ranged all too freely over the formidable array of theologians from the patristic age to the Reformation and the late Renaissance. While there were, of course, favourites—St. Augustine ('the most judicious of all the Fathers'),[1] St. John Chrysostom, St. Bernard of Clairvaux—we must not forget that the history of thought rarely progresses from peak to peak but, more often than not, rolls across hill-tops and frequently descends to the valleys below. Students of the Renaissance generally and of Milton in particular, hesitating to look across such a seemingly endless vista, have often restricted themselves to one figure[2] or even to one minor work,[3] not always with happy results. Perhaps what is needed—at least on occasion—is a cosmic view that embraces the 'characteristicall truthes' of the faith no less than those 'marginal and interlineary notes' which, though of slight consequence to the salvation of the individual, are yet of vital importance in the investigation of the general order of ideas characteristic of the intellectual and spiritual temper of an age.[4] The present study, I should insist, has not necessarily attained to such a cosmic vision; but I have at least glanced at most of the peaks and a number of the hill-tops, including as many as possible of the writers in Peter Sterry's list: 'Commentators, Common-placers, Controversiaries, School-men, all sorts of Divines in general'.[5] My aim has been to write not an exhaustive study, which would be impossible, but only a partial introduction—mere prolegomena—to an utterly fascinating age.

I suppose it is hardly necessary to insist that my concern with the traditional aspects of Milton's thought is not meant to detract from the obvious uniqueness of his achievement. I am well aware—as

Quarterly, vii (1947); R. P. C. Hanson, Origen's Doctrine of Tradition (1954), ch. i, and Tradition in the Early Church (1962); G. W. H. Lampe, in Scripture and Tradition, ed. F. W. Dillistone (1955), ch. ii; and Oscar Cullmann, The Early Church, ed. A. J. B. Higgins (1956), ch. iv.

[1] Daniel Featley, Clavis mystica (1636), p. 409. I do not mention Thomas Aquinas on purpose, for I am not convinced of his popularity during the seventeenth century (notwithstanding John K. Ryan's thesis in NS, xxii (1948), 1–33, 126–208). The only definite instances of his invocation I know are noted below, pp. 81 ff., 89 f.

[2] The latest effort is by Harry F. Robins, If this be Heresy: A Study of Milton and Origen (Urbana, 1962), which I reviewed in JEGP, lxiv (1965), 586–9.

[3] Cf. George C. Taylor, 'Did Milton read Robert Crofts' A Paradise Within Us or the Happie Mind [1640]?' PQ, xxviii (1949), 207–10.

[4] The quoted phrases are from Nicholas Byfield, The Paterne of Wholsome Words (1618), p. 7, and Donne, Sermons, viii. 309.

[5] The Spirit convincing of Sinne (1645), p. 2.

indeed any student of Renaissance literature must be—that Milton's peculiar power consists precisely in this, that he used traditional ideas in such a way that they were transformed into seeming novelties. If this is spectacularly true of *Lycidas*,[1] it is also true of the other minor poems, of *Samson Agonistes*, and of the two epics. Such is the total picture of which these prolegomena presume to consider only a part.

Before I turn to other matters, another word of caution: my references to the Christian tradition are not meant to imply that I shall deal with the 'characteristicall truthes' of Christianity at the expense of the distinctly Protestant aspects of Milton and the thinkers of his persuasion. Indeed, I have been less than sympathetic toward the occasional efforts to make *Paradise Lost*—in the words of one Catholic writer—'capable of being read as a poem embodying theological doctrines in conformity with those of the Catholic Church'.[2] *Paradise Lost* is not a Christian poem generally; it is, rather, a Christian *Protestant* poem, and attempts to make it doctrinally palatable to Catholic readers do violence to its unique position as *the* epic of Protestantism. Assuredly the coincidence of Catholic and Protestant ideas is of considerable significance and may not be overlooked; but their differences, I should think, are of greater import still, and to disregard them is to distort our under-standing of the order of ideas characteristic of the seventeenth century. Hence my repeated stress in the pages that follow on the emphatically Protestant burden of *Paradise Lost*; hence also my refusal to dismiss Milton's constant pleas against the toleration of Catholics, or—further afield—to overlook the persistent Protestant identification of the Pope with the Antichrist. We may not thrill to Calvin's view of Catholic priests ('filthie bastardes'),[3] yet in this and other instances we shall at least glance into the seething cauldron that was the Renaissance, appreciating the fervour of the whole by the intensity of the part. In all, then, the present study encompasses the 'characteristicall truthes' of historical and traditional Christianity

---

[1] See my edition of *Milton's 'Lycidas': The Tradition and the Poem* (1961).

[2] Sister Miriam Joseph, C.S.C., 'Orthodoxy in *PL*', *Laval théologique et philosophique*, viii (1952), 243–84. Cf. Sister Mary Irma Corcoran's essay on *PL*, in *The Great Books: A Christian Appraisal*, ed. H. C. Gardiner (1951), iii. 89–96.

[3] *Sermons . . . upon . . . Galatians*, tr. Arthur Golding (1574), fol. 225ᵛ. The kindest concession was to say that Roman Catholicism contains 'much' Christianity (Joseph Mede, *Diatribæ* (1642), p. 75). Sir Thomas Browne's generosity (*RM*, i. 3) was un-common; normally 'popery' was not allowed one iota of Christianity.

but finally expands so as to include the specifically Protestant manifestation of the cumulative Christian tradition as reflected in the current of thought contemporary with Milton. In this last respect I have followed Miles Mosse's advice to 'all young Diuines' in 1614 to traverse 'the worthie writings of *Luther, Melancthon, Calvin, Beza, Zanchius, Musculus,* and the like'.[1] If I have often strayed from these eminent theologians to the popular writers of the Renaissance and even to less obviously relevant writers—the legendary thrice-great Hermes, the compilers of cabbalistic fantasies and all similar 'human traditions' generally—that was because I was mindful of Irenaeus's dictum that 'with God there is nothing without purpose or due signification' (*nihil enim vacuum, neque sine signo apud Deum*). The way of truth may be one, yet as Clement of Alexandria observed, 'into it, as into a perennial river, streams flow from all sides' (μία μὲν οὖν ἡ τῆς ἀληθείας ὁδός· ἀλλ᾽ εἰς αὐτήν, καθάπερ εἰς ἀέναον ποταμόν, ἐκρέουσι τὰ ῥεῖθρα ἄλλα ἄλλοθεν).[2]

[1] *Iustifying and Saving Faith* (Cambridge, 1614), p. 13.
[2] Irenaeus, *Adversus haereses*, IV. xxi. 3 (*Patr. g.* vii. 1046; *ANCL*, v. 453), and Clement, *Stromata*, I. 5 (*Patr. g.* viii. 720; *ANCL*, iv. 366).

I

The Fountain of Light
THE DOCTRINE OF THE GODHEAD

as the Sunne riseth, not to stand still, but to goe forward,
not to darken, but to enlighten the earth: so thou wast
borne, not to continue a childe, but encrease in true knowledge of thy Creator.

HUMPHREY EVERINDEN[1]

I

THE invitation extended traditionally to increase our 'true knowledge' of God has always been much qualified. The Lord had himself
served notice through Isaiah that

> my thoughts are not your thoughts,
> Neither are your ways my ways . . .
> For as the heavens are higher than the earth,
> So are my ways higher than your ways,
> And my thoughts than your thoughts.
> (Isa. lv. 8–9)

In *Paradise Lost* Raphael repeatedly warns Adam that the divine
secrets should be admired rather than scanned (VIII. 72–75), that

> Heav'n is for thee too high
> To know what passes there; be lowlie wise:
> Think onely what concernes thee and thy being.
> (VIII. 172–4)

Francis Quarles in 1640 reiterated these common exhortations. 'Be
not over curious in prying into Mysteries', he wrote, 'lest, by seeking
things which are needlesse, thou omittest things which are necessary.'[2] Milton's Adam, immediately after his creation, spontaneously

---

[1] *A Brothers Gift* (1623), § 14.
[2] *Enchyridion* (1640), sig. G3ᵛ. See also below, p. 118.

acknowledged the same admonition to the Vision Bright that appeared before him:

> To attaine
> The highth and depth of thy Eternal wayes
> All human thoughts come short, Supream of things.
>
> (VIII. 412–14)

Milton's contemporaries also acknowledged it in a variety of ways. Man, according to one of the most popular, 'whose understanding is only perpendicular, and measures all things by streight lines', cannot possibly comprehend God 'with whom circles are straight lines, and strait lines are Angles'.[1] Numerous writers, typifying the Renaissance fondness for examples, obligingly retold this old story:

> *Simonides* the Poet, being demanded by *Hiero* the Tyrant, what God was, craved a day to deliberate; and not being then able to define the true Nature and Essence of God, hee craved two daies more; that time being past, and himselfe yet unresolved, hee craved four dayes, still doubting his number: and being demanded the reason hereof, hee answered, that the more he studied and dived into that abysse, the lesse able was hee to define what God was; so incomprehensible is Gods Essence.[2]

Too often the fundamental principle involved here was laboriously stated, but Richard Hooker proclaimed it once in the measured strides of a master prose-writer when he wrote:

> Dangerous it were for the feeble braine of man to wade farre into the doings of the most High; whom although to know be life, and ioy to make mention of his name; yet our soundest knowledge is, to know that wee know him not as indeede he is, neither can know him; and our safest eloquence concerning him is our silence when wee confesse with our confession, that his glory is inexplicable, his greatnesse aboue our capacitie and reach. He is aboue, and we vpon earth; therefore it behooueth our words to be warie and few.[3]

---

[1] Sir Richard Baker, *Meditations*, 4th ed. (1640), p. 31.

[2] Charles Anthony, *Gods Presence Mans Comfort* (1646), p. 10. The story, which is mentioned by Cicero (*De natura deorum*, I. 22), is also related by Calvin, *Inst.* I. v. 12; Barnaby Rich, *Faultes* (1606), fol. 32ᵛ, and *Opinion Deified* (1613), p. 1; John Lewis, *Ignis cœlestis* (1620), p. 1; Nicholas Ling, *Politeuphuia* (1626?), p. 4; John Randall, *The Great Mysterie*, 2nd ed. (1630), p. 1; Thomas Heywood, *The Hierarchie of the Blessed Angells* (1635), p. 78; Byshop (below, p. 14, n. 3); David Person, *Varieties* (1635), iv. 191 f.; John Robinson, *Essayes*, 2nd ed. (1638), pp. 4 f.; *et al.*

[3] Hooker, p. 4. Milton in *DDC* also stresses God's incomprehensible nature, invoking Ps. cxlv. 3 and Is. xl. 28 (*Works*, xiv. 60).

Christian apologists, always aware that man's words can hardly be 'warie and few', endorsed two main approaches to all 'things invisible to mortal sight'. In Milton's *De doctrina christiana* these two approaches are simply termed 'negative' and 'affirmative'. John Donne explained them as follows:

Sometimes we represent God by Substraction, by Negation, by saying, God is that, which is not mortall, not passible, nor moveable: Sometimes we present him by Addition; by adding our bodily lineaments to him, and saying, that God hath hands, and feet, and eares, and eyes; and adding our affections, and passions to him, and saying that God is glad, or sorry, angry, or reconciled.[1]

The 'negative' approach, associated commonly with such notable exponents of the *theologia negativa* as the pseudo-Dionysius in the fifth century, Duns Scotus in the thirteenth, and Nicholas of Cusa in the fifteenth, has actually overflowed its partisan bounds to become one with the mainstream of Christian ideas. The 'affirmative' approach proved even more popular, especially when in time it appeared as the theory of 'accommodation'. Donne's statement, just quoted, enjoys support from a host of like pronouncements asserting variously that 'God speaks to us after the manner of men', that he 'illustrate[s] heavenly truths by earthly resemblances', that he 'condescendeth to our capacities in a more familiar and delightful way, so as to teach us by *Comparisons* and *Similitudes*, the better to imprint in our hearts and memories what so nearly concerns us'.[2]

---

[1] *Sermons*, viii. 54. Milton's statement is in *Works*, xiv. 53; on Donne see further Arnold Stein, *John Donne's Lyrics* (Minneapolis, 1962), pp. 175 ff.

[2] Seriatim: Richard Sibbes, *Bowels Opened* (1641), p. 143; Isaac Craven, *The New Paradise* (1658), p. 2; Nehemiah Rogers, *The Good Samaritan* (1640), p. 8. The same notion is asserted by the writers I cited elsewhere ('*PL* and the Theory of Accommodation', *TSLL*, v (1963), 58–63) as well as by Calvin, *Foure Sermons*, tr. John Fielde (1579), fol. 39; Amandus Polanus, *The Substance of Christian Religion*, tr. Elijah Wilcox, 2nd ed. (1597), pp. 6 ff.; Pierre Viret, *A Christian Instruction*, tr. John Shute (1573), p. 418; Pietro Martire Vermigli, *apud* Joseph C. McLelland, *The Visible Words of God* (Edinburgh, 1957), pp. 74 ff.; Gerhard, p. 17; John Woolton, *A Neuue Anatomie* (1576), fol. 42ᵛ; Hugh Roberts, *The Day of Hearing* (Oxford, 1600), pp. 13 f.; John Deacon and John Walker, *Dialogicall Discourses* (1601), p. 17; John Sanford, *Gods Arrowe* (Oxford, 1604), p. 15; John Rawlinson, *Fishermen* (1609), p. 4; Ames, p. 10; Thomas Granger, *The Light of the World* (1616), p. 5; Michael Wigmore, *The Good-Adventure* (1620), p. 20; Immanuel Bourne, *The Anatomie of Conscience* (1623), p. 3; Donne, *Sermons*, ii. 288 f., and ix. 135, 142, 236, etc.; William Laud, *A Sermon preached . . . at White-Hall* (1626), pp. 11 f.; Lewis Bayly, *The Practice of Piety*, 35th ed. (1635), p. 125; John Bond, *Ortus occidentalis* (1645), pp. 15 f.; Anthony (above, p. 8, n. 2), pp. 9 f.; Theophilus Wodenote, *Eremicus theologus* (1654), pp. 19 f.; Robert Mossom, *The Teacher's*

Paradise Lost echoes most emphatically this venerated theory (ἐν παραβολαῖς καὶ ὁμοιώσεσι πολλάκις λαλοῦν τὸ ἅγιον Πνεῦμα)[1] in Raphael's account of the War in Heaven. The account begins by 'like'ning spiritual to corporeal forms' (v. 573), and in conclusion reminds Adam that Raphael's approach consisted of 'measuring things in Heav'n by things on Earth' (vi. 893). If Adam remains unenlightened by Raphael's '*Comparisons* and *Similitudes*' dealing with objects beyond human experience, it is because *Paradise Lost* is a 'comedy' involving a divine mystery best understood—if it can be understood at all—in terms of the ineffable work of grace on both man and the universe at large. What this means I hope to make clear later, in Chapter VII.

The traditional exposition of God's attributes furnishes one of the most enduring aspects of the affirmative approach. 'Every Attribute of GOD', observed Humphrey Sydenham, 'is God him-selfe; and God himselfe is principally discovered by those Attri-butes.' However, theologians have always cautioned against attempts to emphasize any one divine attribute at the expense of the others, reminding their readers that the various attributes are not 'dis-tinguished one from another *really* in Gods nature; but onely formally in our conceptions'. Thus we have lengthy lists of divine attributes as we pass from one 'formal' conception to the next. Milton's own inventory in *De doctrina christiana* is typical in its enumeration and discussion of God's eternity and immutability, unity and truth, infinity and intelligence and will. Notwithstanding, three attributes were most frequently dwelt upon: omnipotence, omniscience, and omnipresence. As Donne assured his congregation, 'often God admits into his owne Name, this addition of Universality, *Omne*, *All*, as though he would be knowne by that especially. He is

---

Tripartite (1657), iii. 122; Baxter, iv. 219; Henry More, *An Apology* appended to *A Modest Enquiry* (1664), p. 485; Robert Sanderson, *XXXV. Sermons*, 7th ed. (1681), i. 156 f.; *et al.* See also the commentaries by Edward R. Dowey, Jr., *The Knowledge of God in Calvin's Theology* (1952), pp. 3 ff., 243 ff.; John M. Steadman, in *Archiv für das Studium der neueren Sprachen*, cxcv (1959), 273–89; and esp. Roland M. Frye, *God, Man and Satan* (Princeton, 1960), *passim*.

[1] Justin Martyr, *Dialogus cum Tryphone*, LXXVII (*Patr. g.* vi. 657). Milton's parallel statement (*DDC, Works*, xiv. 31) echoes such authoritative expositions as those by Clement of Alexandria, *Stromata*, II. 16 (*ANCL*, xii. 43 f.); Origen, *Homiliæ in Numeros*, XXIII. 2 (*Patr. g.* xii. 748); Augustine, *De civ.* xv. 25, and *De Trinitate*, I. i. 2 (*NPNF*, iii. 18); Hilary of Poitiers, *De Trinitate*, VIII. 43 (*Patr. l.* x. 268 f.); Gregory of Nyssa, *Contra Eunomium*, I. 39 (*NPNF*, 2nd ser., v. 93); and John of Damascus, *De fide ortho-doxa*, I. 11 (*Patr. g.* xciv. 841). Cf. Moses Maimonides, *The Guide of the Perplexed*, esp. xlvi (tr. M. Friedländer, 2nd ed. (1956), pp. 59–63).

Omnipotent, There he can doe All; He is Omniscient, There he can know All; Hee is Omnipresent, There he can direct All.'[1]

William Perkins's *Armilla aurea* (1590), one of the most popular theological treatises of the high Renaissance in England, compresses the Biblical verses chiefly employed in expositions of God's omnipotence into this comprehensive statement:

Gods omnipotencie, is that by which he is most able to perform euery worke. Matth. 19. 26. *With men this is impossible, with God all things are possible.* Some things are here to be excepted. First, those thinges, whose action argueth an impotencie, as to lye, to denie his worde. Titus 1. 2. *Which God that cannot lye, hath promised.* 2. Tim. 2. 13. *He cannot denie himselfe.* Secondly, such thinges as are contrarie to the Nature of God, as to destroy himselfe, and not to beget his Sonne from Eternitie. Thirdly, such thinges as implie contradiction. For God can not make a truth false, or that which is, when it is not to be.

Gods power, may be distinguished into an absolute and actuall power. Gods absolute power, is that by which he can do more, then he eyther dooth, or will doe. Matth. 3. 9. *I say unto you, God is able of these stones to rayse up children to Abraham.* Phil. 3. 21. *According to the working, wherby he is able to subdue euen all things unto himselfe.* Gods actuall power, is that by which he causeth all things to be, which he freely will. Psalm. 135. 6. *All things which God will, those he doth in heauen and in earth, and in all depthes.*[2]

In *Paradise Lost* divine omnipotence is implied, rather than directly affirmed, behind every event in the narrative. This is true especially of the act of creation, which, with the sweep of the psalmist, declares God's almightiness: 'he spake, and it was done; he commanded, and it stood fast' (Ps. xxxiii. 9). But never was God's omnipotence more impressively upheld by Milton than in the very style of his Heaven, a style described as 'solid, hardwearing, on the side of the immutable'.[3]

The Biblical *locus classicus* concerning the divine attribute of omniscience is the psalmist's confession:

> O Lord, thou hast searched me, and known me.
> Thou knowest my downsitting and mine uprising.

---

[1] Seriatim: Sydenham, *Sermons upon Solemne Occasions* (1637), p. 155; Robert Mossom, *Sion's Prospect* (1653), p. 9; Milton, *DDC*, *Works*, xiv. 40–61; Donne, *Sermons*, vii. 247. See further Heppe, ch. v.

[2] *A Golden Chaine*, tr. Anon. (1591), sigs. A7–A7ᵛ.

[3] J. B. Broadbent, *Some Graver Subject* (1960), p. 106. Kingsley Widmer also relates Milton's style to God's 'immutable transcendent authority' in *ELH*, xxv (1958), 258–69.

Thou understandest my thought afar off.
Thou compassest my path and my lying down,
And art acquainted with all my ways.
For there is not a word in my tongue,
But, lo, O Lord, thou knowest it altogether.
Thou hast beset me behind and before,
And laid thine hand upon me.
Such knowledge is too wonderful for me;
It is high, I cannot attain unto it.

(Ps. cxxxix. 1–6)

Yet the Bible insists that God's omniscience comprehends all realizations of the divine purpose. 'I know the thoughts that I think toward you, saith the Lord, thoughts of peace, and not of evil, to give you an expected end' (Jer. xxix. 11). 'The Lord', we read in the New Testament, 'knoweth them that are his' (2 Tim. ii. 19); we are indeed elected 'according to the foreknowledge of God' (1 Pet. i. 2). Milton in *De doctrina christiana* observed of such Biblical claims that 'so extensive is the prescience of God, that he knows beforehand the thoughts and actions of free agents as yet unborn, and many ages before those thoughts or actions have their origin.' Since all Christians, and not Protestants alone, count God's prescience in the Fall of Man, the sweeping assertion of Wolfgang Musculus, the great Protestant expositor, accurately generalized that 'all men doe very well agree therin, that the sinne of Adã was frõ euer foreseen & foreknowen to God.' Hieronymus Zanchius, another formidable Protestant commentator, adequately proposed the common assumptions in his statement that

God, *from the beginning of the world*, yea even from Eternitie according to his infinite wisdome foreknew all things to come, both the good, which he would do; and the evil, which he would permit to be done; so farre forth that nothing did or could lye hid from him: And we doubt not *but all things*, whatsoever have been, are, shall or may be, although they never come to passe, *are* and have been alwayes *naked and open in his sight*.[1]

However, Matthew Newcomen, Milton's associate in the war of the pamphlets during the 1640's, postulated the Christian view of God's omniscience in terms that can hardly be bettered:

[1] Seriatim: Milton, *Works*, xiv. 57; Musculus, fol. 17; Zanchius, pp. 19–20 [quoting Acts xv. 18 and Hebr. iv. 13]. For a doctrinal statement consult the Formula of Concord (1577), in Tappert, pp. 616 f. On the problem of God's foreknowledge *v.* man's free-will, see below, pp. 192 ff.

THE DOCTRINE OF THE GODHEAD

the knowledge of God, it reacheth unto *all things*, πάντα, all things: *All things* that are *in God*, and all things that are *without God*. All things, *Divine* and *not Divine*. All things, *Angelicall* or *Humane*: *Heavenly* or *earthly*: All things *good* or *evil*, *great* or *small*: *secret* or *open*. All things that *have been*, or *have not been*: that are, or that are not; that shall be, or that may be, or that never shall, never can be: All things past, present, future, contingent, impossible, *All things are naked and open unto the eyes of him, with whom we have to doe* [Hebr. iv. 13].[1]

In *Paradise Lost* God is claimed to behold all 'past, present, future' (III. 78), and Belial is driven to confess that the Lord 'from Heav'ns highth / All these our motions vain, sees and derides' (II. 190 f.). Milton himself declares that absolutely nothing

> can scape the Eye
> Of God All-seeing, or deceave his Heart
> Omniscient.   (X. 5–7)

God is 'th' Eternal eye, whose sight discernes / Abstrusest thoughts' (V. 711 f.), and even when all Heaven rests, 'th' unsleeping eyes of God' still search the minds of all his creatures (V. 647). This recurring metaphor of the divine eyes bears the approval of tradition and exemplifies also the theory of accommodation. Repeatedly sanctioned by the Scriptures in verses such as Proverbs xv. 3 ('the eyes of the Lord are in every place, beholding the evil and the good'), it was echoed by Donne during the Renaissance when he said that God is 'all eye', while Bishop Guillaume du Vair spoke of 'this All-seeing-eye, which pierceth through ages as the Sunne through the Aire'. To quote again from Matthew Newcomen,

All things are not only *naked*, without clokes or colours, but *ript open*, unbowell'd, anatomised, turned inside outward in the eye of God. There is nothing so reserved, so hidden *in man* or *from man*, but it is *open* to the *eye of God*.[2]

We may approach by way of the familiar psalm quoted earlier the divine attribute of omnipresence:

> Whither shall I go from thy spirit?
> Or whither shall I flee from thy presence?

---

[1] *The All-seeing Vnseen Eye of God* (1647), p. 2. Newcomen was one of the five writers whose initials made up the pen-name 'Smectymnuus'. The others were Stephen Marshall, Edmund Calamy, Thomas Young [Milton's tutor], and William Spurstow.

[2] Seriatim: Donne, *Sermons*, iv. 150; du Vair, *A Buckler against Adversitie*, tr. Andrew Court (1622), p. 70; Newcomen (as before), p. 11.

If I ascend up into heaven, thou art there:
If I make my bed in hell, behold, thou art there. . . .
(Ps. cxxxix. 7–8)

During the Renaissance, and earlier, God's omnipresence was often
visualized in terms of the circle, regarded widely as 'of all formes
. . . the perfectest', 'the most ample of alle figures', 'a clear embleme
of eternity'.[1] A variant was the conception of God as 'an intelligible
sphere, whose center is every where, whose circumference is no
where'.[2] This is related closely to the idea in *Paradise Lost* that 'God
in Heav'n / Is Center, yet extends to all' (IX. 107 f.), upon which
innumerable commentaries exist, from one of Donne's best-known
statements ('God is all Center, as that hee looks to all, and so, all
circumference, as that hee embraces all') to an earlier affirmation by
John Byshop about 'that apt likening of God by the diuine *Platon-
istes* vnto the centre, or midle pricke, all lines do proceede into the
circle and from it returne vnto the centre againe, so also from God all
good things come vnto his creatures, and from them redound backe
vnto his honour and glorie'.[3] Such also is the burden of Raphael's
observations in *Paradise Lost* (V. 469 ff.), reinforced later by Michael
when he assures Adam that his expulsion from Eden shall not
deprive him of God's 'blessed count'nance':

his Omnipresence fills
Land, Sea, and Aire, and every kinde that lives,

[1] Seriatim: Donne, *Sermons*, iv. 51; Caxton, *Mirrour of the World* (tr. 1480), ed.
Oliver H. Prior (1913), p. 58; Fulk Bellers, *Jesus Christ* (1652), p. 10. See also below,
p. 40.
[2] Joseph Hall, *The Character of Man* (1635), p. 17. The most influential statement of
this idea was Nicholas of Cusa's, in *De docta ignorantia*, II. 2 (*Opera* (Basle, 1565),
p. 38); cf. Cassirer, p. 28, and Copleston, iii. 239. For other statements see Jean Pierre
Camus, *A Dravght of Eternitie*, tr. Miles Car (Douai, 1632), p. 64; Richard Hooke,
Davids Diamond (1635), pp. 23 f.; Sydenham (above, p. 11, n. 1), pp. 135 f.; Sir Thomas
Browne, *Christian Morals* (Cambridge, 1716), p. 76; Glanvill, *The Vanity of Dogmatizing*
(1661), p. 241; *Peter Sterry*, ed. V. de S. Pinto (Cambridge, 1934), p. 90; etc. The idea
has been attributed to St. Bonaventura (cf. Sir Herbert Grierson, *The Poems of John
Donne* (Oxford, 1912), ii. 176; Charles Williams, *He Came Down from Heaven* (1938),
p. 105, and *The Figure of Beatrice* (1943), p. 24), but it is doubtless much older (cf., for
example, Scholem, p. 218, and F. L. Huntley, *Sir Thomas Browne* (Ann Arbor, 1963),
pp. 108 f., 139, 262). Variants abound: see Ficino, *Comm.* ii. 3; Pico, 'A Platonick Discourse', tr. Thomas Stanley, *Poems* (1651), p. 235; Oswald Croll, *Mysteries of Nature*,
tr. Henry Pinnell in *Philosophie Reformed* (1657), pp. 55 f.; Donne, *Essays*, p. 39, and
Sermons, v. 325, ix. 406, etc.; Christopher Harvey, *The Synagogue* (1640), p. 11;
Pascal, *Pensées*, § 84; *et al.* See further Dietrich Mahnke, *Unendliche Sphäre und All-
mittelpunkt* (Halle, 1937), esp. ch. iii.
[3] Donne, *Sermons*, vii. 247, and Byshop, *Beautifull Blossomes* (1571), fol. 1.

Fomented by his virtual power and warmd . . .
. . . doubt not but in Vallie and in Plaine
God is as here, and will be found alike
Present, and of his presence many a signe
Still following thee, still compassing thee round
With goodness and paternal Love, his Face
Express, and of his steps the track Divine.

(XI. 336–54)

II

These assumptions—the common property of all orthodox
thinkers of the Renaissance—usually comprehended that 'Sphynx
of Divinitie', the doctrine of the Trinity.[1] Without access to Milton's
theological treatise De doctrina christiana, we should probably have
agreed with Bishop Thomas Newton (1749) that Paradise Lost is
entirely orthodox, and we might have been tempted to accept even
Charles Symmons's verdict (1806) that the poem is 'orthodox and
consistent with the creed of the Church of England'.[2] The discovery
of De doctrina christiana in 1823, however, drastically changed
opinions which were agonizingly reappraised. Henry Todd was not
the only one to retract his old approbation of Milton's orthodoxy
and to charge him now with a number of heresies. By 1855 Thomas
Keightly summed up the considered view of scholars when he
observed that Paradise Lost expounds the Arian heresy in a 'plain
and unequivocal manner'.[3] This view led in 1941 to a study minimiz-
ing the differences between Paradise Lost and De doctrina christiana,
and concluding too readily that the poem is 'an Arian document'.[4]
Certain critics, however, protested against the assumption that 'a
poem is essentially a decorated and beautified piece of prose', and
one argued that the treatise could not have in all respects served
as the blueprint for the poem because of the subtle differences
between them.[5] In time it became equally clear that even the Arian

[1] John Day, Day's Dyall (Oxford, 1614), p. 57.

[2] Ant Oras, Milton's Editors and Commentators . . . 1695–1801 (Dorpat, 1930), p. 227,
and Herbert McLachlan, The Religious Opinions of Milton, Locke and Newton (Manchester, 1941), p. 17; respectively.

[3] McLachlan (previous note), p. 25.

[4] Maurice Kelley, This Great Argument: A Study of Milton's 'DDC' as a Gloss upon
'PL' (Princeton, 1941).

[5] Cleanth Brooks, in English Institute Essays 1946 (1947), pp. 127–8, and Arthur
Sewell, A Study in Milton's Christian Doctrine (1939); respectively. See also the review
of Kelley's book by A. S. P. Woodhouse, PR, lii (1943), 206–8.

element so hastily detected in *De doctrina christiana* is nothing but an extension of the 'subordinationism' upheld by the early Christian writers to the Council of Nicaea and revived by the Cambridge Platonists in Milton's own age.[1] I have elsewhere supported this conclusion by presenting evidence to contradict the relationship assumed to exist between Milton's views and the Arian heresy.[2] At this juncture, therefore, I restrict myself to some further prolegomena only, in part explaining what is really at issue and in part selecting from the family of traditional ideas current during the Renaissance those which relate to Milton's *De doctrina christiana*.

Milton's opinions of the Trinity in his theological treatise are, though couched in the intricate terms of theology, clearly to be understood. The Trinity as such is not rejected. The Father, the Son, and the Holy Spirit are proclaimed to be 'one' in love, communion, spirit, and glory. More important still, each is termed 'God' (*deus*), and each is specifically said to share in the divine substance (*substantia*). Thus the Father 'imparted to the Son as much as he pleased of the *divina natura*, nay of the *substantia natura*'. The Son is made expressly of the Father's *substantia*, and so is the Holy Spirit.[3] Milton does, however, reject their equality in terms of the divine essence (*essentia*). He avoids the term 'three persons', and tells us they are not 'one in essence'. On the contrary, even while they partake of the same *substantia*, each has the *essentia* or *hypostasis* proper to himself ('*essentia* and *hypostasis* mean the same thing').[4]

These conclusions, Milton informs us in the preface to *De doctrina christiana*, are grounded solely on a 'most careful perusal and meditation of the Holy Scriptures'. Their appeal is to the exclusively Protestant doctrine which allows the individual freedom to interpret the Bible guided solely by the *testimonium Spiritus sancti internum*. Were we prepared to accept such a claim at face value, we should perforce have to concede the essential truth of Milton's conclusions, since Biblical scholars now assure us that the Scriptural evidence for the doctrine of the Trinity is 'singularly disconcerting', that 'even the explicit idea of the Trinity is absent from the apostolic

---

[1] This important thesis is argued by William B. Hunter, 'Milton's Arianism Reconsidered', *HTR*, lii (1959), 9–35. A useful seventeenth-century compendium of the early 'subordinationist' ideas is John Biddle's *The Testimonies of Irenæus*, etc. (1649?).

[2] See 'Milton and Arianism', *JHI*, xxv (1964), 423–9.

[3] *Works*, xiv. 193, 187, 403.

[4] Ibid. 401, 221, 43; cf. 311.

witness to the faith'.[1] Yet neither Milton nor 'the whole Protestant church' he invokes in his treatise did in fact by-pass *humanae traditiones* altogether. The following table presenting the various formulations of the doctrine of the Trinity indicates both the highly flexible terminology sanctioned by tradition and the line of descent to Milton's particular conception.[2] The divine 'substratum' constitutes the essence or substance common to the entire Godhead, and the 'mode of existence' designates the specific essence or substance peculiar to each Person within the Godhead:

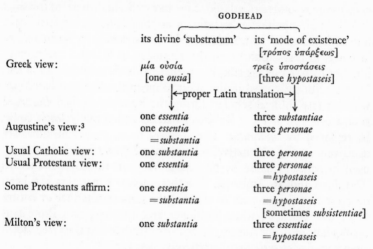

	GODHEAD	
	its divine 'substratum'	its 'mode of existence' [τρόπος ὑπάρξεως]
Greek view:	μία οὐσία [one *ousia*]	τρεῖς ὑποστάσεις [three *hypostaseis*]
	←proper Latin translation→	
	one *essentia*	three *substantiae*
Augustine's view:[3]	one *essentia* = *substantia*	three *personae*
Usual Catholic view:	one *substantia*	three *personae*
Usual Protestant view:	one *essentia*	three *personae* = *hypostaseis*
Some Protestants affirm:	one *essentia* = *substantia*	three *personae* = *hypostaseis* [sometimes *subsistentiae*]
Milton's view:	one *substantia*	three *essentiae* = *hypostaseis*

---

[1] Kenneth E. Kirk, in *Essays on the Trinity and the Incarnation*, ed. A. E. J. Rawlinson (1928), p. 199, and Emil Brunner, *The Christian Doctrine of God*, tr. Olive Wyon (1949), p. 205. The 'triadic pattern' sought by Arthur W. Wainwright in *The Trinity in the NT* (1962) is not quite so readily discerned by Biblical scholars.

[2] The crucial terms *substantia*, *hypostasis*, etc., are explained by J. F. Bethune-Baker, *An Introduction to the Early History of Christian Doctrine*, 2nd ed. (1920), pp. 116 f., 231–8, and E. J. Bicknell, *A Theological Introduction to the Thirty-Nine Articles*, 2nd ed. (1925), pp. 63–65. On the differences between the Greek and Latin views, consult G. L. Prestige, *God in Patristic Thought* (1936), ch. viii–x, and Vladimir Lossky, *The Mystical Theology of the Eastern Church* (1957), ch. iii. Cf. the authorities I cited in *JHI* (above p. 16, n. 2), but see especially the fundamental study by William B. Hunter, 'Some Problems in John Milton's Theological Vocabulary', *HTR*, lvii (1964), 353–65.

[3] Augustine was aware that the correct translation of the Greek formula (one *ousia* and three *hypostaseis*) should be one *essentia* and three *substantiae*, but maintained that 'because with us the usage has already obtained, that by *essentia* we understand the same thing which is understood by *substantia*, we do not dare to say one *essentia*, three *substantiae*, but one *essentia* or *substantia* and three *personae*' (*De Trinitate*, v. viii. 9, and ix. 10; in *Patr. l.* xlii. 917–18, and *NPNF*, iii. 92). In fact, however, Augustine's view was based on usage as much as it was on his failure to grasp the difference between *ousia* and *hypostasis* (*De Trin.* v. viii. 10) since he knew Greek moderately (cf. below, p. 100).

The Catholic Church adopted not Augustine's version but Tertullian's, one *substantia* in three *personae*,[1] which Protestants altered by moving in a number of directions at once. The majority of their commentators adhered to Calvin's lucid exposition: 'vnder the name of God, we vnderstande the one onely and single *essentia* in whiche we comprehende thre *personae* or *hypostaseis*.'[2] Some, however, offered interpretations resembling Milton's in *De doctrina christiana*. But here clarity falters. The term *substantia*, for example, which Milton employed to characterize the divine 'substratum' (the Greek *ousia*), corresponds to Catholic usage but walks in Protestant treatises in bewildering guises: as *essentia*, or as *essentia* in the original Latin but as 'substance' in translation, or as *substantia* in Latin but as 'essence' in translation.[3] Lest the confusion in Milton's age reaches into our own, let us ask simply whether Milton's term *substantia* had been traditionally used in the West to mean the divine substratum, whether any Biblical scholar during the Renaissance had endorsed such a use, whether any Reformer had conceded that *essentia* could be replaced by *substantia*. The answers to all three questions are decisively in the affirmative. The term *substantia* had indeed been used in Milton's sense by numerous Western theologians such as Tertullian and St. Ambrose. The three divine *hypostaseis* had been described by Erasmus as 'of one and the same substaunce or nature or of one essence', while Bullinger and Polanus, two Protestant theologians of major stature, agreed with Luther that the Greek term *ousia* signifies *essentia* or, alternatively, *substantia*.[4]

---

[1] Tertullian, *Adversus Praxeam*, XI–XII (*Patr. l.* ii. 166–8).

[2] *Inst.* I. xiii. 20 [the original Latin in A. Tholuck's edition (Berlin, 1846)]. Thus also Hieronymus Zanchius, *De religione christiana* (Basle, 1585), p. 10; Wolfgang Musculus, *Loci communes* (Basle, 1560), pp. 8 f.; Gulielmus Bucanus, *Institutiones theologicæ* (Geneva, 1609), p. 7; Amandus Polanus (below, n. 4), i. 555; William Ames, *Medulla theologica*, 3rd ed. (Amsterdam, 1628), p. 16; Johann Wolleb, *Compendium theologiæ christianæ* (Cambridge, 1648), p. 9; Johannes van Marck, *Compendium theologiæ christianæ* (Amsterdam, 1690), p. 93; *et al.*

[3] Thus Beza's 'vnam esse diuinam essentiam quam Deus appellamus' (*Tractationum theologicarum* (Geneva, 1570), i. 1) was translated 'there is one onely dyuyne substaunce whych we call God' (*A briefe . . . Summe of the Christian Faith*, tr. Robert Fyll [1565?], sig. B8). Cf. XXXIX Art., I and v. Conversely, Daniel Heinsius's *substantia* (*In Theophania . . . homilia* (Leyden, 1612), p. 9) was translated 'essence' (*The Mirrour of Humilitie*, tr. John Harmar (1618), p. 5).

[4] Seriatim: Tertullian (above, n. 1), and Ambrose, *De fide orthodoxa*, III. 14 (*Patr. l.* xvi. 611); Erasmus, *A Playne . . . Declaration of the Cōmune Crede*, tr. Anon. (1533), sig. B8 [the original Latin is quoted below, p. 20, n. 2]; Luther, *Commentariolus in epistolam divi Pauli Apostoli ad Hebreos* (1517), in *Werke* (Weimar, 1939), LVII [iii]. 100: 'usia, quod "essentiam" seu "substanciam" significat'. Cf. Bullinger,

Milton's *substantia*, like the Greek word *ousia* it is supposed to translate, is not a Biblical term, even though Milton himself claims that his *De doctrina christiana* rests solely upon the Holy Scriptures (*solo Dei verbo*). Aware of this discrepancy, Milton probably turned with considerable relief to another crucial theological term which does occur in the Bible. According to the Epistle to the Hebrews (i. 3), the Son of God is χαρακτὴρ τῆς ὑποστάσεως αὐτοῦ [τοῦ Πατρός], meaning—if we are to trust the Authorized Version—that he is 'the express image of his [the Father's] person'. But the translation of ὑπόστασις (*hypostasis*) as 'person' (*persona*) finds warrant only in Beza's Latin version of the New Testament (1556) and in its English offspring, the Geneva Bible of 1560. Nearly all other versions agree with the Vulgate's translation of *hypostasis* as *substantia*.[1] Milton appears to have taken an independent line. He rejected both Beza's *persona* and the more common *substantia*, and chose instead the term *essentia*. In his words,

the *essentia* of God, being in itself most simple, can admit no compound quality; so that the term *hypostasis* Heb. i. 3. which is differently translated *substantia*, or *subsistentia* [=*persona*], can be nothing else but that most perfect *essentia* by which God subsists by himself, in himself, and through himself. For neither *substantia* nor *subsistentia* makes any addition to what is already a most perfect *essentia*; and the word *persona* in its later acceptation denotes not the *ens* itself, but the essence of the *ens* in the abstract. *Hypostasis*, therefore, is clearly the same as *essentia*, and thus many of the Latin commentators render it in the passage already quoted.[2]

Compendium christianæ religionis (Zürich, 1559), fol. 21, and Polanus, *Syntagma theologiæ christianæ* (Geneva, 1612), i. 370. Later Johann Heinrich Heidegger was to write, 'Deus Pater Filium suum ab æterno ex substantia sua genuit' (*Corpus theologiæ christianæ* (Zürich, 1700), i. 125).

[1] Thus Erasmus, *Nouum Testamentum graece & latine* (Paris, 1543), ii. fol. 105ᵛ; Gwalter in his revision of Erasmus, *Novi Testamenti aeditio postrema* (Zürich, 1547), fol. 256; Sebastian Castellio, *Testamentum Novum* (Basle, 1551), sig. R1; Bullinger, Pellikan, Bibliander, *et al.*, *Biblia sacrosancta* (Zürich, 1543), iii. fol. 95ᵛ; as well as most English versions (Wycliffe, Tyndale, Cranmer, and of course Rheims). Brian Walton's monumental edition (*Biblia sacra polyglotta* (1657), v. 850 f.) translates both the Greek *hypostasis* and its Syriac equivalent as *substantia*, but the Arabic and Ethiopic equivalents as *persona*. Consult also the observations by Cardinal Cajetan, *Epistolæ Pauli* etc. (Paris, 1532), fol. 189ᵛ; Jacques Lefèvre d'Étaples, *Epistole diui Pauli ... cum commentariis* (Paris, 1517), fol. 180; Willem Hessels van Est(ius), Chancellor of the University of Douai (d. 1613), *In omnes d. Pauli epistolas ... commentarii* (Mainz, 1859), iii. 26 f.; the great Biblical scholar Cornelius a Lapide (d. 1637), *Commentaria in omnes divi Pauli epistolas* (Antwerp, 1734), pp. 835 f.; David Dickson, *A Short Explanation of ... Hebrewes* (Aberdeen, 1635), pp. 7 f.; and John Mayer, *A Commentarie upon all the Epistles of ... Paul* (1631), pp. 584 ff.

[2] *Works*, xiv. 41, 43.

Did Milton adopt the equation *hypostasis* = *essentia* because he felt that these terms were occasionally flexible enough to admit of interchange?[1] Did he even assume that Erasmus had actually sanctioned this equation?[2] But Milton himself disposes of our need to speculate. He informs us specifically that the translation of *hypostasis* as *essentia* had already appeared in 'many of the Latin commentators'. Unfortunately he names none, but they must have existed, since Calvin also refers to them as 'some expositours' in his militant observations on the meaning of *hypostasis* in Hebrews i. 3. According to Calvin,

The apostles namyng the sonne, the engraued forme of the *hypostasis* of his father, he vndoubtedly meaneth, that the Father hath some beeyng, wherin he differeth from the sonne. For to take it for *essentia* (as some expositours haue done, as if Christ like a piece of waxe printed with a seale didde represent the substaunce of the Father) were not onely harde but also an absurditie. For sithe the Essence of God is single or one and vndiuisible, he that in hym selfe conteineth it all and not by pecemeale, or by deriuation, but in whole perfection, should very vnproperly yea fondly bee called the engraued forme of hym. But because ẙ father although he be in his own propretie distinct, hath expressed hymselfe wholly in his sonne, it is for good cause sayde, that he hath geuen his *hypostasis* to be seene in hym. ... Surely by the Apostles wordes we gather, that there is a certayn propre *hypostasis* in the father, that shineth in the sonne: whereby also agayne is easily perceiued the *hypostasis* of the sonne that distinguisheth him from the Father. Like order is in the holy ghost. . . Yet this distinction is not of the *essentia*, whiche it is vnlawfull to make manyfolde. Therfore if the Apostles testimonie be credited, it foloweth that there be in God thre *hypostaseis*. This terme seying the Latines haue expressed with the name of *persona*, it were to muche pride and waywardnesse to brawle about so cleere a matter. But if we list worde for worde to translate, we may call it *subsistentia*. Many in the same sense haue called it *substantia*. And the name of *persona* hath not ben in vse among the Latins onely: but also the Grecians, perhaps to declare a consente, haue taught that there are three *prosopa*, that is to say Persons in God. But they, whether they be Grekes or Latins that differ one from an other in the worde, doo very well agree in the summe of the matter.[3]

    [1] Cf. Zacharias Ursinus: 'Filius . . . gignitur a Patre, de essentia Patris: Essentia autem Filii, nõ gignitur . . .' (*Opera theologica* (Heidelberg, 1612), i. 542). See also Bartholomaeus Keckermann's observations on the Son's *essentia*, in *Systema s.s. theologiæ* (Hanau, 1602), pp. 62 f.

    [2] Cf. 'Tres sunt proprietatibus distincti, sed trium eadem est substantia siue natura, aut quod uerbu quidam arbitrantur aptius, essentia' (*Dilucida et pia explanatio symboli* (Basle, 1533), p. 19). But Erasmus, in his annotations on the NT (Basle, 1535, p. 705), accepted only *hypostasis*=*substantia*.

    [3] *Inst.* I. xiii. 2 [the original in Tholuck, as before, p. 18, n. 2]. See further Calvin's

I have quoted Calvin's statement at some length to show that the orthodox arguments are not necessarily the most persuasive. Milton certainly did not find them so, and his dissatisfaction led him to 'many of the Latin commentators', among them, surely, the great Italian Hebraist Emanuele Tremellio (1510–80). Though most often referred to as 'that learned Jew',[1] Immanuel Tremellius had first been converted to the Catholic faith by Cardinal Pole and later to Protestantism by Peter Martyr (Vermigli). Obliged to leave Italy for Germany, he arrived in England at Archbishop Cranmer's invitation. In 1549 he was appointed Regius Professor of Hebrew at Cambridge; but the accession of Queen Mary forced his return to Germany, where in 1561 he obtained the Chair of Old Testament Studies at Heidelberg. After a second visit to England about 1565, Tremellius secured a lasting reputation with his translation of the New Testament from Syriac into Latin, first published in 1569 and dedicated to the *regina potentissima* Elizabeth I. He then collaborated with the celebrated French scholar François du Jon (Junius) to produce a Latin translation of the whole Bible (1575–9) which was 'for long the standard Protestant Latin translation'.[2] Tremellius, in his version of the New Testament, often reprinted since it was so widely acclaimed by many Catholics and almost all Protestants, translates the word *hypostasis* not as *substantia*, or *persona*, but—as Milton translated it in his theological treatise—*essentia*.[3] Search will undoubtedly reveal other precedents, but in the meantime Milton's reference to so important an authority as Tremellius[4] suffices to establish that in *De doctrina christiana* he had not leaned exclusively on the Holy Scriptures but had availed himself of Renaissance Biblical scholarship.

Commentarie on . . . Hebreuues, tr. Clement Cotton (1605), pp. 12 f. Estius (above, p. 19, n. 1) also notes that some expositors translate *hypostasis* as *essentia*.

[1] Gilbert Burnet, *The History of the Reformation* (Oxford, 1865), ii. 256.

[2] *The Oxford Dictionary of the Christian Church*, ed. F. L. Cross (1957), p. 1373. See also Basil Hall, 'Biblical Scholarship', in *The Cambridge History of the Bible*, ed. S. L. Greenslade (Cambridge, 1963), pp. 72 f.

[3] I consulted Tremellius's 1569 translation of the NT (Geneva: ʽΗ Καινὴ Διαθήκη etc., fol. 617) and the first English edition of the Tremellius–Junius Bible (*Biblia sacra*, etc. (1579–80), v. 161; first published in Frankfurt, 1575–9). Since Junius kept revising Tremellius's labours, I checked also some of the seventeenth-century editions of their Bible (the Hanau ed. of 1602 [ii, p. 381]; the Geneva ed. of 1617 [iii, fol. 379]) but found that *hypostasis* continued to appear as *essentia*.

[4] Milton never named Tremellius, but his six references to Junius in DDC (*Works*, xiv. 292; xv. 126, 132, 164; xvi. 358; xvii. 308) are in fact to the Tremellius–Junius Bible (cf. previous note). Kelley (above, p. 15, n. 4 [p. 42]), while convinced that Milton ordinarily followed this Bible, seems not to have realized the importance of his statement.

The hard core of Milton's thesis remains, nevertheless, the 'subordinationism' espoused by the early Fathers whose views Tertullian well summarized: 'Pater enim tota substantia est: Filius vero derivatio totus et portio.'[1] These, then, are among the antecedents of Milton's *De doctrina christiana*.

III

Considered in the light of *De doctrina christiana* and the Christian tradition, *Paradise Lost* is far from 'an Arian document', and does not even espouse the 'subordinationism' of the treatise. Not that the doctrine of the Trinity in *Paradise Lost* is uttered in 'plain and unequivocal' manner, much less in a manner sufficient to confound the ignorant and amaze the very faculties of eyes and ears. The council in Heaven and the differentiation between the Father and the Son clearly evident there (III. 56 ff.) is one of several incidents in *Paradise Lost* which show up so absurdly naïve a conclusion. It will therefore be valuable to examine here some of the differences between *Paradise Lost* and *De doctrina christiana*, and in the poem the expression of ideas present immemorially within the circle of the Christian tradition.

Paradise Lost is a poem, *De doctrina christiana* a treatise. It sounds too obvious, yet we should hardly be well advised—as has been done—to overlook the difference even for a moment. Each work elicits from us a different response because of obvious differences in form, mode of expression, range of language, metaphor, structure. In *De doctrina christiana* we have, for example, the precise theological statement that the Father and the Son are not equal ('non æqualibus').[2] By contrast we have in *Paradise Lost* the Father's assertion that the Son is

> Thron'd in highest bliss
> Equal to God, and equally enjoying
> God-like fruition.

(III. 305-7)

Take the phrase 'God-like fruition'. It has studied generosity, and should be judged according to the sort of metaphorical language that starts off in Book III: 'Hail holy Light, ofspring of Heav'n first

---

[1] *Adversus Praxeam*, IX: 'the Father is the entire substance but the Son is a derivation and portion of the whole' (*Patr. l.* ii. 164; *ANCL*, xv. 349).
[2] *Works*, xiv. 50, 190, 210, 310, 328, 342; xv. 4.

born . . .'.[1] What is afterwards stated not only reinforces the structure of the poem by contrasting the fruition within the Godhead to the sterile and perverse relations within the infernal Trinity—Satan, Sin, and Death (II. 648 ff.)—but testifies also to a divine unity that far outstretches the mere unity in love, communion, spirit, and glory that Milton argues in *De doctrina christiana*. It is not only that the Son reflects the paternal glory in full resplendence (V. 720; X. 65) and that in him dwells the fulness of the divine love (III. 225). Of even greater significance, the Son is said to be the image of the Father in all things (VI. 736), to shine all the Father forth (III. 139; VII. 196; X. 66), and to express 'all his Father full' (VI. 720). The traditional language Milton employs in *Paradise Lost* is partly illuminated for us by John Day in his summary (1614) of the most common metaphors used by patristic writers to set forth the Trinity. Metaphors have been borrowed, we are informed,

as first from the similitude of the *Sunne* and his *Beames*, so *Iustin Martyr*, *Tertullian*, *Cyprian*, and *Lactantius*: From the similitude of the *Fountaine*, *Floud*, and *River*, so *Tertullian* againe, and *Cyprian*, and *Lactantius*; from the similitude of the *Roote*, and *Stem*, and *Bough of a tree*, so *Tertullian* & *Cyprian*: from the *Vnderstanding*, *Memory*, and *Will*, so S. *Austen*: from the three faculties of the Soule, *Rational*, *Irascible*, & *Concupiscible*, so others.[2]

We may better appreciate the differences between *Paradise Lost* and *De doctrina christiana* by reminding ourselves that in his treatise Milton expressly avoided 'the drama of the personalities in the Godhead',[3] yet in his poem that very drama formed the basis of the entire council in Heaven. This distinction might well seem to argue that the 'subordinationism' of *De doctrina christiana* is even more explicit in *Paradise Lost*. But Milton's conception of the heavenly council in *Paradise Lost* makes the poem not less but more orthodox and certainly traditional. We shall later observe how the immemorial allegory of the debate among the four daughters of God was adapted

---

[1] Cf. William B. Hunter's argument that Milton addresses the Son of God at the beginning of Book III (*MLN*, lxxiv (1959), 589–92) but also in the invocations which begin Books I, VII, and IX (*SEL*, iv (1964), 35–42).

[2] *Day's Dyall* (Oxford, 1614), p. 57. On the analogy of the triune Godhead to the tripartite soul, see Donne, *Sermons*, iii. 145, 154; v. 149; ix. 83 f., etc.; the sources mentioned by Mary P. Ramsey, *Les Doctrines médiévales chez Donne*, 2nd ed. (1924), pp. 208 f.; and the writers I cited in *PQ*, xxxix (1960), 120 f. The *locus classicus* is Augustine, *De Trinitate*, x. 17–19. Cf. below, p. 50.

[3] *Works*, xiv. 197.

by Milton and, once joined to the Protestant theory of the Atone-ment, yielded emphatic differentiation among the persons of the Godhead in Book III and elsewhere.[1] But that differentiation may also stem from the theory of accommodation Milton drew upon, or from a widespread idea touching the council said to have been con-vened in Heaven before the creation of man, resting on Genesis i. 26 ('Let *us* make man in *our* image . . .') which is claimed to offer the earliest Biblical evidence for the doctrine of the Trinity.[2] At the same time, Ephesians i. 11 ('[God] worketh all things after the counsel of his own will') was held to argue that God according to the reference in Genesis first 'taketh counsel with his wisdome & vertue', and second, before creating man, called 'a councell, and [did] consult', 'deliberating with himselfe, the Father with the Sonne and the holy Ghost, and they with him'.[3] If the same argu-ments are applicable to the council summoned before the creation of man (*PL*, VII. 505 ff.), they are applicable also to the councils in Book III and elsewhere (VII. 131 ff.; X. 21 ff.).

Milton's differentiation of the persons within the Godhead in *Paradise Lost* derives, I suggest, from four traditions: the allegory of the daughters of God, the Protestant view of the Atonement, the theory of accommodation, and the belief in the convocation of a council before the creation. But these are, I insist, peripheral considerations only; as I earlier argued, *Paradise Lost* as a poem must remain our chief concern. Did Milton achieve any balance between manner and matter, between the poetic utterance and the traditional material that constitutes that utterance? Are we to accept the drama and reject the dogma altogether, claiming that 'we have incautiously misconstrued as dogma what Milton intended as drama'?[4] Are manner and matter after all wedded? The principal

---

[1] See below, pp. 131–142.

[2] For a representative statement see Hilary of Poitiers, *De Trinitate*, IV. 17; consult also Adelheid Heimann, 'Trinitas creator mundi', *Journal of the Warburg Institute*, ii (1938–9), 42–52. Judaism interprets Gen. i. 26 as implying a council between God and the angels (*Talmud*: Sanhedrin, § 38*b* [p. 242]; Ginzberg, i. 5; H. Wheeler Robinson, *JTS*, xlv (1944), 151–7).

[3] Seriatim: the Geneva Bible (1560), marginal note to Gen. i. 26; John Swan, *Speculum mundi* (Cambridge, 1635), p. 496; and Thomas Cartwright, *Christian Religion* (1611), p. 25. For an authoritative statement see Anselm, *Meditationes*, i. 1 (ed. C. C. J. Webb (1903), pp. 55 f.); consult also Humphrey Sydenham, *Natures Overthrow* (1626), pp. 4 f.; Joseph Hall, *A Plaine . . . Explication* (1633), i. 4; and Donne, *Sermons*, i. 289; ii. 337; v. 157; vi. 154, 266, 296; ix. 60, 69, 137.

[4] This thesis is most competently argued by Irene Samuel, 'The Dialogue in Heaven', *PMLA*, lxxii (1957), 601–11.

evidence is a strange 'coincidence': Milton differentiates between the Father and the Son *only* during their verbal exchanges in the various councils that took place in Heaven, but as soon as these councils end and the Godhead acts beyond the confines of Heaven the distinction between the two persons is abruptly dropped. Thus during the council before the creation of the universe the Father and the Son are clearly differentiated (VII. 131 ff.), but once the Creator embarks on his mission outside Heaven he is specifically termed 'God'. During the council after the Fall of Man the Father and the Son are again clearly differentiated (X. 21 ff.), but once the Judge leaves Heaven for the Garden of Eden he is once again termed 'God', even 'the Lord God' (X. 163). The idea underlying all these incidents in *Paradise Lost* may well be 'the common known *Maxim*, constantly and uniformly received in the Catholick Church' as Bishop Robert Sanderson called it, which Samuel Hoard restated in 1636 when he wrote that

it hath been a rule of constant credit among all Divines, that *opera Trinitatis ad extra sunt indivisa*, the externall operations of the Trinity are undivided. But yet it hath pleased God to appropriate as it were, and affixe some of these works to the Father, some to the Sonne, and some to the Holy Ghost, that wee who are of weake capacities in conceiving such deepe mysteries, as that of the Trinity is, might by this meanes be inabled in some measure to apprehend the truth of it.[1]

As I read *Paradise Lost*, Milton achieved the proper balance between matter and manner by preserving the unity of the Godhead even when, for dramatic purposes, he differentiated between the Father and the Son.[2] This does not, however, end the matter, simply begins it.

Grammatici certant et adhuc sub iudice lis est.

---

[1] Sanderson, *XXXV. Sermons*, 7th ed. (1681), i. 42, and Hoard, *The Soules Miserie* (1636), pp. 19–20. See also the statements by Christopher Lever, *The Holy Pilgrime* (1618), pp. 3 f., and Henry King, *A Sermon of Deliverance* (1626), p. 17.

[2] I argued this point at some length in a preliminary study which I hope will elicit a number of replies: 'The Godhead in *PL*: Dogma or Drama?' *JEGP*, lxiv (1965), 29–34. Cf. my observations on *PL* and the language of theology, in *Language and Style in Milton*, ed. R. D. Emma and J. T. Shawcross (1967).

2

The Great Idea

THE DOCTRINE OF CREATION

Almightie God hath first in himselfe the Idæa, or platforme
of all things, and then accordingly frames his workes out of
himselfe.

JOHN YATES[1]

I

CHRISTIAN theologians have traditionally insisted that the allegorical interpretation of the Scriptures may not be advanced at the
expense of the literal meaning. 'We must', urged Thomas Aquinas,
'hold to the historical truth of the narrative as a foundation of whatever spiritual explanation we may offer.'[2] Protestants agreed with
marked enthusiasm, expressly permitting allegorical interpretations
only 'when the matter is before proued by other firme testimonies'
or—in plainer terms—'when the Allegorie is rightly grounded vpon
the literall sense'.[3] A strong minority was even more restrictive,
persuaded with Calvin that 'there hath not bin a more diuelishe
deuice than these allegories, which haue borne such sway in the
world, and as yet still delight many men.'[4] This attitude is not as

---

[1] *A Modell of Divinitie* (1622), p. 103.

[2] *S. th.* I. cii. I. On the rise and development of allegory, see esp. R. M. Grant, *The
Letter and the Spirit* (1959), pt. i; George de F. Lord, *Homeric Renaissance* (1956),
ch. ii; Wolfson (below, p. 29, n. 3), i. 115–38; Beryl Smalley, *The Study of the Bible
in the Middle Ages*, 2nd ed. (Oxford, 1952), *passim*; G. R. Owst, *Literature and Pulpit
in Medieval England*, 2nd ed. (Oxford, 1961), ch. ii; Edgar de Bruyne, *Études d'esthétique
médiévale* (Bruges, 1946), ii. 302–70; and Henri de Lubac, *Exégèse médiévale* (Paris,
1959–64), 4 vols.

[3] Pietro Martire Vermigli, *Commentaries . . . upon . . . Romanes*, tr. H. B. (1568), fol.
327ᵛ; Thomas Jackson, *A Treatise of . . . Faith* (1627), p. 76. On Donne's similar view,
see Helen Gardner, *The Business of Criticism* (Oxford, 1959), pp. 136 f. [quoted and
documented by E. M. Simpson in Donne, *Sermons*, x. 363 ff.], and Dennis B. Quinn,
JEGP, lxi (1962), 313–29. Only one effort exists on Milton: H. R. MacCallum, *UTQ*,
xxxi (1962), 397–415.

[4] *Sermons . . . upon . . . Galatians*, tr. Arthur Golding (1574), fol. 216ᵛ. I cited Calvin
and others to the same effect in *TSLL*, v (1963), 60.

unreasonable as it may seem, for it testifies to the ever-present Christian concern lest the allegorical approach to the Bible should deprive Christianity of its uniquely historical character, reducing it to a mere philosophy or, worse, an aggregate of myths. Heinrich Bullinger, commenting on the popularity of allegory in the early Eastern Church, lucidly stated the peril inherent in its subsequent dissemination:

after they had once tasted the sweetnesse of allegories, as of a more loftie vnderstanding, they vaunted themselues immoderately, and brought euery thing to allegories, so that euerie one thought, that he might lawfully say what he would herein. And this euill did not stay it selfe within the East, but inuaded Afrike, Italie, France, and Spayne also. So by a little and a little the purenesse of Christian Theologie was transformed into a certaine Philosophie.[1]

Bullinger failed to cite the Eastern theologian principally responsible for the dissemination of allegory, but others named him readily and with evident disapproval. He was, of course, Origen—'an *Allegorist*; an vnsound Interpreter'—whose name is rarely absent from the constant admonitions not to transform the Scriptures 'into *Allegories* to the destroying of the letter, which was *Origens* fault'.[2] It is not my purpose here to enumerate all the faults that the Renaissance discovered in Origen, but at least one 'foolish' notion I intend to consider in my last chapter. Another, his exposition of the events in the Garden of Eden 'interpreted philosophically',[3] did not have to wait until the Renaissance before it was condemned. As Jeremy Taylor informs us, it had been instantly dismissed by St. Jerome as a useless allegory because Origen 'took away quite the truth of the Story, and not only *Adam* was turned out of the Garden, but the Garden it selfe out of Paradise'.[4] During the Renaissance a number of wild thinkers, Paracelsus and Boehme among them, strained after allegorical interpretations, and even the substantial John Colet boldly claimed that the account of creation in Genesis is merely 'a high and holy fiction'.[5] In the end all these efforts were, like Origen's,

---

[1] *The Woorthynesse . . . of the Holy Scripture*, tr. John Tomkys (1579), fols. 111ᵛ–112.

[2] Samuel Gibson, *The Only Rule* (1616), p. 11; Nehemiah Rogers, *The Wild Vine* (1632), p. 83. Milton's censure of 'erroneous *Origen*' (*Works*, iii. 34) coincides with the views I quoted in *JEGP*, lxiv (1965), 588.

[3] *C. Cels.* IV. 40; *De pr.* IV. iii. 1. See also below, p. 281.

[4] Θεολογία ἐκλεκτική (1647), p. 69.

[5] Paracelsus, *Three Books of Philosophy*, in Pinnell (below, p. 40, n. 4), pt. ii; Boehme, *Mysterium magnum*, tr. John Ellistone and John Sparrow (1654); and Colet,

shipwrecked on the rock of Christian orthodoxy. To the orthodox the entire Pentateuch beginning with the first chapter of Genesis— written, it was traditionally believed, by Moses—constituted an infallible history of the origin and initial progress of the human race.[1] The warning of the German Reformer, Lucas Trelcatius, not to tamper with that history is commonplace: 'Those thinges which of *Moses* are written down of the forme, and order of things created, are not to bee taken Allegorically, but Physically, (or Naturally).'[2]

The acceptance of the historicity of the Mosaic account of creation is attested by the widespread persuasion that the world was created, as William Perkins estimated late in the sixteenth century, 'between fiue thousand and sixe thousand yeres agoe'.[3] As I have indicated elsewhere, a host of Renaissance chronologists agreed, variously fixing the year of creation at most a century on either side of 4000 B.C.[4] Concurrently, however, the apologists of the faith were reluctant to claim that the creation of the world by God is necessarily self-evident. In fact they had no choice but to concede with Thomas Lushington that 'though it may be evinced by strong arguments that the world was created; yet neither those arguments [nor] the framing of them, are obvious to all men'—whereupon the act of creation was made a matter of faith, not open to discourse, as Donne put it, but 'at once swallowed and devour'd by faith, without mastication, or digestion'.[5] The opposition, we can be certain, were hardly impressed; indeed they were merely irritated by the irrelevant reply to their query concerning God's activities before the creation: 'He made Hell, wherein hee might tormente perpetually suche curious fellowes, as doe demaunde such questions.'[6]

It has never been easy to argue with determined Christians.

Opuscula quaedam theologica, ed. J. H. Lupton (1876), pp. 3–28, as discussed by Israel Baroway, *JEGP*, xxxii (1933), 461–3.

[1] Calvin, *Inst.* I. xiv. 1; Bullinger, *Fiftie . . . Sermons*, tr. H. I. (1587), p. 9; Ursinus, p. 333; Henry Valentine, *Foure Sea-Sermons* (1635), p. 14; Elnathan Parr, *The Grounds of Divinitie*, 8th ed. (1636), p. 122; Thomas Young [Milton's tutor], *The Lords-Day* (1639, tr. 1672), p. 69; *et al.*

[2] Trelcatius, p. 112. See also Williams, p. 43.

[3] Perkins, p. 60. But in his *Specimen digesti* (Cambridge, 1598) Perkins fixed the year of creation more precisely in 3967 B.C.

[4] 'Renaissance Estimates of the Year of Creation', *HLQ*, xxvi (1963), 315–22.

[5] Lushington, *The Expiation of a Sinner* (1646), p. 245; Donne, *Essays*, p. 54.

[6] The story derives from Augustine, *Conf.* XI. 12. I quote it from Daneau (below, p. 30, n. 4), fol. 77ᵛ, though it occurs also in Bucanus, p. 62; Goulart, i. 7; Perkins, p. 61; Samuel Purchas, *Purchas his Pilgrimage* (1613), p. 10; Peter Heylyn, *Cosmographie*, 2nd ed. (1657), p. 1; Petrus de Witte, *Catechizing* (Amsterdam, 1664?), p. 186; *et al.*

II

The Christian doctrine of creation during the Renaissance, claims to the contrary notwithstanding, was not based directly on the account in Genesis. This is not surprising, for the Mosaic narrative, implying belief in an already existing matter out of which God created the world, is essentially dualistic, and commentators over the centuries had to intervene before the doctrine of *creatio ex nihilo* was preferred to that dualism. Even then the difficulties were not eliminated, but continued to plague Christian theologians through the Renaissance and after. Certainly when Donne declared categorically that there was 'no pre-existent matter in the world, when God made the world', his claim could not possibly be substantiated by the first chapter of Genesis, which maintains rather—as modern Biblical scholars have readily conceded—that there *was* a pre-existent mass, 'an amorphous watery mass in which the elements of the future land and sea were commingled'.[1]

The early Christians were aware that the claim for the world's creation *ex nihilo* had already been advanced in the apocryphal Old Testament,[2] but they knew also that the balance overwhelmingly favoured the idea of creation *ex materia praeexistente*. On the one hand was the Mosaic account, which Philo and the Alexandrian Jews were soon to interpret as God's introduction of form and life (*nous*) into a primary pre-existent matter created by God. On the other was the supporting evidence of the Aristotelian thesis touching the eternal coexistence of God and the world, the claims of the fabulous Hermes Trismegistus and of Ovid that the world arose from a prior 'undigested lump', and, above all, Plato's notion that the Demiurge did not create the world in any strict sense of the term but shaped it out of a pre-existent matter.[3] The sheer weight of these authoritative

[1] Donne, *Sermons*, v. 316; but cf. S. R. Driver, *The Book of Genesis* (1904), p. 4, and John Skinner, *Commentary on Genesis* (Edinburgh, 1910), p. 17.

[2] 2 Macc. vii. 28: 'God made [heaven and earth] of things that were not.' Cf. *Talmud*: Hagigah, § 12a (p. 63), and see further Harris F. Fletcher, *Milton's Rabbinical Readings* (Urbana, 1930), pp. 81 ff. But the Wisdom of Solomon xi. 17 differs, asserting that God 'made the world of matter without form'. Consult A. Altmann, *Journal of Jewish Studies*, vii (1956), 195–206.

[3] See *Hermetica*, ed. Walter Scott (Oxford, 1924), i. 146 f. I quote Ovid from George Sandys, tr., *Metamorphosis* (1626), p. 1; see further Davis P. Harding, *Milton and the Renaissance Ovid* (Urbana, 1946), pp. 67 ff. The relevant passages in Plato are collected by Adam Fox, *Plato and the Christians* (1957), pp. 27–66. Until the Renaissance the inestimably influential *Timaeus* was known in Chalcidius's fourth-century version, which was not displaced even by Ficino's popular translation (Raymond Klibansky, *The Continuity of the Platonic Tradition* (1939), pp. 28, 32). On Philo *et al.* see Tixeront,

pronouncements meant that for the early Christians the belief that the world had been formed out of a formless matter (ἐξ ἀμόρφου ὕλης) was at first accepted without qualification.[1]

When the dualism inherent in this attitude was seen to be obviously inconsistent with monotheism, the Christian theologians of Alexandria proposed that God had created the formless matter in advance of the six day's work, a theory which was time and again to save appearances. Thereafter it became reasonably possible to assert that the world was created 'out of what did not previously exist', that 'there was nothing made, except out of nothing'.[2] On a later occasion Augustine, who knew as well as any perceptive theologian that it was useless to deny the possibility of creation out of a pre-existent matter, stated the traditional Christian qualification: 'if the world was made out of some unformed matter, that matter was made of absolutely nothing.'[3] And it was this aspect, more than any other, of the Christian doctrine of creation that had to be 'swallowed and devour'd by faith'.

In 1576 the noted French theologian Lambert Daneau had the impression that a large majority of his contemporaries thought it most probable that before or at the outset of the first day of creation, God made 'of nothyng' a 'matter and masse which was first confusedly brought foorth, and conteined in it the seedes of all other thinges'.[4] Daneau was not mistaken. During the Renaissance the 'matter and masse' he mentions was described variously as 'Nature's gallimauphrey', 'a confused Mass / Of things disordered', a 'confused heape', 'an *empty*, rude, vnshapen, and *indigested* lump'—or, as Luther put it, 'a vast and emptie lump, [*Chaos*] which was dark and without shape'.[5] At least part of the intellectual progeny of this

i. 214; Frederick W. Farrar, *History of Interpretation* (1886, repr. Grand Rapids, 1961), pp. 34 ff.; C. M. Walsh, *The Doctrine of Creation* (1910), pp. 57 ff.; and esp. Harry A. Wolfson, *Philo* (Cambridge, Mass., 1947), i. 300 ff. There are many references to extra-Biblical views in Ficino, *Comm.* i. 3, and a full list in John Ray, *Three Physico-Theological Discourses* (1693), Disc. I, ch. i.

[1] Justin Martyr, *Apologia*, I. 10 (*Patr. g.* vi. 340).

[2] Irenaeus, *Adversus haereses*, II. x. 2 (*ANCL*, v. 145), and Tertullian, *Adversus Hermogenem*, XXXIII (*ANCL*, xv. 103). The theories of creation that Christianity considers unacceptable are surveyed by Athanasius (*De Inc.* II), to whose list we should add Origen's idea of creation *ab aeterno* (*De pr.* III. v. 3). See further R. B. Tollinton, *Alexandrine Teaching on the Universe* (1932), pp. 87 ff.

[3] *De vera religione*, XVIII. 36 (*LCC*, vi. 242).

[4] *Physica christiana* (Geneva, 1576), tr. Thomas Twyne, *The Wonderfull Workmanship of the World* (1578), fols. 46-46ᵛ.

[5] Seriatim: Joshua Poole, *The English Parnassus* (1657), p. 277; Nicholas Billingsley,

chaos was suggested accurately enough by the French scholar Simon Goulart:

by the *Chaos*, is vnderstood the first matter which God created of nothing, and afterwards gaue it forme, drawing therefrom the works which he did in the sixe dayes. Such is the Poets opinion, *Plato* in his *Timeo*, his schollers, and diuers ancient and moderne *Theologians* are of this opinion, and esteeme that *Moses* in the I. verse of the first chapter of *Genesis* teacheth, that God created first of all, the . . . only matter from which the world should take issue, the rich Orchard of the beauties of this whole, the *Embrion* which should bee formed in sixe dayes, in the estate wherein now we see it.[1]

To 'save phenomena' the apologists of the faith postulated *two* creations: a first creation that resulted in the *ex nihilo* production of chaos ('from Absolute Notbeing to Being'), and a secondary creation during which order was imposed upon the 'first matter' ('from Potentiality to Actuality').[2]

Paradise Lost sustains unreservedly the secondary creation. The 'first matter' is twice described, both times in broadly traditional terms. Chaos from the gates of Hell is revealed as

> a dark
> Illimitable Ocean without bound,
> Without dimension, where length, bredth, and highth,
> And time and place are lost; where eldest *Night*
> And *Chaos*, Ancestors of Nature, hold
> Eternal Anarchie, amidst the noise
> Of endless warrs, and by confusion stand.
> For hot, cold, moist, and dry, four Champions fierce
> Strive here for Maistrie, and to Battel bring
> Thir embryon Atoms.   (II. 891–900)

Κοσμοβρεφία (1658), p. 1; Francis Trigge, *Sermon preached at Grantham* (Oxford, 1594), sig. C2ᵛ; John Andrewes, *The Brazen Serpent* (1621), p. 43; Luther, *Table-Talk*, p. 66. Milton's view used to be attributed to Spenser, esp. to *An Hymne in Honour of Love*, ll. 57 f. (cf. Edwin Greenlaw, *SP*, xvii (1920), 335), but others have since indicated its commonplace nature (Whiting, p. 18; Williams, p. 49; Woodhouse, *PQ*, xxviii (1949), 224). There are numerous references in M. Y. Hughes's ed. of Milton (1957), pp. 179 f.; Kirkconnell, pp. 122 f., 440 f.; Svendsen, pp. 50–52; Taylor (below, p. 33, n. 4), pp. 30–32; Itrat Husain, *The Dogmatic and Mystical Theology of John Donne* (1938), p. 49. Thomas Aquinas reported the similar views of Ambrose, Basil the Great, John Chrysostom (*S. th.* I. lxvi. 1). See also Origen, *De pr.* II. i. 4.

[1] Goulart, i. 16.

[2] Thus Trelcatius, pp. 102 f., and—parenthetically—Samuel Gott, *The Divine History* (1670), p. 113. For parallel statements, see Arminius, ii. 355 f., and Heppe, pp. 196 ff. The two-stage creation is essentially Philo's contribution (James K. Feibleman, *Religious Platonism* (1959), p. 112).

From the gates of Heaven, just before God embarks on the creation of 'new Worlds', chaos appears as a

> vast immeasurable Abyss
> Outrageous as a Sea, dark, wasteful, wilde,
> Up from the bottom turnd by furious windes
> And surging waves, as Mountains to assault
> Heav'ns highth, and with the Center mix the Pole.
>
> (VII. 211–15)

This is nature's Womb (II. 911), and the universe is extracted out of it in ordered sequence.[1] The idea bore the stamp of tradition. In the work of creation, according to Gregory of Nyssa, 'the Deity proceeded by a sort of graduated and ordered advance', which is to say, the Biblical scholar John Lightfoot explained, that

God in framing the world, begins aboue and workes downeward; and in three dayes hee layes the parts of the world, and in the three other dayes, he adornes those parts.

The first day hee makes all the heauens, the matter of the earth, and comes downe so low as the light. The second lower, and makes the firmament or aire. The third lowest of all, and makes distinction of earth and water. Thus in three dayes the parts, or body of the world is laid, in three dayes more, and in the same order they are furnished. For on

The fourth day the Heauens which were made the first day are deckt with starrs. The fifth day the Firmament, which was made the second day, is filled with birds. The sixth day, the Earth, which was laid fit the third day, is replenished with beasts, and lastly man. Thus God in the sixe dayes finished all his worke of Creation.[2]

Milton's acceptance of the theory of the first creation was drastically qualified. The traditional doctrine of *creatio ex nihilo* he certainly denied, in his theological treatise explicitly, and in *Paradise Lost* implicitly, since chaos is nowhere said to have been created 'of nothyng'. Not that Milton maintained the eternal co-existence of God and the rude pristine matter, for he had no wish to become the prey of dualism. He claimed instead that chaos 'originated from God at some particular time', so that ultimately all things derive their

---

[1] On the intellectual progeny of the 'chaos' in *PL*, see above (p. 29, n. 2–3, and p. 30, n. 1), but also Walter C. Curry, *Milton's Ontology* etc. (Lexington, Ky., 1957), ch. ii; A. B. Chambers, *MLN*, lxxvi (1961), 693–5, and esp. *JHI*, xxiv (1963), 55–84.

[2] Gregory, *De anima et resurrectione* (*NPNF*, 2nd ser., v. 441); Lightfoot, *Erubhin* (1629), pp. 151 f. Ralegh (p. 12) has a similarly lengthy statement; Donne is quoted below, p. 57. On the Hebraic background of this idea, see Eric C. Rust, *Nature and Man in Biblical Thought* (1953), ch. iii (i).

existence from God (*omnia ex Deo*).[1] Milton's theory may not seem
particularly orthodox, yet it is not heretical either; indeed, the use of
such labels only diverts our attention from the essential fact that
Milton's view of creation *ex Deo*, far from being unique, forms part
of an 'ancient and honourable Christian tradition' that probably began
with Plotinus and was then conveyed by the proponents of the *via
negativa* to the Renaissance.[2] Milton had better reason than the *ex
nihilo* theory or the cabbalistic view of retraction[3] for espousing this
tradition; he had the idea of the world's creation *ex Deo* which to an
incomparable extent impels Christian belief in God's goodness. In
the Father's declaration on the forthcoming creation,

> Boundless the Deep, because I am who fill
> Infinitude, nor vacuous the space.
> Though I uncircumscrib'd my self retire,
> And put not forth my goodness, which is free
> To act or not, Necessitie and Chance
> Approach not mee, and what I will is Fate.

(VII. 168–73)

Essentially these lines argue that the infinite and omnipresent God,
because he has a free nature, is inactive and does not exert his goodness, since he is at rest; or acts and does exert his goodness, thereby
forcing chaos to yield to his beneficence.[4] Thus the creation of the
world was undertaken further to disseminate the goodness latent
within the Godhead.

In the first chapter of Genesis the creation is six times described
as good, a reiteration that ends in an even higher degree of divine

---

[1] *DDC, Works*, xv. 19–20. On Milton's denial of *creatio ex nihilo*, see the 'strictly
linguistic' study by George N. Conklin, *Biblical Criticism and Heresy in Milton* (1949),
ch. v; and on *creatio de Deo*: esp. A. S. P. Woodhouse, *PQ*, xxviii (1949), 216–22. Both
discussions should be read in the light of Adamson's findings (next note).

[2] J. H. Adamson, 'Milton and the Creation', *JEGP*, lxi (1962), 756–78. The esoteric
doctrines often said to be woven into *PL* are rightly dismissed by Madsen, pp. 220 ff.

[3] Proposed by Denis Saurat (*SP*, xix (1922), 136–51; *Milton* (1944), pp. 102–4,
236–8), but disposed of by McColley, i, pp. 222 f.; Joseph L. Blau, *RR*, vi (1941–2),
163–5; Woodhouse (above, n. 1), pp. 227 f.; C. S. Lewis, *A Preface to 'PL'*
(1942), pp. 85–87; R. J. Z. Werblowsky, *JWCI*, xviii (1955), 90–113; and Michael F.
Moloney, *PQ*, xl (1961), 34–43. For a proper understanding of 'retraction'—introduced
by Isaac Luria in the thirteenth century—consult Scholem, pp. 260 ff.

[4] This is basically the interpretation of the passage by George C. Taylor, *Milton's
Use of Du Bartas* (Cambridge, Mass., 1934), pp. 38–42; Maurice Kelley, *This Great
Argument* (Princeton, 1941), pp. 80–82, 209–13; Arthur Sewell, *RES*, xv (1939), 75–78,
and *A Study in Milton's Christian Doctrine* (1939), pp. 124–32. On the phrase 'put forth'
cf. below, p. 208.

approbation: 'God saw every thing that he had made, and, behold, it was *very* good.'[1] In *Paradise Lost* the repeated assertion that each day's work was good yields to the statement that 'all was entirely good' (VII. 549). The Creator is himself impressed as he surveys

> this new created World
> Th' addition of his Empire, how it shewd
> In prospect from his Throne, how good, how faire,
> Answering his great Idea.
> (VII. 554–7)

Not every authority was inclined to believe that God created the world on the basis of a pre-existent idea; Du Bartas, for example, expressly rejected the possibility that the Creator had employed a 'fore-conceited Plot'.[2] Yet a considerable number of writers agreed with Spenser that when

> this worlds great workmaister did cast
> To make al things, such as we now behold,
> It seemes that he before his eyes had plast
> A goodly Paterne, to whose perfect mould
> He fashioned them as comely as he could.[3]

'God created all things', Nicholas Byfield likewise remarked in 1626,

According to the *Idæa* of all things in his owne minde: for as the Carpenter first conceives the frame in his head, and then builds according to that *Idæa* in his minde: so did God build the world according to the eternall patterne which was in Gods minde.[4]

---

[1] In the LXX the divine satisfaction is mentioned eight times. Christian theologians did not fail to note the parallel in *Timaeus*, 37 C: 'When the father and creator saw the creature which he had made . . ., he rejoiced.' Cf. Augustine, *De civ.* xi. 21.

[2] Du Bartas, p. 6. 'George Puttenham' in 1589 also denied that God created the world 'by any paterne or mould, as the Platonicks with their Idees do phantastically suppose' (*Elizabethan Critical Essays*, ed. G.G. Smith (Oxford, 1904), i. 3).

[3] *An Hymne in Honour of Beautie*, ll. 29–33.

[4] *The Rule of Faith* (1626), pp. 145–6. Perhaps the most enthusiastic exponent of this idea was Donne (*Essays*, p. 29; *Sermons*, iv. 98, 240; vii. 60 f.; viii. 120; ix. 49, 73 f., 276); but see also Richard Hooker, *The Nature of Pride* (Oxford, 1612), p. 3; Browne, *RM*, i. 58; Ames, pp. 27–29; Goulart, i. 8 f.; Thomas Vaughan, *Anthroposophia theomagica* (1650), pp. 5 ff.; Henry More, Ψυχωδία *platonica* (Cambridge, 1642), ii. 103; Sir John Pettus, *Volatiles* (1674), p. 77; *et al.* Among the older influential statements are: Gregory of Nyssa, *In Hexaemeron explicatio apologetica* (*Patr. g.* xliv. 72); Thomas Aquinas, *S. th.* I. xv. 3; and Pico, 'A Platonick Discourse', tr. Thomas Stanley, *Poems* (1651), pp. 218 f. Further references in Heppe, p. 192; Whiting, pp. 19 f.; Williams p. 44; Isidore Epstein [on Ronsard], *PMLA*, lxxix (1964), 224; Herbert Agar, *Milton and Plato* (Princeton, 1928), p. 48; Wolfson, (above, p. 29, n. 3), i. 204 ff., and *The Philosophy of the Church Fathers* (Cambridge, Mass., 1956), i. 257 ff. See also Feibleman (above, p. 31, n. 2), pp. 153 ff.

If the Creator appeared to be limited by this notion, it did at least permit comparison between the final result and the original idea, and a declaration that divine expectations had been fully realized.

The execution of the 'great idea' was an act freely performed by God. Goodness is indeed by nature communicative, and in the time-honoured expression, *bonum est diffusivum sui*; yet the Creator was under no compulsion to create: 'nothing', wrote Thomas Palfreyman in 1578, 'nothing did either moue or inforce God, vnto the creation of this world, but onely his owne infinite mercie and goodnesse'.[1] Some Christian writers, among them the ever-memorable John Hales, rather carelessly allowed a degree of necessity on God's part ('his goodness forced him to break out, to communicate himself'), but Christians generally, including Milton, always insisted with St. Augustine that God had created the world neither out of any necessity nor out of any want, but simply 'out of the fulnesse of [his] goodnesse'.[2] Within the Christian tradition the prime reason for the creation of the world has, in the words of St. John of Damascus, generally been that 'God... in his exceeding goodness wished certain things to come into existence which would enjoy his benefits and share in his goodness'.[3]

Behind this traditional view stands not Moses but Plato, 'that *Atticke Moses*'.[4] Exponents of the Mosaic narrative were enormously influenced by a celebrated passage in the *Timaeus*, which declares the reason for the creation to be the Demiurge's wish to pass on to the created his goodness: 'Let me tell you then, why the creator of the world generated and created this universe. He was good, and no goodness can ever have any jealousy of anything. And being free from

---

[1] *The Treatise of Heauenly Philosophy* (1578), p. 797.

[2] Hales, *Sermons preach'd at Eton* (1660), p. 44; Augustine, *Conf.* XIII. 4. Among the representative censures of the 'necessity' theory are: in the early Church, Irenaeus, *Adversus haereses*, IV. xiv. 1; during the Renaissance: Sir John Hayward, *Davids Teares* (1623), p. 152; and in our time: E. L. Mascall, *He Who Is* (1943), pp. 105–12, and Leonard Hodgson, *The Doctrine of the Trinity* (1944), pp. 122–34. On Milton's position see *DDC*, *Works*, xv. 5, 15, and Woodhouse (above, p. 33, n. 1), pp. 212–15.

[3] *De fide orthodoxa*, II. 2 (*NPNF*, 2nd ser., ix. 18). Thus Tertullian, *Adversus Marcionem*, II. 3–4; Origen, *De pr.* II. ix. 6; Augustine, *De civ.* XI. 21.

[4] Edward Chaloner, *Sixe Sermons* (1623), p. 337. Cf. Baxter, ii. 280, and Francis Cheynell, *The Divine Trinunity* (1650), p. 5: '*Plato* was not called the Atticising *Moses* in vaine.' Long before the Platonists of Renaissance Italy seized on the idea (Robb, pp. 51–53), Numenius wrote: τί γάρ ἐστι Πλάτων ἢ Μωϋσῆς ἀττικίζων; (*apud* Clement of Alexandria, *Stromata*, I. 22, 150). Clement also has the best introduction to the early Christian view of Greek 'plagiarisms' from the OT (ibid. v. 14). For a full exposition see Theophilus Gale, *The Court of the Gentiles* (Oxford, 1671), pt. ii, bk. ii, ch. ii et seq.

jealousy, he desired that all things should be as like himself as possible. This is the true beginning of creation and of the world.'[1] Dressed in Christian garb, the Platonic notion appeared in Dante thus:

> In sua eternità di tempo fuore,
>   fuor d'ogni altro comprender, come i piacque,
>   s'aperse in nuovi amor l'eterno amore.[2]

Like statements naturally abound, often transferred from one commentator to another with only slight changes in wording; thus Augustine's 'Because God is good, we are', in 1629 became John Gaule's 'It was the sole Goodness of our God, not onely that we were good, but that we were'.[3] And here is Dr. Walter Charleton's excellent summary of the traditional thesis:

> Such was the Freedom of his Will, that no necessity could constrain him to the production of any thing; such the Bounty, that none could restrain him from the voluntary profusion of his goodness. When twas indifferent to him, or to constitute a World, or to continue alone; he yet was pleased to follow the propensity of his own infinite Benignity, and to create: insomuch as he judged it better that there should be other natures beside his own, to which he might impart the overflowings of his goodness; then not.[4]

The popular question asked of Lambert Daneau ('What cause mooued God specially to make this worlde, hee himselfe lacking nothing') evoked the answer: 'Euen his mere goodnes, that is to saye, his most louing good will to communicate the same his felicitie unto certaine thinges, so farre foorth as the nature of those things whiche hee created, was able to receiue the same.'[5]

It is a question which to readers of *Paradise Lost* has an inescapably familiar ring. Adam likewise desired to know

---

[1] *Timaeus*, 29 E, tr. Benjamin Jowett (1871). The passage is discussed by A. E. Taylor, *A Commentary on Plato's Timaeus* (Oxford, 1928), pp. 75–79, and its influence is stated by Frank E. Robbins, *The Hexaemeral Literature* (Chicago, 1912), pp. 4 f. Cf. above, p. 29, n. 3. Milton's debt to *Timaeus* has been argued by Edward C. Baldwin (*PMLA*, xxxv (1920), 214–16), but as much could be claimed on behalf of every Christian writer.

[2] *Par.* xxix. 16–18: 'In his eternity beyond time, beyond all other comprehension, as was his pleasure, the eternal love revealed himself in new loves.'

[3] Augustine, *De doctrina christiana*, i. i. 32 [*apud* S. J. Grabowski, *The All-Present God* (St. Louis, 1954), p. 156]; Gaule, *Practique Theories* (1629), p. 2.

[4] *The Darknes of Atheism* (1652), pp. 79–80. See also Donne's extended commentary in *Sermons*, vi. 232 ff.

[5] Daneau (above, p. 30, n. 4), fol. 44.

> what cause
> Mov'd the Creator in his holy Rest
> Through all Eternitie so late to build
> In *Chaos*.   (VII. 90–93)

Yet Raphael, unlike Daneau, replies that the decision to create a new
world came as a result of God's desire to repair the 'detriment' caused
by the expulsion of the rebellious angels. In God's own statement,

> [I] in a moment will create
> Another World, out of one man a Race
> Of men innumerable, there to dwell,
> Not here, till by degrees of merit rais'd
> They op'n to themselves at length the way
> Up hither, under long obedience tri'd,
> And Earth be chang'd to Heav'n, and Heav'n to Earth,
> One Kingdom, Joy and Union without end.   (VII. 154–61)

How intriguing! Was mankind created merely because God desired
to repopulate Heaven? The traditional attitude was clearly that God
did create the human race 'in order that the seats in heaven left
vacant by the fall of Lucifer and his rebellious angels might be filled
again'. This statement occurs not in a Renaissance treatise but in *A
Portrait of an Artist as a Young Man* (1916), where Joyce drew upon
a tradition to which any number of theologians subscribed. All concurred with St. Anselm that 'God planned to restore from human
nature, which he made without sin, the number of the angels who had
fallen'.[1] Milton of course had precedents nearer his own day from
which to draw, for example, Spenser's formulation in *An Hymne
of Heavenly Love* (ll. 101 ff.), and Richard Montagu's in 1642, one
of innumerable such statements from prose-writers: 'This breach in
cõmunion, by the fall of Angels, in the Church, then consisting in
the highest heavens, God againe repaired, and made up, creating
man, purposely made and framed by him, to succeed unto the
ruines, which Angels by their fall had made in the Church, that
City of God.'[2] Nevertheless, we must not allow the popularity of the

---

[1] Joyce, *Portrait* (1957), p. 117; Anselm, *Cur Deus homo?* I. 16 (tr. E. S. Prout (1887)).
Thus Augustine, *De civ.* XXII. 1, and *Enchiridion*, XXIX, LXII (*LCC*, vii, 356, 375), and the
host of authorities cited by McColley i, p. 201; ii, pp. 46 f.

[2] *The Acts and Monuments of the Church* (1642), p. 7. Thus also William Jordan, *The
Creation of the World* (1611), ed. Davies Gilbert (1827), p. 26; Henry King, *A Sermon
of Deliverance* (1626), p. 36; Edward Cooke, *Bartas Junior* (1631), p. 6; Edward Leigh,
A Systeme or Body of Divinity (1654), p. 272; *et al.* For a poetic statement besides
Spenser's, see the *York Plays*, ed. L. T. Smith (Oxford, 1885), p. 6.

repopulation theory to beguile us into thinking that it was ever proposed as the capital reason for God's creation of the universe. That capital reason was, both for Milton and for the Christian tradition, the dissemination of divine goodness. The angelic hymn that follows the announcement of God's intention to create man demonstrates it:

> Glorie they sung to the most High, good will
> To future men, and in thir dwellings peace:
> Glorie to him whose just avenging ire
> Had driven out th' ungodly from his sight
> And th' habitations of the just; to him
> Glorie and praise, whose wisdom had ordained
> Good out of evil to create, in stead
> Of Spirits maligne a better Race to bring
> Into thir vacant room, and thence diffuse
> His good to Worlds and Ages infinite.
>
> (VII. 182–91)

Here in quintessence is the Christian doctrine of creation as well as the answer to Adam's query.

The Christian faith has traditionally asserted that 'the principal end of our Creation' is the glory of God,[1] on the basis of the Old Testament view that 'the Lord hath made all things for himself' (Prov. xvi. 4). 'God has made all things for himself', wrote Sir Thomas Browne, 'and it is impossible hee should make them for any other end than his owne glory; it is all he can receive, and all that is without himselfe.'[2] In *Paradise Regained* Satan, pretending not to understand, indignantly charges God with selfishness:

> hee seeks glory,
> And for his glory all things made, all things
> Orders and governs, nor content in Heaven
> By all his Angels glorifi'd, requires
> Glory from men, from all men good or bad,
> Wise or unwise, no difference, no exemption.
>
> (III. 110–15)

---

[1] Nathanael Cole, *Preservatives against Sinne* (1618), p. 69. For representative statements of this belief, see Hooker, p. 4; Donne, *Sermons*, vi. 297 f.; Bellarmine, *Treatise . . . framing a Ladder*, tr. T. B. (Douai, 1616), pp. 29 ff.; Christopher Lever, *The Holy Pilgrime* (1618), p. 261; Richard Sibbes, *The Christians End* (1639), p. 19; and William Spurstow, *The Wels of Salvation* (1655), p. 267. On Luther's constant concern with the divine glory, see Philip S. Watson, *Let God be God!* (1947), pp. 59 ff. There is a good study of Milton's 'sense of glory' by Merritt Y. Hughes, *PQ*, xxviii (1949), 107–24.

[2] *RM*, i. 35.

But Jesus replies 'fervently' that

> his Word all things produc'd,
> Though chiefly not for glory as prime end,
> But to shew forth his goodness, and impart
> His good communicable to every soul
> Freely.
>
> (III. 122–6)

This statement does not contradict the Son's declaration in *Paradise Lost* that man was made for the glory of God (III. 164). Milton in *De doctrina christiana* observes that God created the world 'for the manifestation of the glory of his power and goodness' (*ad patefaciendam potentiae et bonitatis suae gloriam*), implying that we may not distinguish between the diffusive goodness and the glory of God in so far as the one inevitably yields the other.[1] Two Cambridge Platonists help to elucidate. Ralph Cudworth explained:

the *reason* why God made the World, was from his own *Overflowing* and *Communicative Goodness*, that there might be other Beings also *Happy* besides him, and enjoy themselves. Nor does this at all clash, with God's making of the world, for his own *Glory* and *Honour*. . . . God did not make the World, meerly to Ostentate his *Skill* and *Power*; but to communicate his Goodness, which is chiefly and properly his *Glory*, as the *Light* and *Splendor* of the Sun, is the *Glory of it*.[2]

Similarly John Smith:

God does then most *glorifie* and exalt himself in the most triumphant way that may be *ad extra* or out of himself, if I may so phrase it, when he most of all communicates himself, and when he erects such Monuments of his own Majesty wherein his own *Love and Goodness* may live and reign.[3]

Such comments illuminate for us the numerous testimonies to the divine goodness in *Paradise Lost*, from the angels' statement on the basis of experience (V. 826 f.) to the repeated confessions of Adam: in his first speech after his creation (VIII. 278 f.), in his first address to Eve (IV. 412 ff.), in their joint hymn of thanksgiving (V. 158 f.), and

---

[1] *Works*, xv. 5, 15. The distinction is implicit in Woodhouse (above, p. 33, n. 1), p. 214.

[2] *The True Intellectual System of the Universe* (1678), p. 886.

[3] *Select Discourses* (1660), p. 142. Thus Benjamin Whichcote, *Moral and Religious Aphorisms*, ed. W. R. Inge (1930), p. 39.

finally—the climax of the theme of God's constant creation of good
out of evil—in his exclamation:

> O goodness infinite, goodness immense!
> That all this good of evil shall produce,
> And evil turn to good . . .[1]

Renaissance expositors set forth in several ways the goodness
imparted to the natural order by God, though they most frequently
stressed three: perfection, beauty, and order.[2] I need not cite any
comments on nature's beauty, since these were usually trite or,
worse, almost hysterical in their enthusiasm. Of the order pervading
the universe I will have something to say in the next chapter, so here
I confine myself to creation's 'perfection'. In *Paradise Lost* this is
referred to explicitly (v. 472, 524; x. 482 f.), and often through the
use of two familiar symbols, the circle and musical harmony.

'God', declared Donne, 'hath wrapped up all things in Circles.'[3]
Some experimental scientists may have smiled at such naïveté, but
Donne and his tradition-bound contemporaries were in earnest. The
circle, after all, is a 'most perfect, capable, ancient' figure, and on
that basis alone it *had* to be that 'all the works of the Divine goodnesse are circular': the motion of the heavens, 'circular'; the earth,
'circular' again; nature herself, 'a circular line'; and the human body
'for the most part round and orbicular, or comming neere unto that
figure'.[4] This last most curious notion is as sacrosanct as the first and
the second. Vitruvius had explained long since that 'if a man be
placed flat on his back, with his hands and feet extended, and a pair
of compasses centred at his navel, the fingers and toes of his two

---

[1] XII. 469–71; further discussed below, pp. 142 f. The theme is emphasized in *PL*, I.
163–5, 217–19; VII. 187–91, 613–16; XII. 565–6.

[2] For a good summary of this, see Daneau (above, p. 30, n. 4), fols. 80ᵛ–82. Cf.
Williams, pp. 63 f.

[3] Donne, *Sermons*, vii. 396; see also vi. 173 ff.—though in moments of less assured
'devout fitts' Donne was not quite so positive (cf. *The First Anniversary*, ll. 251 ff.). On
the decline and fall of the circle, see Marjorie H. Nicolson's study, *The Breaking of the
Circle*, rev. ed. (1960), and the supplements—notably by F. L. Huntley—I cited in *MP*,
lxi (1964), 244.

[4] Seriatim: Alexander Ross, *Questions and Answers* (1620), p. 2; Oswald Crollius,
Mysteries of Nature, tr. Henry Pinnell in *Philosophy Reformed* (1657), p. 55; Ross,
Arcana Microcosmi (1652), p. 24; Godfrey Goodman, *The Fall of Man* (1616), p. 134;
Ross, *Medicus medicatus* (1645), p. 21; and Charron, *Of Wisdome*, tr. Samson Lennard
(1640), p. 13. Cf. Ficino: 'Every mind lauds the round figure' (Cassirer, p. 63). The
circle is more 'ancient' than even the Renaissance thought; cf. Harold Bayley, *The Lost
Language of Symbolism* (1951), i. 289. On the world's 'round fourme' see esp. the exposition by Andreas Gerardus Hyperius, *Two Common Places*, tr. R. Vaux (1581), pp. 16 ff.

hands and feet will touch the circumference of a circle described therefrom'.[1] Milton fortunately did not make use of this idea, though the compasses are essential in Raphael's account of the creation. As he reports, God

> took the gold'n Compasses, prepar'd
> In Gods Eternal store, to circumscribe
> This Universe, and all created things:
> One foot he centerd, and the other turnd
> Round through the vast profunditie obscure,
> And said, Thus farr extend, thus farr thy bounds,
> This be thy just Circumference, O World.
>
> (VII. 225–31)

The seventeenth-century reader would have realized that this most magnificent expression of a great Renaissance idea[2] was utilized in order to proclaim the perfection of the newly created world.

Music during the Renaissance commanded extensive respect, especially from humanists but also from Protestant theologians. Did not Luther say, 'next unto *Theologia*, I give the place and highest honor to *Musica*'?[3] Enthusiasm for music was generated by the conviction that music, as Milton himself said, 'has a great power over disposition and manners, to smooth and make them gentle from

---

[1] *De architectura*, III. i. 3; tr. Morris H. Morgan (1960), p. 73. I quoted Helkiah Crooke's lengthy paraphrase (1615) in *NQ*, vii (1960), 54 f. See also *The Drawings of Leonardo da Vinci*, ed. A. E. Popham (1952), § 215. The road from Vitruvius through the Renaissance to Blake is mapped by Désirée Hirst, *Hidden Riches* (1964), esp. ch. ii.

[2] Milton naturally knew the precedent in Dante (*Par.* XIX. 40–42), but far more important was that of Prov. viii. 27, where the Creator sets 'a compass upon the face of the depth' (thus the AV; and though the original Hebrew reads 'circle' rather than 'compass', the latter reading was preferred: see Grant McColley, *NQ*, clxxvi (1939), 97 f., and Fletcher (above, p. 29, n. 2), pp. 100–9; cf. Anthony Blunt, *JWCI*, ii (1938–9), 53–63). The tradition is studied further by A. B. Chambers, *ELH*, xxviii (1961), esp. pp. 33–42. Blake's 'Ancient of Days' is only partly relevant, since the compasses are held by the *left* hand (on the symbolism see J. H. Wicksteed, *Blake's Vision of the Book of Job*, 2nd rev. ed. (1924), **App. A**).

[3] *Table-Talk*, p. 501. For the background consult the selections from patristic literature in *Source Readings in Music History*, ed. Oliver Strunk (1952), ch. ii, and the studies by Théodore Gérold, *Les Pères de l'Église et la musique* (Strasbourg, 1931); Hermann Abert, *Die Musikanschauung des Mittelalters* (Halle, 1905); John Hollander, *The Untuning of the Sky: Ideas of Music in English Poetry 1500–1700* (Princeton, 1961), with full bibliography; and Gretchen L. Finney, *Musical Backgrounds for English Literature* (New Brunswick, N.J., 1962). Milton is discussed by Hollander, pp. 315–31; Finney, ch. viii–xi; Sigmund G. Spaeth, *Milton's Knowledge of Music* (Princeton, 1913); and Laurence Stapleton, *UTQ*, xxiii (1953–4), 217–26. The legend of the Puritan opposition to music has been exploded by Percy A. Scholes, *Music and Puritanism* (Lausanne, 1934).

rustick harshness and distemper'd passions'.[1] Yet more important was the theory, traditionally held, that music really pervades the entire cosmic structure. Thus in the animal kingdom, Bishop Godfrey Goodman claimed in 1616,

you have a full, perfect, and compleat Quier; sufficient variety of voices; the little chirping birds, the Wren and the Robin, they sing a treble; the Goldfinch, the Nightingale, they joyne in the meane; the Black-birds, the Thrush, they beare the tenour, while the four-footed beasts, with their bleating and bellowing, they sing a base.[2]

The 'symphony of nature' is a notion very popular in seventeenth-century poetry; it appears, for example, in Vaughan's *The Morning-Watch* and in *Paradise Lost* (v. 164–201). The underlying theory of the *musica mundana* was, if anything, more popular. According to this, the universe (in Isidore of Seville's words) 'is held together by a certain harmony of sounds, and the heavens themselves are made to revolve by the modulation of harmony'.[3] The theory is of great antiquity, going back to Pythagoras and to Hermes Trismegistus, who claimed that God is 'by nature a musician ($\kappa\alpha\tau\grave{\alpha}\ \phi\acute{\upsilon}\sigma\iota\nu\ \mu o\upsilon\sigma\iota\kappa\acute{o}s$), and not only works harmony in the universe at large, but also transmits to individuals the rhythm of his own music'.[4] Adopted readily by Christianity, the theory induced Gregory of Nyssa to state that the harmony of the created order derives from 'the archetypal and true music which the orderer of the universe lets sound'. Earlier still, Clement of Alexandria maintained that the act of creation was

---

[1] *Of Education, Works*, iv. 289; see also *Ad Patrem*, ll. 21–32. Among the *loci classici* on the power inherent in music, see Iamblichus, *De mysteriis*, III. 9; and among the more thorough Renaissance expositions, consult Henry Peacham, *The Compleat Gentleman* (1622), ch. xi; Burton, *The Anatomy of Melancholy*, 6th ed. (1652), pp. 298–301 [part. 2, sect. 2, memb. 6, subs. 3]; Cowley, *Poems*, ed. A. R. Waller (Cambridge, 1905), pp. 274 ff.; and Nathaniel Wanley, *The Wonders of the Little World* (1678), Bk. v, ch. x. The background of this idea is most ably studied by Frances A. Yates, *The French Academies of the Sixteenth Century* (1947), pp. 36 ff., and *passim*.

[2] *The Creatures praysing God* (1622), p. 24 [Goodman copied this passage from his earlier work *The Fall of Man* (1616), p. 78].

[3] *Etymologiae*, III. 17 (in Strunk (above, p. 41, n. 3), p. 94). See further Leo Spitzer's standard work, *Classical and Christian Ideas of World Harmony*, ed. Anna G. Hatcher (Baltimore, 1963).

[4] Walter Scott, ed., *Hermetica* (Oxford, 1924), i. 274–7; G. R. S. Mead, *Thrice-Greatest Hermes* (1949), ii. 288–9. The Pythagoreans, reported Aristotle, 'supposed the elements of numbers to be the elements of all things, and the whole heaven to be a musical scale and a number' (*Metaphysica*, 985b; tr. W. D. Ross (1908)). This idea, with the implicit support of the Wisdom of Solomon (xi. 20), led to the view of God as a 'great Geometrician' (Hales (above, p. 35, n. 2), p. 49); but see also Kepler's *Harmonices mundi* (1619), which I quoted in *Isis*, xlix (1958), 395).

a musical performance in that God 'composed the entire creation into melodious order, and tuned into concert the discord of the elements'.[1] Clement's theory looks, as it were, both before and after; before, to the apocryphal Wisdom of Solomon (xix. 18–20), itself heavily influenced by Greek ideas; and after, to a number of thoroughly traditional Renaissance conceptions, notably those by Sir John Davies in *Orchestra*, by Cowley in the *Davideis*, and later by Dryden in *A Song for St. Cecilia's Day*. This is how Cowley envisaged the transformation of chaos—creation's 'first draught'—into the universe we know:

> Th' ungoverned parts no Correspondence knew,
> An artless war from thwarting Motions grew;
> Till they to Number and fixt Rules were brought
> By the Eternal Mindes Poetique Thought.
> Water and Air he for the Tenor chose,
> Earth made the Base, the Treble Flame arose,
> To th'active Moon a quick brisk stroke he gave,
> To Saturns string a touch more soft and grave.
> The motions strait, and Round, and Swift, and Slow,
> And Short, and Long, were mixt and woven so,
> Did in such artful Figures smoothly fall,
> As made this decent measur'd Dance of all.[2]

Cowley's description of celestial harmony as a dance is hardly original. Among others, Du Bartas also maintained that the planets 'daunce about this Ball', Crashaw wrote that 'the gay starrs lead on their Golden dance', and Milton claimed that the spheres move in a 'starry dance', a 'mystic Dance not without Song'.[3] We have here a variation on the ever-fascinating theme of 'the Pythagoricall Musick of the spheres', which the Renaissance took over with the endorsement of countless authorities like Plato, Macrobius, and Boethius.[4] Shakespeare in *The Merchant of Venice* epitomizes it:

[1] Gregory, *De occursu Domini*, I. 422 (in Abert (above, p. 41, n. 3), p. 81); Clement, *Protrepticus*, I. 5 (tr. G. W. Butterworth (1919)).

[2] *Davideis*, I, §§ 34–36. John Weemes penned a more detailed exposition in his *Observations* (1633), pp. 3 f., and Martin Fotherby quoted a host of precedents in *Atheomastix* (1622), Bk. II, ch. xii, § 4.

[3] Du Bartas, p. 187; Crashaw, *Sospetto d'Herode*, XXVI. 6 (cf. *The Teare*, l. 141); *PL*, III. 579, and v. 178 (cf. v. 620–7; VII. 562; VIII. 123–5; IX. 103). The idea is traditional; see, for instance, Synesius of Cyrene, *Essays and Hymns*, tr. Augustine FitzGerald (1930), ii. 385.

[4] Seriatim: Sir Thomas Browne, *The Garden of Cyrus* (1658), p. 121; Plato, *Republic*, 617; Macrobius, *Comment. in somnium Scipionis*, II. 1–4; Boethius, *De institutione musica*, I. 2. Further references in Spaeth (above, p. 41, n. 3), pp. 144–9, and esp. Fotherby

There's not the smallest orb which thou behold'st
But in his motion like an angel sings,
Still quiring to the young-ey'd cherubins.
Such harmony is in immortal souls;
But whilst this muddy vesture of decay
Doth grossly close it in, we cannot hear it.

(v. i. 60–65)

The last two lines propound a Renaissance dogma which after Shakespeare was restated by Donne ('the musick of the Sphears, whatsoever it be, we cannot hear it'), and by Milton also ('the heavenly tune . . . none can hear / Of human mould with grosse unpurged ear'), though Milton's statement must be distinguished from Shakespeare's, for Shakespeare was probably interested much more in the poetic merit of the idea whereas Milton was as much concerned with its moral purport implicitly in *Arcades*, explicitly in his second prolusion *De sphaerarum concentu*.[1]

Renaissance writers assure us that the man who lacked response to music was 'suspected to be something of a savage Nature' and indeed not 'weel in his wits' but 'wholly unnatural and inhumane'.[2] I quote again from *The Merchant of Venice*:

The man that hath no music in himself,
Nor is not mov'd with concord of sweet sounds,
Is fit for treasons, stratagems, and spoils.
The motions of his spirit are dull as night
And his affections dark as Erebus.
Let no such man be trusted.

(v. i. 83–88)

We are therefore not surprised to find that Renaissance writers often thought of the devils as tone-deaf and given to the production of horrid noises. The 'gastlie rore' of Tasso's devils, for example, is only a few degrees away from Thomas Adams's conclusion that Hell

(n. 2), pp. 313–18. The best essay on the subject is F. M. Cornford's 'The Harmony of the Spheres', in *The Unwritten Philosophy* (Cambridge, 1950), pp. 14–27; but see also Arthur Koestler, *The Sleepwalkers* (1959), pt. I, ch. ii. The opposition was led by Aristotle (*De caelo*, 290[b]), among whose Renaissance disciples was the Flemish musicologist Joannes Tinctoris (in Strunk (above, p. 41, n. 3), p. 198).

[1] The parenthetical quotations are from Donne, *Sermons*, ii. 170, and Milton, *Arcades*, ll. 72–73. My hesitation concerning Shakespeare is not shared by J. P. Brockbank (*SS*, xvi (1963), 38 f.), who invokes the influential statement of Hooker (v. xxxviii. 1).

[2] Seriatim: Robert Herne, *Ros coeli* (1640), p. 262; Castiglione, *The Courtier*, tr. Thomas Hoby (1588), sig. H3; and Scipion du Plessis, *The Resoluer*, tr. Anon. (1635), pp. 292 f. Thus Benlowes, *Theophila*, vi. 99.

is distinguished for its unpleasant sounds ('Man-drakes and Night-rauens still shriking') rather than for any '*Dorian* musicke'.[1] By contrast the fallen angels of *Paradise Lost* parade to the sound of 'the *Dorian* mood' and listen often to 'Dulcet Symphonies and voices sweet', even to 'jocond Music' (I. 550, 712, 787). Yet the music of Milton's Hell is far from perfect, for music, once divorced from its true source, becomes 'partial' (II. 552), a *concordia discors* wherein the martial sounds predominate (I. 540 ff.) and jarring noises tear Hell's concave with increasing frequency.[2] What a difference between the 'deafning shout' that greets Satan's decision to destroy man (II. 520) and the response of the heavenly angels when the Son offers to save mankind:

> all
> The multitude of Angels with a shout
> Loud as from numbers without number, sweet
> As from blest voices, uttering joy, Heav'n rung
> With Jubilee, and loud Hosanna's filld
> Th' eternal Regions.
>
> (III. 344–9)

Milton could hardly have chosen a more eloquent method of affirming the essential goodness of the created order in continuing loyalty to the orderer of the universe.

III

The creation of the universe has traditionally been conceived of as a work performed together by the three Persons in the Godhead. The formula of St. Athanasius (ὁ γὰρ Πατὴρ διὰ τοῦ Λόγου ἐν τῷ Πνεύματι κτίζει τὰ πάντα) occurs repeatedly up to the Renaissance, as in Johann Gerhard's principal theological treatise ('[everything was] wrought by *God* through the *Sonne* in the *Holy Ghost*').[3] Here is the explanatory statement of the influential William Perkins, joined to the relevant passages in *Paradise Lost*: 'the father is the cause that

---

[1] Tasso, *Gerusalemme liberata*, IV. 18 (tr. Edward Fairfax, *Godfrey of Bulloigne* (1600), p. 58); Adams, *Workes* (1629), p. 242.

[2] See esp. I. 541–3; II. 539–41; and the discussion by J. B. Broadbent, *Some Graver Subject* (1960), pp. 120–2. Garland Ethel has related Hell's marching music to Plutarch's account of the Spartan order of battle (*MLQ*, xviii (1957), 295–302).

[3] Athanasius, *Epistola ad Serapionem*, III. 5 (*Patr. g.* xxvi. 632); Gerhard, p. 40. The Logos was traditionally regarded as the agent of creation—God's 'hand'—in accordance with John i. 3. See Tixeront, i. 214–20, and Henry Bettenson, ed., *The Early Church Fathers* (1956), pp. 117, 390.

beginneth the worke [VII. 154 ff., 514 ff.], the sonne puts it in execution [III. 390 f.; V. 836 f.; VII. 216 f.], the holy Ghost is the finisher
of it [I. 19–22; VII. 234 ff.].'[1]

The angels were the first of the countless beings created by the
Godhead, though the time of their creation is not specified in the
Bible, nor has this time ever been defined by dogma. Augustine,
Gregory the Great, Thomas Aquinas, and Peter Lombard supported
the view that the angels were 'concreated' with the heavens and light;[2]
while Origen, John Chrysostom, Basil the Great, and Ambrose held
that the creation of the angels occurred 'long before the rest of the
corporall world'.[3] Milton, curiously enough, subscribed to the
second of these two views in both *Paradise Lost* and *De doctrina
christiana*,[4] although Protestant inclination was to reject all opinions
as mere speculations without any Scriptural support whatsoever.
As William Alley stated in 1571 on behalf of the Protestant majority,
'concerning the tyme, when [the angels] were made & created,
whether it were together with the light, before man or after man,
and after all the rest of the workes of God, let him declare y̆ knoweth
any certayntie of it, more then the Scriptures do teach.'[5]

Milton's angelology has been the concern of scholars principally
because of 'two little heresies' detected in *Paradise Lost*. The first
(V. 404 ff.) reveals that the angels are capable of assimilating food,
and the second (VIII. 615 ff.) that love-making in Heaven resembles
love-making on earth. Did Milton admit the corporeity of the angels?

[1] Perkins, p. 53. Thus Erasmus, *Exposition . . . of the Cōmune Crede* (1533), sig. E6;
Luis de la Puente, *Meditations*, tr. John Heigham (St. Omer, 1619), ii. 751; and the
references in H. Pinnard, *Dictionnaire de théologie catholique* (Paris, 1908), iii. 2111–15.

[2] John Yates, *A Modell of Divinitie* (1622), p. 118. The most significant poetic use of
this theory is in Dante, *Par.* XXIX. 22–45. See also Heppe, pp. 202 f.; Ursinus, p. 347;
Ames, p. 39; Wolleb, p. 40; John Day, *Day's Dyall* (Oxford, 1614), pp. 84 f.; Robert
Mossom, *Sion's Prospect* (1653), pp. 28, 42; and the more cautious statements of Perkins,
p. 73, and John Deacon and John Walker, *Dialogicall Discourses* (1601), p. 24. Donne's
report that this view was 'ordinarily received' (*Sermons*, ii. 294) is not accurate and was
altered later (*Sermons*, iii. 266; viii. 105, 360 f.). On the background consult Ginzberg,
i. 16–18.

[3] John Salkeld, *A Treatise of Angels* (1613), p. 9. For summaries of the various
opinions see Salkeld, ch. iii; Andrew Willet, *Hexapla in Genesin* (Cambridge, 1605),
p. 17; Thomas Heywood, *The Hierarchie of the Blessed Angells* (1635), pp. 334–6; and
esp. Sigmund Feyerabend, *Theatrum diabolorum* (Frankfurt, 1569), fols. 14ᵛ ff.

[4] *PL*, I. Argument; *DDC*, *Works*, xv. 33. On this tradition, see the numerous precedents cited by McColley i, pp. 184 f.

[5] Πτωχομουσεῖον (1571), i. 122ᵛ. Thus Du Bartas, p. 17; Gerhard, p. 46; Musculus,
fol. 11; Edmund Bunny, *Of Divorce* (1610), pp. 27 f.; Lever (above, p. 38, n. 1),
pp. 19 f.; John Hart, *The Fort-Royal* (1649), p. 473; Edward Sparke, Θυσιαστήριον, 3rd
ed. (1663), p. 550; *et al.* See further Williams, pp. 61 f.

Here is the question fundamental to both his 'heresies', and the answer must be emphatically affirmative, though not without qualification. In Raphael's exposition of the scale of Nature, the first matter is said to be

> Indu'd with various forms, various degrees
> Of substance, and in things that live, of life;
> But more refin'd, more spiritous and pure,
> As neerer to [God] plac't or neerer tending.
>
> (v. 473–6)

Other writers who make similar statements include Donne, with his observation that in comparison with God both angels and human souls are 'but grosse bodies', and Gulielmus Bucanus, who made the sophisticated declaration that the angels

are not altogether and indeed without matter, as neither is the soule of man; for God alone is without matter. For there is nothing created which is not also compounded, either by natural composition, as consisting of matter and forme: or else metaphysical, namely, of the essence, or of the act and the power. Yet because they do not consist of any corporall matter, which is palpable, and subiect to the sight, but rather spirituall altogether, and (as they say in the schooles) onely of the power and the act, they are said to be without matter. But God alone is a power or pure Act: as Aristotle said verie well in the II. booke of his Metaphysiks, chap. 7.[1]

Even clearer are the observations of Henry Lawrence, the Lord President of the Council under Cromwell and the man so highly praised by Milton. Wrote Lawrence in 1646:

If you aske . . . whether the Angells have bodies, or are altogether incorporall, it is a question controverted betweene the Philosophers, the Schoolmen, and the Fathers; the Platonists would have them have bodies, to which many of the Fathers adhere; Aristotle and the Schoolmen would have them altogether incorporall. . . . But if they have any such composition, as may be called a body, it is certainly of the greatest finenesse and subtilty a spirituall body, and therefore not like to be of that grossenes that either the air is, or those heavens that are framed out of the Chaos, but neerer the substance of the highest heavens, which seeme to have bene made at the same time: To conclude, it will be safe to say that in comparison to God they are bodies, in comparison of us they are pure and mighty spirits.[2]

---

[1] Donne, *Sermons*, vii. 344, and Bucanus, pp. 64–65.

[2] *Of our Communion and Warre with Angels* (1646), p. 9. Lawrence—the 'virtuous Father' of Sonnet XX—was also praised by Milton for his scholarship (*Works*, viii. 234).

The supporting views of innumerable Fathers and medieval theologians were readily available in a series of works, among them Noël
Taillepied's *Psichologie* or *Traité de l'apparition des esprits* (1588),
John Salkeld's *Treatise of Angels* (1613), Burton's *Anatomy of Melancholy* (1621), Robert Shelford's *Five Pious and Learned Discourses*
(1635), Robert Gell's Ἀγγελοκρατία Θεοῦ (1650), Henry More's
Apology (1664), and Cudworth's *True Intellectual System of the
Universe* (1678).[1] These summaries of opinion did not quote theologians only. Often cited was the important eleventh-century
Byzantine Platonist Michael Psellus, whose treatise *De dæmonum
operatione*, widely disseminated in the 'Platonic Collection' edited
by Ficino (1497), played a large part in gaining 'the unanimous consent of all Platonists' concerning the angels' corporeity.[2] By Milton's
time the tradition was so well established that Henry More thought
'there is little question to be made' regarding its basic soundness.[3]

Even fewer questions were raised in connexion with the proud
claim that man was the Creator's 'Maister work' (VII. 505). Man was
indeed created last, but that was because 'in a certaine manner hee
was the end and perfection of the rest: and thus beside other interpretations, this also may be admitted of the philosophicall axiome,
quod est primum in intentione, est ultimū in executione'.[4] More important

---

[1] Taillepied, ch. xvi; Salkeld, ch. vi; Burton: part. i, sect. 2, memb. i, subs. 2;
Shelford, pp. 158–62; Gell, esp. pp. 13 f.; More (below, n. 3), ch. iii; Cudworth:
pt. i, ch. v, sect. 3. Among the *loci classici* are: Tertullian, *Adversus Marcionem*, II. 8,
and *De carne Christi*, VI; Basil the Great, *De Spiritu Sancto*, XXXVIII; John of Damascus,
De fide orthodoxa, II. 3; and further: Justin Martyr, *Dialogus cum Tryphone*, LVII. 2;
Tertullian, *De anima*, I–IX; and Lactantius, *Divinae institutiones*, II. 15. Numerous
references are given by Louis Coulange [Joseph Turmel], *The Life of the Devil*, tr. S. H.
Guest (1929), ch. viii–ix; Arturo Graf, *The Story of the Devil*, tr. E. N. Stone (1931),
pp. 24–27; Edward Langton, *Supernatural* (1934), esp. pp. 26, 31, 38, 44, 51; Marjorie
H. Nicolson, *SP*, xxii (1925), 433–52; Walter C. Curry, *Shakespeare's Philosophic Patterns*
(Baton Rouge, 1937), pp. 175 ff., and *Milton's Ontology* etc. (Lexington, Ky., 1957),
pp. 160 ff.; P. L. Carver, *RES*, xvi (1940), 414–20; C. S. Lewis, *A Preface to 'PL'* (1942),
ch. xv; McColley i, pp. 228 f., and ii, p. 70; Rajan, p. 149; and by Robert H. West in
three studies: *PQ*, xxviii (1949), 477–89; *JHI*, xiv (1953), 116–23; and *Milton and the
Angels* (Athens, Ga., 1955), *passim*. The Jewish and early Christian background is
surveyed by Langton, *Good and Evil Spirits* (1942), and *Essentials of Demonology* (1949).

[2] The last phrase is from Agrippa, *Three Bookes of Occult Philosophy*, tr. J. F. (1651),
p. 20. I consulted Psellus in Ficino's edition, *Iamblichus . . . Proclus*, etc. (Leyden,
1607), pp. 334 ff., and in *Patr. g.* cxxii, 836 ff. [tr. Marcus Collisson (Sydney, 1843),
pp. 27 ff.].

[3] *The Apology*, appended to *A Modest Enquiry* (1664), p. 496. More, like Milton,
upheld the angels' 'amorous propension' (*The Immortality of the Soul* (1659), Bk. III,
chs. iv–xi); but see in addition Beaumont's *Psyche*, quoted by McColley ii, p. 85. Even
more relevant is the erotic language of the Johannine Apocalypse.

[4] John Salkeld, *A Treatise of Paradise* (1617), p. 85.

was John Swan's consideration, advanced in 1635: 'God onely spake his powerfull word, and then the other creatures were produced; but now he calls a councell, and doth consult, not out of need, but rather to shew the excellencie of his work.'[1] Observations of this nature were merely the prologue to the Renaissance panegyric on man's outward beauty and inner perfection. Of ideas often repeated and upheld by the greatest thinkers from ancient Greece to the Renaissance in England, one of the most sacrosanct is echoed in *Paradise Lost* and insists that Adam and Eve were created 'not prone / And Brute as other Creatures' but 'erect and tall, / Godlike erect' (IV. 288 f.; VII. 506 f.). Even Calvin among the Reformers decided not to oppose the widespread conviction that 'where al other lyuynge creatures doo grouellyngwise beholde the grounde, to man is geuen an vpright face, and he is commaunded to loke vpon the heauē, and to aduaunce his countenaunce towarde the starres.' More expansively phrased, the idea reappears in a sermon preached in 1627 by Bishop Henry King:

the verie forme of the Bodie [is] built in that streight vpright figure, to make vs vnderstand, that as our future aboad, so our present Contemplation must be Heauen. When other Creatures, in signe of Homage to the earth that bare them, decline downewards, and with deiected postures, confesse their whole Parentage to bee nothing else but Dust . . .; Man, like a Monument of Honour, like a Pillar or Pyramid, erected for the glorie of his Creatour, points vpwards at Him.[2]

Writers of the Renaissance may have waxed enthusiastic over Adam's upright stature, but they grew almost delirious in their praises of his inner perfection, especially of his creation in God's image, though not everybody agreed on the precise meaning of this image. Indeed, interpretations so proliferated that Sir Walter Ralegh's estimate of the situation ('there is much dispute among the Fathers, Schoole-men, and late Writers') strikes us as positive understatement.[3] An adequate summary of the more popular theories was made available by Andrew Willet in 1605:

[1] *Speculum mundi* (Cambridge, 1635), p. 496. Parallel statements abound; see above, pp. 24 f.
[2] Calvin, *Inst.* I. xv. 3; King, *Two Sermons preached at White-Hall* (1627), ii. 11–12. I cited numerous references to this view in 'Renaissance Ideas on Man's Upright Form', *JHI*, xix (1958), 256–8.
[3] Ralegh's discussion of the 'image' (pp. 22–25) is expounded by Arnold Williams, *SP*, xxxiv (1937), 202 f. See also Heppe, pp. 232 ff., and Donne, *Sermons*, ix. 76 ff. Among the fuller Renaissance treatments are: John Weemes, *The Purtraiture of the*

Basil, Chrysostome, doe vnderstand this image of the dominion which man hath ouer the other creatures.

Augustine of the immortalitie of the soule,[1] wherein it is like vnto God, *lib. de quantitat. anim. c.* 2. Nyssenus in Hexemeron. herein saith this image consisteth, because the soule is capable of all goodnesse: Damascene, because man hath freewill, *lib.* 2. *de fide. c.* 12. The Master of Sentences, distinct. 16. because man hath reason and vnderstanding, and therein excelleth all other creatures . . .

I will also set downe more at large the diuers conceits of Augustine, of this creating of man according to Gods image.

1 He thinketh this image and similitude chiefly to consist in the soule, and secondarily in the bodie, because it was made to be obedient to the soule, and of an vpright forme to behold the heauens. lib. 83. quest. q. 51.

2 He placeth Gods image in man in this, that as all things are of God, so all men had their beginning from Adam. qv. 45. ex vet. test.

3 He thinketh this image to consist, in mans dominion ouer the creatures. de Genes. cont. Manich. c. 22.

4 The soule is like vnto God, because it is whole in the whole bodie, and in euery part thereof, it neither encreaseth, nor decreaseth with the bodie.

5 The soule expresseth the image of the Trinitie, in the vnderstanding, will, memorie, which are three faculties, yet make but one soule.

6 The soule liueth by it selfe, and doth also quicken the bodie, as God quickneth all things.

7 The soule beareth the image of God in reason, the similitude or likenes of God in charitie. lib. de spirit. & anim. c. 39.

Thus Augustine varieth, placing this image sometime in one thing, sometime in another. But to put all out of doubt, the Apostle sheweth, how we are to vnderstand the image of God in man, Eph. 4. 24. *Which after God is created in righteousnes and true holines.* Coloss. 3. 10. *Put on the new man, which is renewed in knowledge, after the image of him that created him.*[2]

Mindful of the same Biblical verses invoked by Willet, Milton in the *Tetrachordon* described God's image in man as incorporating

---

Image of God (1627), and Thomas Hooker, *The Paterne of Perfection* (1640), pp. 1–207; among modern studies: Corcoran, ch. v; David Cairns, *The Image of God in Man* (1953); and Dominique Barthélemy, *Dieu et son image* (Paris, 1963). Further references in *TS*, xx (1959), 62 f.

[1] The creation of the soul was a matter of controversy; the various theories are outlined by Thomas Wilson, *Theologicall Rules* (1615), ii. 30 f., and esp. E[dward] W[arren], *No Praeexistence* (1667). On Milton's espousal of traducianism see above, p. 3, and the background studies by William B. Hunter, *JEGP*, xlv (1946), 68–76, 327–36. The basic sources are in Kelly, pp. 175, 345.

[2] Willet (above, p. 46, n. 3), pp. 14–15.

'Wisdom, Purity, Justice, and rule over all creatures'; in *De doctrina christiana* as 'natural wisdom, holiness, and righteousness'; and in *Paradise Lost* as 'Truth, Wisdom, Sanctitude severe and pure, / Severe, but in true filial freedom plac't'.[1] Clearly Milton throughout *Paradise Lost* laid the greatest emphasis on free will, and the use to which Adam put his 'permissive freedom' immediately after his creation first demonstrates this in the poem's sequence of action.[2] 'A Gold-smith', wrote Thomas Tuke in 1609, 'makes a costly Iewell, beset with pearles and precious stones, and voyd of all deformitie, but yet so makes it, that if it fall, it may be crackt and broken: so God made man most perfect, and garnished his nature with excellent graces, and gaue him power to continue in the same perfection if hee would: yet did he not make him so vnchangeable, but that hee might both fall, and by falling breake and loose his excellencie'.[3] Raphael's last words to Adam in *Paradise Lost* deal with just this mutability of his nature:

> stand fast; to stand or fall
> Free in thine own Arbitrement it lies.
> Perfet within, no outward aid require;
> And all temptation to transgress repell.
>
> (VIII. 640–3)

IV

In his celebrated work on natural theology, William Paley argued that if we found a watch and inspected its mechanism, the logical conclusion would be that sometime and somewhere there existed 'an artificer or artificers who formed it for the purpose which we find it actually to answer'; and by analogy we must deduce from the universal order that it must have had a maker.[4] Yet, as further consideration indicates, it was an unfortunate analogy, because it implies abandonment of the world after its creation, an idea which, if it is appropriate to a number of philosophical views, is nevertheless remote from the main stream of Christian tradition. 'He who

---

[1] *Works*, iv. 74, and xv. 53; *PL*, IV. 293 f., and further: IV. 363 f., 566 f.; VII, 519 f., 526 ff., 627; VIII, 219 ff., 441.

[2] The best reading of Adam's exchanges with the Creator in Bk. VIII is by Charles M. Coffin, 'Creation and the Self in *PL*', *ELH*, xxix (1962), 1–18. The major discourses on free will in the epic are in III. 98 ff.; v. 234 ff., 524 ff.; IX. 343 ff.; X. 43 ff.

[3] *The High-VVay to Heauen* (1609), p. 56.

[4] *Natural Theology* (1802), ed. Henry Lord Brougham and Sir Charles Bell (1845), i. 7.

created Nature also guides it; the boat he built he did not desert',
wrote Jean Fernel, physician to Henri II of France. 'All that which
aforetime God created, whether in the heavens or on the earth, he
cherishes and rules.' Walter Charleton, Charles I's physician, in
concurring also gave warning against the misleading rhetoric that
labels God a pilot, an emperor, or a general; for a pilot, Charleton
pointed out, 'is not *ubiquitary* in all parts of his ship, nor an *Emperour*
actually *omnipresent* in all places of his dominions, nor a *General*
locally present in all quarters and stations of his Army; yet God is
intimately omnipresent in every particle of the world'.[1] God did not
retire after the creation of the universe, leaving us 'alone scipping &
leaping here below vp & downe like Frogs'; on the contrary, the
Creator of the cosmic structure is now its 'guider' and 'house-keeper'
as he was once its 'builder'.[2] John Robinson, the pastor of the Pilgrim
Fathers, in anticipation of Paley, readily admitted that the Creator
is indeed a 'skilfull Artificer' and that his work may be compared to a
watch, but he was careful to add that 'this differenee must always be
minded, that the Artisan leaves his worke being once framed to it
selfe; but God by continuall influx preserves, and orders both the
being, and *motions* of all Creatures.'[3]

The similarity of this thesis to the modern theory of *creatio con-*
tinua springs from our adoption of a traditional idea familiar enough
during the Renaissance. Peter Sterry's version may appear modern;
it is in truth ancient:

> Learned men and Divines teach us; that the Preservation of the world
> is *continuata Creatio*, a continued Creation. In every moment of Time
> from the Beginning of the world to the end, the Divine Act of Preserving,
> and Governing the world according to the Present form proper to it for
> that Season is entirely the same with the Act of Creation.[4]

Here we have a variation of the traditional theme that God's

---

[1] Ferne, *De abditis rerum causis* (Utrecht, 1656), i. 10, 448 f. [tr. Sir Charles Sherring-
ton, *Man on his Nature*, 2nd ed. (Cambridge, 1951), pp. 26, 27]; Charleton, *The Dark-*
nes of Atheism (1652), pp. 114–15.

[2] Seriatim: Calvin, *Sermon . . . on the Historie of Melchisedech*, tr. Thomas Stocker
(1592), p. 91; Sir James Perrott, *The Consideration of Humane Condition* (Oxford,
1600), p. 1; and Herbert (below, n. 4), p. 281.

[3] *Essayes*, 2nd ed. (1638), pp. 31–32.

[4] *The Kingdom of God in the Soul of Man* (1683), pp. 409–10. The idea of *creatio*
continua is also stated by George Herbert, *Works*, ed. F. E. Hutchinson (Oxford, 1941),
p. 281; Anon., *Heautonaparnumenos* (1646), p. 40; and Ralph Venning, *Orthodox Para-*
doxes (1647), p. 25 [also quoted by R. L. Colie, *JWCI*, xxiii (1960), 129]; *et al.*

providence extends 'euen to the basest worme, and least flie, as well as to the Angels in heauen', and thus expressly ostracizes chance from the created order ('nothing is done at aduenture').[1] It is a theme that we shall take up again in the chapter following.

[1] Elnathan Parr, *The Grounds of Diuinitie* (1615), p. 122, and Pierre Viret, *A Christian Instruction*, tr. John Shute (1573), p. 7.

3

The Book of Knowledge Fair

THE NATURE OF NATURE

that huge tome, that great *Manuscript* and worke of nature,
wherein are written the characters of Gods omnipotencie.
HUMPHREY SYDENHAM[1]

I

IN the censure of nature as 'stark blind' in Chapman's *Bussy D'Ambois*, it is maintained that

> Nature lays
> A mass of stuff together, and by use,
> Or by the mere necessity of matter,
> Ends such a work, fills it, or leaves it empty
> Of strength, or virtue, error or clear truth;
> Not knowing what she does.
>
> (v. iii. 12–17)

The thesis advanced here stands—and has in fact always stood—in diametric opposition to Christian thought on nature. While readily granting the existence of evil within the created order, Christianity—as I indicated in the previous chapter—has never conceded that any segment of nature is either purposeless or deprived of the constant supervision of God. The sum total of creation, it is affirmed, lives and moves and has its being under the shadow of the Most High: he is the 'Superintendent Principle over Nature', and nature herself 'nothing else but Gods instrument', his 'vicaire' as Chaucer maintained, or—to use some of Donne's metaphors—'Gods immediate commissioner', 'foreman', 'Lieutenant', and 'Vicegerent'.[2] Hence

---

[1] *Natures Overthrow* (1626), p. 2. I noted this precedent to Sir Thomas Browne's famous statement (*RM*, i. 16) in *Neophilologus*, xlvii (1963), 217.

[2] Seriatim: Henry More, *An Antidote against Atheism*, 2nd ed. (1655), i. 46; Hooker, p. 9; Chaucer, *The Parliament of Fowls*, l. 379; and Donne: *Devotions*, ed. John Sparrow (Cambridge, 1923), pp. 47, 87; *Goodfriday*, 1613, l. 19; *Sermons*, iii. 215.

Dante's statement that 'natura lo suo corso prende / dal divino intelletto'[1]—a conviction which during the English Renaissance was rephrased by Hooker as follows:

it cannot be, but nature hath some Directer of infinite knowledge to guide her in all her wayes. Who the guide of Nature, but onely the God of Nature? *In him we liue, moue, and are* [Acts xvii. 28]. Those things which nature is said to doe, are by diuine Arte performed, vsing Nature as an instrument: nor is there any such Arte or Knowledge diuine in Nature her selfe working, but in the guide of natures worke.[2]

Writing at about the same time, one of the most popular of the continental apologists, Pierre de la Primaudaye, similarly affirmed that

we say with *Iustin Martyr*, that Nature (in which the steps of the diuinitie shine and are liuelie represented) is that spirit or diuine reason, which is the efficient cause of naturall works, and the preseruing cause of those things that haue being, through the onely power of the heauenlie word, which is the workmaister of nature, and of the whole world, and hath infused into euery thing a liuely vertue and strength, wherby it encreaseth and preserueth it selfe by a naturall facultie. Or to speake more briefly, Nature is the order and continuance of the works of God, obeying the deitie, and his words and commandments, and borrowing his force and strength from thence, as from hir fountaine and originall.[3]

In sum, by differentiating sharply between God and nature, the Renaissance perpetuated the traditional distinction between God as *natura naturans* (nature 'naturing' or creative) and the created order as *natura naturata* (nature 'natured' or created).[4]

The thesis that nature is totally subordinate to the Divine Purpose has inevitably led Christianity to an emphatic denial that we are the

---

[1] *Inf.* XI. 99–100: 'nature takes her course from the Divine Intellect'.

[2] Hooker, p. 8. The other great English statement of this idea is by Ralegh, sig. E2ᵛ [quoted in *TZ* (below, p. 74, n. 1), p. 129].

[3] *The French Academie*, tr. T. B. [Thomas Bowes?] (1586), p. 172. The other great continental statement of this idea is by Livinus Lemnius, *Occulta naturæ miracula* (Antwerp, 1559), fol. 3ᵛ [the French version by Jacques Gohorry (Paris, 1574) is quoted by D. B. Wilson, *Ronsard* (Manchester, 1961), p. 59].

[4] For the distinction, see H. Siebeck, in *Archiv für Geschichte der Philosophie*, iii (1890), 370–8; David G. Ritchie, *Natural Rights*, 3rd ed. (1916), pp. 70–74; Henry A. Lucks, *NS*, ix (1935), 1–24; Leon Roth, *Spinoza* (1954), pp. 77–79; *et al.* The orthodox view is summed up in the *Interlude of the Four Elements* where Natura Naturata describes herself as God's 'minister' (*Old English Plays*, ed. W. C. Hazlitt (1874), i. 11). On Bruno's use of this idea, see Copleston, iii. 260; on Spinoza's celebrated identification of *natura naturans* with God, consult his *Ethics*, I, § 29, Schol.

slaves of chance and flies of every wind that blows. As has been said on behalf of medieval theology, 'In the Christian universe nothing ever happens save in the name of a rational order, nothing exists save as depending on it. *Nihil igitur casu fit in mundo*: nothing happens by chance: that is the ultimate Christian attitude to the universal order.'[1] The Reformers, in unqualified agreement with this conviction, could always turn to Calvin for a lucid restatement of their own: 'nothyng commeth by chaunce, but what soeuer commeth to passe in the world, commeth by the secrete prouidence of God.'[2] As we shall see later, this and similar affirmations were finally directed against the Renaissance obsession with 'the ever-whirling wheele of Change' which Christian apologists viewed with mounting alarm and which resulted often in such passionate denunciations as the following by Justus Lipsius:

Thinkest thou that CHAVNCE or FORTVNE beareth any sway in this excellent frame of the world? Or that the affaires of mortall men are caried headlong by chance-medley? I wot well thou thinkest not so, nor any man els that hath either wisdome or wit in his head.[3]

Instead of 'chance-medley', the expositors of the faith maintained that the universe is pervaded by an order which—in the words of Sir Thomas Elyot—'lyke a streyghte lyne issueth oute of prouydence, and passethe directely throughe all thynges'.[4]

The Renaissance belief in cosmic order has been made so abundantly clear by a host of scholars that we have no need to dwell on it here at length.[5] A statement by Thomas Wilson summarizes the standard thesis of the Renaissance:

al things stande by order, and without order nothing can be. For by an order we are borne, by an order we liue, and by an order we make our ende. By order and rule as head, and other obey as members. By an order Realmes stande, and Lawes take force. Yea, by an order the whole worke of Nature, and the perfite state of all the Elements haue their appointed course.[6]

---

[1] Étienne Gilson, *The Spirit of Mediæval Philosophy*, tr. A. H. C. Downes, 2nd ed. (1950), p. 369.
[2] *Commentaries . . . upon the Prophet Daniell*, tr. Arthur Golding (1570), fol. 65.
[3] *Tuuo Bookes of Constancie*, tr. Sir John Stradling (1595), p. 32. On the 'wheele' see below, p. 255.
[4] *Of the Knowledge which maketh a Wise Man*, ed. E. J. Howard (Oxford, Ohio, 1946), p. 103.
[5] See my references in *Isis*, xlix (1958), 391, and *NQ*, x (1963), 282.
[6] *The Arte of Rhetorique* (1553; rev. 1560), ed. G. H. Mair (Oxford, 1909), pp. 156–7.

As may be expected, such statements multiplied to an intimidating degree in the numberless treatises directed against atheism. But the essential point of their prolonged arguments was best—and at any rate most economically—set forth in Milton's *De doctrina christiana* as follows:

There can be no doubt that every thing in the world, by the beauty of its order, and evidence of a determinate and beneficial purpose which pervades it, testifies that some supreme efficient Power must have pre-existed, by which the whole was ordained for a specific end.[1]

Milton is to be numbered among the principal Renaissance thinkers who expounded the concept of universal order in all its glory. In *Paradise Lost* the principle is maintained in Uriel's account of God's imposition of order on the 'formless mass' of chaos:

> at his Word the formless Mass,
> This Worlds material mould, came to a heap:
> Confusion heard his voice, and wilde uproar
> Stood rul'd, stood vast infinitude confin'd;
> Till at his second bidding darkness fled,
> Light shon, and order from disorder sprung:
> Swift to thir several Quarters hasted then
> The cumbrous Elements, Earth, Flood, Aire, Fire,
> And this Ethereal quintessence of Heav'n
> Flew upward, spirited with various forms,
> That rowld orbicular, and turnd to Starrs
> Numberless, as thou seest, and how they move;
> Each had his place appointed, each his course.
>
> (III. 708–20)

In the fuller account of creation by Raphael, the emphasis is again on the termination of the discord between the warring elements. In addition, Milton fully substantiated the widespread opinion concerning 'the Order which God himselfe seems to have observed in the Creation'[2]—which is to say that in erecting the universal edifice God adhered to a specific pattern, progressing gradually and systematically upwards until its culmination in the creation of man.

---

[1] *Works*, xiv. 27; cf. *Artis logicae*, *Works*, xi. 470. For lengthier discussions see William Perkins, *The Cases of Conscience* (1636), pp. 119 ff.; Edward Stillingfleet *Origines sacrae* (1662), pp. 401 ff.; More (above, p. 54, n. 2), ii. 63–157; Walter Charleton, *The Darknes of Atheism* (1652), ch. ii, lect. iii; *et al.* On such treatises cf. Pascal's realistic comments in *Pensées*, § 366.

[2] Donne, *Ignatius his Conclave*, ed. Charles M. Coffin (1941), p. 134.

But it is not merely through the accounts of creation by Uriel and Raphael that Milton stressed the common tenet of the Renaissance that God is 'the God of Order'.[1] *Paradise Lost* in its entirety illustrates Lancelot Andrewes's belief that order is 'highly pleasing' to God. The efforts of the Godhead are constantly bent toward creation, in direct opposition to the activities of Satan, for whom 'Save what is in destroying, other joy / . . . is lost' (IX. 478 f.). The first adverse interference of Satan with the natural order occurs as early as the War in Heaven, when the rebellious angels, in order to secure the necessary materials to build their instruments of destruction,

> up they turnd
> Wide the Celestial soile, and saw beneath
> Th' originals of Nature in thir crude
> Conception.
>
> (VI. 509–12)

This rape of the created order may have been intended as a parallel to the excavation of 'the quiet wombe' of nature in *The Faerie Queene*, which Sir Guyon, not surprisingly, regarded as a sacrilege.[2] In any case, the express violation of nature by the rebellious angels and the subsequent havoc created by their uprooting of the hills are set in striking contrast to the action of the Son of God:

> At his command th' uprooted Hills retir'd
> Each to his place, they heard his voice and went
> Obsequious, Heav'n his wonted face renewd,
> And with fresh Flourets Hill and Valley smil'd.
>
> (VI. 781–4)

Milton indeed emphasizes on countless occasions God's endless efforts to prevent the cosmic structure from collapsing into discord. Early in the War in Heaven, for example, the embattled angels would have spread destruction far and wide

---

[1] On this commonplace (based on 1 Cor. xiv. 33) see Isaac Bargrave, *A Sermon* (1627), p. 2; Daniel Dyke, *Tuuo Treatises*, 5th impr. (1631), pp. 340 f.; Thomas Gataker, *Certaine Sermons* (1637), ii. 188; Donne, *Sermons*, iv. 241, and vii. 230; Quarles, *Enchyridion* (1640), sig. E9; Francis Cheynell, *The Man of Honour* (1645), p. 7; Sir James Harrington, *A Holy Oyl* (1669), p. 142; Baxter, iv. 171; and the twenty references I cited in *JHI*, xx (1959), 164, and *NQ*, x (1963), 284.

[2] II. vii. 17. The well-known Renaissance disapproval of mining (Svendsen, pp. 120f.; I. G. MacCaffrey, *PL as 'Myth'* (Cambridge, Mass., 1959), pp. 160 f.) is utilized by Milton to emphasize Satan's perversion of 'blameless matter' (Kester Svendsen, *Bucknell Review*, ix (1960), 130–42).

Had not th' Eternal King Omnipotent
From his strong hold of Heav'n high over-rul'd
And limited thir might.

(VI. 227-9)

When later the War enters another violent stage, Heaven would
again have 'gone to wrack'

Had not th' Almightie Father where he sits
Shrin'd in his Sanctuarie of Heav'n secure,
Consulting on the sum of things, foreseen
This tumult, and permitted all.

(VI. 671-4)

In still another instance, this time in the sublunary world, the fearful
combat between the mighty Gabriel and Satan would have con-
founded both heaven and earth

had not soon
Th' Eternal to prevent such horrid fray
Hung forth in Heav'n his gold'n Scales.

(IV. 995-7)

Satan, fully aware of the sign's import, promptly retired murmuring.
Yet neither this incident nor the others conclude Milton's concern
with the larger theme of God's constant preservation of the universal
order. The apex of that theme, as we shall see later, is not reached
until the restoration of man by the incarnate God.

II

When Renaissance writers maintained with Sir Thomas Elyot that
all creation is pervaded by a 'streyghte lyne', their metaphor was not
accidental but purposely designed for its appeal to the widely disseminated belief of the age in the hierarchical structure of the
universe. According to this commonplace, all levels of existence
were thought to be tightly knit through an elaborate system of
interdependent 'degrees', extending vertically 'from the lowest earth
to the highest heavens', 'from the footstoole to the throne of God',
'from the Mushrome to the Angels'.[1] In *Paradise Lost* the concept is
expounded by Raphael:

[1] Seriatim: Pico, *De hominis dignitate*, x (*RPM*, p. 229); Hooker, p. 55; Samuel Ward,
The Life of Faith, 3rd ed. (1622), p. 2. See further below, p. 62, n. 4.

O *Adam*, one Almightie is, from whom
All things proceed, and up to him return,
If not deprav'd from good, created all
Such to perfection, one first matter all,
Indu'd with various forms, various degrees
Of substance, and in things that live, of life;
But more refin'd, more spiritous, and pure,
As neerer to him plac't or neerer tending
Each in thir several active Sphears assignd,
Till body up to spirit work, in bounds
Proportiond to each kind. So from the root
Springs lighter the green stalk, from thence the leaves
More aerie, last the bright consummat floure
Spirits odorous breathes: flours and thir fruit
Mans nourishment, by gradual scale sublim'd
To vital spirits aspire, to animal,
To intellectual, give both life and sense,
Fansie and understanding, whence the Soule
Reason receives, and reason is her being,
Discursive, or Intuitive; discourse
Is oftest yours, the latter most is ours,
Differing but in degree, of kind the same.

(v. 469–90)

All created things, it is argued here, are severally distinguished by 'various forms, various degrees', rising 'by gradual scale' through the kingdom of plants and animals to culminate in the 'intellectual' creatures, men and angels, alike endowed with the faculty of reason, which is intuitive in spiritual beings but necessitates 'discourse' in men.[1] This entire 'scale of Nature'—to use Adam's 'traditional' phrase (v. 509)—is pervaded by order, each of its numerous steps being assigned to a specific sphere of action under the providential supervision of God, 'from whom / All things proceed, and up to him return'.

Few other concepts appealed more to the thinkers of the Renaissance than this '*Scale* of *Creatures*', this 'great chaine' stretching through a myriad of interconnected links 'from Heaven to Earth, from Angels to Brutes'.[2] Time and again the writers of the period

[1] Cf. Bishop Robert Mossom: 'what they [the angels] know, is not apprehended in parts, by a *discursive* reasoning, but comprehended at once in a present *intuition* of their understanding' (*Sion's Prospect* [1653], p. 46). But see Heppe, pp. 203 ff.

[2] Seriatim: Charleton (above, p. 57, n. 1), p. 130; Donne, *Sermons*, v. 374; Henry More, *Divine Dialogues* (1668), p. 16. Svendsen (pp. 114 f.) quotes a formulation similar to Milton's by Mercator.

stood transfixed before the wonder of 'those degrees which God
hathe set in the order of nature', before the miraculous 'agreement
and well hanging togither' of all things in such 'excellent correspon-
dence' each to each that, jointly, they declare unity to be 'the ground-
worke of nature, the very *Atlas* of the Beeing of all things'.[1] The
various levels of existence, furthermore, are so 'knit together', so
'linckt and tyed together', that there is no 'emptinesse', 'no where
any leap or gap', 'no *vacuum*, or vacuity in the world'.[2] In the
detailed 'explanation' of this *connexio rerum* by John Weemes in
1627,

God hath ioyned all things in the world, *per media*, by middles; as
first, hee hath coupled the *earth* and the *water* by *slime*; so the *ayre* and the
water by *vapours*; the *exhalations* are a middle betwixt the *ayre* and the
fire; *argilla*, or *marle*, a middle betwixt *slime* and *stones*; So the *chrystall*
betwixt *water* and the *diamond*; *mercury* or *quicksiluer*, betwixt *water* and
mettels; *Pyrrhites* the *firestone* or *marcasite*, betwixt *stones* and *mettles*; the
corall betwixt *roots* and *stones*, which hath both a roote and branches;
Zoophyta, or plants resembling liuing creatures (as the *Mandrage* resembling a man, the hearbe called the *scythian lambe*, resembling a lambe) are
a middle betwixt *animals* and *plants*; So *amphibia*; (as the seale and such)
betwixt the *beasts* liuing on earth, and in the sea; so *Struthiocamelus* the
Ostrich betwixt *fowles* & *beasts*; So the *fleeing fishes* are a middle, betwixt
the *fowles* and the *fishes*; the *batt* betwixt *creeping things* and the *fowles*;
the *hermaphrodite* betwixt *man* and *woman*; the ape betwixt a *man* and a
beast, and *man* betwixt the *beast* and *angels*.[3]

Where Weemes depended for his 'evidence' on the natural sciences
—or what he mistook to be the natural sciences—others leaned for
support on the pronouncements of 'authorities' and on the series of
analogies that tradition had already made sacrosanct. So far were
commentators prepared to go that they even invoked such 'authorities' as the mythical Hermes Trismegistus, who had maintained—
much to the delight of Renaissance writers—that the various parts of
the universe are arranged in 'a straight line' extending from the top
of the natural order to its very bottom (ἔστιν ἡ διάταξις αὕτη κατ᾽

[1] Seriatim: Calvin, *Sermons . . . upon the Booke of Iob*, tr. Arthur Golding (1574),
p. 49; Anthony Fletcher, *Profitable Similies* (1595), p. 35; John Randol, *A Sermon*
(Oxford, 1624), p. 3; Charles Herle, *Contemplations* (1631), p. 499.

[2] Seriatim: Henry Ainsworth, *The Orthodox Foundation of Religion* (1641), p. 20;
Godfrey Goodman, *The Fall of Man* (1616), p. 427; Nicholas Byfield, *The Rule of Faith*
(1626), p. 163; Peter Sterry, *The Freedom of the Will* (1675), p. 158; Michael Sendi-
govius, *A New Light*, tr. John French (1650), p. 88.

[3] *The Pourtraiture of the Image of God* (1627), p. 49.

εὐθυτενῆ γραμμὴν ἄνωθεν κάτω ἀκολλητὶ τὴν φύσιν).[1] Two of the analogies employed are of interest to us here because they occur in *Paradise Lost*: the golden chain (II. 1051 f.) and the ladder of Jacob (III. 502 ff). The ultimate source of the first is *The Iliad* (VIII. 19–27), and of the second the Book of Genesis (xxviii. 10–15), yet despite their varied origin they testify to the way that seeming opposites were often drafted into the service of one and the same comprehensive scheme. Milton's own use of them was anticipated by a host of writers, all in essential agreement with Bernardino Ochino's statement that 'the creatures be vnyted so to gethers that eche one hangeth on other, & al of god, in such wise that they make a ladder.'[2] If other writers saw fit to displace the ladder by the chain—or, like Milton, to use both[3]—the principle remained the same and was equally acceptable to all.

One of the most thorough expositions of the Scale of Nature is to be found in Comenius's *Physicæ ad lumen divinum reformatæ synopsis*, first published in Leipzig in 1633. Milton could have formulated his version of the widely known concept without having read Comenius, but he may have been acquainted with the work and may even have met Comenius during his visit to England in 1641 at the invitation, possibly, of Parliament. While in England Comenius met Hartlib, with whom he had been corresponding—and Hartlib, we must remember, was the person to whom Milton addressed his educational treatise in 1644. In the epilogue of his work, Comenius summarized his entire theme as follows:[4]

[1] *Hermetica*, ed. Walter Scott (Oxford, 1924), i. 512. Cf. the statement of the thirteenth-century Cabbalist Moses de Leon, quoted by Scholem, p. 223. For a more authoritative statement see Clement of Alexandria, *Stromata*, VII. ii. 9 (*LCC*, ii. 98).

[2] *Certayne Sermons*, tr. Richard Argentine (1550?), sig. A8ᵛ.

[3] For example, Anthony Maxey, *The Sermon preached . . . at VVhite-Hall* (1605), sig. E2, and Andrew Willet, *Hexapla in Genesin* (Cambridge, 1605), p. 300. On Jacob's ladder, see also below, p. 227.

[4] *Naturall Philosophie reformed by Divine Light*, tr. Anon. (1651), pp. 238–40. The best-known expositions of this commonplace are in *Troilus and Cressida*, I. iii. 85–124, and *An Essay on Man*, i. Among other formulations: Nicholas of Cusa, *De concordia catholica* (I, §§ 1–4), ed. Simon Schardius, *De iurisdictione . . . imperiali*, etc. (Basle, 1566), pp. 478 ff.; *Hom. I*, Hom. x; Sir Richard Barckley, *The Felicitie of Man* (1598), pp. 532 ff.; John Weemes, *Observations* (1633), pp. 3 ff.; John Swan, *Redde debitum* (1640), pp. 16 ff.; Comenius, *The Gate of Languages*, tr. Thomas Horn (1650), ch. iii et seq.; and the sermons by George Meriton (1611), John Randol (1624), and Barten Holyday (1626). The classic study is Arthur O. Lovejoy's *The Great Chain of Being* (Cambridge, Mass, 1936). See also the supporting evidence I cited in 'The Numerological Approach to Cosmic Order during the English Renaissance', *Isis*, xlix (1958), 391–7, and 'The Scale of Nature and Renaissance Treatises on Nobility', *SN*, xxxvi (1964), 63–68.

the created World is a meer harmony. All things by one, all things to one; the highest and the lowest, the first and the last, most straightly cleaving together, being concatenated by the intermediate things, and perpetuall ties, and mutuall actions and passions inevitable, so that the world being made up of a thousand thousand parts, and particles of parts, is nevertheless one, and undivided in it selfe . . . . We have seen also that admirable scale of creatures, arising out of the principles, and ascending by a septenary gradation. For we have vnderstood, that whatsoever there is besides God, it is either an Element, or a Vapour, or a Concrete, or a Plant, or an Animall, or a Man, or an Angell; and that the whole multitude of creatures is ranked into these seven classes, or great Tribes. In every of which there is some eminent virtue flowing from the essence of the Creatour (yet every latter including the former.) For

In {
  Elements, Being
  Vapours, Motion
  Concretes, Figure, or Quality
  Plants, Life.
  Living Creatures, Sense.
  Men, Reason.
  Angels, Understanding
} is eminent.

Comenius's recognition of a 'septenary gradation' in the Scale of Nature was dictated by his belief in the mystical significance of the number seven. But other commentators, while in express agreement with the principle of 'gradation', differed in thinking that there are not seven levels of existence but four or even simply three. The latter view was adequately set forth by Pico when he observed that Platonists—though actually not merely Platonists—

distinguish Creatures into three degrees. The first comprehends the corporeal and visible, as Heaven, Elements, and all compounded of them: The last the invisible, incorporeal, absolutely free from bodies which properly are called Intellectual (by Divines Angelical) Natures. Betwixt these is a middle nature, which though incorporeal, invisible, immortal, yet moveth bodies, as being obliged to that office; called, the rational soul; inferiour to Angels, superiour to Bodies; subject to those, regent of these.[1]

Considering further this threefold distinction, we may glance first at the topmost step in the universal scale, the angels.

[1] 'A Platonick Discourse upon Love', tr. Thomas Stanley, *Poems* (1651), p. 216. Among the older exponents of the 'three degrees' are Augustine, *De libero arbitrio*, II. iii. 7 ff., and Macrobius, *Comment. in somnium Scipionis*, I. xiv. 10 ff. Further references in *NQ*, x (1963), 283 f.

When Milton maintained in *Paradise Lost* that there are specific 'orders' and 'degrees' in Heaven (v. 586–91), he was restating his earlier view that the angels are 'distinguisht and quaterniond into their celestiall Princedomes, and Satrapies'.[1] Yet, apart from an occasional reference to some of their titles—'Thrones, Dominations, Princedoms, Vertues, Powers' (v. 601, 840)—Milton refused to name all the angelic orders, still less commit himself to the widely accepted ninefold arrangement proposed by Dionysius the Areopagite.[2] This attitude, far from indicating 'independence of mind',[3] resulted from two developments in the late fifteenth and early sixteenth centuries. First, a number of humanists, notably Valla, Cajetan, and Erasmus, agreed with some medieval thinkers in denying that the works attributed to Dionysius the Areopagite were written by St. Paul's convert in Athens (Acts xvii. 34); they were penned, according to more recent scholars, by a disciple of Proclus late in the fifth century. Secondly, Luther and Calvin rejected the pseudo-Dionysius's speculations as 'vain babblings' without any Biblical support whatsoever.[4] By Milton's time the tendency among Protestants was to reject the 'palpable follie' of the 'high soaring (though counterfeit) *Dionysius*', but to maintain, just as categorically, that the angels are indeed 'Legioniz'd in Rankes'.[5] The Protestant refusal to be precise concerning the celestial orders even extended to the traditional elevation of Michael to the highest rank among the angels, now denied because, as Thomas Adams pointed out, 'it can neuer bee proued, that hee was, is, or shall be Monarch, or head of

---

[1] *RCG, Works*, iii. 185. The celestial 'degrees' are also upheld in *DDC, Works*, xv. 37, III.

[2] According to *De coelesti hierarchia*, VII–IX, the nine orders are: seraphim, cherubim, thrones, dominations, virtues, powers, principalities, archangels, angels. Two other schemes were initiated by Gregory the Great (*Homiliæ*, II. xxxiv. 7; *Moralia*, XXXII. xxiii. 48), one of which was popularized by Bernard of Clairvaux (*De consideratione*, v. 4), and the other by Isidore of Seville (*Etymologiæ*, VII. 5). The Gregory–Bernard scheme is the same as the Areopagite's, but reverses the virtues and principalities. The Gregory–Isidore scheme is: seraphim, cherubim, powers, principalities, virtues, dominations, thrones, archangels, angels. There may be a remote reference to the latter in *PL*, v. 749 f.

[3] Rex Clements, 'The Angels in *PL*', *Quarterly Review*, cclxiv (1935), 289.

[4] Valla, *Opera* (Basle, 1543), fol. 852; Cajetan, *Evangelia cum commentariis* (Paris, 1532), fol. 283ᵛ; Erasmus, *In Novum Testamentum . . . annotationes* (Basle, 1519), fol. 225; Luther, *Works*, i. 235, and *Table-Talk*, p. 356; Calvin, *Inst.* I. xiv. 4. See my fuller discussion in 'Renaissance Thought on the Celestial Hierarchy: The Decline of a Tradition', *JHI*, xx (1959), 155–66, and xxiii (1962), 265–7. Cf. *Sophia*, xxxiii (1965), 341–8.

[5] Seriatim: John Deacon and John Walker, *A Summarie Answere* (1601), p. 142; Joseph Mede, *Diatribæ* (1642), p. 172; John Davies of Hereford, *The Holy Roode* (1609), sig. 14.

all Angels'.[1] In *Paradise Lost* Michael does indeed appear as 'Prince of Angels' during the War in Heaven (VI. 281), but that appearance, I think, is justifiable on the basis of another tradition acceptable to Protestants, of Michael as a type of the Christ to come.[2]

Below the angels in the Scale of Nature stands man, widely and overwhelmingly hailed as the 'mean' or 'middle peece' in the universal structure, 'the bond or buckle of the world', 'the knot of all', the 'amphibious piece betweene a corporall and spirituall essence', 'the Golden Clasp whereby Things Material and Spiritual are United', 'that Hymen of eternall and mortall things, that Chaine together binding vnbodied and bodily substances'.[3] Renaissance writers, supporting their panegyric of man as the beauty of the world and the paragon of animals, delighted to invoke the psalmist's statement that man was created 'a little lower than the angels' (Ps. viii. 5).[4] But other authorities could be—and were—quoted to advantage, among them Gregory the Great, who had maintained man's 'middle state, inferior to angels and superior to beasts', and Nemesius of Emesa, who had asserted that God placed man 'on the boundary between the intelligible order and the phenomenal order' so that 'the entire universe should form one agreeable unity, unbroken by internal incoherences'.[5] Yet man, it was further claimed, fills a gap

[1] *Workes* (1629), p. 548.

[2] I cited to this effect Bullinger, Marlorat, *et al.*, in *The Phoenix and the Ladder* (Barkeley, 1964), p. 99. See also the marginal note on Rev. xii. 7 in the Geneva Bible (1560); Wolleb, p. 51; etc.

[3] Seriatim: Pomponazzi, *De immortalitate animae*, I (*RPM*, p. 282); Guillaume du Vair, *A Buckler against Adversitie*, tr. Andrew Court (1622), p. 152; Oswald Croll, *Mysteries of Nature*, tr. Henry Pinell in *Philosophy Reformed* (1657), p. 54; Donne, *Sermons*, ii. 342; Browne, *RM*, i. 34; Traherne, *Christian Ethicks* (1675), p. 205; and William Drummond of Hawthornden, *Flouures of Sion* (Edinburgh, 1623), p. 66. The last of the statements quoted above was the most popular (cf. Donne, *Essays*, p. 30), lifted almost verbatim from Pico's celebrated apostrophe (see *RPM*, p. 224, and 'Platonick Discourse' (above, p. 63, n. 1), p. 223). Parallel statements abound: Ralegh, p. 30; Goodman (above, p. 61, n. 2), p. 427; John Davies of Hereford, *Humours* (1609), p. 245; William Loe, *The Mystery of Mankind* (1619), p. 144; Samuel Purchas, *Purchas his Pilgrim* (1619), pp. 137 f.; John Doughty, *A Discourse*, etc. (Oxford, 1628), i. 14; Charron, *Of Wisdome*, tr. Samson Lennard (1640), p. 33; John Swan, *Speculum mundi* (Cambridge, 1635), pp. 427 f.; Henry Church, *Miscellanea* (1637), ii. 81 f.; Richard Carpenter, *Experience*, etc. (1642), ii. 67; James I, *Regales aphorismi* (1650), p. 126; *et al.* See also Ficino, *Theologia platonica*, III. 2 (*JHI*, v (1944), 227–32). Robb (pp. 116 f.) quotes the representative formulation of Girolamo Benivieni; but see further Ernst Cassirer, *JHI*, iii (1942), 319 ff.; Paul O. Kristeller, *JHI*, v (1944), 220–6, and *Italica*, xxiv (1947), 93–112; and esp. Eugenio Garin, 'La "Dignitas homini" e la letteratura patristica', *La Rinascita*, i (1938), § 4, pp. 102–46.

[4] See further 2 Enoch xxx. 10–12 (*OT Pseud.*, p. 449).

[5] Gregory, *Dialogi*, III (tr. Philip Woodward (Paris, 1608), p. 357); Nemesius, *De*

in the Scale of Nature not merely because he is part angel and part beast but particularly because he incorporates within himself elements from every rung in the cosmic ladder. Thomas Heywood agreed readily that man is indeed made cunningly of elements and an angelic sprite:

> Man is a ligament,
> And folding vp in a small continent,
> Some part of all things which before were made;
> For in this Microcosme are stor'd and layd
> Connexiuely, as things made vp and bound,
> Corporeall things with incorporeall.[1]

As David Person ventured to explain this popular notion in 1635,

the earth is not unfitly compared unto a living mans body, the rocks and stones whereof are his bones, the brookes and rivers serpenting through it, the veynes and sinewes conveying moistnesse from the fountaines unto all the members; the hollow of our bowells and of the trunke of our bodies, to the vast and spacious cavernes and caves within the body of this earth ... within the which hollow of our bodyes our vitious windes are enclosed, which if they have no vent, presently they beget in us *Iliak* passions, collicks, &c. whereby our whole body is cast into a distemper and disturbed; even as the windes closed in these cavernes, and hollow subterranean places, pressing to have vent, and not finding any, making way to themselves, do then beget these earth-quakes.[2]

Even if the major writers of the Renaissance disagreed with the excessive enthusiasm of this statement, they were still prepared to accept its basic premise. The idea of the microcosm of man—what in *Paradise Regained* is unoriginally termed 'mans lesse universe' (IV. 459)—was so widely disseminated during the Renaissance that, as we are assured by a writer of the 1620's, it was at the time 'in all mens mouthes'.[3] Here as elsewhere, supporting evidence was sought in the most unlikely places, including the intriguing possibility that

---

natura hominis, II and IV (*LCC*, iv. 229, 235). For the representative view of the Reformers see Zwingli's statement in Frye, p. 125.

[1] *The Hierarchy of the Blessed Angells* (1635), p. 338. Cf. Herbert, *Man*, ll. 13–15.

[2] *Varieties* (1635), i. 27. For the original Hebrew idea see Ginzberg, i. 49 f.; for the standard Christian view: John of Damascus, *De fide orthodoxa*, II. 12.

[3] William Struther, *Christian Observations*, 2nd century (Edinburgh, 1629), p. 177. I have cited well over 120 references to this notion in 'The Microcosm of Man', *NQ*, vii (1960), 54–56, and x (1963), 408–10. The most thorough study of the idea is by Rudolf Allers, 'Microcosmus: From Anaximandrus to Paracelsus', *Traditio*, ii (1944), 319–407.

the four letters of Adam's name designate—in Greek at any rate—the four parts of the world: $A(\nu\alpha\tau o\lambda\dot{\eta})$, $\Delta(\dot{\upsilon}\sigma\iota\varsigma)$, $A(\rho\kappa\tau o\varsigma)$, $M(\epsilon\sigma\eta\mu\beta\rho\acute{\iota}\alpha)$.[1]

Within the rung in the universal ladder occupied by man are a number of interlocking orders, finally reducible—as in Johann Gerhard's detailed exposition—to three: 'The Ecclesiasticall, Politicall, and Oeconomicall: The First, of the Church; the Second, of the Common-wealth; the Third of the private familie'.[2] The last of these is of particular concern to the student of Milton, partly because the poet's consistent view that man is naturally superior to woman, that man's is indeed 'the perfeter sex',[3] has not endeared him to the enlightened ages since the Renaissance. Milton's attitude coincides with the predominant view of his contemporaries and immediate predecessors, including the humanists who like Vives in *De institutione feminae christianae* (1529) asserted that 'all lawes, both spirituall and temporal, & nature her self crieth and commandeth that the woman shall be subiect and obedient to the man.'[4] The subordinate status of women was accepted as part of the Scale of Nature; indeed, 'to deny this', according to one typical warning, 'is to resist the Councell of the Highest.'[5]

Further down in the universal structure, beneath the middle state assigned to man, is the aggregate of animals, plants, and inanimate nature generally. The principle of gradation, however, was thought to be evident even here, for as Leonard Pollard asserted in 1556 in a series of rhetorical questions,

> Do ye not see in the firmamente dyuers bryghtnes to be in the starres, and yet the sonne to be the bryghtest of them al? Are there not degrees amongst the fowles: and yet the Eegle kynge of them all. Do not beastes one excell another, and are not they all vnder the Lyon? What shulde I speke of the Cranes when they flye, haue they net theyr Capitayne and guyde: Is there not amongst the bees one master bee, vnto whome all the residue be obedient?[6]

---

[1] 'East, West, North, South'. The idea is mentioned, for example, by Pontus de Tyard, *L'univers* (Lyon, 1557), p. 116; Griffith Williams, *The True Church* (1629), p. 829; and Sir Miles Sandys, *Prudence* (1634), p. 23. For precedents see the Sibylline Oracles iii. 24–26 and 2 Enoch xxx. 13 (*OT Pseud.*, pp. 379, 449, with further references to Augustine, Bede, *et al.*). A variation on this theme is quoted by Svendsen, p. 279.

[2] *Divine Aphorismes*, tr. Ralph Winterton (Cambridge, 1632), chs. xx–xxiii.

[3] *An Apology*, etc., *Works*, iii. 306.

[4] *The Instruction of a Christian Woman*, tr. Richard Hyrd (1592), sig. P3.

[5] Daniel Touteville, *St. Pauls Threefold Cord* (1635), p. 33. See further below, p. 179.

[6] *Fyve Homiles* (1556), sig. G2ᵛ. Further references by Anthony G. Petti, *ESEA*, 1963, pp. 69 f.

Only one group of beings was specifically excluded from the Scale of Nature: the fallen angels. Some commentators, in fact, went as far as to deny that there is any order in Hell at all,[1] though most of them, in agreement with the majority of the Fathers and medieval theologians, maintained that there is 'a difference of degrees in evill Angels', perhaps even a 'ladder' and a ninefold infernal hierarchy 'contrary to the nine orders of the Angels'.[2] Milton, having avoided the precise arrangement of the angels, eschewed also that of the devils. However, he readily accepted the notion of infernal degrees: in his theological treatise on the basis of the traditional theory of *pœnis disparibus*,[3] and in his major epic because he wished to emphasize Satan's constant efforts to imitate the Most High. Hence the similarities between the parades in Heaven and in Hell, as well as the identical titles of the angels and devils.[4]

III

In one of his most influential statements, St. Paul affirmed that even pagans cannot pretend to be unaware of God's ways, since 'that which may be known of God is manifest in them; for God hath shewed it unto them. For the invisible things of him from the creation of the

---

[1] For example, Richard Eburne, *The Tuuo-folde Tribute* (1613), i. 19; Lewis Bayly, *The Practice of Piety*, 35th ed. (1635), p. 88; and esp. John Deacon and John Walker, *Dialogicall Discourses* (1601).

[2] Paul Baynes, *Commentary upon . . . the Ephesians* (1643), p. 722; William Sclater, *A Sermon* (1616), p. 3; Heywood (above, p. 66, n. 1), p. 411; Johann Gerhard, *The Soules VVatch*, tr. Richard Bruck, 3rd ed. (1621), p. 51; Sir William Alexander, *Doomesday*, xi. 25, in *Recreations* (1637); Joseph Hall, *The Invisible World* (1659), p. 143; Witte (below, p. 84, n. 2), p. 196; Benjamin Camfield, *Discourse of Angels* (1678), pp. 39 f. 45 f.; *et al.* For a collection of views on Hell's 'degrees' see Sigmund Feyerabend, *Theatrum diabolorum* (Frankfurt, 1569), fols. 57 ff. The 'ladder' is referred to in *The English Faust-Book of 1592*, ed. H. Logeman (Gand and Amsterdam, 1900), p. 27. The 'nine degrees', which are mentioned in *Ioannes Coletus super opera Dionysii*, ed. J. H. Lupton (1869), pp. 43, 193, are discussed fully by Agrippa, *Three Bookes of Occult Philosophy*, tr. J. F. (1651), pp. 397 ff. See further Arturo Graf, *The Story of the Devil*, tr. E. N. Stone (1931), pp. 43 ff.; Rudwin (below, n. 4), ch. vii; Edward Langton, *Supernatural* (1934), pp. 153 ff.; and Robert H. West, *The Invisible World* (Athens, Ga., 1939), pp. 23 f., 81 f., 217, etc.

[3] *Works*, xvi. 373: 'Punishment . . . varies according to the degree of guilt.' Cf. Bullinger: 'there be degrees of punnishement, after the qualitie of the crime' (*Sermons upō the Apocalips*, tr. John Daws (1561), p. 585). Among the precedents are Origen, *De pr.*, I. viii. 1, and Gregory the Great, *Moralia*, ix. 98.

[4] *PL*, v. 583 ff. (cf. I. 544 ff.); v. 601 (cf. x. 460). On the traditional theory of Satan's imitation of God see Maximilian Rudwin, *The Devil in Legend and Literature* (Chicago, 1931), pp. 39 f., and ch. xii.

world are clearly seen, being understood by the things that are made, even his eternal power and Godhead.' (Rom. i. 19 f.)[1] This sanction of the study of nature as revelatory of God, which later ages termed 'natural theology', manifested itself during the Renaissance in a variety of related ways: in some instances, quite simply through a reiteration of the idea that 'universus mundus nihil aliud est quam Deus explicatus';[2] on other occasions, through an affirmation of the divine 'signatures' and 'hieroglyphicks' said to be engraven on the created order;[3] and at last through an appeal to the popular metaphor of 'the book of nature'. The following statement, written in 1638, is commonplace:

> The great volume of nature, the book of the creatures is laid open before us; and in every leafe, and page, and line of it, God hath imprinted such evident characters of his divine properties, such lively representations of his glory, that we may runne and reade his excellency therein.[4]

The variations of this theme are endless. To some writers nature seemed not merely a book but a 'manuscript'; to others, a 'folio' published in 'capitall letters'; and to still others—with mounting enthusiasm—a 'great and glorious Library', a 'Colledge', and even an 'immense Universitie'.[5] Milton, far more restrained, averred in *Paradise Lost* that the heavens 'speak / The Makers high magnificence' (VIII. 100 f.), and that indeed the totality of the created order comprises 'the Book of Knowledge fair' (III. 47). In Raphael's statement to Adam,

---

[1] Elaborations of the Pauline view abound; among the *loci classici* are Gregory of Nazianzus, *Theological Orations*, II. 6 (*LCC*, iii. 139), and Basil the Great, *Hexaemeron*, I. 6 (*NPNF*, 2nd ser., viii. 55).

[2] *Apud* Griffith Williams, *The Best Religion* (1636), p. 305: 'the whole world is nothing els but an explication of God.' Once quoted by Ralegh (p. 2), this statement was bound to be cited again—as by Robert Barrell, *Spirituall Architecture* (1624), p. 10; Daniel Featley, *The Summe of Saving Knowledge* (1626), sig. A3; Henry King, *Two Sermons* (1627), i. 9; Sibbes, *A Glance of Heaven* (1638), ii. 31; Peter Heylyn, *Cosmographie*, 2nd ed. (1657), p. 1; *et al.* The obvious source is Ps. xix. 1–2.

[3] Ralegh, p. 2; Browne, *RM*, i. 17; Quarles, *Emblemes* (1658), 'To the Reader'; More (above, p. 54, n. 2), p. 101; Glanvill, *The Vanity of Dogmatizing* (1661), p. 30; *et al.*

[4] William Bloys, *Adam in his Innocencie* (1628), pp. 8–9.

[5] On the 'manuscript' see: Richard Carpenter, *Experience*, etc. (1642), ii. 156, and above, p. 54, n. 1. On the 'capitall letters': Joseph Hall, *The Character of Man* (1635), p. 14; Richard Montagu, *Acts and Monuments* (1642), p. 38; William Hodson, *The Divine Cosmographer* (Cambridge, 1640), p. 30; and the references in *Neophilologus*, xlvii (1963), 218. On the last three metaphors: Nicholas Byfield, *The Rule of Faith* (1626), p. 164; William Pulley, *The Christians Taske* (1619), p. 379; Charles Goldwell, *Choyce and Applications* (1621), pp. 47 f., as well as Ferdinando Parkhurst, *Masorah* (1660), p. 4.

> Heav'n
Is as the Book of God before thee set,
Wherein to read his wondrous Works.
(VIII. 66–68)

The theory underlying the affirmations of Milton and his contemporaries was adequately set forth by that 'great secretary of nature
and all learning', Sir Francis Bacon:

> *Naturall Theology*, is truly called *Divine Philosophy*. And this is defined
> to be a Knowledge, or rather a spark and rudiment of that Knowledge
> concerning God; such as may be had by the light of Nature; and the
> Contemplation of the Creature; which Knowledge may be truly termed
> *Divine* in respect of the Object; and *Naturall* in respect of the Light.[1]

This is not to say that orthodox Christian thinkers have ever
maintained the self-sufficiency of natural theology. St. Paul, indeed,
made it quite clear that we can never know God perfectly this side of
Heaven; for now, as he wrote, 'now we see through a glass, darkly;
but then face to face: now I know in part; but then shall I know even
as also I am known' (1 Cor. xiii. 12). For the best summary statement
of this point of view we may turn to Donne:

> Certainly, every Creature shewes God, as a glass, but glimmeringly and
> transitorily, by the frailty both of the receiver, and beholder: Our selves
> have his Image, as Medals, permanently, and preciously delivered. But by
> these meditations we get no further, then to know what he *doth*, not what
> he *is*.

Donne's attempt to balance the book of nature with the written one
of the Scriptures is a Renaissance commonplace. Here, for example,
is the statement of Andreas Gerardus (Hyperius), professor of theology at Marburg:

> to the intente that menne might at all times aspire to the knowledge and
> vnderstandyng of the power and will of *God*, *God* himselfe hathe set forth
> openly in the sight of all men, two large and ample bookes, stuffed and
> replenished with manifolde doctrine, whereout all things pertayning to
> the same his diuine power and will, are fully and sufficiently to be learned.
> The one of them is all this vniuersall worlde, whiche of vs is inhabited,
> and lyeth open on euerye side to the surveyall of oure senses: the other is
> the word of *God*, comprised in the bookes and writings of the Prophets
> and Apostles.[2]

---

[1] *Of the Advancement and Proficience of Learning* (Oxford, 1640), p. 137 [Bk. III,
ch. ii]. Cf. Erasmus, *De lib. arb.*, p. 24.

[2] Donne, *Essays*, p. 20, and Hyperius, *The Course of Christianitie*, tr. John Ludham
(1579), pp. 5–6. Of the numerous parallel statements see esp. Sir George More,

The constant emphasis on the two books of God was indirectly aimed at such extremists as Raymond of Sebonde, author of the *Theologia naturalis sive liber creaturarum*, a popular work written in the early fifteenth century. The Spanish theologian has been kept alive for posterity by Montaigne, who translated the *Theologia naturalis* but then penned an 'Apology for Raymond of Sebonde', the longest of his *Essays* and the vehicle for his scepticism. Nevertheless, Raymond himself contributed to his place in Christian thought by popularizing the idea of 'the book of the creatures' with which the mind of the Renaissance was so preoccupied and by first employing the term 'natural theology' as the title of a work.[1] Yet in his excessive enthusiasm over the book of nature Raymond came perilously near affirming the superfluity of God's written book, which caused the most controversial portion of his work, the Prologue, to be placed on the Index in 1595. Some Protestants like Francis Quarles went even further than the Vatican, bluntly dismissing Raymond's labours as 'Folly'. But the more common Protestant view is represented by Donne, who cautiously remarked that Raymond 'may be too abundant in affirming, that *in libro creaturarum* there is enough to teach us all particularities of Christian Religion', and then went on to observe that Raymond's thesis should be supplemented by taking a 'further step' from the book of nature to the written book of the Scriptures.[2] Hence the common celebration of the two books of God, the one—as Milton observed in the 1640's—the one 'all his visible works', and the other 'those recited decrees' contained in the Bible.[3] The same balance appears in *Paradise Lost*, where 'the Book of Knowledge fair' is at last subordinated to the revealed will of God in 'those writt'n Records pure' (XII. 513).

Behind the Renaissance persuasion that the natural order reveals the purposes of God stands the Judaeo-Christian view of nature. The Hebrew and early Christian attitude to nature was conditioned by

---

Demonstration, etc. (1579), p. 23; Richard Middleton, *The Heauenly Pro:gresse* (1617), pp. 186 f.; John Preston, *Life Eternall* (1631), i. 34; Alexander Grosse, *Suueet . . . Inducements* (1632), pp. 434 f.; William Price, *Ianitor animæ* (1638), pp. 253 ff.; Michael Jermin, *A Commentary upon . . . Ecclesiastes* (1639), pp. 81 f.; Sibbes, *Beames of Divine Light* (1639), i. 116 f.; George Hall, *Two Sermons* (1641), p. 26; and Richard Whitlock, *Ζωοτομία* (1654), p. 236.

[1] See C. C. J. Webb, *Studies in the History of Natural Theology* (Oxford, 1915), pp. 292–312.

[2] Quarles, *Divine Fancies* (1632), p. 88; Donne, *Essays*, p. 8.

[3] DDD, *Works*, iii. 420.

the conviction that the omnipotent Most High has absolute jurisdiction over every aspect of creation. This belief, magnificently phrased in God's address to Job out of the whirlwind, was stated as poetically, if more briefly, by Amos:

> Seek him that maketh the seven stars and Orion,
> And turneth the shadow of death into the morning,
> And maketh the day dark with night:
> That calleth for the waters of the sea,
> And poureth them out upon the face of the earth:
> The Lord is his name.
>
> (Amos v. 8)

From this belief the Hebrews advanced to the conclusion that in some way all of nature's 'singularities and discontinuities' are vitally important in the gradual revelation of the Divine Purpose in history.[1] Accordingly, when the psalmist meditated on the righteousness of God, he alluded spontaneously to the joys of nature:

> Let the heavens rejoice, and let the earth be glad;
> Let the sea roar, and the fulness thereof.
> Let the field be joyful, and all that is therein:
> Then shall all the trees of the wood rejoice.
>
> (Ps. xcvi. 11–12)

The anger of God was associated with convulsions in nature:

> The mountains saw thee, and they trembled:
> The overflowing of the water passed by:
> The deep uttered his voice,
> And lifted up his hands on high.
> The sun and moon stood still in their habitation.
>
> (Hab. iii. 10–11)

In the celebrated Song of Deborah the imminent destruction of Barak's enemies is said to have been anticipated by upheavals in the natural order:

> Lord, when thou wentest out of Seir,
> When thou marchedst out of the field of Edom,
> The earth trembled, and the heavens dropped,
> The clouds also dropped water.
> The mountains melted from before the Lord.
>
> (Judges v. 4–5)

---

[1] See F. W. Dillistone, *Christianity and Symbolism* (1955), ch. ii, and the references in *TZ* (below, p. 74, n. 1), p. 126.

This attitude toward nature was shared by the early Christians. Throughout the New Testament, the terms of total reference appropriate to the omnipotent God are employed again; and again we find nature reacting benevolently or adversely, in either case reflecting the purposes of the Most High. The most striking manifestation of this attitude is, of course, nature's violent reaction upon the Crucifixion, beginning with the darkness at the height of noon, and progressing through an earthquake to the resurrection of the dead (Matt. xxvii. 45 ff., Mark xv. 33 ff., Luke xxiii. 44 ff.).

The continuity of tradition throughout the age of Milton is testified by countless treatises of the Renaissance. Most frequently—almost habitually—nature's reaction to contemporary events was said to have been parallel to incidents recounted in the Scriptures.[1] But even when the reference was not directly to a specific Biblical event, the language used was often largely, and at times exclusively, derived from the Old Testament. Here is George Wither's typical description of the angry Lord:

> from about
> His eye lids, so much terror sparkled out,
> That ev'ry circle of the Heav'ns it shooke,
> And all the World did tremble at his looke;
> The prospect of the *Skie*, that earst was cleare,
> Did with a lowring countenance appeare:
> The troubled *Ayre*, before his presence fled;
> The *Earth* into her bosome shrunke her head;
> The *Deeps* did roare; the *Heights* did stand amaz'd;
> The *Moone* and *Stars* upon each other gaz'd;
> The *Sun* did stand unmoved in his path;
> The Hoast of Heav'n was frighted at his wrath.[2]

The widespread Renaissance belief that nature fully reflects the divine intentions is particularly evident in the commentaries on the upheavals that accompanied the death of Jesus. This is how Erasmus described the events at Calvary:

The very Sunne felte the punishement of the innocent, and coulde not abyde to beholde so wicked a dede. He couered his face with a blacke

---

[1] Cf. nature's reputedly favourable response during the victory of Elizabeth I over the Spaniards as of Deborah over the Canaanites (Judges v. 20; cf. Lodowick Lloyd, *The Tragicocomedie of Serpents* (1607), p. 11), and the mourning of the created order upon the death of Prince Henry as of Jonathan (1 Sam. i. 21; cf. Daniel Price, *Lamentations* (1613), p. 1).

[2] *Britain's Remembrancer* (1628), fol. 17ᵛ.

cloude, and all that cuntrey was couered with darkenes, frō sixe of the clocke vntill nyne. . . . The yearth also did quake, stones brake assondre and euerie parte of nature trembled at so horrible a dede of crueltee.[1]

This viewpoint is also encountered in Quarles's poem on the Passion:

> The earth did tremble; and heav'ns closed eye
> Was loth to see the *Lord of Glory* dye;
> The Skyes were clad in mourning, and the Spheares
> Forgot their *harmony*; The Clouds dropt *teares* . . .
> Th' affrighted heav'ns sent down elegious *Thunder*;
> The *Worlds Foundation* loos'd, to lose their *Founder*.[2]

Yet the Renaissance held not only that God's attitude is revealed through nature during a given incident or shortly after it, but also that God employs nature to divulge occurrences of the future. Here, it may be thought, we touch upon Renaissance astrology, whose capital rule—to quote Francis Quarles—was that 'Heav'ns seldome shine / With idle fires; like Prophets they devine / Stupendious events.'[3] But the disciples of astrology were not the only ones to attach significance to nature's 'singularities and discontinuities'. In the 1580's, to quote John Harvey, this view was shared by 'the common people' no less than by 'the learneder, and wiser sort', while in the next generation, according to George Hakewill, the 'common opinion' was still that comets and similar disturbances in the heavens 'haue allwayes prognosticated some dreadfull mishaps to the world, as outragious windes, extraordinary drought, dearth, pestilence, warres, death of Princes and the like'.[4] That such convictions

---

[1] *Paraphrase . . . upon the Newe Testamente* (1548), i. 106, 166ᵛ. See further my survey, 'Renaissance Commentaries on the Passion', *TZ*, xx (1964), 125–35, and the lengthy observations in Thomas Milles, *The Treasurie . . . of Times* (1613), Bk. VII, ch. 7; Antonio de Guevara, *The Mount of Caluarie*, tr. Anon. (1618), pt. i, chs. 38, 43–45; Luis de la Puente, *Meditations*, tr. John Heigham (St. Omer, 1619), ii. 298 f., 316 ff.; Anthony Stafford, *The Day of Salvation* (1635), pp. 133 ff.; Peter Hausted, *Ten Sermons* (1636), Serm. I; *et al.* One of the *loci classici*: Jerome, *Commentaria in evangelium S. Matthæi*, IV. xxvii. 45 (*Patr. l.* xxvi. 212).

[2] 'On our Saviours Passion', *Divine Fancies* (1641), p. 165. For another poetic account see Giles Fletcher, *Christs Victorie and Triumph*, iii. 38–39.

[3] *Hosanna*, ed. John Norden (Liverpool, 1960), p. 6. On Renaissance astrology consult Cassirer, ch. iii (2); Caroll Camden, *The Library*, xii (1931), 83–108, 194–207; Willard Farnham, *The Medieval Heritage of Elizabethan Tragedy*, rev. ed. (1956), esp. ch. iii; Moriz Sondheim, *JWCI*, ii (1938–9), 243–59; Lynn Thorndike, *A History of Magic* (1941), vols. v–vi, *passim*; Jean Seznec, *The Survival of the Pagan Gods*, tr. B. F. Sessions (1953), Bk. I, ch. ii; Clyde L. Manschreck, *Melanchthon* (1958), ch. viii; and the references in Svendsen, p. 264.

[4] Harvey, *A Discoursive Probleme* (1588), p. 1; Hakewill, *An Apologie*, etc. (1627), p. 119.

were widely spread is not necessarily surprising; for if nature is indeed the book of God, may it not be that disorders in the skies and on earth are 'signes of his wrath' over 'our sinnes'? Calvin was by no means the only one to reply that this is so;[1] this was repeatedly proclaimed by the vast majority of Christians, Protestants as well as Catholics, who held that comets and eclipses and earthquakes are 'not to be thought trifles', being rather significant events that 'foreshewe somewhat to follow'.[2] Although the apologists of the faith were by the early seventeenth century fully aware that 'unnatural' phenomena could be explained scientifically, they insisted that 'though some naturall reasons may bee probably rendred, yet being extra-ordinarie, they do proclaime, in their kinde, Gods anger, and threaten some judgement'.[3]

Certain facts, it would seem, do not support the contention that the Renaissance view of nature is essentially Biblical in origin. The reported occurrences during the death of Jesus, for example, are by no means unique; extra-Biblical literature teems with parallel reports of nature's adverse reaction, particularly in connexion with the death of popular epic heroes like Beowulf, Roland, Digenis Akrites, Prince Rostislav Vsevolodich in *The Song of Igor's Campaign*, and even Affonso Henriques in *Os Lusíados*.[4] In addition, there is the convention of nature's lamentation in nearly every pastoral elegy since Theocritus, Bion, and Moschus,[5] and also the numerous occasions in Shakespeare's plays when the natural order reacts adversely before or after an 'unnatural' event. Particularly noticeable in the Shakespearean corpus are the eclipses, each of which is accompanied by a 'paraphrase'. Prince Escalus, for example, observes that 'The sun,

---

[1] *Sermons . . . upon the Booke of Iob*, tr. Arthur Golding (1574), p. 707. See further S. K. Heninger, Jr., *A Handbook of Renaissance Meteorology* (Durham, N.C., 1960), pp. 23 ff.

[2] Abraham Fleming, *A Bright Burning Beacon* (1580), sig. D4ᵛ. This treatise is a collection of 'a huge multitude of examples . . . to verifie this matter'. For others like it, see William Vaughan, *The Golden-Grove* (1600), ch. liii; Martin Parker, *A True and Terrible Narration* (1638); and Nathaniel Wanley, *The Wonders of the Little World* (1678), Bk. VI, ch. ix.

[3] Thomas Jackson, *Judah must into Captivitie* (1622), pp. 22–23. See further Svendsen, ch. iii.

[4] *Beowulf*, l. 3146, ed. F. P. Magoun (Cambridge, Mass., 1959), p. 89; *La Chanson de Roland*, ll. 1423–37, ed. F. Whitehead (Oxford, 1942), p. 42; *Digenis Akrites*, ed. and tr. John Mavrogordato (Oxford, 1956), p. 244; *The Song of Igor's Campaign*, ll. 799–802, tr. Vladimir Nabokov (1960), p. 69; *Os Lusíados*, III, lxxxiv. 1–4, ed. J. D. M. Ford (Cambridge, Mass., 1946), p. 100.

[5] For references consult the bibliography, and J. H. Hanford's essay, in *Milton's 'Lycidas': The Tradition and the Poem*, ed. C. A. Patrides (1961), pp. 27 ff., 238 ff.

for sorrow, will not show his head'; of the eclipse on the day after King Duncan's murder, an old man says it is 'unnatural, / Even like the deed that's done'; in *Antony and Cleopatra*, Antony himself thinks that the disappearance of the sun 'portends alone / The fall of Antony'; and finally, in *King Lear*, there are the 'late eclipses in the sun and moon' of which Gloucester declares they will 'portend no good to us'.[1] Shakespeare dwelt on many other signs in nature besides eclipses, among them the staggering number of portents preceding the assassination of Julius Caesar, restated by Horatio in *Hamlet* (I. i. 113–25), and the 'unnatural' events on the night of the murder in *Macbeth*:

> The night has been unruly. Where we lay,
> Our chimneys were blown down; and, as they say,
> Lamentings heard i' th' air; strange screams of death,
> And prophesying with accents terrible
> Of dire combustion and confus'd events
> New hatch'd to th' woeful time. The obscure bird
> Clamour'd the livelong night; some say, the earth
> Was feverous and did shake.
>
> (II. iii. 59–66)

Yet the similarities between this Shakespearean theme and the Biblical view of nature are apparent at least as often as they are real. The evidence suggests that Shakespeare always subordinated ideas to his dramatic art—never vice versa[2]—and his conception of nature must therefore be seen as related only coincidentally to the Biblical theory accepted by Christians till the Renaissance. After all Shakespeare could—and did—gather as much from Plutarch and the extra-Biblical tradition generally, just as Camões is indebted not to the Bible but to Virgil for his account of nature's mourning at the death of Affonso Henriques,[3] and poets working within the conventions of the pastoral elegy utilized the 'pathetic fallacy' because of the cumu-

---

[1] *R. and J.* v. iii. 306; *Macb.* II. iv. 10 f.; *A. and C.* III. xiii. 154 f.; *K. L.* I. ii. 112 f. On Shakespeare's view of nature see E. C. Knowlton, *PMLA*, li (1936), 718–44; G. Wilson Knight, *The Crown of Life* (1947), ch. iii; R. C. Bald, in *J. Q. Adams Memorial Studies* (Washington, D.C., 1948), pp. 337–49; Robert E. Heilman, *This Great Stage* (Baton Rouge, 1948); John F. Danby, *Shakespeare's Doctrine of Nature* (1949); Theodore Spencer, *Shakespeare and the Nature of Man*, 2nd ed. (1951); George W. Williams, *SQ*, ii (1951), 57–71; Robert Speaight, *Nature in Shakespearean Tragedy* (1955); and L. C. Knights, *Some Shakespearean Themes* (1959), chs. v–vi.
[2] See Frye's excellent study (above, p. xii), which ought to curtail the more extreme attempts to christianize Shakespeare.
[3] Sir Maurice Bowra, *From Virgil to Milton* (1945), p. 105.

lative classical precedents. The attitude toward nature characteristic of the pastoral elegists, of Camões, of Shakespeare, may coincide with the traditional Christian view, but differs significantly from it by envisaging nature poetically, or occasionally as a dynamic force in her own right, but rarely as God's commissioner, vicar, or vice-regent in agreement with the specifically Christian claim upheld during the English Renaissance by Hooker, Ralegh, Donne, and Milton.

Milton's use of the convention of 'pathetic fallacy' in *Lycidas* (ll. 39 ff., 134 ff.) may seem to argue against his espousal of the Christian view of nature, but in fact the lamentation of the natural order for the dead poet is not an end in itself; it is rather a step in the progress of the poem from the secular to the sacred, from the non-Christian to the Christian, culminating in the vision of him that walked the waves. In retrospect, this appearance of the Lord of nature in *Lycidas* transforms even the conventional mourning of nature from a mere 'pathetic fallacy' to a categorical affirmation of its transcendental significance. We can be certain that Milton would have agreed with La Primaudaye's statement, quoted earlier, that nature is totally subservient to God, 'borrowing hir force and strength from thence, as from hir fountain and originall'.

The Christian view of nature was upheld by Milton not only in *Lycidas*, but earlier in the *Nativity Ode*[1] and subsequently in *Paradise Lost*. Nature participates in the happiness of Adam and Eve upon their marriage:

> all Heav'n,
> And happie Constellations on that houre
> Shed thir selectest influence; the Earth
> Gave sign of gratulation, and each Hill;
> Joyous the Birds; fresh Gales and gentle Aires
> Whisperd it to the Woods, and from thir wings
> Flung Rose, flung Odours from the spicie Shrub,
> Disporting, till the amorous Bird of Night
> Sung Spousal, and bid haste the Eevning Starr
> On his Hill top, to light the bridal Lamp.
>
> (VIII. 511–20)

When Eve eats of the forbidden fruit, however, the violent reaction of nature, set forth by Milton in a preponderance of monosyllables, indicates all too clearly the attitude of God's 'vicaire':

[1] On nature's attitude upon the birth of Jesus, see below, p. 143.

> Earth felt the wound, and Nature from her seat
> Sighing through all her Works gave signs of woe,
> That all was lost.   (IX. 782–4)

Likewise, the moment that Adam shared the disobedience of his wife,

> Earth trembl'd from her entrails, as again
> In pangs, and Nature gave a second groan,
> Skie lowr'd, and muttering Thunder, som sad drops
> Wept at compleating of the mortal Sin
> Original.[1]   (IX. 1000–4)

The theory underlying these lines reappears in two other instances in *Paradise Lost*. The first occasion is during the passage of Sin and Death through the constellations on their way to our world after the Fall, when

> the blasted Starrs lookd wan,
> And Planets, Planet-strook, real Eclips
> Then sufferd.   (X. 412–14)

The second forms part of the War in Heaven 'accommodated' to our understanding. When Lucifer's rebellion aroused the divine wrath,

> Clouds began
> To dark'n all the Hill, and smoak to rowl
> In duskie wreathes, reluctant flames, the signe
> Of wrauth awak't.   (VI. 56–59)

Milton approached cautiously the other Renaissance view that 'unnatural' phenomena 'foreshewe somewhat to follow'. In his *History of Britain*, admittedly, he reports a series of portents—eclipses, comets, and even midnight 'barbarous noises' and 'hideous howlings'—but these, as I shall argue later, were dictated by the practice of Renaissance historiographers.[2] Otherwise, there is no evidence to suggest that Milton was so uncritical as to believe with Comenius that comets and all other apparent disorders in the heavens 'indeed are wont to portend no good'.[3] In *Paradise Regained*

---

[1] Precedents occur anywhere from rabbinic literature (Ginzberg, i. 79) to Grotius's *Adamus Exul* (Kirkconnell, p. 184)—but do not include the remote 'parallel' in Hesiod cited by C. G. Osgood, *The Classical Mythology of Milton's English Poems* (1900), p. 61.

[2] See the 'signs' enumerated in *Works*, x. 65 f., 169, 171, 177, 180, 249, and cf. below, p. 256.

[3] *Orbis sensualium pictus*, tr. Charles Hoole (1659), p. 304. This work was one of the most popular school-books of seventeenth-century Europe.

Milton even more cautiously indicated that some 'signs' are instigated not by God but by Satan (I. 393 ff.; IV. 489 ff.), though in
other instances, when it was certain that they had been caused by
God, he accepted them as forerunners of the Divine Purpose. Thus
after the Fall in *Paradise Lost*, when Eve naïvely thinks that she is to
remain with Adam in the Garden, Milton intervenes to observe that

> Fate
> Subscrib'd not; Nature first gave Signs, imprest
> On Bird, Beast, Aire; Aire suddenly eclipsd
> After short blush of Morn; nigh in her sight
> The Bird of *Jove*, stoopt from his aerie tour,
> Two Birds of gayest plume before him drove:
> Down from a Hill the Beast that reigns in Woods,
> First Hunter then, persu'd a gentle brace,
> Goodliest of all the Forrest, Hart and Hinde;
> Direct to th' Eastern Gate was bent thir flight.
>
> (XI. 181–90)

Adam, no longer able to read the book of nature as infallibly as he
used to (cf. VIII. 273–9), now resolves to await a direct revelation
from God. His observation to Eve, therefore, though seemingly a
restatement of Raphael's earlier assurance that the natural order is
'the Book of God', is distinctly more cautious:

> O *Eve*, some furder change awaits us nigh,
> Which Heav'n by these mute signs in Nature shews
> Forerunners of his purpose. . . .
>
> (XI. 193–5)

After Milton caution declined noticeably. Nearly a century later,
when 'wicked' Lisbon was shattered by the violent earthquake of
November 1755, the traditional theory that nature's upheavals are
signs of the divine wrath reached hysterical proportions. But at
last powerful voices were raised in dissent—notably Voltaire's[1]—
and the Biblical view of nature, already twisted beyond recognition,
died a mute, inglorious death.

IV

Natural theology during the Renaissance was extended significantly to comprehend the traditional theory of 'natural law', the

---

[1] See T. D. Kendrick, *The Lisbon Earthquake* (1956), and Theodore Besterman,
Voltaire Essays (1962), ch. iii.

immemorial persuasion that nature incorporates a moral law evident
to those within as well as to those without the Church. Christian
considerations of this law inevitably begin with St. Paul's statement
that 'not the hearers of the law are just before God, but the doers of
the law shall be justified. For when the Gentiles, which have not the
law, do by nature the things contained in the law, these, having not
the law, are a law unto themselves: which shew the work of the law
written in their hearts, their conscience also bearing witness, and
their thoughts the mean while accusing or else excusing one another'
(Rom. ii. 13–15). Unfortunately the term 'natural law', as Donne
justifiably complained, is 'so variously and unconstantly deliver'd,
as I confess I read it a hundred times before I can understand it
once, or can conclude it to signifie that which the author should at
that time meane'.[1] Notwithstanding the labyrinth of interpretations,
the main line of tradition is clearly visible, and to follow it may help,
us, as Ariadne's thread helped Theseus, to emerge from darkness
into light.[2]

One of the finest Greek affirmations of the divine origin of all laws
is to be found in *Oedipus Rex*. As the chorus sings in that tragedy,

> Let all my words and actions keep
> The laws of the pure universe
> From highest Heaven handed down;
> For Heaven is their bright nurse,
> Those generations of the realms of light;
> Ah, never of mortal kind were they begot,
> Nor are they slaves of memory, lost in sleep:
> Their father is greater than Time, and ages not.[3]

---

[1] *Biathanatos* (1646?), i. 36.
[2] On the development of 'natural law', see Otto Gierke, *Political Theories of the Middle Ages*, tr. F. W. Maitland (Cambridge, 1900), pp. 73 ff., 172 ff.; David G. Ritchie, *Natural Rights*, 3rd ed. (1916), ch. ii; Sir Frederick Pollock, *Essays in the Law* (1922), ch. ii; Charles G. Haines, *The Revival of Natural Law Concepts* (Cambridge, Mass., 1930), ch. i; Ernest Barker, 'Introduction' to Gierke's *Natural Law and the Theory of Society* (Cambridge, 1934), I. xxxiv-l; Joseph Dalby, *The Catholic Conception of the Law of Nature* (1943); A. R. Vidler and W. A. Whitehouse, *Natural Law*, 2nd ed. (1946); Heinrich Rommen, *The Natural Law*, tr. T. R. Hanley (St. Louis, 1949), chs. i–iii; George W. Paton, *Jurisprudence*, 2nd ed. (Oxford, 1951), ch. iv; Robert M. Grant, *Miracle and Natural Law* (Amsterdam, 1952), ch. ii; A. P. d'Entrèves, *Natural Law* (1952); W. Friedmann, *Legal Theory*, 3rd ed. (1953), chs. iii–vii; Robert Ornstein, *JEGP*, lv (1956), 213–29; and Jacques Ellul, *The Theological Foundation of Law*, tr. Marguerite Wieser (1961). On natural law in the Bible, consult C. H. Dodd, *NT Guides* (Manchester, 1953), ch. vi.
[3] *Oedipus Rex*, ll. 865–72; tr. Dudley Fitts and Robert Fitzgerald (1951). See also *Antigone*, ll. 455 ff.

Three centuries later the same idea was restated by Cicero, though now the vagueness of the unwritten laws celebrated by Sophocles was replaced by a definite theory of natural law. According to Cicero,

> True law is right reason in agreement with nature; it is of universal application, unchanging and everlasting; it summons to duty by its commands, and averts from wrongdoing by its prohibitions. . . . We cannot be freed from its obligations by senate or people, and we need not look outside ourselves for an expounder or interpreter of it. And there will not be different laws now and in the future, but one eternal and unchangeable law will be valid for all nations and all times, and there will be one master and ruler, that is, God, over us all, for he is the author of this law, its promulgator, and its enforcing judge. Whoever is disobedient is fleeing from himself and denying his human nature, and by reason of this very fact he will suffer the worst penalties.[1]

Upon its advent, Christianity almost at once adopted the Stoic formulation of the law of nature and merged it with the Decalogue; and though there were distinct differences between the pagan and the Christian views—notably Christianity's occasional denial that moral principles can be grasped by human reason without divine revelation—the fusion of the two currents of thought exercised a profound influence upon all subsequent expositions of the *lex naturae*. The fully developed Christian position has been summarized as follows:

> The source of our being and the Artificer of our nature is God Himself. That 'law of nature', which, as the Apostle said, is written on the hearts even of the heathen, is an expression of the Reason which of itself is a reflection of the wisdom and 'eternal law' of God. First, then, comes the 'eternal law' of God; second, as reflecting it, the 'law of nature', and third, the customary and statute law of men, which has no validity except as an approximation of the 'law of nature'. From the Being and Nature of God Himself is derived man's innate sense of justice; and justice may be called man's 'natural' law, because, where he commits injustice, he does despite to his human nature, he falls short of the meaning and purpose of humanity.[2]

The clearest statement of the Christian philosophy of law was penned by St. Thomas Aquinas. When St. Thomas summarized and

---

[1] *De republica*, III. 22; tr. C. W. Keyes (1928). On the Ciceronian position consult Huntington Cairns, *Legal Philosophy* (Baltimore, 1949), pp. 132 ff.; and on other Greek and Roman formulations: James L. Adams, *JR*, xxv (1945), 97–118.

[2] Nathaniel Micklem, *The Theology of Politics* (1941), pp. 60–61.

perfected the views of his predecessors, he not only reaffirmed the christianized persuasion of the Greeks and the Romans that 'all laws proceed from the eternal law', but simultaneously upheld the specifically Christian claim of the necessity for revelation by asserting that 'there is in us the knowledge of certain general principles, but not proper knowledge of each single truth, such as that contained in the Divine Wisdom.'[1] The hierarchy of laws that St. Thomas went on to expound—the primal *lex aeterna* and, deriving thence, the *lex naturalis* and the *lex humana*—was set forth so brilliantly that no later discussion within the framework of the Christian faith is far removed from his formulation. Moreover, the *lex aeterna* was held to be immutable and binding upon God himself, meaning in the terminology of medieval scholasticism that God acts in accordance with his 'obediential power' (*potentia obedientialis*), which is inviolate since its institution and the fundamental principle in the divine government of the universe.[2]

St. Thomas Aquinas cast his net wide, and if he missed Marsilius of Padua, he managed to catch in it almost every Christian writer to the later seventeenth century. We must note especially the Spanish Jesuit Francisco Suárez among Catholics,[3] and among Protestants the entire array of Reformers led by Luther, Calvin, Zwingli, and Melanchthon.[4] The continuity of tradition is well attested, but here is the statement of the popular Protestant theologian Wolfgang Musculus:

the law of nature is not called such a thing, which either besides or aboue

---

[1] *S. th.*, II. xci. 3, and xciii. 3. On the philosophy of law from Augustine to Thomas Aquinas see the excellent surveys by Anton-Hermann Chroust in *PR*, liii (1944), 195–202, and *NS*, xx (1946), 26–71; and further: Odon Lottin, *Le Droit naturel chez Saint Thomas d'Aquin et ses prédécesseurs*, 2nd ed. (Bruges, 1931); A. P. d'Entrèves, *La Filosofia politica medioevale* (Turin, 1934), pt. ii, ch. i, and *The Medieval Contribution to Political Thought* (1939), ch. ii; Walter Ullmann, *Medieval Papalism* (1949), chs. ii–iii; Dalby (above, p. 80, n. 2), ch. iv; Albert H. Olson, *ATR*, xxxiii (1951), 149–57; and Jean-Marie Aubert, *Le Droit romain dans l'œuvre de Saint Thomas* (Paris, 1955), with full bibliography.

[2] Gilson (above, p. 56, n. 1), pp. 377–81.

[3] See the *Selections* from Suárez, *De legibus* (Coimbra, 1612), tr. G. L. Williams *et al.* (Oxford, 1944), esp. ii. 39 ff. Consult also Copleston, iii, ch. 23, and Bernice Hamilton, *Political Thought in Sixteenth-Century Spain* (Oxford, 1963), esp. ch. i.

[4] See August Lang, *Calvin and the Reformation* (1909), pp. 56 ff.; Philip S. Watson, *Let God be God!* (1947), pp. 110 ff.; Bernard Erling, *Nature and History* (Lund, 1960), pp. 259 ff.; Frye, pp. 96 ff.; but esp. the two brilliant studies by John T. McNeill in *CH*, x (1941), 211–27, and *JR*, xxvi (1946), 168–82. The conclusions of Ernst Troeltsch are inaccurate (*The Social Teaching of the Christian Churches*, tr. Olive Wyon (1931), pp. 528–39).

that eternall lawe which is in God, is prescribed by our nature it selfe, but that which is by God himself naturally fastened and established in al men, and very agreable vnto his eternal law. . . . Now the law of nature is that light & iudgement of reason, wherby we doe discerne betwixt good & euil. Thomas Aquinas sayth, ỹ ỹ law of nature is nothing els, but ỹ participatiõ of the eternal law, in a reasonable creature.

A century later, in England, Nathanael Culverwell linked his eloquent restatement of the Thomistic formulation to the Homeric *aurea catena* we noted earlier. 'The golden chain of Lawes', wrote Culverwell, is 'tied to the chair of *Jupiter*, and a command is only vigorous as it issues out, either immediately or remotely from the great Sovereigne of the world. So that τὸ ὄν, is the sure bottome and foundation of every Law.' Then, continuing in the manner of Musculus and a host of other apologists, Culverwell indicated clearly the derivation of the *lex naturae* from the *lex aeterna* by discoursing on 'the spring and original of all Lawes',

the eternal Law, that fountain of Law, out of which you may see the Law of *Nature* bubbling and flowing forth to the sons of men. For, as *Aquinas* does very well tell us, the Law of *Nature* is nothing but *participatio Legis æternæ in Rationali creatura*, the copying out of the eternal Law, and the imprinting of it upon the breast of a Rationall being; that eternal Law was in a manner incarnated in the Law of *Nature*.[1]

But the greatest English exponent of the Thomistic conception of law remains Richard Hooker. For him, as for nearly every one else, the affirmation of St. Paul I quoted earlier was fundamental. As Hooker maintained in one of his sermons,

Vnder the name of the Lawe wee must comprehend not only that which God hath written in tables and leaues, but that which nature also hath engraven in the hearts of men. Else how shall those heathen which never had bookes but heaven and earth to looke vpon be convicted of perversenesse? But the Gentiles which had not the law in bookes, had, saith the Apostle, the effect of the law written in their harts.[2]

'All things', declared Hooker in his majestic *Laws of Ecclesiastical Polity*, 'doe worke after a sort according to Law'; and though, he added, though there are a number of laws operative at the various levels of the created order, they do not differ from each other in kind

[1] Musculus, fols. 29ᵛ–30, and Culverwell, *Discourse of the Light of Nature* (1654), pp. 20, 25. See also the parallel statements by Robert Bolton, *Two Sermons* (1639), pp. 7 f., and Theophilus Gale, *The Court of the Gentiles* (Oxford, 1669), i. 5 f.
[2] *A Learned Sermon of the Nature of Pride* (Oxford, 1612), p. 5.

since they have a common source in God, who is 'a law both to himselfe, and to all other things besides'.[1] The theme was reiterated by
endless writers, from the catechizer Petrus de Witte, who maintained
that properly speaking 'there is but one Law of God, an eternal &
unchangeable rule of righteousness', to the greater apologist of the
faith John Donne, who categorically affirmed the existence of 'a certain Divine soul, and spark of Gods power, which goes through all
Laws and inanimates them'.[2] The tradition flowed on to the very end
of the seventeenth century, when Benjamin Whichcote, on behalf of
the Cambridge Platonists, succinctly stated that 'The Law of Nature
is that, which is Reason: which is Right, and Fit.'[3]

But between Hooker and the Cambridge Platonists new ideas
were already opposing the mainstream of tradition. Confusion, in
the form of a distinction drawn between the law of nature and the
law of reason, set in early in the seventeenth century through the
discourses of Sir Henry Finch.[4] More seriously still, Hobbes secu-
larized natural law by denying the validity of its traditional theological framework. This is not to say that Hobbes rejected the law of
nature outright; on the contrary, the terminology of his *Leviathan*
(1651) conforms strictly to orthodox usage. Yet in spite of appearances natural law was 'shorn of all its power',[5] partly because in the
pristine state envisaged by Hobbes man proved himself not a rational

---

[1] Hooker, pp. 3, 4. On Hooker's philosophy of law, see Norman Sykes in *The Social
and Political Ideas of . . . the 16th and 17th Centuries*, ed. F. J. C. Hearnshaw (1926),
pp. 63–89; A. P. d'Entrèves, *Riccardo Hooker* (Turin, 1932), and *Med. Contribution*
(above, p. 82, n. 1), ch. vi; E. T. Davies, *The Political Ideas of Richard Hooker* (1946),
ch. iii; F. J. Shirley, *Richard Hooker and Contemporary Political Ideas* (1949), ch. iv;
Peter Munz, *The Place of Hooker in the History of Thought* (1952), pp. 175 ff.

[2] Witte, *Catechizing upon the Heidelbergh Catechisme* (Amsterdam, 1664?), p. 25
[first published in Dutch, 1658]; Donne, *Sermons*, v. 225 (cf. vii. 217.) See further the
lengthy expositions by Jeremy Taylor, *Ductor dubitantium* (1660), Bk. II, and Walter
Charleton, *The Harmony of . . . Laws* (1682), as well as the commentary by Thomas
Wood, *English Casuistical Divinity during the Seventeenth Century* (1952), pp. 79 ff.

[3] *Moral and Religious Aphorisms*, ed. W. R. Inge (1930), p. 65. See also Whichcote's
Select Sermons (1698), p. 302, and for the statement of another Cambridge Platonist:
John Smith, *Select Discourses* (1660), p. 156.

[4] *Law: or, A Discourse Thereof* (1613), Bk. I, chs. i–ii. Another alteration of the
traditional viewpoint—almost imperceptible—set in with Charron; see Eugene F. Rice,
Jr., *The Renaissance Idea of Wisdom* (Cambridge, Mass., 1958), pp. 192 ff. Once I
thought that Grotius had also abandoned the Thomistic formulation, but Anton-
Hermann Chroust convinced me this was not so (*NS*, xvii (1943), 101–33).

[5] W. Friedmann, *Legal Theory*, 3rd ed. (1953), p. 42. For a survey of recent studies of
Hobbes see J. B. Stewart, *Political Science Quarterly*, lxxiii (1958), 547–65. Developments in the late seventeenth and early eighteenth centuries are outlined by Paul Hazard,
The European Mind, tr. J. L. May (1953), pt. iii, ch. iii, and Francis Oakley, *CH*, xxx
(1961), 433–57.

being but an animal of extreme brutality, and partly because Hobbes, like Machiavelli and Bodin, ascribed the source of all laws to the sovereign, thus reducing them to a singular law whose nature was strictly civil.

Milton's quite contrary view is too well known for detailed consideration here;[1] but much remains to be said of his adherence to the tradition of natural law. Milton set out his fundamental generalization in *De doctrina christiana*, where in discussing the law of God—written and unwritten—he declared that the latter is 'no other than that law of nature given originally to Adam, and of which a certain remnant, or imperfect illumination, still dwells in the hearts of mankind'. Elsewhere he maintained that the *lex naturae* has always been—together with the *lex aeterna* whence it derives— 'immutable' as well as 'commensurat to right reason', which accounts for its being 'the only law of laws truly and properly to all mankinde fundamental'. Moreover the revelation of the written law did not invalidate the law of nature, which retains 'the same obligatory force' as the Decalogue and the Gospel, though when the book of nature cannot be read accurately—a common enough predicament since the Fall—then the individual must resort to 'the light of grace, a better guide than nature'.[2] Jesus, in *Paradise Regained*, makes precisely this point. Satan had observed that

> All knowledge is not coucht in *Moses* Law,
> The *Pentateuch* or what the Prophets wrote,
> The Gentiles also know, and write, and teach
> To admiration, led by Natures light.
>
> (IV. 225–8)

Satan is not wrong, but only half right. He is not wrong because he has shrewdly paraphrased St. Paul's endorsement of the idea that the heathen were guided 'by nature'; but he is only half right because, not prone to Christian apologetics, he failed to state Paul's further argument that the written law is superior to the natural. The balance is restored in the 'sage' reply of Jesus:

> Think not but that I know these things, or think
> I know them not; not therefore am I short

---

[1] On Milton and Hobbes consult Marjorie H. Nicolson, *SP*, xxiii (1926), 405–33, and Don M. Wolfe, *SP*, xli (1944), 410–26.

[2] Seriatim in *Works*: DDC, xvi. 101; DDD, iii. 440 and 480; *The Readie and Easie Way*, vi. 113; DDC, xvi. 109; *Animadversions*, iii. 142. Cf. *Tetrachordon*, iv. 135, 176; DDC, xv. 117.

Of knowing what I ought: he who receives
Light from above, from the fountain of light,
No other doctrin needs, though granted true;
But these are false, or little else but dreams,
Conjectures, fancies, built on nothing firm.

(IV. 286–92)

Many a reader of *Paradise Regained* has viewed the disparagement of Greek philosophy and literature by Jesus as 'most puzzling', and often thought it an opinion to which Milton was driven late in life by 'the reproving voice of his Puritan conscience'.[1] That disparagement does not seem to me either puzzling or Puritan, because Jesus utters a commonplace of Christian thought: that after the Fall the *lex naturae* is almost always an 'imperfect illumination', an uncertain guide likely to mislead us unless we take the further step in the direction of 'those writt'n Records pure'. Here is no self-righteous assertion that Christians will inevitably conduct themselves in a morally upright manner, but the expectation that they are more capable of attaining the highest standards of morality because their moral code comes 'bubbling and flowing forth' from God while that of the others is merely 'natural', 'built on nothing firm', and so subject to error. As Milton well knew, such a viewpoint can be demonstrated historically to include the possibility of Greeks and Romans being morally superior to those within the Judaeo-Christian tradition. Whenever they did manifest this moral superiority it was because they had obviously read aright the law of nature. In *Paradise Regained* Jesus expressly commends those 'from God inspir'd' no less than those in whom 'moral vertue is exprest / By light of Nature not in all quite lost' (IV. 351 f.).

For Milton the 'unwritten lawes and ideas which nature hath ingraven in us' comprised a corpus of material he had studied well and used on a number of occasions, notably in the divorce tracts with which we shall deal later,[2] and in defending the execution of Charles I on 29 January 1649. 'No understanding man can be ignorant', declared Milton within a month of the regicide, 'that Covenants are ever made according to the present state of persons and of things; and have the more general laws of nature and of

---

[1] E. M. W. Tillyard, *Milton* (1930), pp. 307–10, and H. J. C. Grierson, *The Background of English Literature* (1925), p. 21. But John M. Steadman has since demonstrated conclusively that the 'pattern of systematic rejection' in *PR* is 'a standard method of Western ethical tradition' (*UTQ*, xxxi (1962), 416–30).

[2] See below, pp. 184 ff. On the relevance of this tradition to *Comus*, see Madsen, pp. 198 ff.

reason included in them, though not express'd. If I make a voluntary
Covnant as with a man, to doe him good, and he prove afterward a
monster to me, I should conceave a disobligement.'¹ Milton's initial
argument is plain enough: since Charles I violated the law of nature
through tyranny, neither the rebellion nor the regicide were infrac-
tions of God's will. Two years later Milton reiterated his thesis in
full before an international audience. Opposed by the formidable
Salmasius, who had likewise appealed to natural law, Milton devoted
the fifth chapter of his *Defensio pro populo anglicano* to an analysis of
the concept. Salmasius had defined the law of nature as 'a principle
implanted in all men's minds, to regard the good of all mankind in
so far as men are united together in societies. But it cannot procure
the common good unless, as there are people that must be governed,
it also ascertain who shall govern them.' Readily subscribing to this
definition, Milton proceeded to employ it against Salmasius. The
crux, he pointed out, lies in the words 'all mankind'; and since
Charles was not inclined toward the welfare of all his subjects—
always 'by nature supreme'—his deposition was fully justified. It is
quite true that 'the obedience of superiours', as Donne had written,
'is of the law of Nature'; but this truism, Milton affirmed, must not
be accepted without qualification. The law of nature, he insisted,
cannot possibly be invoked to sustain a tyrant in power, for tyranny
is contrary 'to the will of God, to nature, and to reason'; according
to the celebrated dictum of Suárez, *lex injusta non est lex*. As Milton
summarized his theory of the ruler, from which he never once
deviated, there can be 'no king by the law of nature except him who
excels all the rest in wisdom and courage. . . . For unto the wisest
man nature gives command over men less wise, not unto the
wicked man over good men, a fool over wise men: and consequently
they that take the government out of such men's hands, act quite
according to the law of nature.'² This is precisely what Abdiel states

---

¹ *The Tenure of Kings and Magistrates, Works*, v. 35. The first republican to appeal to
the law of nature was Henry Parker (*Observations*, 1642); others soon followed suit:
among republicans, esp. John Goodwin; and among royalists, Sir Dudley Digges and
Henry Ferne. See William Haller, *The Rise of Puritanism* (1938), ch. x, but also Arthur
Barker, *Milton and the Puritan Dilemma* (Toronto, 1942); William J. Grace, *JHI*, xxiv
(1963), 323–36; and Ernest Sirluck, 'Introduction' to Milton's *Complete Prose Works*
(New Haven, 1959), ii. 12–52, and *MP*, lxi (1964), 209–24.

² Seriatim: Milton, *Works*, vii. 269, 271–3; Donne, *Devotions*, ed. John Sparrow
(Cambridge, 1923), p. 61; Milton, *Works*, vii. 427; Suárez, *De legibus*, III. 19 [quoted by
Ritchie (above, p. 80, n. 2), p. 42]; Milton, *Works*, vii. 273. Cf. the case of Nimrod
in *PL*, XII. 27–29.

in *Paradise Lost* after Satan has accused the faithful angels of servility to God:

> Unjustly thou deprav'st it with the name
> Of *Servitude* to serve whom God ordains,
> Or Nature; God and Nature bid the same,
> When he who rules is worthiest, and excells
> Them whom he governs. This is servitude,
> To serve th' unwise, or him who hath rebelld
> Against his worthier.

(VI. 174–80)

V

The Biblical and the Renaissance attitudes toward nature, for all their similarities, diverge drastically in at least one significant respect. While the Hebrews and the early Christians upheld the direct relationship between God and nature, the divine realm and the natural order were divorced from each other as a result of a profound change which gradually set in. Thus St. Augustine, who represents the earlier Christian view, affirmed a 'continuous chain of causality', refusing to separate nature from supernature but preferring to regard them as 'interpenetrating one another in all the phenomena of the world'.[1] By the time St. Thomas Aquinas made his influence felt, and through the Renaissance, nature came to be regarded as a closed immutable order whose powers, once granted by God upon the creation of the world, became in a sense autonomous. In effect, as against the Biblical conviction of the 'living relatedness' between God and nature,[2] now the Creator was to his creation as a monarch to his lieutenants who are the delegates of his authority. In the express statement of Pierre Charron early in the seventeenth century, 'God and nature are in the world, as in a state, the king, the author and founder, and the fundamentall law which hee hath made for the preservation and government of the said estate.' Even more pertinent and explicit is Bacon's observation that the 'Laws of nature, which now remaine, and governe inviolably till the end of the world, began to be in force when God rested from his works, and ceased to create, but received a revocation in part by the curse since which time they change not'. For this reason, Bacon added, God's providential supervision of the natural order is 'not immediate, and

---

[1] T. A. Lacey, *Nature, Miracle and Sin* (1916), pp. 31, 72.
[2] Evgueny Lampert, *The Divine Realm* (1946), p. 115.

direct, but by compass, not violating nature'. Milton, like Bacon, affirmed in *De doctrina christiana* that 'certain immutable laws' have been enacted, by which every part of the creation is administered.[1]

But the delegation of immutable laws to nature does not prevent God from interfering in the creation directly. This can and does happen, the result being a miracle. Here we have the clearest possible indication of the change in the trends of Christian thought on nature since Augustine. To Thomas Aquinas miracles were a violation of nature, a special intervention on God's part in order to effect some end which the creation was not originally endowed with the ability to perform. According to Augustine, however, every aspect of the universal structure is miraculous, though familiarity has deprived it of its wonder for us. As he observed on a memorable occasion, 'is not the world a miracle? Yet visible, and of his making. Nay, all the miracles done in this world are less then the world it selfe, the heauen and earth and all therein'. Indeed, he went on, 'though these visible miracles of nature, bee now no more admired, yet ponder them wisely, and they are more admirable then the strangest: for man is a greater miracle then all that hee can worke.'[2] Quite the contrary, declared Thomas Aquinas, miracles are rather 'against the order of the whole created nature' in that they are 'works that are sometimes done by God outside the usual order assigned to things'.[3]

The Thomistic interpretation of miracles was gradually assimilated into Christian orthodoxy and persisted through the seventeenth century. There were, to be certain, a number of eloquent statements of the Augustinian thesis,[4] but on the whole the Renaissance adhered to the Thomistic conception that miracles are performed by God 'above' or 'against' nature. Richard Bernard's statement in 1642 represents the common point of view: '*Miracles* are workes above the strength of Nature, and can be effected of none, but by the Authour of Nature, who only doth them either above or against the

---

[1] Charron, *Of Wisdome*, tr. Samson Lennard (1640), p. 270; Bacon, *The Confession of Faith* (1641), p. 4; Milton, *Works*, xv. 91.

[2] *De civ.* X. 12. On the Biblical view of miracles, see Harold Knight, *SJT*, v (1952), 355–61, and the references in *TZ*, xx (1964), 132. On the development of the concept since Augustine, consult John A. Hardon, *TS*, xv (1954), 229–57. See also Heppe, pp. 264 ff.

[3] *S. th.* I. cx. 4; *S. c. Gent.* III. ci.

[4] See, for instance, John Swift, *Divine Echo* (1612), sig. I5 f., and—in part at least— Donne, *Essays*, pp. 81 ff. Elsewhere Donne subscribed to the post-Augustinian thesis (*Sermons*, vii. 300, 373 f., etc.).

power of Nature.'[1] Milton, once again, concurred: a miracle, he wrote in *De doctrina christiana*, is the production of 'some effect out of the usual order of nature', and its primary author is always God, since 'he only is able to invert the order of things which he has himself appointed'.[2]

For one kind of inversion, however, God was not directly responsible. This, as we shall see next, was the 'breach disloyal' of angels and of man.

[1] *The Bibles Abstract* (1642), p. 25. Further references in *TZ*, xx (1964), 132 f.
[2] *Works*, xv. 95. See further Maurice Kelley, *MLN*, liii (1938), 170–2.

4

The Breach Disloyal

THE FALL OF ANGELS AND MAN

breake vnity once, and farewell strength.

WILLIAM LAUD[1]

I

RENAISSANCE expositors accepted the theory of the angels' rebellion in Heaven as a fact. Unfortunately the Biblical evidence for this theory is distressingly inadequate, consisting of a passage in Isaiah and a few verses in the Book of Revelation.[2] In Isaiah the reference is to the fall of the King of Babylon, whom Christian theologians displaced in favour of Satan on the evidence of an incidental statement by Jesus ('I beheld Satan as lightning fall from Heaven' [Luke x. 18]). Thus Isaiah:

How art thou fallen from heaven, O Lucifer, son of the morning!
How art thou cut down to the ground, who didst weaken the nations!
For thou hast said in thine heart, 'I will ascend into heaven,
I will exalt my throne above the stars of God:
I will sit also upon the mount of congregation, in the sides of the
north:
I will ascend above the heights of the clouds; I will be like the Most
High.'
Yet thou shalt be brought down to hell, to the sides of the pit.

(Isa. xiv. 12–15)

The other major 'evidence' given in verification of the War in Heaven, one of the poetic visions in the Johannine Apocalypse, is just as questionable:

And there appeared another wonder in heaven; and behold a great red dragon, having seven heads and ten horns, and seven crowns upon his

---

[1] *A Sermon preached . . . at Westminster* (1625), p. 9.

[2] For one of the most lucid expositions of the relevant passages, see John Fosbroke, *Six Sermons* (Cambridge, 1633), iii. 3 ff. Among the earlier statements, consult Innocent III, *The Mirror of Mans Lyfe*, tr. H. Kerton (1576), Bk. II, ch. xxix.

heads. And his tail drew the third part of the stars of heaven, and did cast
them to the earth. . . . And there was war in heaven: Michael and his
angels fought against the dragon; and the dragon fought and his angels,
and prevailed not; neither was their place found any more in heaven. And
the great dragon was cast out, that old serpent, called the Devil, and Satan,
which deceiveth the whole world: he was cast out into the earth, and his
angels were cast out with him.   (Rev. xii. 3-4, 7-9)

The constant Protestant demand for the adjustment of *humanae
traditiones* to 'the standard of Scripture' is not audible in connexion
with the War in Heaven. Here, more than anywhere else, Protestants
fell silent before the cumulative voices of their predecessors. Lucifer,
for example, was accepted as leader of the apostate angels and thought
to have occupied a position 'more excellent than all the Angels of
heaven in resplendent brightnesse', 'highest of all in the *orders* of
Angels'.[1] Tradition also provided the cause of Lucifer's revolt, as we
see from this typical exposition by John Salkeld, the learned Catholic
reportedly converted by James I:

> Amongst other very curious Questions which *Theodoretus* vpon
> *Genesis* propoundeth, one is this: *Quam ob causam è cœlo Diabolus
> decidit?* What was the cause why the Diuell (who before was a glorious
> Angell in all naturall beauty) fell from heauen? To which hee answereth,
> *That . . . the cause of his fall was pride, as* Esaias *testifieth*; Cogitauit apud
> semetipsum, supra nubes locabo solium meum, & ero similis altissimo;
> *Hee thought with himselfe, I will place my Throne aboue the clouds, and I
> will be like unto the Highest.* Which opinion of *Theodoretus*, may be con-
> firmed out of diuers places of Scripture, *Iob* 41. [34] *Eccles[siasticus]* 10.
> [12 ff.] *Tob.* 4. [13] *Esay.* 14. [12–15] *Ezech.* 28. [2 ff.] For although this
> of *Esaias* is literally to be vnderstood of the King of Babilon, and the other
> of *Ezechiel* of the King of Tyre, yet this doth not hinder, but that also
> they may be vnderstood of the Diuell, as head of all the proud and wicked;
> according to the exposition of *Hierome, Austine, Ambrose* and *Gregory* the
> Diuine.[2]

---

[1] Thomas Tymme, *A Silver Watch-Bell*, 18th impr. (1638), p. 67, and Richard Gove,
The Saints Hony-comb (1652), p. 163. Lucifer's high rank is a very old idea; it is repeatedly mentioned in orthodox as well as in apocryphal literature (see, for instance,
the Book of John the Evangelist in *NT Apocr.*, p. 188).

[2] *A Treatise of Angels* (1613), pp. 335–6. Behind this summary stands nearly every
commentary on Isa. xiv, commencing with Origen (*De pr.* I. v. 5; *Homiliæ in Numeros*,
XII. 4) and including Jerome (*Commentariorum in Ezechielem liber IX*, 28), Ambrose (*In
Psalmum David CXVIII Expositio*, VII. 7), *et al.* See also the views of the Fathers and
Protestant theologians collected by Sigmund Feyerabend, *Theatrum diabolorum* (Frankfurt, 1569), fols. 26 ff., and Heppe, pp. 216 f. One of the few dissenting commentators
was Joseph Hall, *The Invisible World* (1659), p. 140.

Protestant commentators, well aware that the Bible does not 'plainly discover' or 'peculiarly define' the sin of Lucifer and his disciples,[1] more often than not resorted to an enumeration of the various possibilities: 'some say, it was pride in affecting Divinity: Some say it was envy stirred by the decree of exalting mans nature above Angels, in and by Christ: Some say a transgression of some commandments in particular, not exprest, as *Adams* was.'[2] But once these theories were mentioned and debated at length, nearly every commentator concluded that pride, the sin of the angels chosen by tradition, was the most probable. As Donne pointed out,

the Schoolemen, when they have tyred themselves in seeking out the name of the sin of the Angels, are content at last for their ease to call it Pride, both because they thought they need goe no farther, for, where pride is, other sins will certainly accompany it; and because they extended the name of Pride to all refusals and resistances of the will of God, and so pride, in effect, includes all sin.[3]

Milton's statement of Lucifer's sin condenses within a few lines the whole tradition from Isaiah to the theologians of the Renaissance:

> his Pride
> Had cast him out from Heav'n, with all his Host
> Of Rebel Angels, by whose aid aspiring
> To set himself in Glory above his Peers,
> He trusted to have equald the Most High.
>
> (I. 36–40)

Given the all-inclusive nature of pride ('there is no sinne almost but pride doth participate with it'),[4] Milton variously analysed Lucifer's

---

[1] Robert Mossom, *Sion's Prospect* (1653), p. 49, and Bullinger, *Fiftie . . . Sermons*, tr. H. I. (1587), p. 745.

[2] John Trapp, *A Commentary . . . upon the Epistles* (1647), p. 659. For another list see Edward Leigh, *A Systeme or Body of Divinity* (Oxford, 1654), pp. 280 f. On the rabbinic attitude consult Ginzberg, i. 62–64.

[3] *Sermons*, v. 308–9. On this tradition, see Edward J. Montano, *The Sin of the Angels* (Washington, D.C., 1955); and on Milton's use of it: Robert C. Fox, *TSLL*, ii (1960), 261–80. The allegory of Sin and Death (*PL*, II. 648 ff.) is also traditional, demonstrating 'the beginning and proceeding of sinne' (Bullinger, *Fiftie . . . Sermons*, tr. H. I. (1587), p. 486). See further R. C. Fox, *MLQ*, xxiv (1963), 354–64, but esp. John M. Steadman, *MP*, liv (1957), 217–20, and *PQ*, xxxix (1960), 93–103, as well as the commentary by Roland M. Frye, *Perspective on Man* (Philadelphia, 1961), pp. 47–50.

[4] Miles Smith, *Sermon, preached at Worcester* (Oxford, 1602), p. 15. Cf. Augustine: pride is 'the beginning of all sinne' (*De civ.* XIV. 13).

disobedience and mentioned the fallen archangel's ingratitude toward the Creator (IV. 42–57). The reiterated censure of ingratitude
during the Renaissance as a marble-hearted fiend, as 'worse then
Heathenish; yea more then *Brutish*', reveals the kind of response the
poet was expecting of his readers. In Donne's reminder, 'No book
of Ethicks, of morall doctrine, is come to us, wherein there is not,
almost in every leafe, some detestation, some Anathema against
ingratitude.'[1]

According to a Talmudic theory occasionally revived during the
Renaissance, there are precisely 301,655,172 angels.[2] We are not
told whether this census was taken before or after the rebellion in
Heaven; if before, Renaissance commentators must have thought
(on the basis of the claim that the dragon 'drew the third part of the
stars' [Rev. xii. 4]) that Lucifer's disciples numbered at least one
hundred million angels. The Biblical claim itself, at any rate, was
'generally interprete[d]' as referring to the fall of the angels,[3] which
is the reason why Milton specifies in *Paradise Lost* that Lucifer was
joined in his revolt by 'A third part of the Gods' (VI, 156).

The details of the War in Heaven were the despair of nearly every
expositor in Milton's age. Some, like Milton himself in *De doctrina
christiana*, elected to lapse into silence; others, like Donne, simply
gave up in frustration ('what kinde of battle soever it were').[4] Yet
one literal-minded poet, Thomas Heywood, boldly decided to
allow the embattled spirits 'No Lances, Swords, nor Bombards'
but only 'spirituall Armes'. This was the result:

> *Lucifer*, charg'd with insolence and spleene;
> When nothing but Humilitie was seene,
> And Reuerence towards God, in *Michaels* brest,
> By which the mighty Dragon he supprest. . . .[5]

As I noted earlier, Milton's solution of the problem in *Paradise Lost*
was attempted in terms of the theory of accommodation.[6] If that

---

[1] Nehemiah Rogers, *The Penitent Citizen* (1640), p. 88, and Donne, *Sermons*, vi. 42.
Luther's view is quoted by Frye, pp. 187 f.; but see esp. E. Catherine Dunn, *The Concept of Ingratitude in Renaissance English Moral Philosophy* (Washington, D.C., 1946).

[2] This cabbalistic fancy is reported by Francesco Giorgio, *Tria millia problemata*
(Paris, 1622), fol. 373; Antoine Le Grand, *An Entire Body of Philosophy*, tr. Richard
Blome (1694), i. 83 f.; *et al.* Various other estimates are cited by Feyerabend (above,
p. 92, n. 2), fols. 16ᵛ f., and Maximilian Rudwin, *The Devil in Legend and Literature*
(Chicago, 1931), ch. ii.

[3] Donne, *Sermons*, viii. 370.   [4] Ibid. iv. 79.

[5] *The Hierarchie of the Blessed Angells* (1635), p. 341.   [6] See above, pp. 9–10.

attempt is not beyond reproach, we must nevertheless credit Milton with such wisdom as he manifested in choosing a method of presentation somewhat less absurd than Heywood's and more in conformity with tradition.

The introduction of evil into a universe controlled by an omnipotent God was a problem that Renaissance apologists endeavoured to explain by the traditional theory of 'permissive evil'. 'The Will of God', as Peter Sterry put it, 'is commonly and rightly distinguished into *positive* and *permissive*. Evil is by the permissive, Good from the positive Will of God.'[1] This customary assumption appears also in Milton's *De doctrina christiana*, where God is said to permit the existence of evil 'by throwing no impediment in the way of natural causes and free agents'.[2] In *Paradise Lost* not only is the War in Heaven 'permitted', 'sufferd' by God (VI. 674, 701), but whatever else Satan undertakes is by the 'high sufferance', the 'high permission of all-ruling Heaven' (I. 212, 366). The temptation and fall of man are foreknown and foretold (III. 92), the very stairs leading to the earth are permissively let down to allow Satan access to Eden (III. 523 ff.), Satan's deception of Uriel is in accord with God's 'permissive will' (III. 685), and the entry of Sin and Death into the fallen world is 'suffered' by 'the will of Heav'n' (II. 1025; X. 622 ff.). Why is God so tolerant of evil? Orthodox apologists replied to the inevitable question by listing a number of possibilities. As John Carpenter wrote in 1597,

it pleaseth the Lorde of heauen to permit and suffer (for a time) this instrument of his wrath to rage in the worlde: partly for the exercise of the Church in this her pilgrimage through the huge wildernesse of this worlde: that the godly being tryed, may runne vnto his mercie for comforte, and by the same resist the enemie, and resisting, may get the victorie, and hauing the victorie, they may bee crowned: for were there not an enemy, there could bee no battaile: Were there not a battaile, there should bee no victorie: and were there not a victorie, there would be no Crowne: partly, hath the Lorde thus suffered his Enemie to raigne ouer the children of disobedience, and to rage in the worlde for the punishment of transgressions and sinnes, for a scourge to beate and to humble the

---

[1] *A Discourse of the Freedom of the Will* (1675), p. 23. On permissive evil see esp. Augustine, *Enarrationes in Psalmos*, XXXI. ii. 26 (*ACW*, XXX. 95); Ambrose, *Epistolae*, XX. 15 (*LF* [1881], p. 132); Thomas Aquinas, *S. th.* I. xxii. 2 (2); Tappert, p. 617; Heppe, pp. 274 ff.; etc. Some writers were rather careless. Cf. Thomas Sutton: 'when God suffers sin to be done, hee also wils it to be done' (*Lectures* (1632), p. 149).

[2] *Works*, xv. 67.

children of men, chiefely them which knowing God, doe neither glorifie God, as God; nor bee thankfull in their hearts for the benefite of his Sonne; but waxing full of Vanitie in their carnall imaginations, doo walke their owne wayes in the lewdnesse of their mindes. But aboue all, that the highest God might be glorified, as well in the horrible confusion & destruction of his proud enemies; as in the wonderfull deliuery and saluation of his elected Saints.[1]

But this is not to say that according to the theory of permissive evil God is merely passive. As Milton makes clear in *Paradise Lost*, God is from time to time also restrictive, limiting or forbidding certain events. He therefore limits the duration of the War in Heaven (VI. 699–703), and he prohibits the clash between Gabriel and Satan, whereupon Gabriel pointedly observes,

> *Satan*, I know thy strength, and thou knowst mine,
> Neither our own but giv'n; what follie then
> To boast what Arms can doe, since thine no more
> Then Heav'n permits, nor mine.
>
> (IV. 1006–10)

In *Paradise Regained* Jesus similarly informs Satan that

> Thy coming hither, though I know thy scope,
> I bid not or forbid; do as thou find'st
> Permission from above; thou canst not more.
>
> (I. 493–6)

Though this sounds ominously Calvinistic it is in conformity with tradition. Behind Milton's thesis in both epics stands the Christian claim that God's permissiveness in no way reduces control over the created order. On the contrary, as Christian apologists have repeatedly maintained, 'the Angels degenerating into Devils do not cease to be under the Dominion of God'; indeed, Satan is himself 'but a *slave* to God', 'serviceable to Gods end, whether he will or no', for God (to use a popular metaphor) holds all the devils and evil men 'in a chaine, and will not suffer them to goe one inch beyond his appointment, to doe the least point of their owne will'.[2] Claims of

---

[1] *A Preparative to Contentation* (1597), pp. 3–4. Parallel summaries abound, but see esp. Thomas Taylor, *Christs Victorie* (1633), p. 439.

[2] Seriatim: Henry More, *Divine Dialogues* (1668), p. 19; Donne, *Sermons*, x. 135; Richard Sibbes, *The Christians Portion* (1638), p. 17; and Miles Smith, *Sermons* (1632), p. 101. To the references I have cited elsewhere ('Milton and his Contemporaries on the Chains of Satan', *MLN*, lxxiii (1958), 257–60) may be added the following: Lancelot Andrewes, *The Wonderfull Combate* (1592), fol. 97ᵛ; John King, *Lectures upon Ionas*

this nature may raise more problems than they settle, but at least they manage to combat the pernicious heresy of dualism that an excessive stress on permissive evil would inadvertently introduce.

The fallen angels, after their expulsion from Heaven, are committed by Satan to a course of action which he retails for us:

> To do aught good never will be our task,
> But ever to do ill our sole delight,
> As being contrary to his high will
> Whom we resist. If then his Providence
> Out of our evil seek to bring forth good,
> Our labour must be to pervert that end,
> And out of good still to find means of evil.
>
> (I. 159–65)

But Milton observes that Satan was destined to witness

> How all his malice serv'd but to bring forth
> Infinite goodness, grace and mercy shewn
> On Man by him seduc't.
>
> (I. 217–19)

The principle stated here is fundamental not only to *Paradise Lost* but to Christian theology. As Timothy Rogers wrote in 1653, 'Satan and wicked ones fetch evill out of good; yea turn good into evill, as much as lyes in them: but God contrary wise, turns evill into good; and fetches good out of evill.'[1]

II

If the rebellion of the angels is a tradition not explicitly supported by the Scriptures, we expect that there is certainly ample Biblical evidence for the Christian attitude toward man's disobedience and its consequences. Not quite. The Christian doctrine of sin is indeed supported by St. Paul's exposition in Romans v. 12–21, but the Christian doctrine of *original* sin ('omnes peccaverunt Adama peccante') was erected by inference rather than direct reference to the Scriptures, and may even be regarded as 'entirely absent from

(Oxford, 1597), p. 56; Andrew Willet, *Catholicon* (Cambridge, 1602), p. 33; John Rawlinson, *Quadriga salutis* (Oxford, 1625), ii. 12; Daniel Dyke, *Tuuo Treatises*, 5th impr. (1631), p. 217; Sibbes, *The Saints Safetie* (1633), i. 112; John Stoughton, *XI. Choice Sermons* (1640), i. 44; Rutherford (below, p. 109, n. 3), p. 208; and esp. Donald Lupton, *Obiectorum reductio* (1634), § 9, 'Of a *Dogge* in a *Chaine*'.

[1] *A Faithfull Friend* (1653), p. 126.

the Bible'.[1] The account in Genesis is silent on the possibility of hereditary guilt, and Judaic apocalyptic and rabbinical literature omits to mention the transmission of Adam's sin to his descendants. The psalmist had indeed asserted, 'Behold, I was shapen in iniquity,/ And in sin did my mother conceive me' (Ps. li. 5), but even here the argument more concerns the fact of the universality of sin than any specific belief in the biological propagation of Adam's sin.[2] The theory of *peccatum ex origine* is intimated neither in the New Testament nor in the commentaries of the apologists until Tertullian.

Tertullian's starting-point was his theory that both soul and body are 'conceived, and formed, and perfected simultaneously, as well as born together; and that not a moment's interval occurs in their conception, so that a prior place can be assigned to either'. But since Tertullian also regarded the soul as matter, he concluded that the soul no less than the body is transmitted from parent to offspring; from which we infer that, in view of Adam's sin, there is in us all 'an antecedent, and in a certain sense natural, evil which arises from its corrupt origin'.[3] Here, for the first time in the history of Christian dogma, we come across the term *originis vitium*. The door to the darker side of the theory of original sin was thrown wide open to welcome St. Augustine.

Christian hamartiology just before Augustine's time was divided more or less evenly between two points of view, represented by Western and Eastern Christendom. The spokesmen for the Eastern Church, and Jerome in the West, did not on the whole believe in hereditary sin but adhered to the creationist theory of the soul's origin, according to which each soul is separately created by God

[1] E. La B. Cherbonnier, *Hardness of Heart* (1956), p. 87. My survey hereafter is based largely on N. P. Williams, *The Ideas of the Fall and of Original Sin* (1927); F. R. Tennant, *The Sources of the Doctrines of the Fall and Original Sin* (Cambridge, 1903); Joseph Turmel, *Histoire du dogme du péché originel* (Macon, 1904); and a number of briefer studies such as Robert Mackintosh, *Christianity and Sin* (1913), ch. ix, and J. M. Shaw, *Christian Doctrine* (1953), ch. xi. On Augustine I have additionally consulted Tixeront, ii. 460–76; T. A. Lacey, *Nature, Miracle and Sin* (1916), chs. iii, vi; *et al.* For Calvin I am especially indebted to T. F. Torrance, *Calvin's Doctrine of Man* (1949), chs. vii–viii.

[2] Only 2 Esdras vii. 48 is explicit ('O Adam, what hast thou done? for though it was thou that sinned, thou art not fallen alone, but we all that come of thee'). Yet this reference was useless to Protestants, who commonly considered the OT Apocrypha to be uncanonical (XXXIX Art. [VI]; *West. Conf.* i. 3). Indeed, while Catholics accepted the Apocrypha as 'Gods owne word' (Nicholas Sanders, *The Rocke of the Church* (St. Omer, 1624), p. 9), Protestants thought them 'contrary to their selues, variable, foolishe' (John Barthlet, *The Pedegrewe of Heretiques* (1566), fol. 10).

[3] *De anima*, xxvii and xli (*ANCL*, xv. 474 and 505). See further Tertullian's *De carne Christi*, 11.

and bestowed upon the individual at birth. The Western Church, and Gregory of Nyssa in the East, adopted in general a milder form of Tertullian's traducianist views. Neither segment of Christendom went to extremes: while avowing the gravity of Adam's offence, they nevertheless denied that its consequences to posterity meant more than limited weakness. Of all the Fathers of the Church, only Tertullian anticipated Augustine in any marked degree, though at the border-line of the Augustinian era we find Ambrose emphasizing the solidarity of the human race in Adam and claiming that the freedom of the will was considerably impaired by the sin of the first man.

The Augustinian thesis was formulated in the heat of controversy. The first British theologian, Pelagius, provided the opposition. His aims, noble enough at the outset, managed ultimately to outdistance all previous attempts to minimize the effect of Adam's sin on his descendants. According to Pelagius,

Everything good and everything evil, in respect of which we are either worthy of praise or of blame, is done by us, not born with us. We are not born in our full development, but with a capacity for good and evil; we are begotten as well without vice as without virtue, and before the activity of our own personal will there is nothing in man but what God has stored in him.[1]

In an attempt to counteract the destructive implications of Pelagianism, Augustine shifted the emphasis from the human plane to the divine by stressing mankind's dependence upon the Creator, the inability of the human race to raise itself unaided, and the primacy of divine grace in each and every act undertaken by man. The Augustinian doctrines of depravation and predestination, of free will and the damnation of unbaptized infants, cannot be divorced from his reiterated conviction that divine grace through the Son of God is the fundamental tenet of the Christian faith.

One of Augustine's major contributions was his insistence that sin originates from the will of man and is therefore entirely voluntary. 'But the quality of mans will', he further realized, 'is of some moment, for if it be bad, so are all those motions [of the soul], if

---

[1] *Pro libero arbitrio, apud* Augustine, *De peccato originali*, XIV; in *Documents of the Christian Church*, ed. Henry Bettenson (1954), p. 75. Pelagius has not fared well among theologians, but I might recommend the essay by A. H. Birch in *Hibbert Journal*, xlvi (1947), 56–62, and esp. John Ferguson's sympathetic study, *Pelagius* (Cambridge, 1956).

good, they are both blamelesse, and praise-worthy'.[1] The conclusion he ultimately reached was that the will is naturally inclined toward evil:

I enquired what . . . Iniquity should be: But I found it not to bee a substance, but a swarving meerely of the will, crookt quite away from thee, O God, (who art the supreme substance) towards these lower things; which casts abroad its inward corruption, and swels outwardly.[2]

This disposition of the will toward evil applies not only to a few individuals but to the whole human race considered as the direct successors of Adam and heirs of his sin. Mankind, Augustine maintained, was present in the first man *in semine* or *in germine*; and as a result of Adam's heinous crime, we have all inherited the *originis reatus* no less than the *originale peccatrix*, becoming a *massa peccatrix*, indeed a *universa massa perditionis*.[3] God, stated Augustine,

made man vpright: who being willingly depraued and iustly condemned, begot all his progeny vnder the same depriuation and condemnation: for in him were we all, when as, he beeing seduced by the woman, corrupted vs all: by her that before sinne was made of himselfe. Wee had not our particular formes yet, but there was the seede of our naturall propagation, which beeing corrupted by sinne must needs produce man of that same nature, the slaue to death, & the obiect of iust condēnation: and therefore this came from the bad vsing of free will, thence arose all this teame of calamity, drawing al men into misery (excepting Gods Saints) frō their corrupted originall, euen to the beginning of the second death which hath no end.[4]

Central to Augustine's thesis is St. Paul's statement in Romans v. 12 that sin exists 'for that all have sinned' (AV). But Augustine's knowledge of Greek was exiguous enough for him to misconstrue the phrase ἐφ' ᾧ πάντες ἥμαρτον ('because all have sinned') as referring to Adam and as meaning *in quo omnes peccaverunt* ('in whom all sinned').[5] About this error pivoted the Western Christian doctrine of original sin.[6]

---

[1] *De civ.* XIV. 6. See further *De vera religione*, XIV.   [2] *Conf.* VII. 16.

[3] The last of these phrases is the most celebrated; it occurs in *De gratia Christi et de peccato originali*, II. 34 (*Patr. l.* xliv. 402).   [4] *De civ.* XIII. 14.

[5] The error occurs in *De peccatorum meritis et remissione*, I. 11 (*Patr. l.* xliv. 116). A similar misunderstanding has been noted in Ambrosiaster (see Kelly, p. 354; Williams (above, p. 98, n. 1), p. 308) as well as in the Reformers (see Heppe, p. 347). Augustine speaks of his limited knowledge of Greek in *De Trinitate*, III, Preface (*NPNF*, iii. 55).

[6] Kelly, p. 354. On the differences between the Eastern and Western views on original sin, see esp. Tixeront, iii. 202 ff.

Augustine's interpretation of original sin, and particularly his graver views on predestination and the deprivation of free will, were accepted neither widely nor at once. Eastern Christendom was cool because a milder version of the doctrine better suited the Hellenic temper, and because the Christological controversy occupied the whole attention of the Eastern Fathers, allowing less time for a consideration of the problems related to the Fall. But in the West Augustinianism attained gradual acceptance,[1] and though later St. Thomas Aquinas emphasized the goodness inherent in mankind and asserted that the freedom of the will was not seriously impaired by man's first disobedience, St. Augustine's views were again revived in the early fifteenth century through Thomas Bradwardine and, especially, Gregory of Rimini. Then, riding high on the wave of the Reformation, Augustinianism returned to reassert itself in even harsher terms in the theology of the Reformers, notably Luther and Calvin.

In its most extreme form, the post-lapsarian state of man was set forth in 1619 by William Whately, the 'roaring' vicar of Banbury, as follows:

A man in the state of corrupt nature, is nothing else but a filthy dung-hill of all abominable vices: hee is a stinking rotten carrion, become altogether vnprofitable and good for nothing: his heart is the diuels store-house, an heape of odious lusts; his tongue is a fountaine of cursing and bitternesse, and rotten communication; his hand is a mischieuous instrument of filthinesse, deceit, and violence; his eyes great thorowfares of lust, pride, and vanity; his feet are swift engins, mouing strongly to reuenge, wantonnesse and lucre; his life a long chaine of sinfull actions, euery later linke being more wicked then the former: yea it is but (as it were) one continued web of wickednesse, spun out, and made vp, by the hands of the diuell and the flesh, an euill spinner, and a worse weauer.[2]

Luther's view was just as unequivocal: 'Whatsoeuer is in our wil, is euil: whatsoeuer is in our vnderstanding, is errour. Wherefore in spirituall matters man hath nothing but darknes, errours, ignor-

---

[1] Cf. the crucial decrees of the Council of Orange in 529 (Denzinger, §§ 174 ff.). The treatises most often used by Protestants were Augustine's *De gratia et libero arbitrio* and *De correptione et gratia*, the defence of Augustinianism in *De vocatione* (attributed to Prosper of Aquitaine), and Bernard of Clairvaux's *De gratia et libero arbitrio*. On the attitude of the Greek Church consult the decrees of the Synod of Jerusalem in 1672 (Schaff, ii. 410 ff.). On the two precursors of the Reformers I cite later, see esp. Gordon Leff, *Bradwardine and the Pelagians* (1957), and *Gregory of Rimini* (1961).

[2] *The Neuu Birth* (1618), pp. 7–8. There is an even lengthier castigation of fallen man in Gabriel Powel, *The Resolved Christian* (1616), pp. 5 ff. See also Heppe, pp. 336 ff.

aunce, malice, and peruersenes both of wil and vnderstanding.'[1]
For his part, Calvin redefined the Augustinian doctrine of original
sin as 'the inheritably descendynge peruersnesse and corruption of
our nature, poured abroade into all the partes of the soule'.[2] The
sin committed by Adam, Calvin insisted, was 'not a lighte negligence,
but a detestable wicked acte', a 'monstruous wickednesse'; and we
are all directly responsible for that act in the unity of our descent
from Adam: 'Adam was not onely the progenitour, but also the
roote of mans nature, and therefore in his corruption was all
mankynde worthelye corrupted.' Moreover, mankind was present
in Adam not merely 'seminally', as Augustine held, but 'federally',
so that we are 'all borne euell and corrupted', 'we bryng with vs
from ẙ wombe of our Mother a viciousnesse planted in our be-
getting'. We have become 'in all partes of our nature corrupted and
peruerted', the image of God has been twisted into an 'vggly
deformitie', and as the slaves of sin we 'can doe nothinge but sinne'.
Man is so completely severed from God that he 'conceiueth,
coueteth, and enterpriseth all wickednesse, filthinesse, vncleanesse,
and mischiefe'; his heart, indeed, is 'so throughly soked in poison of
sinne, that it can breathe out nothing but corrupt stinke'.[3]

   However much one interpretation happened to vary from the next,
Protestants were agreed that original sin, in the sense of 'an hereditary vitiousnesse' or '*homogeneall* corruption' or '*epidemicall* contagion' issuing from Adam, must be accepted as 'a maine principle
of the Christian faith'.[4] Milton's exposition of this principle in
De doctrina christiana has, accordingly, no surprises in store for us,
for it differs only in length from such earlier statements as Joshua
Sprigge's ('*Adam* falling cast us all down') or John Donne's ('man
was sour'd in the whole lump, poysoned in the fountain, perished at
the chore, withered in the root, in the fall of *Adam*').[5] Underlying all
these affirmations is the Augustinian thesis readily adopted by the
Reformers and clearly set forth by Thomas Tuke in 1609:

[1] *A Commentarie . . . upon . . . Galatians,* tr. Anon. (1575), fol. 82.

[2] *Inst.* II. i. 8. Calvin's view is 'properly a corollary of [his] doctrine of grace' (T. F.
Torrance, *Calvin's Doctrine of Man* (1949), chs. vii–viii). Cf. below, ch. vii.

[3] *Inst.* I. xv. 4; II. i. 4, 5, 6, 8; ii. 6; v. 19.

[4] Seriatim: Trelcatius, p. 509; Ames, p. 67; Anthony White, *Truth and Error* (Oxford,
1628), p. 41; and Thomas Bilson, *The Survey of Christs Sufferings* (1604), p. 147.

[5] Seriatim: Milton, *Works,* xv. 191–3; Sprigge, *A Testimony,* etc. (1648), p. 85;
Donne, *Sermons,* viii. 176. For a particularly lucid statement of the Protestant position,
see Bishop Edward Reynolds, *Three Treatises* (1631), pp. 134 ff. For a dogmatic affirmation consult *Conf. Aug.,* art. ii.

Adam was no priuate person, but represented all mankinde. And therefore we stood and fell with him. For hee was the root, and we are his branches: he was the spring, and we the streams: he was the head, and wee are as the members. As the King, his Nobles, Knights and Burgesses doe represent the whole realme in the Parliament: euen so did *Adam* represent the person of his whole posteritie. Whatsoeuer he receiued of God, he receiued it for himselfe and for them all; as wee see a man by high treason doth taint his blood, and disgrace his posteritie.[1]

The precise extent to which Adam's disobedience affected both his own free will and that of his descendants was a matter of earnest controversy, in the 1520's argued by Luther in his bitter controversy with Erasmus ('a real Proteus for elusiveness'), subsequently by Calvinists and Arminians as by Jansenists and Molinists, and later in the seventeenth century by Bishop Bramhall, ambitiously endeavouring to quell the loosed leviathan Thomas Hobbes.[2] Nonetheless, no orthodox Protestant expositor was prepared to minimize the gravity of Adam's rebellion. In fact, unlike some of Milton's critics who think that Adam had committed some readily definable sin, Milton and his contemporaries believed that man's first disobedience was a *summa omnium vitiorum*, 'no light, trivial, or single sin, but indeed a *mass* or *heap* of hainous, horrid, and manifold impieties, even to a violation of the whole *Decalogue*'.[3] The reiterated claim that the sin of Adam and Eve was 'diuers and manifolde' wound its way into both *Paradise Lost*, where Milton speaks of that sin as 'manifold' (x. 16), and *De doctrina christiana*, where he inquires:

what sin can be named, which was not included in this one act? it comprehended at once distrust in the divine veracity, and a proportionate

---

[1] *The High-uuay to Heauen* (1609), pp. 56–57.

[2] On the Hobbes–Bramhall controversy see Samuel I. Mintz, *The Hunting of Leviathan* (Cambridge, 1962), ch. vi. There is a good introduction to Arminianism by Carl Bangs, *CH*, xxx (1961), 155–70; see further: A. W. Harrison, *Arminianism* (1937); Herbert D. Foster, *HTR*, xvi (1923), 1–37; James H. Elson, *John Hales* (1948), ch. iv; and R. L. Colie, *Light and Enlightenment* (Cambridge, 1957). If seventeenth-century accounts are mostly prejudiced (e.g. Daniel Featley, *Pelagius redivivus* (1626), or John Owen, Θεομαχία αὐτεξουσιαστική (1643)), so are many modern discussions of the Luther–Erasmus controversy (usually in Luther's favour: e.g. Robert H. Murray, *Erasmus and Luther* (1920), ch. vii, or Gordon Rupp, *The Righteousness of God* (1953), ch. xii). Balanced accounts have been attempted by Preserved Smith, *Erasmus* (1923), ch. xii; James Mackinnon, *Luther and the Reformation* (1929), iii. 211–73; E. G. Schwiebert, *Luther and his Times* (St. Louis, 1950), pp. 683 ff.; and Jean Boisset, *Érasme et Luther* (Paris, 1962). The Italian humanists are discussed by Cassirer, ch. iii; the Molinists *et al.*, by Copleston, iii. 342 ff., and Harnack, iv. 89 ff.

[3] Robert Mosson, *Sion's Prospect* (1653), p. 63. Modern interpretations are listed by Millicent Bell, *PMLA*, lxviii (1953), 866.

credulity in the assurances of Satan; unbelief; ingratitude; disobedience; gluttony; in the man excessive uxoriousness, in the woman a want of proper regard for her husband, in both an insensibility to the welfare of their offspring, and that offspring the whole human race; parricide, theft, invasion of the rights of others, sacrilege, deceit, presumption in aspiring, fraud in the means employed to attain the object, pride, and arrogance.[1]

The eating of the forbidden fruit, Milton further asserted, was 'in its own nature indifferent'; its significance accrued from its prohibition 'as a test of fidelity', 'in order that man's obedience might be thereby manifested'.[2] Milton's interpretation is validated by the tradition which St. John of Damascus summed up: 'The tree of knowledge was for trial, and proof, and exercise of man's obedience and disobedience.'[3] Tradition also supports another notion of Milton's that the tree of knowledge derives its name from the event. The tree, Johann Gerhard similarly observed, 'was so called from the *Event*: For by tasting of the fruit thereof man learnt by wofull experience, what a great good he had deprived himself of, by reason of his sin; and what a great evil he drew upon himself, by his disobedience'.[4] Gerhard's statement reminds us of Adam's tragic realization after the Fall:

> since our Eyes
> Op'nd we find indeed, and find we know
> Both Good and Evil, Good lost, and Evil got.
> (IX. 1070–2)

---

[1] *Works*, xv. 181–3. Of the numerous parallel statements, see Perkins, pp. 109 f.; Ursinus, p. 130; Musculus, fol. 21; Wolleb, p. 61; Bartholomaeus Keckermann, *A Manuduction to Theologie*, tr. Thomas Vicars (1622?), pp. 34–36; Andrew Willet, *Synopsis papismi* (1594), pp. 810 f.; Holland (below, p. 109, n. 3), fols. 10 f.; Thomas Cartwright, *Christian Religion* (1611), p. 57; and Petrus de Witte, *Catechizing* (Amsterdam, 1664?), p. 53. See also Williams, pp. 121 f.

[2] *DDC, Works*, xv. 113–15. On the 'cause' of the Fall in *PL*, see Leon Howard, *HLQ*, ix (1946), 149–73, and John M. Steadman, *JHI*, xxi (1960), 180–97.

[3] *De fide orthodoxa*, II. 11 (*NPFN*, 2nd ser., ix. 29). See *PL*, III. 95; IV. 428, 520; VIII. 325; and the statements by Arminius, ii. 369 f., and the writers I have cited in 'The Tree of Knowledge in the Christian Tradition', *SN*, xxxiv (1962), 239–42.

[4] Gerhard, p. 79. Thus Milton, *Works*, xv. 115, and among his predecessors esp. Luther, *Works*, i. 93, who in turn invoked Augustine, *De genesi ad litteram*, viii. 15–16. Cf. *De civ.* XIV. 13: 'man desiring more became lesse.' Speculations concerning the precise genus of the forbidden fruit go back to the *Talmud*: Berakoth, § 40a (pp. 248 f.), and Sanhedrin, § 70a (p. 478). Perkins (p. 109) was intentionally vague: 'an apple or some such fruit.' In *PL* Satan is at least far more positive (x. 487).

The irony within this confession extends to the Father's subsequent declaration:

> O Sons, like one of us Man is become
> To know both Good and Evil . . .
>
> (XI. 84–85)

According to Andrew Willet's explanatory comment in 1605, 'here the Lord speaketh (ironically) not that man was now become like indeed in knowledge of God, (for it is not to be thought, that mans knowledge was encreased by his sinne . . .) but the Lord derideth mans follie, that was brought into such a foolish conceit by breaking the commandement, to be made like to God'.[1]

Since the fruit was prohibited to man as a test of fidelity, it is not surprising that Satan's capital aim was to undermine man's faith in God by inducing him to question the terms of that prohibition. As Lancelot Andrewes observed of Satan's scheming, 'It is our faith that he aimes at. . . . For having ouerthrowne that, disobedience soone will follow.'[2] Concurring, Milton demonstrated the success, and failure, of Satan's approach: its success in the case of Eve; its failure when the Lady was tempted by Comus, Samson by Harapha, and Jesus by Satan. Both Milton and his contemporaries regarded Eve as prejudiced toward Satan's arguments, as partly fallen before she actually ate the forbidden fruit. Already preoccupied with herself to a dangerous degree, she was 'inflamed', 'fired' by Satan's flattering terms of address ('Goddesse'), while his promise of divinity proved 'an argument suteable to her humour'.[3] These traditional aspects of Eve's temptation are all present in *Paradise Lost*. Milton added another incident, her demonic dream (V. 30–93). Adam, though suspicious that the dream is 'of evil sprung', decides nonetheless that

> Evil into the mind of God or Man
> May come and go, so unapprov'd, and leave
> No spot or blame behind: Which gives me hope

[1] *Hexapla in Genesin* (Cambridge, 1605), pp. 28–29. What Willet interpreted as irony Peter Hausted regarded as 'Sarcasme' (*Ten Sermons* (1636), p. 143).
[2] *Seven Sermons* (1627), pp. 28–29. See also Luther's observations in *Works*, xxiv. 343.
[3] Seriatim: Henry King, *An Exposition upon the Lords Prayer* (1634), p. 277; Sir Henry Spelman, *The History and Fate of Sacrilege* (1698 [written c. 1632]), p. 3; Stephen Jerome, *A Serious Fore-warning* (1613), p. 4; and William Vaughan, *The Soules Exercise* (1641), p. 9. Milton's Satan flatters Eve as much and more (ix. 532 ff., 538, 547, 612, 626, etc.).

That what in sleep thou didst abhorr to dream,
Waking thou never wilt consent to do.

(V. 117–21)

Adam's argument is clear: according to the pattern of 'unapprov'd' evil in the mind of God, man may also entertain evil thoughts yet remain blameless so long as he does not approve them. The argument may or may not be valid.[1] At any rate, Adam errs in his curious conviction that Eve abhorred her dream. This is her claim, but in reality, or subconsciously, she was so impressed by her 'high exaltation' of the night that her account throbs with excitement, offering us one of the most poetic passages in *Paradise Lost*. The dream, though instigated by Satan (IV. 800 ff.), is yet a projection of her innermost desires and aspirations. The point is not in the least modern. 'A Dreame', wrote Thomas Nash in 1594, 'is nothing els but the Eccho of our conceipts in the day'. As Robert Sanderson also observed in 1632, 'our *Dreames* for the most part looke the same way, which our *freest thoughts* encline'. Thomas Adams with equal pertinence quoted Augustine ('What a man desires in the day, he dreames in the night') and then went on to say that 'if you desire to make any vse of dreames, let it be this. Consider thy selfe in thy dreaming, to what inclination thou art mostly carried: and so by thy thoughts in the night, thou shalt learne to know thy selfe in the day'.[2]

Perhaps the most fascinating aspect of Eve's encounter with the tempter is the lore surrounding the serpent. The Book of Genesis does not identify the serpent with Satan; that was a later development in Judaic thought, leading to the Renaissance belief, which Milton shared, that the serpent was 'but the outward instrument

[1] Cf. Robert Bruce: 'Suppose thou hast euill cogitations & motions, yet if . . . thou resist them, thou art not guiltie before God' (*The Way to True Peace* (1617), p. 333). Yet the opposite was also part of the tradition: 'Sins in thought, are great sins' (William Fenner, *Practicall Divinitie* (1650), p. 4). Augustine's theory that both Adam and Eve were 'secretly' corrupted before the Fall (*De civ.* XIV. 13) underlies the debate between Millicent Bell and Wayne Shumaker, 'The Fallacy of the Fall in *PL*', *PMLA*, lxx (1955), 1185–1203. Perhaps the answer may be found in Jerome's ranking of sins (*Commentaria in Amos*, I. i. 5; in *Patr. l.* xxv. 996).

[2] Seriatim: Nash, *The Terrors of the Night* (1594), sig. C4; Sanderson, *Tuuelve Sermons* (1632), p. 504; and Adams, *Workes* (1629), pp. 842 f., whose statement was quoted later by John Spencer, Καινὰ καὶ παλαιά (1658), p. 237. On the 'conservative' dreamlore tapped by Milton, see esp. William B. Hunter, *ELH*, xiii (1946), 255–65; *MLQ*, ix (1948), 277–95. Cf. Irene Samuel, *JEGP*, lxiii (1964), 441–9. L. L. Whyte, in *The Unconscious before Freud* (1962), esp. ch. v, discusses the early awareness of the mysterious realm within man, a realm 'amplum et infinitum' (Augustine, *Conf.* X. 8).

which the Deuill vsed'.¹ Just as old is the tradition that before the Fall the serpent was beautiful and could in fact walk 'vpright vpon his feet'.² Milton, like Donne, was not quite prepared to credit that the serpent had feet ('we are not sure of that; nor is it much probable')³. But he emphasizes the beauty and upright posture of the serpent in *Paradise Lost*, where it appears

> not with indented wave,
> Prone on the ground, as since, but on his reare,
> Circular base of rising foulds, that tour'd
> Fould above fould a surging Maze, his Head
> Crested aloft, and Carbuncle his Eyes;
> With burnisht Neck of verdant Gold, erect
> Amidst his circling Spires, that on the grass
> Floted redundant: pleasing was his shape,
> And lovely, never since of Serpent kind
> Lovelier.

(IX. 496–505)

Eve did not run away from such a sight because—so it was usually explained—before the Fall 'all serpents and beasts were gentle, meeke, and subiect to mans command and gouernment, so that as they had no power to doe any harme to man, so neither did they appear horrible in their aspect'. Although Eve's restraint in *Paradise Lost* has to be justified on grounds of this kind, Milton wisely refrained from over-taxing our credulity by restating Luther's improbable notion that Adam, Eve, and the serpent 'durst dallie and plaie' together before the Fall.⁴

Eve plucked and ate the forbidden fruit at high noon (IX. 739), 'in the face of the sun, in open defiance of God'.⁵ Adam joined her in

---

¹ George Gifford, *A Discourse of the Subtill Practises of Deuilles* (1587), sig. F2ᵛ. For a commentary on Satan's disguises in *PL*, see Raymond B. Waddington, *TSLL*, iv (1962), 390–8.

² Johann Michael Dilherr, *Contemplations*, tr. William Style (1640), p. 24, and John Salkeld, *A Treatise of Paradise* (1617), p. 217. The serpent's erect posture is mentioned in the *Talmud*: Sotah, § 9b (p. 40); see further Harris F. Fletcher, *Milton's Semitic Studies* (Chicago, 1926), pp. 130–2. Renaissance serpent lore is also discussed by Svendsen, pp. 165 ff.   ³ Donne, *Sermons*, x. 184.

⁴ *Table-Talk*, p. 70. The other statement is John Chrysostom's, quoted by Salkeld (above, n. 2). Another improbable idea that Milton avoided is the tradition that the serpent's face resembled Eve's. On this see Paul and André Bergouignan, *Le Péché originel* (Paris, 1952), figs. 1, 14–16, 19–20.

⁵ On this tradition, based on 'the noonday devil' (Ps. xc. 6 in the Douai OT, xci. 6 in AV [which reads: 'the destruction . . . at noonday']), see the admirable essay by Albert R. Cirillo in *ELH*, xxix (1962), 372–95; further discussed by Jackson I. Cope, *The*

eating the fruit a little later. All in all, their stay in the Garden of Eden was 'very short'.[1]

III

The most disastrous consequence of the Fall of Man is stated at the outset of *Paradise Lost*: Adam's disobedience 'Brought Death into the World' (I. 3). According to tradition, man had been created immortal: 'if he had not sinned', as Tertullian put it, 'he certainly would not have died'.[2] The obvious problem of how our physical frame could have withstood the effect of centuries does not seem to have troubled commentators. Most of them were content to maintain that after man was created, God 'ordained him a law, by observation of which, as the Angels by *Jacobs* Ladder, he should ascend up to supernatural and heavenly bliss'.[3] In *Paradise Lost* Raphael is less dogmatic. As he tells Adam,

> time may come when men
> With Angels may participate, and find
> No inconvenient Diet, nor too light Fare:
> And from these corporal nutriments perhaps
> Your bodies may at last turn all to spirit,
> Imploy'd by tract of time, and wingd ascend
> Ethereal, as wee, or may at choice
> Here or in Heav'nly Paradises dwell.
>
> (V. 493–500)

Metaphoric Structure of 'PL' (Baltimore, 1962), pp. 130 ff. My quotation is from Jeremy Taylor, by way of Cope's study.

[1] Thus Perkins (below, p. 109, n. 1), p. 180, with whom Milton evidently agreed. Others thought that Adam was in the Garden either a few days (thus Laurentius Codomannus, *Chronographia*, 3rd ed. (1596), p. 10; Thomas Morton, *The Three-fold State* (1629), p. 8), or less than a day (thus Donne, *Sermons*, x. 48; John Gaule, *Practique Theories* (1629), p. 17; Quarles, *Divine Fancies* (1632), p. 181; John Lightfoot, *The Harmony . . . of the OT* (1647), p. 4; Rutherford (below, p. 109, n. 3), p. 185; Zacheus Montague, *The Jus Divinum* (1652), p. 17; de Witte (above, p. 104, n. 1), p. 50), or even 'very few houres' (thus Henry King, *Two Sermons preached at White-Hall* (1627), i. 4; Cristóbal de Fonseca, *Devout Contemplations*, tr. James Mabbe (1629), p. 273; Luther, *Table-Talk*, p. 364). According to Jewish lore, Adam lived in Eden anywhere from five and a half hours (*OT Pseud.*, p. 451; cf. *Talmud*: Sanhedrin, § 38b (p. 242)) to seven years (*OT Pseud.*, p. 16).

[2] *De anima*, LII (*ANCL*, xv. 526).

[3] John Hales, *Sermons preach'd at Eton* (1660), p. 44. Earlier views are noted in McColley i, pp. 201 f., 220 f. See also Gregory the Great, *Moralia*, IV. 54 (*LF*, xviii. 220), and among statements nearer to Milton's age: Luther, *Table-Talk*, pp. 57, 477; John Woolton, *A Neuue Anatomie* (1576), fol. 13ᵛ; Humphrey Sydenham, *Natures Overthrow* (1626), pp. 6 f.; Donne, *Sermons*, x. 187. Cf. Williams, pp. 104 ff.

But as the state of innocence did not last long, suffice it to say with Milton's contemporaries that Adam was 'the cause of murthering the whole world', and so a criminal, the 'first Criminal' in history.[1]

More immediate than the invasion by death of the created order was nature's adverse reaction. This, as we noted earlier, was felt at once,[2] though its precise effects were not observed until some time later. The relevant passage in *Paradise Lost* (x. 651–714) expresses agreement with numerous Renaissance affirmations that after the Fall mere anarchy was loosed upon the world and nature was 'turned vp side downe', became 'motionsick', 'out of frame', 'out of order'.[3] Here is part of Francis Quarles's detailed exposition:

> The Aire that whisper'd, now begins to rore,
>   And blustring Boreas blows the boyling Tide;
> The white-mouth'd Water now usurps the shore,
>   And scorns the pow'r of her tridental guide;
> The Fire now burns, that did but warm before,
>   And rules her ruler with resistless pride:
>   Fire, Water, Earth, and Aire, that first were made
>   To be subdu'd, see how they now invade;
> They rule whom once they serv'd, command, where once obey'd.[4]

As often as not, Renaissance writers set forth nature's disorder in musical terms. Nathanael Culverwell's view of the Fall as a discordant note in the harmony of the universe is typical: 'When God first tun'd the whole creation, every string, every creature praised him; but man was the sweetest and loudest of the rest, so that when that string apostatized, and fell from its first tuning, it set the whole creation a jarring.'[5] Milton's statement in *At a Solemn Musick* is similar:

---

[1] Seriatim: John Preston, *Sermons* (1630), sig. Q4ᵛ; Jean-François Senault, *Man become Guilty*, tr. Henry Earl of Monmouth (1650), p. 6 [the original French title was *L'Homme criminel* (1644)]; and Joseph Glanvill, *The Vanity of Dogmatizing* (1661), p. 1. On Adam as a 'murtherer', see also William Perkins, *Works* (Cambridge, 1605), p. 11; Richard Fowns, *Trisagion* (1618), p. 42; and Browne, *RM*, ii. 4.

[2] See above, pp. 77–78.

[3] Seriatim: William Chub, *The True Trauaile* (1585), sig. B6ᵛ; Samuel Rutherford, *Christ Dying* (1647), p. 12; Henry Holland, *The Historie of Adam* (1606), fol. 10; and William Smith, *The Neuu-Creation* (1661), p. 22. Further references in Michael Macklem, *The Anatomy of the World* (Minneapolis, 1958), pp. 103 f. For a penetrating analysis of the violation of order in *PL*, see Arnold Stein, *Answerable Style* (Minneapolis, 1953), pp. 89–108.

[4] *Emblemes* (1658), p. 10 [I. ii. 4]. For a parallel statement in prose, see Sydenham (above, p. 108, n. 3), p. 5. The background may be observed in *OT Pseud.*, pp. 17, 477 f., cf. 555 f.

[5] *The Light of Nature* (1654), p. 105. Parallel statements abound: Christopher Lever, *Heaven and Earth* (1608), p. 17; Sterry (above, p. 95, n. 1), pp. 30, 157; etc., but esp.

> disproportion'd sin
> Jarr'd against natures chime, and with harsh din
> Broke the fair musick that all creatures made
> To their great Lord, whose love their motion sway'd
> In perfet Diapason, whilst they stood
> In first obedience, and their state of good.
>
> (ll. 19–24)

Another popular way of expounding the same idea was in terms of the 'Homeric' golden chain. For this we may turn to Sir Richard Barckley's formulation in 1598:

where all the meane causes of things euen from the vppermost heauen, vnto the lowest part of the earth, depended each vpon other in such an exact order & vniformity to the production of things in their most perfection and beautie, so as it might well be likened to that *Aurea Cathena* as *Homer* calleth it, by the grieuous displeasure, which God conceiued against man, he withdrew the vertue which at the first he had giuen to things in these lower parts, and nowe through his curse the face of the earth and all this elementarie world, doth so much degenerate from his former estate, that it resembleth a chaine rent in peeces, whose links are many lost and broken, and the rest so slightly fastened as they will hardly hangtogether.[1]

Barckley's statement opens the way to a belief widespread in Renaissance literature that nature has progressively decayed since the Fall and has already become 'an olde ruinous buildyng', 'a decrepit wretch'.[2] But this belief need not detain us here, partly because a host of scholars have already attended to it, and partly because more and more seventeenth-century thinkers, including Milton, refused to believe that God's providence would have permitted nature to degenerate. Their champion was George Hakewill, whose *Apologie or Declaration of the Power and Providence of God* (1627) was later hailed by John Ray as having 'fundamentally confuted' the notion of nature's decay.[3]

Jacob Revius's poem 'Creation', in Frank J. Warnke, *European Metaphysical Poetry* (New Haven, 1961), pp. 212 f.

[1] *A Discourse of the Felicitie of Man* (1598), pp. 5–6. For a similar statement, see Godfrey Goodman, *The Fall of Man* (1616), p. 17. Cf. Donne, *Sermons*, vii. 231.

[2] Pierre Viret, *The Worlde possessed with Deuils*, tr. Thomas Stocker (1583), sig. B5, and Daniel Tuvil, *Essayes* (1609), p. 220. The most celebrated exponent of this idea is Donne (*Sermons*, vi. 323; cf. vii. 271). Elsewhere I noted John Dove's revision of Hooker to the same effect (*Neophilologus*, xlvii (1963), 219 f.).

[3] *Three Physico-Theological Discourses* (1693), pp. 278 ff. Milton's statement is in *Naturam non pati senium*. The idea of nature's decay is discussed by George Williamson,

The effect of Adam's disobedience on the macrocosm of nature corresponds to its effect on the little world of man. Adam's conduct after the Fall, when he raves and grows more fierce and wild at every word, demonstrates an idea often repeated that sin is 'anomy',[1] and expresses dramatically the sort of behaviour castigated in innumerable Renaissance treatises on the passions. Hence the significance of Adam's description in *Paradise Lost* as one who is 'in a troubl'd Sea of passion tost' (x. 718). Earlier the metaphor was applied to both Adam and Eve:

> They sate them down to weep, nor onely Teares
> Raind at thir Eyes, but high Winds worse within
> Began to rise, high Passions, Anger, Hate,
> Mistrust, Suspicion, Discord, and shook sore
> Thir inward State of Mind, calme Region once
> And full of Peace, now tost and turbulent.
>
> (IX. 1121–6)

The metaphor reached Milton and the Renaissance with impressive credentials since it was St. Augustine's 'master image' and had Biblical sanction in Isaiah's affirmation that 'the wicked are like the troubled sea, when it cannot rest' (Isa. lvii. 20).[2] The restatement of John Smith, the Cambridge Platonist, reads like a commentary on *Paradise Lost*:

ELH, ii (1935), 121–50; Richard F. Jones, *Ancients and Moderns*, 2nd ed. (St. Louis, 1961), ch. ii; Charles M. Coffin, *John Donne and the New Philosophy* (1937, repr. 1958), pp. 130 ff., 264 ff.; Ernest L. Tuveson, *Millennium and Utopia* (Berkeley, 1949), esp. ch. ii; Victor Harris, *All Coherence Gone* (Chicago, 1949); Hiram Haydn, *The Counter Renaissance* (1950), pp. 525 ff.; Herschel Baker, *The Wars of Truth* (1952), pp. 65 ff.; Joseph A. Bryant, in *SAMLA Studies in Milton*, ed. J. M. Patrick (Gainesville, Florida, 1953), pp. 1–19; Geoffrey I. Soden, *Godfrey Goodman* (1953), ch. vii; Paul H. Kocher, *Science and Religion in Elizabethan England* (San Marino, Calif., 1953), pp. 82 ff.; Ronald W. Hepburn, *Cambridge Journal*, vii (1954), 424–34, and *JHI*, xvi (1955), 135–50; Marjorie H. Nicolson, *The Breaking of the Circle*, rev. ed. (1960), pp. 65 ff., 105 ff., and *Mountain Gloom and Mountain Glory* (Ithaca, N.Y., 1959), ch. ii; and John L. Mahoney, *CLA Journal*, v (1962), 203–12. Luther's acceptance of this idea, as against Calvin's rejection of it, is discussed by T. F. Torrance, *Kingdom and Church* (Edinburgh 1956). Later developments are considered by Macklem (above, p. 109, n. 3), chs. ii–iii.

[1] From 1 John iii. 4 (ἡ ἁμαρτία ἐστὶν ἡ ἀνομία), variations on which occur in Perkins, p. 103; Arminius, ii. 155; Donne, *Sermons*, vii. 230; John Terry, *The Trial of Truth* (Oxford, 1602), ii. 12; William Foster, *The Means to Keepe Sinne*, etc. (1629), p. 3; Thomas Sutton, *Lectures* (1632), p. 406; Hugo Grotius, *A Defence of the Catholick Faith*, tr. W. H. (1692), p. 11; and the writers I cited in *NQ*, x (1963), 284.

[2] On Augustine *et al.*, see D. C. Allen, *MLN*, lxxvi (1961), 308–12. There is another authoritative statement in Luther, *Werke* (Weimar, 1886), iv. 602. On Shakespeare's use of the idea consult G. Wilson Knight, *The Shakespearian Tempest* (1932).

The mind of a wicked man is like the Sea when it roares and rages through the striving of severall contrary winds upon it. Furious lusts and wild passions within, as they warre against Heaven and the more noble and divine part of the Soul, so they warr amongst themselves, maintaining perpetuall conflicts, & contending which shall be the greatest.[1]

The condition of mind described by John Smith was usually held to be the result of conscience ('See in the troubled Sea, the Emblem of a troubled conscience').[2] Thus in *Paradise Lost*, no sooner is Adam said to be 'in a troubl'd Sea of passion tost' than he acknowledges spontaneously the role of conscience:

> O Conscience, into what Abyss of fears
> And horrors hast thou driv'n me; out of which
> I find no way, from deep to deeper plung'd!
>
> (x. 842–44)

The ascription to Satan of the same crisis of conscience is a familiar parallel (IV. 23); and the two instances, we realize, are meant to remind us of the promise made by the Father immediately after the Son's offer to die for fallen man:

> I will cleer thir senses dark,
> What may suffice, and soft'n stonie hearts
> To pray, repent, and bring obedience due . . .
> And I will place within them as a guide
> My Umpire *Conscience*, whom if they will hear,
> Light after light well us'd they shall attain,
> And to the end persisting, safe arrive.
>
> (III. 188–97)

Conscience was variously described by Milton's contemporaries as God's 'Messenger', 'Deputie', 'Embassador', 'Sergeant', 'Notary', 'Vicar', 'Register', 'Chancellor', and 'Vice-Roy', though at least one writer, Samuel Purchas, anticipated Milton's metaphor by asserting that conscience is 'a iust Vmpire betwixt God and Man, giuen as a Guardian to the Soule and Vertues keeper'.[3] The effect of this

---

[1] *Select Discourses* (1660), p. 421.

[2] Jeremiah Dyke, *Tuuo Treatises*, 6th ed. (1635), i. 220.

[3] *Purchas his Pilgrim* (1619), p. 222. The other metaphors occur, seriatim, in Baxter, iii. 115; John Weemes, *Exercitations* (1632), p. 39; Anthony Cade, *A Sermon of . . . Conscience* (1621), p. 19; Perkins, p. 104; Dyke (previous note), i. 11; Richard Sibbes, *Bowels Opened* (1641), p. 139; William Strong, Ἡμέρα ἀποκαλύψεως (1645), p. 21; Immanuel Bourne, *The Anatomie of Conscience* (1623), p. 11; and Nicholas Billingsley, *A Treasury of Divine Raptures* (1667), p. 155. The Biblical background is set forth by W. David Stacey, *The Pauline View of Man* (1956), ch. xvi, and esp. by C. A. Pierce, *Conscience*

umpire on the mind of man was also variously represented, though the most common approach coincides with Milton's exposition of the 'inner Hell' that is generated first in Satan and then in Adam.[1] The rich tradition involved here may be gathered from such a summary statement as Jeremiah Dyke's, that 'A good conscience makes a Desert a Paradice, an evill one turnes a Paradice into a Desert'. The great French apologist Pierre Viret similarly affirmed that 'the faithfull beginneth alreadie his paradise in this worlde, and the infidell and vnfaithfull hys hell.'[2]

Another way of looking at the effects of the Fall was stated in an Elizabethan homily: 'In stede of the ymage of GOD, [man] was become nowe the ymage of the Deuyll.'[3] As Michael observes in *Paradise Lost*, referring to the descendants of Adam,

> Thir Makers Image . . .
> Forsook them, when themselves they villifi'd
> To serve ungovernd appetite, and took
> His Image whom they serv'd, . . . since they
> Gods Image did not reverence in themselves.
>
> (XI. 515–25)

Expanding this theme, Michael subsequently informs Adam that

> Since thy original lapse, true Libertie
> Is lost, which alwayes with right Reason dwells
> Twinnd, and from her hath no dividual being:
> Reason in man obscur'd, or not obeyd,
> Immediatly inordinate desires
> And upstart Passions catch the Goverment
> From Reason, and to servitude reduce
> Man till then free.
>
> (XII. 83–90)

As we have seen, Milton demonstrates the principle enunciated here in terms of the 'high Passions' that transformed the minds of Adam

---

in the NT (1955). I would not recommend O. Hallesby's *Conscience*, tr. C. J. Carlsen (1939).

[1] *PL*, IV. 18 ff., 73 ff.; X. 842 ff. As critics have often noted, a variation on this theme is the state of 'inner Chaos'. See, for example, Arthur Sewell, *A Study in Milton's Christian Doctrine* (1939), pp. 147 f., and A. B. Chambers, *JHI*, xxiv (1963), 57 f.

[2] Dyke (above, p. 112, n. 2), i. 229; Viret, *The Christian Disputations*, tr. John Brooke (1579), fol. 248ᵛ. See also below, p. 176.

[3] *Hom. II*, sig. zzz4. The idea is Biblical; cf. John viii. 34 ('whosoever committeth sin is the servant of sin'), Rom. vi. 16, 2 Pet. ii. 19.

and Eve into regions 'tost and turbulent'. Milton's explanation at the time was that

> Understanding rul'd not, and the Will
> Heard not her lore, both in subjection now
> To sensual Appetite, who from beneath
> Usurping over sovran Reason claimd
> Superior sway.
>
> (IX. 1127–31)

The roots of this passage stretch back to Plato's tripartite division of the soul in the *Republic* (439–42) as interpreted by various Renaissance writers, particularly Sir Thomas Elyot. According to Elyot, whenever reason, understanding, or will ceases to exercise its appointed tasks, the soul

loseth hir dignite, & bicõmith ministre vnto the sences which before were her slaues who vsurping the preeminēce & hauing the affectis & Wylle holly at their cõmandment do possede the body as theyr propre mancion, leauynge nothynge to the soule, but to vse onely her powers after theyr sensuall appetites. And so Man bireft of that portion wher in he was lyke vnto god, is become equalle or rather inferior to brute beastes.[1]

For Milton the most authoritative statement yet penned was Spenser's, that 'better teacher than Scotus or Aquinas'. Spenser maintained in *The Faerie Queene* that

> in a body, which doth freely yeeld
> His partes to reasons rule obedient,
> And letteth her that ought the scepter weeld,
> All happy peace and goodly gouernment
> Is setled there in sure establishment.
>
> (II. xi. 2)

But when man's god-like reason is disobeyed, the body becomes

> fowle and indecent,
> Distempred through misrule and passions bace:
> It growes a Monster, and incontinent
> Doth loose his dignitie and natiue grace.
>
> (II. ix. 1)

These lines, as well as the passages from both Elyot and Milton,

---

[1] *Of the Knowledge which maketh a Wise Man* (1533), ed. E. J. Howard (Oxford, Ohio, 1946), pp. 119–20. See also Burton's detailed exposition in *The Anatomy of Melancholy*, pt. 1, sect. 1, memb. 2, subs. 5–11. A variation of this idea seems to have been worked into *The Tempest* (see James E. Phillips, *SQ*, xv (1964), 147–59).

appeal to yet another tradition which conceives of man as the 'middle peece' in the Scale of Nature. Augustine phrased it in this way: 'The life of man is the middle between Angels and beasts: if man takes pleasure in carnal things, he is compared to beasts; but if he delights in spiritual things, he is suited with Angels.'[1] There are hundreds of similar statements in Renaissance literature. Here is an elaborate exposition by Joseph Hall:

Man, as he consists of a double nature, flesh and spirit, so is he placed in a middle rank betwixt an angel, which is spirit, and a beast, which is flesh; partaking of the qualities, and performing the acts of both: he is angelical in his understanding, in his sensual affections, beastial: and to whether of these he most enclineth, and conformeth himself, that part wins more of the other, and gives a denomination to him; so as, he that was before half angel, half beast, if he be drowned in sensuality, hath lost the angel, and is become a beast; if he be wholly taken up with heavenly Meditations, he hath quit the beast, and is improved angelical.[2]

This commonplace became a particular favourite of the Cambridge Platonists, for whom sin was nothing else than 'The sinking of a Mans Soul from God into a Sensual Selfishness'. They were persuaded with Whichcote that 'no Man that is immers'd in a sensual Brutish Life, can have any true Notion of Heaven or of Glory',[3] a viewpoint holding good not only for man's fallen state in *Paradise Lost* but for the situation Milton had earlier depicted in *Comus*.

Milton in *Comus* is concerned with moderation in general but selects temperance for particular treatment. As with other issues that preoccupied the thinkers of the Renaissance, these involve not only man's microcosm but the greater world of nature also. Bishop Hall voiced the common sentiment when he declared that moderation is 'the silken string that runs through the pearl-chain of all vertues'. He also added that moderation is the cornerstone upon which universal order rests:

what goodnesse can there be in the world without Moderation, whether in the use of Gods creatures, or in our own disposition and carriage?

---

[1] *Apud* Quarles, *Emblemes* (1658), p. 91. Augustine's variation on this theme in *De Trinitate*, XII. xi. 16, is the source for Pascal's observation in *Pensées*, § 329.
[2] *Select Thoughts* (1648), pp. 177–8. On this common idea see, e.g., Pico (*apud* Copleston, iii. 213 f.).
[3] John Smith, *Select Discourses* (1660), p. 394, and Whichcote, *Select Sermons* (1698), p. 33.

Without this, Justice is no other then cruell rigour; mercy, unjust remisnesse; pleasure, bruitish sensuality; love, frenzy; anger, fury; sorrow, desperate mopishnesse; joy, distempered wildnesse; knowledge, saucy curiosity; piety, superstition; care, wracking distraction; courage, mad rashnesse; Shortly, there can be nothing under heaven, without it, but meere vice and confusion: Like as in nature, if the elements should forget the temper of their due mixture, and incroach upon each other by excesse, what could follow but universall ruine? . . . It is therefore Moderation, by which this inferiour world stands.[1]

Comus appears quite prepared to agree, for he counsels the Lady against the extreme of abstinence, 'lean and sallow Abstinence' as he terms it. Here is part of his argument:

> Wherefore did Nature powre her bounties forth,
> With such a full and unwithdrawing hand,
> Covering the earth with odours, fruits, and flocks,
> Thronging the Seas with spawn innumerable,
> But all to please, and sate the curious taste?
>   . . . if all the world
> Should in a pet of temperance feed on Pulse,
> Drink the clear stream, and nothing wear but Freize,
> Th' all-giver would be unthank't, would be unprais'd,
> Not half his riches known and yet despis'd.
>
>   (ll. 710–24)

The argument may sound eminently convincing but does not bear close scrutiny. Comus, employing a characteristically shrewd tactic, has equated abstinence with temperance. But the Lady, not in the least deceived, calmly reiterates the traditional view that 'holy' temperance is opposed both to 'lean and sallow Abstinence' and to 'lewdly-pamper'd Luxury':

> do not charge most innocent nature,
> As if she would her children should be riotous
> With her abundance, she good cateress
> Means her provision onely to the good
> That live according to her sober laws,
> And holy dictate of spare Temperance:
> If every just man that now pines with want
> Had but a moderate and beseeming share
> Of that which lewdly-pamper'd Luxury
> Now heaps upon som few with vast excess,

---

[1] *Christian Moderation* (1640), i. 3–4, 6.

Natures full blessings would be well dispenc't
In unsuperfluous eeven proportion,
And she no whit encomber'd with her store,
And then the giver would be better thank't,
His praise due paid.

(ll. 762–76)

Thus the Lady upholds what Joseph Hall called the 'lawfull and allowed latitude of just pleasure' wherein the approved *via media* between gluttony and abstinence consists.[1] Far from championing abstinence, her argument resembles that of a contemporary of Milton's, that 'Mans wisdome consists not in the not using, but in the well using of what God and the world affords him.'[2] Michael argues similarly in *Paradise Lost* when he admonishes Adam to

observe
The rule of not too much, by temperance taught
In what thou eatst and drinkst, seeking from thence
Due nourishment, not gluttonous delight.

(XI. 530–3)

Yet the Lady is even more the captive of tradition than Michael, for she echoes a theme that was to be favoured by the Cambridge Platonists: 'swinish gluttony / Ne're looks to Heav'n amidst his gorgeous feast' (776 f.).

Paradise Lost, however, is concerned more specifically with one aspect of the theme of moderation, the temperance of knowledge. Raphael is sufficiently explicit:

Knowledge is as food, and needs no less
Her Temperance over Appetite, to know
In measure what the mind may well contain,
Oppresses else with Surfet, and soon turns
Wisdom to Folly, as Nourishment to Winde.

(VII. 126–30)

The Christian faith has not always maintained a position either clearly defined or consistent toward the acquisition of knowledge. The inclination has been mostly toward Milton's opinion that 'the contemplation of natural causes and dimensions' cannot compare with 'the only high valuable wisdom' that is the knowledge of 'any thing distinctly of God, and of his true worship, and what is infallibly good and happy in the state of mans life, what in it selfe evil and

---

[1] Ibid. i. 33.   [2] Robert Herne, *Ros coeli* (1640), p. 284.

miserable'.[1] The idea is given voice in *Paradise Lost* when Raphael advises Adam:

> Sollicit not thy thoughts with matters hid,
> Leave them to God above, him serve and feare;
> ... Heav'n is for thee too high
> To know what passes there; be lowlie wise:
> Think onely what concernes thee and thy being.
>
> (VIII. 167–74)

The knowledge of ourselves, wrote Pierre de la Primaudaye, is 'the store-house of all wisdome, and beginning of salvation'. 'The true science and study of man', echoed Charron as though he were anticipating Pope, 'is man himselfe.' Du Bartas agreed:

> Ther is no Theam more plentifull to scan,
> Then is the glorious goodly Frame of MAN.[2]

With Sir John Davies leading the way among the poets, the literature of the Renaissance abounds in expositions of the *nosce teipsum* theme. But the popular writers on theology stand closer to *Paradise Lost*, arguing as they did that 'When we are willingly ignorant, of that which God would not haue vs know; this is a learned ignorance, as it is a blockish knowledge, when wee are curious to vnderstand things hid from vs.'[3]

This, however, does not imply that Milton was as naïve as the popular theologians. He knew from experience that the thirst for knowledge forms an irrepressible component of human nature, just as he knew many literary testimonies of it, whether the Faust legend or Marlowe's apostrophe in *Tamburlaine* on the 'aspiring minds' of men in constant search of 'knowledge infinite' (pt. I, II, vii, 18–29). Accordingly in *Paradise Lost* Adam is presented as desirous of knowledge for its own sake, notwithstanding his own claim that he seeks it in order to praise God, 'the more / To magnifie his works, the more we know' (VII. 96 f.). Before the purpose of Raphael's mission in Eden is even announced, Adam expresses his wish 'to know / Of things above this World' (V. 454 f.). After the initial exchanges Adam presses the archangel further, with 'more desire

---

[1] *RCG, Works*, iii. 229. See further Eugene F. Rice, Jr., *The Renaissance Idea of Wisdom* (Cambridge, Mass., 1958), esp. ch. v; Antonio V. Romuáldez, *SR*, xi (1964), 133–50; and Robert Hoopes, *Right Reason in the English Renaissance* (Cambridge, Mass., 1962).

[2] Seriatim: La Primaudaye, *The French Academie*, tr. T. B. (1586), p. 11; Charron, *Of Wisdome*, tr. Samson Lennard (1640), p. 1; and Du Bartas, p. 155. Cf. above, pp. 7 ff.

[3] Thomas Wilson, *Ænigmata sacra* (1615), p. 139; appended to *Theologicall Rules*.

to hear' of matters beyond his ken (v. 555). Raphael then gives his account of the War in Heaven, and as he ends we become aware that Adam's desire to know has not at all been exhausted (VII. 61). Milton at this juncture introduces a meaningful simile. Adam, we are told, is

> as one whose drouth
> Yet scarce allayd still eyes the current streame,
> Whose liquid murmur heard new thirst excites.
>   (VII. 66–68)

Raphael next sets forth the creation of the world, whereupon Adam declares that his thirst for knowledge has been largely but by no means fully quenched (VIII. 6 f.). Something yet remains to be satisfied, and he inquires after the movement of the heavens. The obliging Raphael obliges once again, and Adam at last assures him that he is now fully satisfied (VIII. 180). Yet within a second he is qualifying his assurance:

> But apt the Mind or Fansie is to roave
> Uncheckt, and of her roaving is no end.
>   (VIII. 188–9)

It is only much later, after the Fall and after Michael has revealed the future, that Adam declares with finality that he has had his fill of knowledge and that it was folly to aspire beyond the knowledge within bounds earlier advocated by Raphael (XII. 558–60; VII. 120).

V

Renaissance apologists never tired of stressing the vast difference between God's attitude toward fallen man and his attitude toward the rebellious angels. Lucifer and his disciples were 'cast downe', but Adam and Eve 'cast out'. The angels were expelled from Heaven 'immediately' and condemned to Hell 'for ever', but the man and woman lingered in the Garden until after God's visit, and even then 'were not cast into condemnation without hope, without mercy, as the Angels were; but had a hope given [them] to be again restored'.[1] The Augustinian thesis that 'man had sinned less than the devil' was used to account for such differences in the penalties doled out.

---

[1] Seriatim: John Wall, *Alæ seraphicæ* (1627), p. 61; Luis de la Puente, *Meditations*, tr. John Heigham (St. Omer, 1619), i. 246; Richard Sibbes, *Light from Heaven* (1638), ii. 17; and Christopher Lever, *The Holy Pilgrime* (1618), p. 81.

The distinction was made because the angels disobeyed through 'willfull pride' whereas man was merely 'misse-lead': 'the Angels fell of themselves, but man by the suggestion of another.'[1] In the words of the Father in *Paradise Lost*, the angels

> by thir own suggestion fell,
> Self-tempted, self-deprav'd: Man falls deceiv'd
> By th' other first: Man therefore shall find Grace,
> The other none.
>
> (III. 129–32)

We now see why a drastic difference exists between the two judgements described by Milton. When the angels are judged after the War in Heaven, the Son of God appears 'full of wrauth', 'Gloomie as Night', with a terrible countenance 'too severe to be beheld', and mercilessly drives them out of Heaven (VI. 824 ff.). When Adam and Eve are judged, God appears 'without revile', 'gracious', 'mild', and so compassionate that he covers their nakedness with the skins of beasts (X. 96, 118, 211 ff.; cf. 1046–8). And still more important, as we shall see in the next chapter, God proclaims the 'mysterious terms' of the woman's seed.

[1] Seriatim: Augustine, *De libero arbitrio*, III. 10 (tr. C. M. Sparrow (Charlottesville, Va., 1947)); Sir John Stradling, *Divine Poems* (1625), p. 5; and Richard Field, *Of the Church*, 3rd ed. (Oxford, 1635), p. 5.

5

Deeds above Heroic

THE RESTORATION OF MAN

[There are some] that cherish in their bosomes, and enter-
taine with stipends such, as are come to this (*phrensie*, I will
call it) to say; what needs any *satisfaction*? what care we,
whether *Iustice meet* or no? that is (in effect) what needs
CHRIST? Cannot GOD *forgive* offences to Him made, of
His free *goodnesse*, of His meere *mercy*, without putting His
SONNE to all this pain? Fond men! If He would quit His
Iustice, or wave His *truth*, He could: But, His *Iustice* and
truth are to Him as *essentiall*, as *intrinsecally essentiall*, as His
Mercy: of equall regard every way as deare to Him. *Iustice*
otherwise remains unsatisfied: and satisfied it must be,
either on Him, or on us.

LANCELOT ANDREWES[1]

I

THE midnight of man's first disobedience was followed by the
dawn of God's mighty wrath. In *Paradise Lost* the Most High
addresses the sad and mute sanctities of Heaven in harsh, metallic
language:

> fall'n he is, and now
> What rests, but that the mortal Sentence pass
> On his transgression, Death denounc't that day,
> Which he presumes already vain and void,
> Because not yet inflicted, as he feard,
> By some immediat stroak; but soon shall find
> Forbearance no acquittance ere day end.
> Justice shall not return as bountie scornd.

(X. 47–54)

Milton, far from being singular in this unattractive conception of
Divine Awe, has merely rephrased the recurrent Protestant stress

---

[1] *XCVI. Sermons*, 4th ed. (1641), p. 101.

on the 'fire' and 'fury' of the Almighty's 'dradfull angre and wrath'.[1]
To be certain, a number of Protestants were distressed by this
conduct of the Most High ('Gods threatenings, I confess, have
sometimes a fearful browe, and like a skie troubled & shak'd with
red, intimate fire and bloud'),[2] but in the end all of them declared
that conduct to be essentially just.

To the 'dradfull angre' of God, however, was almost always joined
a consideration of the divine mercy. Thus in Book III of *Paradise
Lost* the Father is said to be concerned with both justice and mercy
(132 ff., 401 ff.), and the 'metallic' address just quoted from Book X
concludes with yet another attempt to 'collegue' the two:

> But whom send I to judge them? whom but thee
> Vicegerent Son, to thee I have transferrd
> All Judgement, whether in Heav'n, or Earth, or Hell.
> Easie it may be seen that I intend
> Mercie collegue with Justice, sending thee
> Mans Friend, his Mediator, his design'd
> Both Ransom and Redeemer voluntarie,
> And destind Man himself to judge Man fall'n.
>
> (X. 55–62)

The assumption underlying these lines was stated by John Gaule in
1629: 'Our good God was prone to Mercy, euen when prouoked to
wrath.'[3] An attractive theory, we feel, but hardly convincing, even
when stated in the persuasive manner of John Donne, that God has
made no decree to distinguish the seasons of his mercies. Deeds
being more eloquent than words, the occasion called for an immediate
and substantial demonstration that in Paradise, as Donne would
have us think, the fruits of mercy were indeed ripe the first moment
after the Fall.[4]

This demonstration, as it happens, was provided by Protestants
in a manner unparalleled in the teaching of other Christians. As I
have explained elsewhere at some length,[5] the most relevant passage

---

[1] Seriatim: Daniel Featley, *Clavis mystica* (1636), p. 43; Humphrey Sydenham, *Iacob and Esau* (1626), p. 20; and Melanchthon, *The Iustification of Man*, tr. Nicholas Lesse (1548), fol. 16ᵛ.

[2] Humphrey Sydenham, *Sermons upon Solemne Occasions* (1637), p. 172.

[3] *Practique Theories* (1629), p. 5.

[4] *Sermons*, vi. 172.

[5] 'The "Protevangelium" in Renaissance Theology and *PL*', *SEL*, iii (1963), 19–30. Of nearly one hundred primary and secondary sources quoted or cited in this study, I have borrowed here only seven. The rest constitute additional documentation.

is embedded in the sentence that God passes on Satan in Genesis iii. 15, restated by Milton thus:

> Between Thee and The Woman I will put
> Enmitie, and between thine and her Seed;
> Her Seed shall bruise thy head, thou bruise his heel.
>
> (x. 179–81)

To prevent any misunderstanding, Milton proceeded to explain that these 'mysterious terms' were

> verifi'd
> When *Jesus* son of *Mary* second *Eve*,
> Saw Satan fall like Lightning down from Heav'n,
> Prince of the Aire; then rising from his Grave
> Spoild Principalities and Powers, triumphd
> In op'n shew, and with ascension bright
> Captivitie led captive through the Aire,
> The Realme it self of *Satan* long usurpt,
> Whom he shall tread at last under our feet.
>
> (x. 182–90)

If later ages have by and large doubted whether Genesis iii. 15 is a Messianic text at all, Protestants and Catholics of the Renaissance alike considered the promise of the woman's seed to be 'the fyrst declaration of the gospell' and in fact 'the great promise that contains all the rest'.[1] Moreover, the swiftness with which the prophecy was proclaimed ('immediatlie after the transgression'[2]) impressed every apologist of the faith as incontrovertible evidence that the mercies of God know indeed no season.

The universal persuasion that Genesis iii. 15 is the 'first gospel'— the *protevangelium*—was marred only by the controversy concerning the exact reference of the pronoun in the phrase 'it shall bruise' (AV). The varied interpretations, with a censure of the obvious culprits, were summarily stated by Nicholas Gibbens in 1601:

[the pronoun] may onlie be translated, as some doe, *it*; that is, that same seed; but much better, *he*: namelie, that one person; as manie other, &

---

[1] Thomas Lanquet, *An Epitome of Chronicles* (1559), fol. 6ᵛ, and Mark Frank, *LI Sermons* (1672), p. 66. Cf. Pascal's comment on 'the Christ promised from the beginning of the world' (*Pensées*, § 776). Recent discussions of Gen. iii. 15 are cited by Dominick J. Unger, *The First-Gospel* (St. Bonaventure, N.Y., 1954); Josef Haspecker and Norbert Lohfink in *Scholastik*, xxxvi (1961), 357–72.

[2] Zanchius, p. 44. The word 'immediatly' is also stressed in *Hom. II*, sig. Aaaa1.

euen *Hierom* himselfe, and the Septuagint translation, and our English[1] hath it. But some of the Fathers, misguided by the translations of *Aquila*, of *Symmachus*, and *Theodotion*, which chieflie in their time were in vse, doe read it, *she shall breake*: so also doth the Iewish Targhum which those translatours followed, as Iewish heretikes: yet none of these expound it of any other woman then of *Heua*, sauing that in a mysticall sense, they take it for the affections of the minde. But the church of Rome will needes read it, *she shall breake*, & vnderstand it of the virgin *Marie*, giuing vnto her the glorie of breaking the Serpents head.[2]

Few aspects of Catholic devotion succeeded in stimulating the ire of Protestants more than the elevation of the Virgin to the rank of 'mediatrix nostra et interventrix ad Filium.'[3] 'They haue made her', sneered Bishop Miles Smith, 'the very dore by which we enter into Paradise, shut by *Eue*, opened by her.' But under no circumstances, Bishop Smith continued, should Mary be regarded as 'the Mediatresse of Reconcilement and Propitiation'—not even if, added Richard Sheldon in 1612, 'if all *Austens*, all *Bernards*, all *Gregories*, all *Angells* from heauen should affirme it'. Donne was equally explicit:

I know the Fathers are frequent in comparing and parallelling *Eve*, the Mother of Man, and *Mary* the Mother of God. But, God forbid any should say, That the Virgin *Mary* concurred to our good, so, as *Eve* did to our ruine. . . . *Mary* had not the same interest in our salvation, as *Eve* had in our destruction; nothing that she did entred into that treasure, that ransom that redeemed us.[4]

[1] The Geneva Bible, which is the only version to use 'he'. Wycliffe and the Douai OT read 'she'; the Bishops' Bible and AV, 'it'. In three cases the pronoun was cleverly by-passed: Tyndale and Rogers ('that seed shall tread'); Coverdale ('the same [seed] shall tread'). Yet the recent translation of the Jewish Publication Society of America (*The Torah* (Philadelphia, 1962), p. 7) reads, '*They* shall strike', etc.

[2] *Questions and Disputations* (1601), p. 146. Catholics have since reconsidered their interpretations (Unger (above, p. 123, n. 1), pp. 7, 30 ff.); but see P. Duncker, O.P., 'Our Lady in the OT', in *Mother of the Redeemer*, ed. Kevin McNamara (Dublin, 1959), ch. i.

[3] Thus Peter of Blois, *Sermones*, xii (*Patr. l.* ccvii. 597); cf. St. Bernard, *apud* Harnack, vi. 316. See further G. G. Coulton, *Five Centuries of Religion* (Cambridge, 1923), i, chs. ix–x. In some sense at least, Catholics still regard the Virgin as co-redemptrix with the Christ; see Denzinger, § 1978a, and the papal statements—none made *ex cathedra*—quoted in *TS*, xxi (1960), 219.

[4] Seriatim: Smith, *Sermones* (1632), p. 53; Sheldon, *The First Sermon* (1612), p. 42; and Donne, *Sermons*, i. 200. The violent Protestant disapproval of 'the gross and abominable superstitions' concerning the Virgin (Calvin, *Comm.: John 1–10*, p. 47) was an attack on Mariolatry, not Mariology. The interested reader should consult the studies by René Laurentin (tr. 1956), Hugo Rahner (tr. 1961), Max Thurian (tr. 1963), and Otto

Concurring with the prevalent Protestant opinion, Milton expressed himself in violent opposition to the occasional Catholic claim that 'the obedience of *Mary* was the cause of salvation to her selfe, and all mankind.'[1] His contrary view, as we have seen, took the form of the explicit equation of the seed with the Christ, which is precisely the identification insisted upon by his contemporaries and immediate predecessors.[2] Thereafter in *Paradise Lost* the prophecy is recollected at a crucial moment in the relations of our 'grand parents'. Long after it was first uttered by God, Adam attempts to console his repentant wife with these words:

> let us seek
> Som safer resolution, which methinks
> I have in view, calling to minde with heed
> Part of our Sentence, that thy Seed shall bruise
> The Serpents head.
>
> (X. 1028–32)

For the time being, however, the terms are still mysterious to both. But not for long. The archangel Michael was already receiving his charge from God to

> reveale
> To *Adam* what shall come in future dayes,
> As I shall thee enlight'n, intermix
> My Cov'nant in the Womans seed renewd. . . .
>
> (XI. 113–16)

In line with the divine behest, Michael—'milde', 'benigne', 'gentle' —unfolds the future before an expectant Adam. But the key word is not mentioned until the appearance of Abraham in the vision, whereupon Michael states that 'in his Seed / All Nations shall be blest' (XII. 125 f.). Shortly after that, the word is repeated—with a significant addition:

Semmelroth (tr. 1964), but also E. L. Mascall and H. S. Box, eds., *The Blessed Virgin Mary* (1963), and esp. Hilda Graef, *Mary: A History of Doctrine and Devotion* (1963–5), 2 vols.

[1] *Of Prelaticall Episcopacy*, in *Works*, iii. 94. On the nature and limits of Milton's concern with the Virgin in the two epics, see Mary Christopher Pecheux on *PL* (*PMLA*, lxxv (1960), 359–66) and Herbert H. Petit on *PR* (*Papers of the Michigan Academy of Science, Arts, and Letters*, xliv (1959), 365–9).

[2] For example: Pietro Martire Vermigli, *In primum librum Mosis . . . commentarii* (Zurich, 1579), fols. 15–16; Francis Kett, *The Glorious . . . Glorification* (1585), sig. B2; Henry Holland, *The Historie of Adam* (1606), fol. 11ᵛ; Josias Nichols, *An Order of Houshold Instruction* (1596), sigs. D2 f.; and the forty authors cited in *SEL* (above, p. 122, n. 5), pp. 20 f.

all Nations of the Earth
Shall in his Seed be blessed; by that Seed
Is meant thy great deliverer, who shall bruise
The Serpents head; whereof to thee anon
Plainlier shall be reveald.

(XII. 147–51)

Michael's failure to be precise is calculated: being an excellent story-
teller, he increases the suspense by withholding the information
Adam is seeking until the appropriate moment. So the gradual
identification of the seed continues. The intricate science of typology
is next resorted to, so that Adam is informed

by types
And shadowes, of that destind Seed to bruise
The Serpent, by what meanes he shall achieve
Mankinds deliverance.

(XII. 232–5)

At the mention of David, Michael pauses to look both before and
after:

of the Royal Stock
Of *David* (so I name this King) shall rise
A Son, the Womans Seed to thee foretold,
Foretold to *Abraham*, as in whom shall trust
All Nations, and to Kings foretold, of Kings
The last, for of his Reign shall be no end.

(XII. 325–30)

Then, at long last, the Nativity:

His place of birth a solemn Angel tells
To simple Shepherds, keeping watch by night;
They gladly thither haste, and by a Quire
Of squadrond Angels hear his Carol sung.
A Virgin is his Mother, but his Sire
The Power of the most High; he shall ascend
The Throne hereditarie, and bound his Reign
With Earths wide bounds, his glory with the Heav'ns.

(XII. 364–71)

As Michael falls silent, Adam joyously exclaims:

O Prophet of glad tidings, finisher
Of utmost hope! now clear I understand
What oft my steddiest thoughts have searcht in vain,

Why our great expectation should be calld
The seed of Woman. . . .
                              (XII. 375-9)

But Adam has not in fact 'understood' as yet. Patiently, therefore,
Michael explains what is meant by the stroke that is to 'bruise the
Victors heel'. This leads to an account of the redemption, to Adam's
acknowledgement of that wondrous mystery, and to Michael's final
statement explicitly linking his narrative with the mysterious terms
of the *protevangelium*:

> The Womans Seed, obscurely then foretold,
> Now amplier known thy Saviour and thy Lord.
>   (XII. 543-4)

In the moving confession of faith that follows, Adam acknowledges
the seed to be his 'Redeemer ever blest' (XII. 573). He has finally
'understood'. At last he has become a Christian.

Milton's interpretation is securely grounded upon the peculiarly
Protestant doctrine of justification *sola fide*. Adam, it was repeatedly
maintained,[1] was not merely aware of the future advent of the
Messiah, but apprehended its precise nature 'by faith alone' and
was saved. As the dramatist and divine Peter Hausted observed in
1636, no sooner did Adam fall—and we in him—'but *presently*
Christ adventures after us, for although hee was not *exhibited* untill
the *fulnesse* of time; yet the *vertue* of his *conception, nativity, passion*,
and *resurrection*, was in efficacie to *beleeving Adam*'. The popular
Swiss theologian Rudolph Gwalter was even more positive: there
was 'no doubte', he affirmed, that Adam believed in the revealed
Christ; indeed, he added,

it is euident that he dyd put his whole hope and trust in Jesus Chryst
alone, which was that promised seede of the woman. Therefore *Adam* was
a christian man, and beleeued that he and his posteritie should be deliuered
and saued from the tyrannie of the Diuell, through the merite of Chryst
onely.[2]

'*Adam* was a christian man'—yet not only Adam, we are further
assured, but all the other patriarchs who similarly 'obteined saluation by faith alone in Christ' and subsequently 'declared and spred

---

[1] Notably by Luther (*Works*, xlv. 203; xxvi. 351; etc.) no less than by Anabaptists
(The Dordrecht Confession (1632), iii, in *Creeds of the Churches*, ed. J. H. Leith (1963),
p. 295). On 'justification by faith alone' see below, pp. 187 ff.

[2] Hausted, *Ten Sermons* (1636), p. 142; Gwalter, *Homelyes . . . uppon the Actes*, tr.
John Bridges (1572), pp. 852 f. See also Zanchius, pp. 61 ff., 132 f.

about with great diligence the promise of the seed which in tyme to come should be shewed'. For Protestants, then, the history of salvation began with Adam—appropriately regarded as 'ordained Bishop and Doctor, by the Promise made, of the Womans seede'— while thereafter (as the Scotch Confession of Faith in 1560 phrased it) the *protevangelium* continued to be 'maist constantlie received of al the faithfull, from *Adam* to *Noe*, from *Noe* to *Abraham*, from *Abraham* to *David*, and so forth to the incarnatioun of *Christ*'.[1] The vision of the future in *Paradise Lost* unfolds precisely in terms of such faithful individuals,[2] culminating at last in the incarnation of the Son of God whom Adam accepts as his redeemer 'by faith alone'.

II

Writing in 1599, Bishop Thomas Bilson maintained that 'as well Patriarks as Prophets, yea all the godlie from *Abel* to Christ did by their sacrifices and seruice of God professe and confirme their faith to be this, that they looked for the Seede of the woman, who by his death and bloud should purge their sinnes, and make peace betweene God and them.'[3] Such a statement reaffirms the straight line leading from the promise of redemption made in Paradise to its fulfilment upon the advent of the Christ, while asserting also that the prophecy of the *protevangelium* was subsequently reinforced by the 'types and shadowes' alluded to by Michael in *Paradise Lost* (XII. 239 f.). In this respect, Benjamin Whichcote was not in the least original when he advanced from a consideration of the 'first gospel' to an affirmation of typology in general:

The Promise of the *Messias* doth bear the most ancient Date. No sooner . . . is Man become guilty; but the Promise is made, *That the Seed of the Woman shall break the Serpent's Head*. Which St. *John* comments upon, in these Words, *For this Cause the Son of God was manifested, to destroy the Works of the Devil* [1 John iii. 8].

---

[1] Seriatim: Bullinger, fols. 45–45ᵛ; Simon de Voyon, *A Discourse*, etc., tr. John Golburne (1598), p. 12; and *Confessio fidei scoticana*, IV (Schaff, iii. 442). On the extended statements by Melanchthon, Reuchlin, Bullinger, *et al.*, see John E. Parish, *Rice Institute Pamphlet*, xl (1953), §3, pp. 1–24, and *JEGP*, lviii (1959), 241–7; John M. Steadman, *SP*, lvi (1959), 214–25, and *Anglia*, lxxvii (1959), 12–28; and *SEL* (above, p. 122, n. 5).

[2] In Book XI, notably Abel (436 ff.), Enoch (665 ff., 700 ff.), Noah (719 ff.); and in Book XII, Abraham (113 ff.), Isaac (153 ff.), Moses (169 ff.), Joshua (310 ff.), and David (321 ff.). Cf. Luther, *Works*, xiii. 88.

[3] *The Effect of Certaine Sermons* (1599), p. 55.

And this Promise is often repeated to the Patriarchs successively one after another; to *Abraham*, to *Isaac*, to *Jacob*: As also in the Types and Shadows that were under the Mosaical Dispensation; as the Apostle tells us (*Heb.* 1:1) *God who at sundry Times, and divers Manners, spake unto our Fathers by the Prophets, hath in these last Days spoken unto us by his Son,* &c. That which is now plainly declar'd unto us by the *Messias*, was darkly represented by the Prophets.[1]

The orthodox thinkers of the Renaissance maintained the validity of 'types and shadowes' with a unanimity impressive in its contrast to our own scepticism. 'When, and in what', they used to inquire, 'was not Christ typed, or prophecied? Each Type was a silent Prophecie of him; each Prophecie a speaking Type.'[2] Before his advent the Christ did not merely speak 'by the mouthes of his holy seruants since the world beganne', but was further 'presignified, premonstrated, and foretold' in the infinite 'typicall prefigurations', the numberless 'darke riddles and figures' contained in the Old Testament.[3] Bishop Griffith Williams adequately summarized the conventional attitude:

[The Christ] is the *First*, hee is the *Last*, he is α *Legis*, & ω *Euangelij*, The beginning of the *Law*, and the end of the *Gospell*; *Velatus in Veteri, reuelatus in Nouo Testamento*:[4] Veyled and shadowed in the Old, reueiled and exhibited in the New Testament; *promised* in that, *preached* in this; there *shewed* vnto the Fathers in *Types*, here *manifested* vnto vs in *Truths*: for the *Tree* of *Life*, the *Arke* of *Noah*, the *Ladder* of *Iacob*, the *Mercy Seat*, the *Brazen Serpent*, and all such mysticall *Types*, and typicall *Figures* that we reade of in the Old *Testament*; what were they else but *Christ*; obscurely *shadowed* before he was fully *reueiled*; and so all the men of Note, *Noah, Isaac, Ioseph, Moses, Aaron, Iosua, Sampson, Dauid, Salomon*, Kings, Priests, Prophets, Titles of Dignities, Names of Honour, or whatsoeuer else was ascribed to them to expresse their *Soueraignty*; they were onely vsed to expresse those *transcendent excellencies*, which these personall types did *adumbrate*, and shew most properly to belong vnto this *King of Kings*.[5]

---

[1] *Select Sermons* (1698), p. 331.

[2] John Gaule, *Practique Theories* (1629) p. 21.

[3] Seriatim: William Loe, *Vox clamantis* (1621), 'To the Reader'; Richard Sheldon, *The First Sermon* (1612), p. 4; Fulk Bellers, *Jesus Christ* (1652), p. 7; and Erasmus, *Exposition . . . of the Cōmune Crede* (1533), sig. A7ᵛ.

[4] This commonplace is a paraphrase of Augustine's celebrated statement in *Quæstionum in Heptateuchum*, II. 73 (*Patr. l.* xxxiv. 623).

[5] *Seven Goulden Candlestickes* (1624), p. 258. For the most thorough seventeenth-century expositions of typology in English consult William Guild, *The Harmony of all the Prophets* (1619) and *Moses Vnuailed* (1620); Charles Herle, *Contemplations* (1631); Thomas

Of the types mentioned here, two in particular are of interest to the student of Milton. Firstly, Samson was said to have prefigured the Christ 'both by his life and deedes'.[1] Secondly, Jacob's Ladder, which is introduced in *Paradise Lost*, III. 501–15, was accepted not only as a prefiguration of the dual nature of the Christ but also of his reconciliation of heaven and earth.[2]

Typology is by no means peculiar to Protestantism. It is on the contrary broadly Christian, having been introduced by the early apologists in their attempts to 'prove' that Jesus was the very Messiah 'premonstrated' in the Old Testament ($\acute{o}$ $\pi\acute{a}\lambda\alpha\iota$ $\delta\iota$' $a\grave{\iota}\nu\iota\gamma\mu\acute{a}\tau\omega\nu$ $\zeta\omega\gamma\rho\alpha\phi o\acute{\nu}\mu\epsilon\nu os$).[3] However, novelty lay in the Protestant interpretation of the *protevangelium*, which, once wedded to typology, provided the substantial demonstration required to proclaim that the winter of divine wrath was indeed overwhelmed by the spring of divine mercy—overwhelmed, moreover, 'immediatlie after the transgression'. For Donne, this became one of the great themes expounded from the pulpit of St. Paul's; for Milton, one of the pillars supporting his justification of the ways of God to men.

III

The fusion of Protestant novelties with sacrosanct traditions continued apace, leading next to the theory of the Atonement advanced by the early Reformers, elaborated further by subsequent Protestant apologists, and woven finally into the fabric of *Paradise Lost*. Here the traditional element was the theme of the 'four

---

Taylor, *Christ Revealed* (1635); Richard Montagu, *Acts and Monuments* (1642), ch. iii; and Samuel Mather, *The Figures or Types of the OT* (1685). The best secondary sources are Patrick Fairbairn, *The Typology of Scripture* (repr., 1953); Leonhard Goppelt, *Typos* (Gütersloh, 1939); A. G. Hebert, *The Throne of David* (1941); G. W. H. Lampe and K. J. Woollcombe, *Essays on Typology* (1957); and Jean Daniélou, *From Shadows to Reality*, tr. Wulstan Hibberd (1960).

[1] Niels Hemmingsen, *The Faith of the Church*, tr. Thomas Rogers (1581), p. 25. Among other writers who attended to the Samson–Christ typology are Melanchthon, *LC*, p. 221; Edwin Sandys, *Sermons* (1585), p. 330; William Perkins, *Commentarie upon . . . Reuelation*, 2nd ed. (1606), p. 178; Thomas Myriell, *The Devout Soules Search* (1610), pp. 84 f.; John Andrewes, *Christ his Crosse* (Oxford, 1614), pp. 71 f.; William Hull, *The Mirrour of Maiestie* (1615), pp. 96 f.; Joseph Hall, *A Recollection*, etc. (1621), i. 939; Quarles, *Divine Fancies* (1632), pp. 52 ff.; and Mather (previous note), pp. 131 ff. The rich tradition underlying *SA* is fully set out by F. Michael Krouse, *Milton's Samson and the Christian Tradition* (Princeton, 1949).

[2] See below, p. 227, n. 2.

[3] Cyril of Alexandria, *Commentarium in Evangelium Joannis*, I. 29 (*Patr. g.* lxxiii. 192).

daughters' of God, ultimately based on Psalm lxxxv. 10 ('mercy and
truth are met together: righteousness and peace have kissed each
other'). Of extraordinary popularity during the Middle Ages, this
allegory was adopted by Protestants mainly because of its espousal
by their favourite medieval theologian, St. Bernard of Clairvaux,[1]
whose lucid exposition of the 'severe contention' among the four
daughters was restated typically in 1617 by Charles Richardson:

the cause of man was from al eternity debated in heauen: where the
iustice[2] & *truth* of God stoode on the one side; and his *mercy* and *peace* on
the other: and his *wisedome* was the Iudge and vmpire. The *iustice* and
truth of God pleaded hard against man, and called for punishment
according to his deserts. But his *mercy* and *peace* pleaded for him, and
defended him. In the end, his *wisedom* found out a way, whereby both his
iustice might be satisfied, & his *mercy* might take place.[3]

More often than not, however, Protestants reduced the four
daughters to two—justice and mercy[4]—reminding us of their violent
strife in the first part of Giles Fletcher's *Christs Victory and Triumph*
and of the 'severe contention' between the Father and the Son in
Book III of *Paradise Lost*.

To appreciate the natural way in which the tradition of the
contending daughters of God became part of the Protestant theory
of the Atonement, we must glance at the development of orthodox
thought concerning the work of the Christ.[5] But the term 'orthodox'

[1] *Sermones de Sanctis: in festo Annuntiationis B. Mariæ*, 1. 9–14 (*Patr. l.* clxxxiii.
387–90; tr. W. B. Flower (1861), pp. 185–9). The allegory has been studied by
Richard Heinzel, 'Vier geistliche Gedichte', *Zeitschrift für deutsches Alterthum*, xvii
(1874), 1–57; Hope Traver, *The Four Daughters of God* (Bryn Mawr, 1907), and *PMLA*,
xl (1925), 44–92; and Arthur Långfors in *Notices et extraits des manuscrits de la Biblio-
thèque Nationale*, xlii (1933), 139 ff. Though Traver's is the fullest account available in
English, see also Honor Matthews, *Character and Symbol in Shakespeare's Plays* (Cambridge, 1962), pp. 71 ff., and Grace Frank, *The Mediaeval French Drama* (Oxford, 1954),
pp. 179 ff. I may cite two fifteenth-century precedents: Feo Belcari, *Rappresentazioni*
(Florence, 1833), pp. 94 ff. ('Annunziazione', § 18 et seq.), and Nicholas Love, *The
Mirror of the Blessed Life of Jesu Christ*, tr. Anon. (1926), pt. i, ch. i. Cf. the forensic
approach to the Atonement in the popular literature of the Middle Ages, outlined by
Paul Vinogradoff, *Roman Law in Mediaeval Europe*, 2nd ed. (Oxford, 1929), pp. 128 ff.,
in turn based on Roderich Stintzing, *Geschichte der populären Literatur des römisch-
kanonischen Rechts in Deutschland* (Leipzig, 1867), pp. 259 ff.
[2] Rather than 'righteousness': a common variant, warranted by tradition (as in the
Douai OT version of Ps. lxxxiv. 11).
[3] *The Price of our Redemption* (1617), p. 65.
[4] See, for example, George Wither, *Britain's Remembrancer* (1628), fols. 21ᵛ ff.
[5] The following paragraphs (to p. 142) draw upon my thesis in 'Milton and the
Protestant Theory of the Atonement', *PMLA*, lxxiv (1959), 7–13, here restated with
additional documentation.

may not be entirely appropriate here, for the Atonement has never been defined by the Church in the sense that the triune Godhead and the dual nature of the Christ have been dogmatically affirmed. As has been said, 'no theological theory is binding upon Christians, no explanation of the Cross is a Christian dogma. We may reject all the theologies of the Atonement, if we will, on the ground that they are inadequate to the mystery of the Crucifixion of Him who was God as well as man, but the mystery itself is at the heart of the Christian faith'.[1] It is a mystery whose capital aim is to uphold the 'at-one-ment' of God and man—'the creation of the conditions whereby God and man come together'[2]—through the Christ Jesus.

Of the four major theories of the Atonement normally distinguished by historians of dogma, the earliest revolved about the Pauline statement that 'as by one man's disobedience many were made sinners, so by the obedience of one shall many be made righteous' (Rom. v. 19). This view of Jesus as the second Adam was enforced during the early history of the Church by such apologists as Justin Martyr, who introduced the concept of Mary as the second Eve, and Irenaeus, who stressed the parallel between the tree of knowledge in Eden and the tree of Calvary that was used to build the Cross.[3] From this premiss it was argued that the Christ 'recapitulated' in his Person the entire human race and that he achieved our redemption as the representative of mankind. Biblical support for the idea of the Christ as the *recapitulator generis humani* was forthcoming from St. Paul's statement that upon the entry of the Son of God into history there were gathered 'together in one all things in Christ, both which are in heaven, and which are on earth' (Eph. i. 10). According to Irenaeus, Justin Martyr was the first to restate this Pauline thesis and to view the Son of God as 'summing up his own handiwork in himself'; yet such was Irenaeus's enthusiasm for the theory that its dissemination was largely the result of his own extensive expositions.[4]

---

[1] Nathaniel Micklem, *What is the Faith?* (1936), pp. 204 f. Cf. Kelly, p. 163.

[2] Whale I, p. 75. Cf. Calvin: 'God is at one wyth vs' (*Tuuo . . . Sermons preached . . . in the Yere. 1555*, tr. Anon. (1576), sig. F6).

[3] Justin, *Dialogus cum Tryphone*, iii; Irenaeus, *Adversus haereses*, v. xvii. 3. Cf. the Gospel of Bartholomew iv. 6 (*NT Apocr.*, p. 173). On the numerous reaffirmations of Justin's concept (as by Irenaeus, *Adv. haer.*, III. xxi. 10; Tertullian, *De carne Christi*, XVII; etc.) see Hugo Koch, *Virgo Eva–Virgo Maria* (Berlin, 1937).

[4] See the passages from Irenaeus in *The Early Christian Fathers*, ed. Henry Bettenson (1956), pp. 110–14, and the discussions by Adhémar d'Alès, *RSR*, vi (1916), 185–211; Emmeran Scharl, *Recapitulatio mundi* (Freiburg i.B., 1941); John I. Hochban, *TS*, vii (1946), 525–57; John Lawson, *The Biblical Theology of St. Irenaeus* (1948), ch. xi; Roland

The view prevailed in the Church for many centuries. It was again summarized by Anselm as follows:

it was fitting that as by a man's disobedience death entered the human race, so by a man's obedience should life be restored. And just as sin, which was the cause of our condemnation, had its beginning from a woman, so should the author of our righteousness and salvation be born of a woman. And as the devil had conquered man by the tasting of a tree, to which he persuaded him, so by the suffering endured on a tree, which he inflicted, should he, by a man, be conquered.[1]

The second interpretation of the Atonement, initially propounded by Irenaeus,[2] is the 'ransom' theory, according to which the Son of God gave his life as a ransom for many and was incarnated so 'that through death he might destroy him that had the power of death, that is, the devil' (Mark x. 45; Matt. xx. 28; Heb. ii. 14). Thus the ransom for our acquittal was paid really to Satan. Irenaeus was supported in the East by Basil the Great and Gregory of Nyssa, and in the West by Ambrose and Jerome; yet all were foreshadowed by Origen, who suggested the same possibility when he inquired: 'But to whom did Christ give his soul as a ransom for many? Certainly not to God; possibly then to the Evil One ($\tau \hat{\omega} \ \pi o \nu \eta \rho \hat{\omega}$)? For he had power over us, until the soul of Jesus was given to him as ransom for us.'[3] Soon, however, this theory deteriorated into a grotesque view of the work of the Christ. As Gregory of Nyssa saw it,[4] though God sought to rescue us from Satan's captivity by 'no arbitrary method' but by one that was 'consistent with justice', he was actually 'clothed with flesh' so that Satan 'might not be affrighted at the near approach of the superior power'. Expressed differently, since 'it was not in the nature of the hostile power to come into contact with the untempered presence of God and endure his unveiled presence, in order that he might be within easy grasp of him who sought to exchange on our behalf, the Divine Being concealed himself with the veil of our nature, that, just as is the case with greedy fish, the hook of the Deity might be swallowed

Potter, *Dominican Studies*, iv (1951), 192–200; Gustaf Wingren, *Man and the Incarnation*, tr. Ross Mackenzie (Philadelphia, 1959), pp. 79 ff.; and Daniélou (above, p. 129, n. 5) ch. iii.

  [1] *Cur Deus homo?* I. 3; tr. Edward S. Prout, 2nd ed. (1887).

  [2] *Adversus haereses*, V. i. 1. On the development of this theory see Jean Rivière, *The Doctrine of the Atonement*, tr. Luigi Cappadelta (1909), chs. xxi–xxiv.

  [3] *Commentaria in Evangelium Matthæum*, XVI. 8 (*Patr. g.* xiii. 1397).

  [4] *Oratio catechetica*, xxii–xxix; tr. James H. Srawley (Cambridge, 1903).

along with the bait of the flesh'. Gregory confessed to an implication
here of 'a kind of deceit and trickery' on God's part, yet he insisted
there is justice in it all the same since 'the action of rewarding the
deceiver according to his desert, by deceiving him in turn, is a
display of justice'. Gregory of Nyssa was not the only one to maintain
this perverse notion. Augustine himself was of the opinion that Jesus
'held out his Cross as a mouse-trap and set as bait upon it his own
blood', while Gregory the Great argued at some length that the
God-man 'made, as it were, a kind of hook of himself for the death
of the devil'.[1] Such extreme statements, however, were indignantly
denounced by other Fathers, among them Gregory of Nazianzus
when he wrote, 'since a ransom belongs only to him who holds in
bondage, I ask to whom was this offered, and for what cause? If to
the Evil One, fie upon the outrage!'[2] The theory was denounced
again by Anselm, and though Bernard of Clairvaux accepted it in
modified form, it continued to decline until the Reformation. When
the Reformers gave it new life, however, they sensibly divested it
of its most unpleasant aspects.[3]

But the most popular theory of the Atonement was destined to be
St. Anselm's interpretation in his celebrated treatise *Cur Deus
homo?* 'The entire will of a rational creature ought to be subject to
the will of God', wrote Anselm. 'The man who does not render to
God this honour, which is his due, takes away from God what is his
own, and dishonours God, and that is to sin' (I. 11). Adam, he went
on, 'allowed himself, by persuasion alone, to be voluntarily overcome
in accordance with the will of the devil, and against the will and
honour of God' (I. 22). Man's first disobedience, then, was a
violation of the honour of God, and before normal relations with
the Deity could be re-established, 'satisfaction', in the sense of
reparation for the dishonour caused, had to be rendered. Since the

---

[1] Augustine, *Sermones*, cxxx. 2 (tr. Sidney Cave, *The Doctrine of the Work of Christ* (1937), p. 119); Gregory, *Moralia*, xxxiii. 14 (*LF*, xxxi. 569). Other references in Tixeront, iii. 347; Philip H. Wicksteed, *Reactions between Dogma and Philosophy* (1920), pp. 93–103; and J. A. MacCulloch, *The Harrowing of Hell* (Edinburgh, 1930), ch. xii. For the adaptation of the idea in art see Meyer Schapiro, ' "Muscipula Diaboli": The Symbolism of the Mérode Altarpiece', *Art Bulletin*, xxvii (1945), 182–7.

[2] *Oratio*, xlv, 22 (*NPNF*, 2nd ser., vii. 431).

[3] Only thrice have I encountered Protestant expositions of the idea that the Christ's flesh was 'the baite of Satan' (John Andrewes, *The Brazen Serpent* (1621), pp. 25 f.; John Wall, *The Lion in the Lamb* (Oxford, 1628), pp. 39 f.; and Gaule (above, p. 122, n. 3), p. 211). But the notion that God had 'utterly befoold' Satan persisted and was carried to New England (Edward Taylor, *Christianographia*, ed. N. S. Grabo (New Haven, 1962), p. 255).

affront to God had been offered by man, man had to offer the required satisfaction; but since no individual could be said to overcome the devil, the initiative had to remain with God. In Anselm's terms, since no one could satisfy God except God himself, and since no one ought to do so save man, the task necessarily had to be assigned to 'one who is God-man' (II. 6). Hence the incarnation of the Son of God: 'the rationale of the incarnation', as has been said, 'is in the Atonement.'[1] Anselm's theory of satisfaction remained substantially unaltered throughout the Middle Ages, though Peter Abailard, and Bernard of Clairvaux in more emphatic form, set out another view whose purpose was to stress God's love as the principal motive for the incarnation of the Son.

With the Reformation the current of thought began to move in still another direction. Elements of the previous theories persisted: Jesus continued to be regarded as the second Adam, recapitulating in his Person the entire human race; the Atonement was again viewed in accordance with the ransom theory, though this ransom was now regarded as paid to the Father rather than to Satan;[2] and finally the Anselmic theory of satisfaction was, outwardly at least, upheld with considerable enthusiasm. But on the whole a new theory emerged, befitting the spirit of the times. Juridical terms, until then used casually, now became the exclusive language of Protestant apologists bent on a concerted interpretation of the Atonement as a legal transaction, as a 'contract'—to use Donne's favourite word[3]— whereby the debt paid to the Supreme Judge was considered to be both the satisfaction demanded by divine justice and the just punish- ment required for our sins. Jesus substituted for us, according to the Reformers, and in a just payment of our sins diverted the wrath of God upon himself. In support of this theory, appeal was normally made to the apostolic statements that Jesus 'took our infirmities', that 'he bare our sins in his body on the tree', and that he was made 'to be sin for us, who knew no sin; that we might be made the

[1] James Denney, *The Christian Doctrine of Reconciliation* (1917), p. 65. Anselmic hamartiology is discussed by W. F. Ewbank, *CQR*, cxlvi (1948), 61–67, and John McIntyre, *St. Anselm and his Critics* (Edinburgh, 1954), ch. ii. Within half a century after Anselm a similar theory of the Atonement was formulated independently in the East by Nicholas of Methone (Christos Androutsos, Δογματικὴ τῆς Ὀρθοδόξου Ἀνατολικῆς Ἐκκλησίας, 2nd ed. (Athens, 1956), p. 199).

[2] Typical instances of this are Kimedoncius (below, p. 137, n. 4), p. 7, and Parr (p. 138, n. 3), p. 130.

[3] *Sermons*, vi. 169, 340; vii. 437, 441; etc. Another popular word was 'pact' (Heppe, pp. 376 ff.).

righteousness of God in him' (Matt. viii. 17; 1 Pet. ii. 24; 2 Cor. v. 21). Commenting on these and similar passages, Luther declared that the Christ 'assumed in his body the sins we committed, to make satisfaction for them by his own blood';[1] there was, Luther insisted on a number of occasions, no other way to 'placate' divine justice but through the death—one might even say the execution—of the Son of God.[2] In Calvin's similar exposition of this 'penal-substitutionary' theory of the Atonement,

> our reconciliation with God was this, that man which had lost [himself] by his disobedience, shuld for remedie set obedience against it, should satisfie the iudgement of God, & paye the penaltie of sinne. Therfore there came forth the true man, our Lord, he put on the persone of Adam, & took vpon him his name to entre into his stede in obeyeng his father, to yeld our fleshe the pryce of the satisfaction to the iust iudgement of God, and in the same fleshe suffer the peyne that we had deserued.

'This is our acquittal', Calvin stated further on, 'that the giltynesse which made vs subiect to punishment, is remoued vpõ the head of the sonne of God.'[3] Calvin and Protestants generally accepted that the honour of God was no longer at stake and in need of reparation. They considered that divine justice demanded satisfaction in accordance with the established and unalterable law of God. Anselm had claimed that it was necessary for our restoration that 'either the honour taken away be repaid or punishment follow';[4] but for the Reformers no alternatives between satisfaction and punishment existed: punishment *is* satisfaction.

The 'dradfull angre and wrath' of God which I noted at the outset of this chapter now merits greater attention. Only by examining the Protestants' recurrent stress on the divine wrath can we penetrate

---

[1] *In epistolam S. Pauli ad Galatas commentarius*, III. 3 (tr. Hastings Rashdall, *The Idea of Atonement* (1919), p. 399). On the occasional earlier use of the ideas of substitution and satisfaction, see Cyril of Alexandria, Eusebius, Origen, Cyprian, Ambrose, Augustine, *et al.* (in Kelly, pp. 177 f., 186, 384 f., 389, 392, 398; Harnack, iii. 310 ff.; Whale II, p. 60). Yet the forensic view of the Atonement never appealed to the Catholic and the Orthodox Churches (Wilhelm Niesel, *Reformed Symbolics*, tr. David Lewis (1962), pp. 136 ff.).

[2] Ibid. iv. 19 (*Werke* (Weimar, 1911), XL. i. 650). See further the passages collected by Hugh T. Kerr, *A Compend of Luther's Theology* (Philadelphia, 1943), pp. 52 ff., and the detailed account in Whale II, pp. 74–80.

[3] *Inst.*, II. xii. 3, and xvi. 5. See further the passages collected from Calvin by Johann Piscator, ed., *Aphorismes*, tr. Henry Holland (1596), chs. x and xiii, and the accounts by John F. Jansen, *Calvin's Doctrine of the Work of Christ* (1956), *passim*, and Paul van Buren, *Christ in our Place* (Edinburgh, 1957), esp. pt. ii.

[4] *Cur Deus homo?* I. 13.

to the emotional core of their theory of the Atonement. And that wrath was certainly stressed—stressed, moreover, in language seemingly calculated to confirm the idea of God not as Love but as Fury, all too readily dispensing 'blowes of an iron rod' and all too often prepared 'to breake and bruise the hardest heart, and crush it in peeces'.[1] Characteristically, after Adam's disobedience, this deity displayed all the 'heate', 'all the fiery fiercenesse of his wrath', and flatly declared that 'he would not be reconciled to us' unless his justice had 'full satisfaction'.[2] As that 'blest man', Richard Sibbes, explained in one of the mildest expositions of the Protestant theory,

> God would restore us by a way sutable to his own excellency every way, wherein no Attribute of his might be a looser: he would bring us to riches and friendship with him, by a way of satisfaction to his justice, that wee may see his justice shine in our salvation (though indeed grace, and mercy triumph most of all, yet notwithstanding) justice must bee fully contented. There was no other way wherein wee could magnifie so much the unsearchable, and infinite wisdome of God (that the Angels themselves prie into) whereby justice and mercy seeming contrary Attributes of God, are reconciled in Christ: by infinite wisedome, justice, and mercy meete together, and kisse one another, justice being satisfied, wisedome is exalted; but what set wisedome on worke? the grace, and love, and mercy of God, to devise this way to satisfie justice, it could not have been done any other way: for before we could be made rich, God must be satisfied: reconciliation supposeth satisfaction, and there could bee no satisfaction but by blood, and there could bee no equall satisfaction, but by the blood of such a person as was God.[3]

This is the burden of all similar affirmations: 'God would not be satisfyed but by sacrifice, & no sacrifice vnlesse it were infinite, could suffice.'[4] Hence the 'contract' between the Father and the Son,

---

[1] Abraham Fleming, *The Foot-path of Faith* (1619), p. 126, and James Forsyth, *The Bitter Waters of Babylon* (1615), p. 13.

[2] Seriatim: *Hom. II*, sig. Dddd3ᵛ; Anthony White, *Truth and Error* (Oxford, 1628), p. 20; Jeremy Taylor, *Deus justificatus* (1656), p. 61; Lancelot Andrewes (above, p. 120, n. 1), p. 582.

[3] *Light from Heaven* (1638), ii. 23. Sibbes expounded the Atonement further in *The Saints Safetie* (1633), i. 260 ff., 267 ff.; *Two Sermons upon . . . Christs Last Sermon* (1636), pp. 31 f.; *The Fountaine Opened* (1638), i. 10, 75, 255 f., and ii. 18 f., 23 f.; *Beames of Divine Light* (1639), i. 17 f., 36, 177 ff., and ii. 32 ff., 72, etc.; and esp. *A Miracle of Miracles* (1638), *passim*.

[4] John Dove, *A Confutation of Atheisme* (1605), p. 87. Among the more substantial expositions of the forensic theory of the Atonement are: Richard Baxter, *Universal Redemption* (1694), *passim*; Paul Baynes, *Two Godly and Fruitfull Treatises* (1619), pp. 210 ff.; Thomas Bilson, *The Survey of Christs Sufferings* (1604), pp. 227 ff., 280ff., etc.;

whereby the God-man was appointed 'the principall debtter for vs, and therby dischargeth vs before God'—paying, it was expressly said, 'paying the *vtmost farthing*, wherein mankinde had runne into *arrerages*'.[1] This legal terminology typifies 'the atmosphere of the criminal law-court' suffusing the theory advanced by the Reformers.[2] Their two basic terms were explicitly forensic: 'satisfaction', which Jeremy Taylor interpreted ('in the modern sense of the word') to mean 'a full payment to the Divine Justice'; and 'justification', which the popular divine Elnathan Parr typically regarded as 'a tearme, or word taken from the bench of the Judge, and signifies by way of sentence, to pronounce a person arraigned, to be cleare, quit and guiltlesse'. Whereupon Parr added:

Wee must then know that Christ is our Surety: and looke, as the debter is discharged by the payment performed by the Surety, and such payment made, is imputed to the Debter, and reckoned as if hee had payed it himselfe: So God in sentence giuing, imputeth unto us that which our Surety hath done or suffered for us, and (whatsoeuer we are in our selues) respecteth us as if it had beene done by us, and so dischargeth us.[3]

There is an affinity between these statements and the recurrent legal

Bullinger, fols. 108 ff.; Nathanael Cole, *The Godly Mans Assurance* (1615), pp. 58 ff., 70 ff.; Thomas Collier, *The Exaltation of Christ* (1646), pp. 49 ff.; Donne, *Sermons*, 293 f., ix. 259 ff., etc.; Richard Fowns, *Trisagion* (1618), Bk. I, chs. 7–13, 31–36, 50–51; Alexander Gil, *Sacred Philosophie* (1635), chs. 20–24; Thomas Goodwin, *Christ Set Forth* (1642), pp. 53 ff., 61 ff.; Joseph Hall, *Heaven upon Earth* (1606), pp. 37 ff.; Sir James Harrington, *An Holy Oyl* (1669), pp. 61 ff., 340 ff.; *The Heidelberg Catechism* (1563) (in Schaff, iii. 311 ff.); Niels Hemmingsen, *The Way of Life*, tr. Nicholas Denham (1579), pp. 67 ff.; Charles Herle, *Wisdomes Tripos* (1655), ii. 43 ff.; *Hom. I*, 'Of the Saluation of all Mankynde', and *Hom. II*, 'Of the Natiuitie' and 'Of the Passion'; Jacobus Kimedoncius, *Of the Redemption of Mankind*, tr. Hugh Ince (1598), esp. Bk. I, ch. v; Edward Leigh, *A Systeme or Body of Divinity* (Oxford, 1654), pp. 181 ff., 395 ff., 415 ff.; Donald Lupton, *Obiectorum reductio* (1634), pp. 29 ff.; John Mayer, *The English Catechisme*, 4th ed. (1630), pp. 35 ff.; Samuel Rutherford, *Christ Dying* (1647), *passim*; Ursinus, pp. 233 ff.; James Ussher, *Immanuel* (1638); and Pierre Viret, *A Christian Instruction*, tr. John Shute (1573), pp. 116 ff. For a dogmatic statement, see *West. Conf.* viii. 5; cf. xi. 3.

[1] Calvin, *Sermon . . . on the Historie of Melchisedech*, tr. Thomas Stocker (1592), p. 34, and John Prideaux, *Eight Sermons* (1621), iv. 18.

[2] David M. Ross, *The Cross of Christ* (1928), p. 189. This 'atmosphere' is essentially St. Paul's contribution; see esp. Rom. iii. 21–26, where 'deliverance takes the form of an acquittal in court' (C. H. Dodd, *The Epistle of Paul to the Romans* (1949), p. 52). See further D. E. H. Whiteley, 'St. Paul's Thought on the Atonement', *JTS*, N.S. viii (1957), 240–55.

[3] Taylor, *Vnum necessarium* (1655), p. 644; Parr, *The Grounds of Diuinitie*, 2nd ed. (1615), pp. 209, 213. Thus at length Trelcatius, p. 226: 'Iustification . . . is properly a free iudiciall action', etc.

metaphors in the poetry of George Herbert, notably including the sonnet *Redemption*, perhaps the finest brief exposition of the Protestant theory of the Atonement in English poetry.

After the heavy stress placed on the 'greuous', 'heauy', 'horrible' wrath of the Father, Protestant apologists at last turned to a consideration of the infinite love displayed by the Son, whereupon the stern guardian of divine justice was said to have become 'of a terrible Justicer a tender father toward vs'.[1] This reported transformation had a singularly unfortunate result since it implied a 'severe contention' not among any allegorical 'daughters' but within the Godhead itself, particularly evident in the constant emphasis on the Son's efforts to 'appease' and 'placate' the initially implacable Father.[2] A number of Protestant apologists, fully aware that their theory inadvertently tended to distinguish between the Father and the Son, pleaded with the faithful not to conceive of 'a bare naked God, but of God invested with a sweet relation of a Father in Christ'. Donne was even more emphatic: 'Never consider the judgement of God for sin alone', he counselled his congregation, 'but in the company of the mercies of Christ.' Was it posssible to translate such a counsel into practice, given a deity so very partial to 'blowes of an iron rod'? A glimpse of the answer is afforded by Joshua Sprigge's significant complaint in 1648 that the love of the Father 'is scarce eyed by most men, but they think that the worke of their salvation proceeds from the kind heart of Jesus'.[3] That had been the implicit Protestant claim for some time.

The inadvertent distinction between the Father and the Son passed from the theological treatises of the period into devotional literature[4] and later into Book III of *Paradise Lost*. In addition, however, Milton's epic reflects other aspects of the Protestant interpretation of the Atonement. Elements of the previous theories were retained by Milton as by the Reformers: the Anselmic stress on

---

[1] John Foxe, *A Sermon of Christ Crucified* (1570), fols. 6, 8ᵛ, 11, 29ᵛ.

[2] These telling metaphors were used repeatedly. Some significant examples: Luther (above, p. 136, n. 2); Melanchthon, *apud* L. W. Grensted, *A Short History of the Atonement* (Manchester, 1920), p. 207; Zwingli, *An Exposition of the Faith*, in *LCC*, xxiv. 250; *Hom. II*, sig. Bbbb1; William Perkins, *A Golden Chaine* (1591), sig. D6ᵛ; and the popular works by Stephen Egerton, *A Briefe Method of Catechizing*, 38th ed. (1631), p. 6, and John Norden, *A Pensiue Mans Practise*, 41st impr. (1635), pp. 218, 221.

[3] Seriatim: Richard Sibbes, *The Christians Portion* (1638), p. 163; Donne, *Sermons*, viii. 207; Sprigge, *A Testimony*, etc. (1648), p. 41.

[4] See Helen C. White, *English Devotional Literature [Prose] 1600–1640* (Madison, 1931), pp. 192 ff.

satisfaction, drastically qualified, is present at every turn; the ransom theory is also stated explicitly, with the Father as the recipient of that ransom (III. 221; X. 61; XII. 424); and the recapitulation theory is likewise expounded, not only with the Christ regarded as the second Adam (III. 285 f.; XI. 383), but also with Mary viewed as the second Eve (V. 387; X. 183). At the same time Milton recreated the very atmosphere of the criminal law-court already present in Protestant theology. Man, we are told again, disobeyed the divine behest and brought death upon himself and posterity; the divine decree which created him immortal could not be revoked, being, like all heavenly laws once enacted, 'Unchangeable, Eternal';[1] to rescind it was to go against the prescribed standards of divine justice: 'Die hee or Justice must' (III. 210); someone had to substitute for man and thereby pay the 'rigid satisfaction, death for death',[2] since 'without such satisfaction', as Milton observed in De doctrina christiana, 'not the least portion of grace could possibly have been vouchsafed'.[3] The forensic terminology employed in Book III of the epic recurs in Book XII, when Michael outlines for Adam the nature of the Christ's satisfaction that is to achieve the restoration of man:

> hee, who comes thy Saviour, shall recure,
> Not by destroying Satan, but his works
> In thee and in thy Seed: nor can this be,
> But by fulfilling that which thou didst want,
> Obedience to the Law of God, impos'd
> On penaltie of death, and suffering death,
> The penaltie to thy transgression due,

[1] PL, III. 127. God's decrees were unanimously regarded as 'unchangeable', 'essentiall and unchangeable', 'steaddie', 'absolute and irrevocable' (seriatim: John Bunyan, The Doctrine of the Law and Grace (1659), pp. 37 f.; Henry Ainsworth, The Orthodox Foundation of Religion (1641), p. 17; Samuel Rutherford, Christ Dying (1647), p. 8; and John Hales, Golden Remaines, 2nd impr. (1673), i. 95). Cf. John Bridges: 'God is not sutche an vnconstant God, to will a thing, and afterwards to be vnwilling in the same thing, he will and he will not, this is boe peepe in dede' (A Sermon preached . . . in Whitson Weeke (1571), p. 29).

[2] PL, III. 212. This phrase has been judged to have 'all the weight of [Milton's] personal emphasis behind it' (A. J. A. Waldock, 'PL' and its Critics (Cambridge, 1947), p. 104). But Milton's contemporaries also state that the satisfaction exacted by the Father was 'severe' and 'strict', that divine justice is distinguished by its 'rigour', its 'high and strict rigour', its 'rigour and seueritie'. Thus Charles Odingsells, The Pearle of Perfection (1637), p. 36; Griffith Williams, The Best Religion (1636), p. 192; Richard Carpenter, Experience, etc. (1642), i. 195; Donne, Sermons, vii. 437; Bartholomäus Keckermann, A Manuduction to Theologie, tr. Thomas Vicars (1622?), p. 38; Richardson (above, p. 131, n. 3), p. 69; John Stoughton, XI. Choice Sermons (1640), ii. 27; et al.

[3] Works, xv. 321-3.

And due to theirs which out of thine will grow:
So onely can high Justice rest appaid.
The Law of God exact he shall fulfill
Both by obedience and by love, though love
Alone fulfill the Law; thy punishment
He shall endure by coming in the Flesh
To a reproachful life and cursed death,
Proclaming Life to all who shall believe
In his redemption, and that his obedience
Imputed becomes theirs by Faith, his merits
To save them, not thir own, though legal works.
For this he shall live hated, be blaspheam'd,
Seis'd on by force, judg'd, and to death condemnd
A shameful and accurst, naild to the Cross
By his own Nation, slaine for bringing Life;
But to the Cross he nailes thy Enemies,
The Law that is against thee, and the sins
Of all mankinde, with him there crucifi'd,
Never to hurt them more who rightly trust
In this his satisfaction.

(XII. 393–419)

There are few opinions that Milton held more sincerely or more consistently than his view of the Atonement. The forensic interpretation of the work of the Christ in *Paradise Lost* is identical with the one set forth in *De doctrina christiana*, which Milton had years before expounded while still in his early twenties. Then, in *Upon the Circumcision*, he wrote that the God-man 'satisfi'd' the transgressed covenant 'intirely'

And the full wrath beside
Of vengeful Justice bore for our excess.[1]

More than four centuries after its initial formulation by the Reformers, the Protestant theory of the Atonement has been called 'immoral'.[2] We cannot be absolutely certain whether some such notion had not occurred to Milton as well; we can only suspect that it might have, principally because nearly every time God appears

---

[1] *DDC, Works*, xv. 315 ff.; *Upon the Circumcision*, ll. 22–24. The conclusion of Amadeus P. Fiore, O.F.M., that Milton's views are 'conformable to orthodox Catholic dogma' is totally unacceptable ('The Problem of 17th Century Soteriology in Reference to Milton', *FS*, xv (1955), 48–59, 257–82).

[2] G. W. H. Lampe, 'The Atonement', in *Soundings*, ed. A. R. Vidler (Cambridge, 1962), pp. 186–7.

in *Paradise Lost* the poetry responds adversely, becoming flat, dull, monotonous. Certainly an impressive number of Milton's contemporaries were quite troubled by the 'fire and bloud' so often intimated by their God, while even before the middle of the sixteenth century the very word 'satisfaction' was—in the telling complaint of the humanist Urbanus Rhegius—'hated to al christen eares'. By 1661 finally, only six years before the publication of *Paradise Lost*, George Rust protested that 'modern Theology', suffering from 'an excess of complement to the Justice of God', had become 'as rude and troublesome as the Ass in the Fable, who did not fawn upon, but invade his master'.[1]

IV

Richard Carpenter in 1642, noting one of the most persistent themes in Christian theology, reported that 'God hath so play'd the good Alchymist, with the sinne of our first Parents, extracting many goods out of one evill, that some curiously question, whether wee may, or may not be sorry, that *Adam* sinn'd.[2] He refers here to the well-known paradox of the 'fortunate' Fall[3] which in *Paradise Lost* is reiterated by Adam immediately after the termination of Michael's prophecy of the Incarnation:

> O goodness infinite, goodness immense!
> That all this good of evil shall produce,
> And evil turn to good; more wonderful
> Then that which by creation first brought forth
> Light out of darkness! full of doubt I stand,
> Whether I should repent me now of sin
> By mee done and occasiond, or rejoyce
> Much more, that much more good thereof shall spring,
> To God more glory, more good will to Men
> From God, and over wrauth Grace shall abound.
> (XII. 469–78)

Most commentators did not question the theory of Adam's 'happy sinne' because they wished to establish that the work of the Christ

---

[1] Rhegius, *A Cōparison betwene the Olde Learnynge & the Newe*, tr. William Turner (1537), sig. B1ᵛ, and Rust, *A Letter of Resolution concerning Origen* (1661), p. 74.

[2] *Experience, Historie, and Divinitie* (1642), i. 68.

[3] Most ably studied by Arthur O. Lovejoy, 'Milton and the Paradox of the Fortunate Fall', *ELH*, iv (1937), 161–79. I gave additional evidence in 'Adam's "Happy Fault" and XVIIth-Century Apologetics', *FS*, xxiii (1963), 238–43.

'encreased Mans excellency', that we have gained a garden 'far exceeding that of *Eden*', 'a better estate then *Adam* was in before his fall'.[1] But Milton, aware of the theological traps inherent in the paradox, sagaciously allowed Adam to give tongue to it while remaining 'full of doubt' about its validity, and to accept also an accompanying tradition that man's salvation is more wonderful than the act of creation, mindful as Milton was of 'all the good auncient Doctours' who 'preferre the worke of mannes redemption, to the same of his creation'.[2]

The redemption of man was decided outside history by the omniscient God and revealed to the angels in advance of the Fall.[3] Within history the process of salvation commenced 'immediatlie after the transgression' with the prophecy of the woman's seed and progressed through countless 'types and shadowes' to the Incarnation. Milton celebrated the Incarnation, the last crucial event in this process, in the ode *On the Morning of Christ's Nativity*. The fundamental theme of this poem, 'universal Peace' (l. 52), unfolds largely in terms of three legends associated traditionally with the Nativity: nature's serenity, the absence of war, and the cessation of pagan oracles. The legend of peaceful nature (ll. 61 ff.) might have had its source in the apocryphal Book of James (xviii. 2), though it was most likely inspired by the customary view of nature as God's 'vicaire' we noted earlier.[4] The second legend upon which Milton drew, the absence of war (ll. 53 ff.), reflects the widespread conviction that at the birth of Jesus there was 'vniuersall *Peace*', 'the face of the whole world, with a generall content of peace did smile'. As Quarles put it,

> when the Olive Branch of Peace was showne
> Then, not before, the Prince of Peace came downe![5]

[1] Seriatim: Richard Sheldon, *The First Sermon* (1612), p. 20; Harrington (above, p. 137, n. 4), p. 150; Thomas Savile, *Adams Garden* (1611), p. 1; and Robert Snawsel, *A Looking Glasse* (1610), sig. F6. Adam's 'happy fall' is also mentioned by John Salkeld, *A Treatise of Paradise* (1617), p. 154.
[2] Pierre Viret, *The Christian Disputations*, tr. John Brooke (1579), fol. 97. This tradition is documented in *FS* (above, p. 142, n. 3).
[3] See *PL*, III. 72 ff., and the authorities cited by McColley I, p. 186.
[4] Above, pp. 54 ff. The Book of James was made available in the sixteenth century by Guillaume Postel (*NT Apocr.*, p. 46). Numerous other legends concerning the Nativity and the Passion are collected in Pedro Mexía's popular *Silua de varia lection* (Valladolid, 1551), Bk. II, ch. 33, translated into French by Claude Gruget (*Diverses leçons* (Lyon, 1592; 1st ed., 1552), Bk. II, ch. 32) and into English by Thomas Fortescue (*The Foreste* (1571), Bk. III, ch. 16).
[5] Seriatim: George Warburton, *King Melchizedech* (1623), pp. 33 f.; Anthony Maxey,

However, the history surrounding the legend of the oracles' cessation is by far the most fascinating history of all.[1] Beginning in Plutarch's *De defectu oraculorum* (ch. xvii), it continued its tortuous journey through Eusebius's *Praeparatio evangelica* and numerous other works, to be treated—and very often mistreated—by an impressive array of poets and prose-writers during the Renaissance, only to be dashed to pieces against Fontenelle's *Histoire des oracles* (1687). Milton stands among the traditionalists who, like his admirer Sir Henry Wotton, were 'stupefied' that upon the Christ's advent the oracles were miraculously 'strucken mute, and nothing [was] to be heard at *Delphos* or *Hammon*'.[2] Milton devoted no less than seven stanzas of the *Nativity Ode* to this legend (XIX–XXV), yet reverted to it still later in life in the Christ's statement to Satan in *Paradise Regained*:

> No more shalt thou by oracling abuse
> The Gentiles; henceforth Oracles are ceast,
> And thou no more with Pomp and Sacrifice
> Shalt be enquir'd at *Delphos* or elsewhere,
> At least in vain, for they shall find thee mute.
> God hath now sent his living Oracle
> Into the World, to teach his final will,
> And sends his Spirit of Truth henceforth to dwell
> In pious Hearts, an inward Oracle
> To all truth requisite for men to know.
>
> (I. 455–64)

The circumcision is the second event in the Saviour's life which commanded Milton's attention. Earlier we noted affinities between *Upon the Circumcision* and the Protestant theory of the Atonement, and it may now be added that Milton's contemporaries also regarded the Christ's circumcision as having 'satisfied' the wrath of God. Perhaps the most interesting parallel occurs in a short poem by Herbert's enthusiastic disciple, Christopher Harvey, who maintained likewise that the circumcision served to 'asswage / The wrath of heaven'.[3] The legal terminology in which Harvey and Milton

---

Certaine Sermons, 7th ed. (1634), p. 195; Quarles, *Hosanna*, ed. John Horden (Liverpool, 1960), p. 4.

[1] See my account, 'The Cessation of the Oracles: The History of a Legend', *MLR*, lx (1965), 500–7.

[2] *Reliquiæ Wottonianæ*, 2nd ed. (1654), pp. 321–2.

[3] *The Circumcision*, in *The Synagogue* (1640), pp. 24 f. Harvey's debt to Herbert is discussed in general by A. C. Howell, *SP*, xlix (1952), 229–49.

couched their poems recurs in nearly every other Protestant reference to the circumcision. A statement by Zacharias Ursinus is typical:

Christ was circumcised, 1. *That he might signifie that he was also a member of that circumcised people*. 2. *That he might shew that he received & tooke our sins on himselfe, that he might satisfie for them*. 3. *That he might testifie that he did entirely and fully fulfill the law in our behalfe*. 4. *The circumcision of Christ was a part also of his humiliation and ransome.*[1]

Milton shares the attitude of his contemporaries in viewing the circumcision as the first event in the Passion (l. 25). Bishop Henry King, for example, regarded the circumcision as the first of several 'payments' to divine justice, and Edward Sparke termed it the Passion's '*Tragick-Prologue*' since the Christ then 'began . . . to take away the Sins of the world'.[2]

Milton did not succeed in his attempt to describe the Passion poetically. As he himself observed in a note: 'This Subject the Author finding to be above the yeers he had, when he wrote it, and nothing satisfi'd with what was begun, left it unfinisht.' But unfinished though *The Passion* is, Milton did not hesitate to publish it at the first available opportunity (1645). Was this his way of warning the world not to expect devotional poetry from him? And was his lack of ardour for the Passion just personal idiosyncrasy or Protestant? While the Catholic and Orthodox Churches have usually shown preference for the Passion and Easter ('drunk of the dear wounds'),[3] Protestantism has in practice shown preference for the Nativity and Christmas. Milton himself, even before he wrote *The Passion*, indicated which subjects he was never to find 'above his yeers'. The comprehensive frame of reference of the *Nativity Ode*, the emphasis on obedience in *Upon the Circumcision*, the theme of temptation enunciated in *Comus*, all seem inevitably to propel Milton toward the one event in the life of Jesus which appealed to him, I mean the temptation in the wilderness set forth in *Paradise Regained*.

Paradise Regained does not pretend to celebrate the God-man's redemption of mankind. In harmony with common sentiment that the encounter in the wilderness marked 'the entraunce of Christ into

---

[1] Ursinus, p. 681. Cf. Ames, p. 94.

[2] King, *A Sermon of Deliverance* (1626), p. 20; Sparke, Θυσιαστήριον, 3rd ed. (1663), pp. 137, 139.

[3] Crashaw, *Sancta Maria Dolorum*, xi. 3. While there is such a thing as Protestant devotional poetry, it was of course written largely by Anglicans allied to the Catholic tradition.

the execution of his office',[1] Milton's epic focuses on the initial
stages of the Saviour's ministry, the 'rudiments' of his achievement
(I. 157), which the angels clearly proclaim in their concluding hymn
of praise:

> Hail Son of the most High, heir of both Worlds,
> Queller of Satan, on thy glorious work
> *Now* enter, and *begin* to save mankind.
>
> (IV. 633–5; my italics)

Milton's contemporaries judged these 'rudiments' to be of supreme
practical significance to the lives of men. The God-man was de-
signated invariably as the most perfect exemplar of the conduct
expected of all men, 'our patterne', 'a patterne to vs how we ought to
walke', 'our Teacher by his words, and Accomplisher by his deedes'.[2]
The Christ's temptation in the wilderness was thus seen as *the*
example that 'might give vs direction whereby to know the speciall
temptations wherewith the Diuell assaults the Church, as also how
to withstand and repell the same'.[3] The central question here is
how far we, mere mortals, can imitate 'our patterne', since 'our
patterne' was not man but God-man. It is tantamount to asking,
'Was Christ really tempted?'[4]

The traditional answer has of necessity emphasized the Christ's
humanity even while cautioning against the negation of his divinity.
In the words of one commentator, 'if we are to express this in human
language, we are forced to assert that within the *sphere* and *period* of
His incarnate and mortal life, He . . . cease[d] from the exercise of
those divine functions and powers, including the divine omniscience,
which would have been incompatible with a truly human experience.'[5]
It is this 'truly human experience' that *Paradise Regained* endeavours

---

[1] John Udall, *The Combate betwixt Christ and the Deuill* (1590?), sig. A6.

[2] Seriatim: Calvin, *Foure Sermons*, tr. John Fielde (1579), fol. 19; Robert Jenison,
The Christian Apparelling (1625), p. 114; and John Lesly, *An Epithrene* (1631), p. 19.
The example of Jesus, commended by himself (John xiii. 15, 34; xv. 12; etc.), was welcomed by humanists with marked enthusiasm; see Vives, *An Introduction to Wysedome*,
tr. Richard Morison (1544), sig. E3, and Ficino, *De christiana religione*, XXIII (Robb,
p. 64).

[3] William Perkins, *The Combat betweene Christ and the Diuell*, 2nd ed. (1606), p. 8.

[4] This is the very title of Gerald Vann and P. K. Meagher's *Stones or Bread? A Study
of Christ's Temptations* (1957), ch. i. I may also recommend the survey of early Christian
thought by M. Steiner, *La Tentation de Jésus* (Paris, 1962).

[5] Charles Gore, *Dissertations* (1895), pp. 94–95. See also J. O. F. Murray, *Studies in
the Temptation of the Son of God* (1916), pp. 73–87, and esp. H. G. Hatch, *The Messianic
Consciousness of Jesus* (1939). Cf. Austin Farrer, *The Triple Victory* (1965).

to illuminate because it accords with a belief widespread during the
Renaissance that the Christ's perfect obedience to the will of God
was 'according to his humanity'.[1] But what renders Milton's poem
fascinating theologically as well as dramatically is the gradual
awakening in Jesus of his mediatorial mission and especially of his
divine nature. This progressive development of Milton's God-man
derives not from the poet's imagination but from a traditional
conviction that 'as he [Jesus] grew vp by little and little in his body:
so (in respect of his soule,) the giftes of the minde encreased daily
more and more'.[2] This development was, moreover, held by tradition
to have reached finality at the end of the Christ's temptations in an
open acknowledgement of his divinity.[3] We see it reflected in the
angels' hymn in *Paradise Regained*:

> True Image of the Father, whether thron'd
> In the bosom of bliss, and light of light
> Conceiving, or remote from Heaven, enshrin'd
> In fleshly Tabernacle, and human form,
> Wandring the Wilderness, whatever place,
> Habit, or state, or motion, still expressing
> The Son of God, with Godlike force indu'd
> Against th' Attempter of thy Fathers Throne . . .
> Hail Son of the most High, heir of both Worlds,
> Queller of Satan, on thy glorious work
> Now enter, and begin to save mankind.
>
> (IV. 595–635)

The problem of the Christ's dual nature is far from being the
only thorny problem in *Paradise Regained*, for we must take into
account Jesus's disparagement of Greek literature and philosophy
(IV. 286–364) and also his denunciation of the multitude as 'a herd
confus'd, / A Miscellaneous rabble' (III. 49 f.). Let us seek enlightenment in the traditional view. The truth is that Milton's opinion of
the multitude was shared by a host of his contemporaries and immediate predecessors, among them Guicciardini and Charron,
Philipp Camerarius and Augustin Marlorat, Barnaby Rich and Sir

---

[1] William Perkins, *A Golden Chaine*, tr. Anon. (1591), sig. D6ᵛ.
[2] Niels Hemmingsen, *A Postill, or Exposition of the Gospels*, tr. Arthur Golding (1574), fol. 32. Cf. Samuel Maresius, in Heppe, p. 420.
[3] See Elizabeth M. Pope, *'PR': The Tradition and the Poem* (Baltimore, 1947), esp. ch. ii. Besides this indispensable study, I should recommend the essays by Barbara K. Lewalski, 'Theme and Structure in *PR*', *SP*, lvii (1960), 186–220, and Louis L. Martz, *The Paradise Within* (New Haven, 1964), Ch. iv.

Thomas Browne, Miles Smith and Lancelot Andrewes.[1] If it still causes concern that Milton attributed his own 'undemocratic' sentiments to Jesus, let us recall that in *Paradise Regained* the God-man denounces the multitude for extolling 'Things vulgar, and well weighd, scarce worth the praise', in order to affirm that 'true glory and renown' consist in God's approbation of the faithful few who seek to further the Divine Purpose (III. 60–64). The student of the Gospels hardly needs reminding that the historic Jesus was likewise often wrathful, the ὀργή which the New Testament attributes to him being his way of emphasizing God's violent opposition to disobedience.[2] The *locus classicus* of this viewpoint is, of course, the episode in which Jesus angrily cleanses the Temple.

The disparagement of Greek achievements should likewise be read in the light both of the circumstances in which it was uttered and of the prevailing Christian mode of thought. When Jesus remarks that Greek achievements are 'unworthy to compare / With Sions songs' (IV. 346 f.), his chief intention is not to denigrate classical culture but to uphold the primacy of 'those writt'n Records pure' as *the* depository of 'true wisdom'.[3] Moreover, this had grown into the burden of Christian teaching even before Jerome inquired rhetorically, 'How can Horace go with the psalter, Virgil with the gospels, Cicero with the apostles?'[4] It is conceivable that many people may concur with Jerome's opinion not of style but of content: Milton echoes him in *Paradise Regained*. Alas, seized by enthusiasm, perhaps even fanaticism, both Jerome and Milton dared to propose the Bible's literary superiority, Milton on two occasions. In *The Reason of Church Government* (1642) he claimed that Hebrew lyric poems are incomparable 'not in their divine argument alone, but in the very critical art of composition', and in *Paradise Regained* he asserted that the 'majestic unaffected stile' of the prophets surpasses

---

[1] These are only eight of the numerous writers I quoted or referred to in ' "The Beast with Many Heads": Renaissance Views on the Multitude', *SQ*, xvi (1965), 241–6.

[2] See esp. A. G. Hebert, *The Biblical Doctrine of the Wrath of God* (1951), and A. T. Hanson, *The Wrath of the Lamb* (1957).

[3] See above, pp. 85–86, but especially the excellent studies by Irene Samuel, 'Milton on Learning and Wisdom', *PMLA*, lxiv (1949), 708–23, and Arnold Stein, *Heroic Knowledge* (Minneapolis, 1957), pp. 94–111.

[4] Letter XXII, 29 (*NPNF*, 2nd ser., vi. 35). Jerome's attitude is discussed by Harald Hagendahl, *Latin Fathers and the Classics* (Göteborg, 1958), pt. ii. The relevant patristic statements were collected during the Renaissance by Edward Lively, Regius Professor of Hebrew at Cambridge, in *A True Chronologie* (1597), pp. 13 ff. See also Howard Schultz, *Milton and Forbidden Knowledge* (1955), chs. i–ii, and the quotations from Beza cited by Edna Newmeyer, *Bulletin of the N.Y. Public Library*, lxvi (1962), 485–98.

'all the Oratory of *Greece* and *Rome*'.[1] We are astonished, and increasingly so, as we come to appreciate how mild was Milton's opinion in comparison with that of the insensitive Luther ('The Greek tragedies are not to be compared with the history of David'), and even of men with substantial literary achievements to their credit, like Erasmus. As Donne likewise observed, 'if we would take all those Figures, and Tropes, which are collected out of secular Poets, and Orators, we may give higher, and livelier examples, of every one of those Figures, out of the Scriptures, then out of all the Greek and Latine Poets, and Orators'.[2]

V

In *The Passion* the Christ is called 'Most perfet *Heroe*' (l. 13), and in *Paradise Regained* his deeds are termed 'Above Heroic' (I. 15). Milton is not the innovator of this concept of the God-man's 'heroism'. It was adapted from the 'Hero Christology' of the Bible, which in turn yielded the tradition of Jesus as 'the hero of heroes'.[3] Christian literature thus abounds in references to 'the qualities of a perfectly heroic soul' exemplified by the Christ, the 'heroicall mind' he possessed, the 'heroicall actes of vertue' he performed, the 'noble and heroicall love' he displayed even toward his persecutors.[4] This conduct by 'our patterne' has been seen traditionally as 'an appeal to all that is heroic in man':

Loyalty to His ideals in our personal spiritual life and in our life as citizens of the Kingdom of God brings us into situations in which we are confronted with malign forces, with risks to be run, with seeming impossibilities to be overcome, with sacrifices to be made, with sufferings to be endured. That is, we are continually presented with opportunities of playing the hero. Under the leadership of the Prince of heroes who died

---

[1] *Works*, iii. 238; *PR*, IV. 356–60.

[2] *Sermons*, vi. 56; cf. ix. 252, and x. 103. See also Luther, *Table-Talk*, pp. 237, 242, and the writers quoted by Israel Baroway, *PMLA*, xxxii (1933), 464–72. The claims of Luther and others did not convince everyone, witness Robert Boyle's obligation to plead that the Bible is not 'so unadorn'd', 'so destitute of Eloquence, that it is flat' (*Some Considerations touching the Style of the H. Scriptures* (1661)).

[3] D. M. Ross (below, p. 150, n. 1), p. 270. On the Biblical background, see Wilfred L. Knox, *HTR*, xli (1948), 229–49; William Manson, *The Epistle to the Hebrews* (1951), pp. 102–6; and John M. Steadman, *HTR*, liv (1961), 29–43.

[4] Seriatim: Pascal, *Pensées*, § 741; Lancelot Andrewes, *Seven Sermons* (1627), p. 97; Luis de la Puente, S.J., *Meditations*, tr. John Heigham (St. Omer, 1619), i. 355; and Thomas Goodwin, *Christ Set Forth* (1642), p. 29.

on the Cross in loyalty to the service of his fellows there can never be lacking the stimulus to raise our life, however humble its setting may be, to heroic heights of service and self-sacrifice.[1]

Milton, having accepted the Christ's 'heroism', welcomed also the sacrosanctity of the *imitatio Christi*. As Michael observes in *Paradise Lost*, the disciples of Jesus were charged with the preparation of the faithful 'in mind . . ., if so befall, / For death, like that which the redeemer dy'd' (II. 444 f.). But the redeemer's life and death could also be imitated by the faithful who lived before his advent, 'types' such as Samson. Hence the validity of Milton's ascription of a 'Heroic magnitude of mind' to the protagonist of *Samson Agonistes*, for he, like the historic Christ, exemplified 'the truest fortitude' that consists in the patient acceptance of afflictions even unto death (ll. 654, 1279). Manoa's epitaph on his dead son applies to Samson as to the 'Most perfet *Heroe*':

> *Samson* hath quit himself
> Like *Samson*, and heroicly hath finisht
> A life Heroic.
> (ll. 1709–11)

The 'truest fortitude' celebrated in *Samson Agonistes* is the ideal immemorially commended by the Christian faith: 'an Heroicall fortitude of minde in bearing all grievous Crosses'.[2] But the invitation is not to passive resignation but to action, the action specified by the Congregational minister Jeremiah Burroughs when he remarked in 1638 on the 'true Heroicall spirit' of men sanctified by grace. As he put it, 'none have such brave heroicall spirits as Gods servants have, it is not discouraged by difficulties, it will set upon things a sluggish spirit thinkes impossible, . . . it breakes through armies of difficulties, that it might goe on its way, and accomplish its worke.'[3]

Milton's thoughts on the essence of 'heroism' are admirably summarized in the opening lines of the ninth book of *Paradise Lost*. Just as Virgil had criticized the heroic ideal he inherited, so Milton

---

[1] D. M. Ross, *The Cross of Christ* (1928), pp. 270–1.

[2] Zanchius, p. 123. Behind Zanchius's statement and Milton's exposition stands the tradition of 'heroism' ever-present in the *Vitae Patrum*. The interested student could begin with, say, *The Martyrdom of Polycarp* (*ACW*, vi. 90–102). Milton's attitude to patience is studied by Paul R. Baumgartner, *SP*, xlx (1963), 203–13, and William O. Harris, *ELH*, xxx (1963), 107–20.

[3] *The Excellency of a Gracious Spirit* (1638), pp. 63–64.

claimed that his own argument is 'Not less but more Heroic' than Homer's and Virgil's[1]—more so indeed than the subject-matter of Christian poets such as Tasso, Ariosto, and Boiardo:

> hitherto the onely Argument
> Heroic deemd [was the] chief maistrie to dissect
> With long and tedious havoc fabl'd Knights
> In Battles feignd, . . . or to describe Races and Games,
> Or tilting Furniture, emblazond Shields
> Impreses quaint, Caparisons and Steeds;
> Bases and tinsel Trappings, gorgious Knights
> At Joust and Torneament; then marshald Feast
> Serv'd up in Hall with Sewers, and Seneshals;
> The skill of Artifice or Office mean,
> Not that which justly gives Heroic name
> To Person or to Poem.   (IX. 28–41)

Milton's reproach to the Italian poets resembles that of the humanists' attack on 'depraved' romances that set forth 'open mans slaughter and bold bawdrye'.[2] The humanists would have commended Milton's attitude in Book IX as they would have commended the subsequent commentary by Michael on the 'slaughter and gigantic deeds' destined to sweep the earth:

> To overcome in Battel, and subdue
> Nations, and bring home spoils with infinite
> Man-slaughter, shall be held the highest pitch
> Of human Glorie, and for Glorie done
> Of triumph, to be stil'd great Conquerours,
> Patrons of Mankind, Gods, and Sons of Gods,
> Destroyers rightlier calld and Plagues of Men.
> Thus Fame shall be achiev'd, renown on Earth,
> And what most merits fame in silence hid.
>   (XI. 691–9)

Michael's words are supplemented by Jesus in *Paradise Regained*:

> if there be in glory ought of good,
> It may by means far different be attaind

---

[1] On Virgil's attitude consult C. M. Bowra, *From Virgil to Milton* (1948), pp. 42 ff.; on Milton's: Davis P. Harding, *The Club of Hercules* (Urbana, 1962), ch. iii. I cited numerous studies of Milton's theory of 'heroism' in *Italian Quarterly*, viii, no. 31 (1965), pp. 81–82.

[2] Thus Ascham on Malory (*The Scholemaster* (1570), ed. D. C. Whimster (1934), p. 74). For a later denunciation of 'depraved' romances, including Malory's, see Mathias Prideaux, *An . . . Introduction for Reading . . . Histories* (Oxford, 1648), pp. 343 f. The context of Ascham's censure is thoroughly studied by Robert P. Adams, *The Better Part of Valor* (Seattle, 1962), ch. xiii, condensed from *HLQ*, xxiii (1959), 33–48.

> Without ambition, warr, or violence;
> By deeds of peace, by wisdom eminent,
> By patience, temperance.
>
> (III. 88–92)

Echoes of *Lycidas* in these passages heighten the significance of Milton's claim at the outset of Book IX that his higher argument concerns 'the better fortitude / Of Patience and Heroic Martyrdom' (IX. 31 f.). Within *Paradise Lost* this ideal is celebrated in connexion with the 'true Heroicall spirit' that Adam and Eve manifest when they repent in 'humiliation meek' and later abandon Eden to face the sufferings of an inhospitable world in 'meek submission' before Divine Providence (X. 1092, 1104; XII. 597). Yet such 'heroic' conduct, Milton avers, would have been impossible had not the God-man volunteered his 'unexampl'd love', which enabled the Godhead to send to man the speediest of its winged messengers, 'Prevenient Grace' (III. 410; XI. 3). What Milton and the Christian faith mean by love and what by grace will be our concern in the next two chapters.

6

Because we Freely Love

THE CHRISTIAN IDEA OF LOVE

Christ is serv'd with Voluntaries.

JOHN DONNE[1]

I

THE Protestants of the Renaissance—in theory—upheld the ideal of universal love with the same enthusiasm that marks all other Christians. In practice the ideal was violated on nearly every available opportunity, the burden of intolerance borne by other Protestants, by all Catholics—themselves hardly more liberal—and by the Jews. It is perhaps permissible to wonder how Jews would have fared in Protestant hands, given Luther's opinion of them as 'wicked and ungodly'.[2] If their persecution was less severe than in Catholic Europe the reason might well have been that leading Reformers were already too preoccupied with their fellow Christians. This preoccupation led in time to the well-known series of tragic events that involved the burning of Michael Servetus in Geneva (1553) and particularly the holocaust of Anabaptists.[3]

Protests broke forth. Within a year of Servetus's execution the celebrated treatise *De haereticis* appeared, said to have been written by Sebastian Castellio. It was followed by many eloquent pleas for toleration, among them those by John Dury, who spent a lifetime endeavouring to unite the Protestants, and by Jeremy Taylor, who

---

[1] *Sermons*, vii. 156.

[2] *Table-Talk*, pp. 346–54. See also Hersch L. Zitt, 'The Jew in the Elizabethan World-Picture', *Historia Judaica*, xiv (1951), 53–60.

[3] Calvin's early call for toleration in the *Inst.* (Whale II, p. 150) was ominously eliminated from later editions. See further the full account by Joseph Lecler, S.J., *Toleration and the Reformation*, tr. T. L. Westow (1960), 2 vols., and the eclectic account by Roland H. Bainton, *The Travail of Religious Liberty* (1953). Bainton also translated Castellio's *De haereticis* (in 1935), which he discussed in *Castellioniana* (Leyden, 1951), pp. 25–79.

argued against the persecution of Anabaptists ('they must be left to God') as well as of Catholics ('yet they keep the foundation, they build upon God in Jesus').[1] But the general denunciation of Dury's work as 'visionary nonsense', the severely diminished effectiveness of Taylor's plea because he regarded the Jews as 'the greatest enemies of Christ', and, lastly, the censure of Acontio's invitation to all Christians ('go beyond one another in offices of Love') as nothing less than 'very dangerous',[2] all prescribed the emphatic limits of Protestant tolerance. Milton's prejudices are defined just as emphatically.[3] The author of *Areopagitica* may not openly have denounced the Jews, yet he did not plead on their behalf either; and while he repeatedly and passionately called for the toleration of all Protestants, he refused to extend freedom of conscience to Catholics. Milton's attitude toward Protestants, it may be argued, was far more enlightened than that of his contemporaries, who normally sneered at any proposal to offer 'a full . . . Liberty for all imaginable kindes of false Religion'. It may also be argued that Milton shared his violent anti-Catholicism with most of his contemporaries, who thought it 'vnreasonably charitable' even to identify the Pope with the Antichrist, and who commonly looked upon all Catholics as 'the directest and deadliest enemies that Christs true Church ever had'.[4] But even after granting to such arguments any force they merit, we are left face to face with the omission by Milton, by Renaissance Protestants and Catholics, to practise the Christian ideal of love they all upheld with such enthusiasm.

'Vnity', wrote Charles Herle in 1631, 'is the ground-worke of nature, the very *Atlas* of the Beeing of all things; love and order are the two shoulders of this *Atlas*.'[5] The conception of the universe in terms of love and order is not very common in Protestantism, which rather tended to emphasize order at the expense of love. There were of course many exceptions to this, particularly among Anglican

---

[1] Taylor, Θεολογία ἐκλεκτική. *A Discourse of the Liberty of Prophesying* (1647), esp. §§ 18 and 20. On Dury see Milton Batten, *John Dury: Advocate of Christian Reunion* (Chicago, 1944).

[2] Jacopo Acontio, *Satans Stratagems*, tr. Anon. (1648), p. 87. The adverse opinion is from Francis Cheynell's *The Divine Trinunity* (1650), pp. 442 ff.

[3] The best account is by Don M. Wolfe, *JEGP*, xl (1961), 834–46. See also Bainton, *Travail*, etc. (above, p. 153, n. 3), ch. vii.

[4] Seriatim: Robert Bayly, *Errours and Induration* (1645), p. 36; Robert Sanderson, *Tuuelve Sermons* (1632), p. 424; and William Gouge, *Gods Three Arrowes* (1631), p. 213. See further below, p. 270.

[5] *Contemplations* (1631), p. 499. This was partially quoted earlier, p. 61.

poets. We think of Spenser; we think of devotional poets like Herbert; and I may also quote this persuasive rhapsody by Peter Sterry:

Homer tells us of a *Chain* fastned to the Throne of *Jupiter*, which reacheth down to the Earth. He speaketh to *Neptune*, *Minerva*, and the rest of the *Powers* about him, which reign in the Skies, in the Seas, in the Earth, in Hell below. *If ye should all hang with your whole weight upon the end of this Chain, I would at my pleasure draw you all up to my self.* The *Throne* of the most *High* God, is a Throne of *Grace*, of *Love*. Like a *Chain* doth the whole *Nature* of things descend from this Throne, having its *top* fastned to *it*. What-ever the weights may be of the lowermost links of this Chain, yet that *Love* which sits upon the Throne, with a Divine delight, as it lets down the Chain from it self, so draws it up again by the Order of the successive Links unto a Divine Ornament, an eternal Joy and Glory to it self.[1]

Sterry and other Protestants like him were exceptions. Among Western Christians the Catholics alone have displayed convincingly a belief in love as the axis of the universe, as that which 'knit[s] all the parts of this great world', that 'wherewith the world, the heauens, and the celestiall spirites are vnited & bounde together'.[2] The failure of Protestants to propound a similar scheme was the result of a number of developments. Their rejection of Mariolatry—as distinct from Mariology—was decisive: it obliged them to attenuate the Virgin's role as the Mother of God and therefore to deny the cosmic implications of her experience. The Protestant theory of the Atonement also contributed significantly, for it stressed persistently 'the absolute necessity of satisfaction to divine Justice',[3] virtually excluding thereby the contemplation of love as the absolute lord of life and death. Moreover, the opposition implied between the Father's concern with justice and the Son's with mercy made the sacrifice of the Filial Similitude appear not so much as a demonstration of divine love but as a successful attempt to oppose the decrees of the Most High. This emphasis accounts for the enormous difference between

[1] *A Discourse of the Freedom of the Will* (1675), sigs. c4ᵛ-d1. Nicholas Breton also penned a Dantesque statement in *The Soules Immortall Crowne* (1605), sig. F1.

[2] Cristóbal de Fonseca, Θεῖον ἑνωτικόν, tr. Sir George Strode (1652), p. 1, and Vives, *The Office and Duetie of an Husband*, tr. Thomas Paynell (1550?), sig. O1. Among the earlier affirmations are Ficino's (*Comm.*, esp. iii. 2; see also Robb, pp. 76 ff.) and of course Dante's—particularly *Purg.* XVII–XVIII, which is ably discussed by Joseph A. Mazzeo, *Structure and Thought in the 'Paradiso'* (Ithaca, N.Y., 1958), esp. chs. iii, v. Milton was certainly interested in Dante, but had, I think, no love for him (as K. C. M. Sills claimed in *MP*, iii (1905), 109 ff.).

[3] Jeremiah Burroughs, *Gospel-Revelation* (1660), p. 311. See above, p. 135 ff.

the celestial laughter heard in *Paradise Lost* and the universal smile observed in the *Paradiso*.[1] Where the Catholic Dante proclaims the joyous laughter of the created order in ecstatic union with Love, the Protestant Milton grimly insists on the Almighty's 'great laughter' in derision of the wretches who vainly oppose his inflexible decrees. Does the theory of accommodation ('these things are said grossely for our capacitie, because the Lord in deede can neither laugh nor crie'[2]) justify Milton's conception, as some may claim? Does Psalm ii. 4 constitute a satisfactory precedent?

> Earths haughtie Potentates and Kings,
> 'Gainst God against his Christ conspire . . .
> But God from his cœlestiall Throne
> Shall laugh, and their attempts deride.[3]

Apologists cannot, however, alter the insistence of Milton and his fellow Protestants upon the divine laughter not as love but as scorn.[4] This is not the genuine voice either of the Christian tradition or of Christian experience, for experience and tradition are united in condemning God's convulsions in *Paradise Lost* and in lauding the dazzling smile that lights up the *Commedia*. Dante is still the undisputed poet of divine love; Milton primarily the poet of cosmic order, and of love only to the extent we are now to observe.

II

Protestants unhesitatingly accepted a tradition that the Father was responsible for setting in motion the process of man's redemption. As Ezekiel Culverwell averred: 'GOD the Father mooved by nothing but his free love to mankind lost, hath made a deede of gift and graunt of his Sonne Christ Jesus unto mankinde.' Humphrey Sydenham was even more insistent: 'not because Christ died for vs, God loued, and chose vs, but because God loued and chose vs, therefor Christ died for vs.'[5] *Paradise Lost* is similarly biased. The Father's

---

[1] *Par.* XXVII. 6; *PL*, II. 190 f., v. 736 f., VIII. 78, and XII. 59.

[2] John Boys, *An Exposition of the Proper Psalmes* (1616), i. 85. Cf. above, pp. 9 ff.

[3] From George Sandys's *Paraphrase upon the Divine Poems* (1638), ii. 2. Cf. Wisdom of Solomon iv. 18.

[4] See, for instance, Thomas Playfere, *Ten Sermons* (Cambridge, 1610), p. 119; Richard Webb, *Christs Kingdome* (1611), pp. 73 f.; John Norden, *A Poor Mans Rest*, 12th ed. (1631), p. 306—and almost any Protestant commentary on Ps. ii. 4. One significant precedent is *Talmud*: 'Abodah Zarah, §§ 3*a*–3*b* (pp. 8–9).

[5] Culverwell, *A Treatise of Faith*, 8th ed. (1648), p. 15, and Sydenham, *Iacob and Esau*

first address in Book III concludes with his express resolution to save, not the fallen angels, but man:

> Man . . . shall find Grace,
> The other none: in Mercy and Justice both,
> Through Heav'n and Earth, so shall my glorie excell,
> But Mercy first and last shall brightest shine.
>
> (131–4)

The best commentary on these lines I know was penned by another poet, Robert Frost:

> after doing Justice justice,
> Milton's pentameters go on to say,
> But Mercy first and last shall brightest shine,
> Not only last, but first, you will observe.[1]

Yet the effort to portray the Father as the champion of both justice and mercy splits against the recurrent Protestant thesis that justice is 'much like to God' and mercy 'much like to Christ'.[2] Milton's use of the word 'love' solely in relation to the Son, never in direct relation to the Father, marks his approval of the distinction. The word 'love' first occurs after the Father's opening speech [my italics throughout]:

> Beyond compare the Son of God was seen
> Most glorious, in him all his Father shon
> Substantially exprest, and in his face
> Divine compassion visibly appeerd,
> *Love without end*, and without measure Grace.
>
> (138–42)

The Son displays his lack of enthusiasm over the Father's pre-occupation with justice: 'gracious was that word which *clos'd* | Thy sovran sentence, that Man should find Grace' (144 f.). But the Father unheeding proceeds to outline his theory of salvation, demanding 'rigid satisfaction' for Adam's disobedience, and asking for a volunteer:

> Say Heav'nly Powers, where shall we find such *love*,
> Which of ye will be mortal to redeem

(1626), p. 7. This attitude did not prevent Sydenham from being worried by 'Gods threatenings' (above, p. 122).

[1] *A Masque of Mercy*, in *Collected Poems* (1949), pp. 626 f.

[2] Thomas Peyton, *The Glasse of Time* (1623), i. 69. Cowley ascribed to the Father 'Power' and to the Son 'Love' (*Poems*, ed. A. R. Waller (Cambridge, 1905), p. 306).

> Mans mortal crime, and just th' unjust to save?
> Dwels in all Heaven *charitie* so deare?
>
> (213–16)

The *theological* blunder involved in the Father's incredible question and the even more incredible silence that greets it make comment superfluous. But in the end the 'blest Kingdoms meek of joy and love' do manage to yield at least one Person prepared to save man, and Milton loses no time in delineating his nature. It is love—'immortal *love*' (267), 'Heav'nly *Love*' (298), 'the fulness . . . of *love* divine' (225), *love* in excess of glory (312). The paean to the Son concludes with the angels' magnificent hymn of praise that culminates in Milton's personal address to the Saviour:

> O unexampl'd *love*,
> *Love* no where to be found less than Divine!
> Hail Son of God, Saviour of Men, thy Name
> Shall be the copious matter of *my* Song
> Henceforth . . .
>
> (410–14)

Milton kept his promise.[1] The celebration of the Son's 'unexampl'd love' in Book III links up with his display of 'Love / Immense' during the creation (VII. 195 f.) but especially with his attitude toward fallen man in Book X. There his response to the Father's invitation to pass sentence on Adam and Eve is said to be 'divinely . . . mild' (X. 67). In Eden he appears as 'the gracious Judge' (118), 'the mild Judge and Intercessor both' (96), and carries out his mission with a 'look serene', a 'mild / And gracious temper' 'Without wrauth or reviling' (1046–8, 1093–7). Two incidents now occur which anticipate directly the Incarnation. The first is the prophecy of the woman's seed; the second is the covering of Adam and Eve's nakedness with the skins of beasts. The second of these incidents has not elicited the attention it deserves. The Son, having sentenced Adam and Eve, is observed

> pittying how they stood
> Before him naked to the aire, that now
> Must suffer change, disdaind not to begin
> Thenceforth the forme of servant to assume,
> As when he washd his servants feet, so now
> As Father of his Familie he clad

[1] See below, esp. pp. 259ff.

Thir nakedness with Skins of Beasts . . .
And thought not much to cloathe his Enemies.

(X. 211–19)

The Son's assumption of servant's form harks back to his 'meek aspect' in Book III (266) and foresees his humble obedience prophesied by Michael in Book XII. It is also related directly to his self-abasement in the *Nativity Ode* (l. 12) and *Upon the Circumcision* (l. 20) but particularly to his humility in *Paradise Regained* as he returns home victorious yet 'unobserv'd' (IV. 638). Milton's clear intent was to confirm the validity of the traditional invitation to regard the God-man as 'our patterne',[1] while at the same time asserting the significance of the Christian paradox that humility is not a degradation but an exaltation, 'the beginning of sanctification', 'a stage towards greatness'.[2] Satan's reproach of Jesus in *Paradise Regained* points how contrary is this claim to the way of the world:

> all thy heart is set on high designs,
> High actions; but wherewith to be atchiev'd?
> Great acts require great means of enterprise,
> Thou art unknown, unfriended, low of birth,
> A Carpenter thy Father known, thy self
> Bred up in poverty and streights at home;
> Lost in a Desert here and hunger-bit:
> Which way or from what hope dost thou aspire
> To greatness?   (II. 410–18)

Tradition in providing the answer to such questions stipulates that man must imitate God's way of accomplishing great things by lowly means of enterprise, 'ludibrious things'.[3] This is well illustrated in the statement made in 1628 by John Wall, the 'quaint preacher' of Oxford:

God hath chosen the weake things of *this world*, to confound the *mightie*. For it is his infirmitie, that makes vs strong. Neither are wee saved by the glorious maiestie of his soveraigne Deitie, but rather indeed, by the perfect obedience, of his despised humanitie. His power did create vs; his weakenes hath redeemed vs. We are framed by his omnipotencie; we are freed by his impotencie. Hee was humbled, that we might be

---

[1] See above, pp. 146, 150. Augustine's *De fide et symbolo*, VI, contains a classic statement on Jesus as the foremost exemplar of humility.

[2] Donne, *Sermons*, ix. 153, and Pascal, *Pensées*, § 392. Cf. Donne's *Hymne to God my God*, l. 30: 'that he may raise the Lord throws down.'

[3] Stephen Marshall, *Gods Master-piece* (1645), p. 20.

exalted: he was blasphemed, that we might be honoured: he was scourged, that wee might bee healed. He was crucified, that wee might bee glorified.[1]

Milton accepted the paradox with undeviating consistency. As early as 1642, in *The Reason of Church Government*, he emphasized 'the weak things which Christ hath made chois to work by', and repeatedly contrasted 'the mighty weakness of the Gospel' with 'the weak mightiness of mans reasoning'. In ampler exposition he stated:

who is ther almost that measures wisdom by simplicity, strength by suffering, dignity by lowliness, who is there that counts it first, to be last, somthing to be nothing, and reckons himself of great command in that he is a servant? yet God when he meant to subdue the world and hell at once, part of that to salvation, and this wholly to perdition, made chois of no other weapons, or auxiliaries then these whether to save, or to destroy. It had bin a small maistery for him, to have drawn out his Legions into array, and flankt them with his thunder; therefore he sent Foolishness to confute Wisdom, Weakness to bind Strength, Despisednes to vanquish Pride. And this is the great mistery of the Gospel made good in Christ himself, who as he testifies came not to be minister'd to, but to minister.[2]

Ten years later, while defending the republican cause before an international audience, Milton answered in these terms the biting remarks on his blindness ventured by his opponent Alexander More:

Neither am I concerned at being classed, though you think this a miserable thing, with the blind, with the afflicted, with the sorrowful, with the weak; since there is a hope, that, on this account, I have a nearer claim to the mercy and protection of the sovereign father. There is a way, and the Apostle is my authority, through weakness to the greatest strength. May I be one of the weakest, provided only in my weakness that immortal and better vigour be put forth with greater effect; provided only in my darkness the light of the divine countenance does the more brightly shine: for then I shall at once be the weakest and the most mighty; shall be at once blind, and of the most piercing sight. Thus, through this infirmity should I be consummated, perfected; thus, through this darkness should I be enrobed in light.[3]

---

[1] *The Lion in the Lambe* (Oxford, 1628), pp. 38–39. The concluding sentences echo a theological commonplace first argued by St. Athanasius: ὁ τοῦ Θεοῦ Λόγος . . . ἐνηνθρώπη-σεν ἵνα ἡμεῖς θεοποιηθῶμεν (*De Inc.* LIV, in *Patr. g.* xxv. 192). Cf. John Lewis: 'the Sonne of *God* was made the Sonne of man that the sonnes of men might be made the sonnes of God' (*Ignis cœlestis* (1620), p. 35).

[2] *RCG, Works*, iii. 243, 248 f.

[3] *Defensio secunda, Works*, viii. 73. This attitude was to sustain Milton during the subsequent vicious attacks by individuals like Sir Roger L'Estrange (*No Blinde Guides* (1660), reprinted in William R. Parker, *Milton's Contemporary Reputation* (Columbus, 1940), pp. 245–60). Cf. *SA*, ll. 1294–6.

Milton's last prose statement of this theme was written in 1659. As he then asserted, 'it is the councel and set purpose of God in the gospel by spiritual means which are counted weak, to overcom all power which resists him.' Men may do no less: 'Gods glory in the whole administration of the gospel according to his own will and councel ought to be fulfilled by weakness.'[1]

The same paradox is woven into *Paradise Lost*.[2] Michael's prophecy of the future leads to Adam's acknowledgement that God is

> by small
> Accomplishing great things, by things deemd weak
> Subverting worldly strong, and worldly wise
> By simply meek.
>
> (XII. 566–9)

Adam's immediate appeal to the Christ's example (572) looks ahead to *Paradise Regained* where 'the weak things which Christ hath made chois to work by' are defined in advance of his victory as

> Humiliation and strong Sufferance:
> His weakness shall orecome Satanic strength
> And all the World, and mass of sinful flesh.
>
> (I. 160–2)

Here we have the best exposition of the claim that Jesus performed 'deeds / Above Heroic' (I. 14 f.). As we noted earlier, that demonstration of 'heroism' involved the active exercise of patience before 'armies of difficulties'.[3] But it also involved obedience, the obedience 'unto death, even the death of the Cross' that in the historic Christ sprang out of his desire to seek, as he said, 'not mine own will, but the will of the Father which hath sent me' (Phil. ii. 8; John v. 30). Milton did not deviate from the witness of the New Testament. In *Paradise Regained* Jesus is always as ready to comply with the divine will as he is to add to divine glory (II. 259; III. 106 f.), notwithstanding his full awareness that his mission lies 'Through many a hard assay eev'n to the death' (I. 264).

Obedience to God has traditionally been interpreted in the light of the divine love revealed in and through the Christ. Its revelation ensures, therefore, that obedience is not tainted by servility but is

---

[1] *Of Civil Power*, *Works*, vi. 24, 33.

[2] There is a good summary of this theme in Thomas Greene, *The Descent from Heaven* (New Haven, 1963), pp. 388–94.

[3] See above, pp. 149 ff.

the free worship of God, arising from our gratitude for the love he displayed 'while we were yet sinners' (Rom. v. 8). 'Obedience', it has been said, 'means no more than love, and love fulfils every legitimate obedience.'[1] Jesus himself grounded obedience squarely on love: '*If* a man love me, he *will* keep my words' (John xiv. 23). St. Paul was just as insistent on the 'necessity' of our loving obedience to God and our loving service to our fellow men. As a commentator has observed,

> Obedience for Paul is the glad obedience of the son to the Father who has revealed Himself in Christ. It is the attitude of the recipient of free, unmerited grace to the gracious Giver. The new law is the love of Christ 'who loved me and gave Himself for me', which constrains a man to obey Him and serve all men.[2]

Love is free and yet 'constraineth' (2 Cor. v. 14). This paradox, one of the great commonplaces in Christian theology, appears in the religious literature of the Renaissance with appropriate frequency. We are '*bound*' by love, it was variously said, because 'love hath a compulsive facultie', 'an *Adamantine power*, that is able to draw the hardest heart'; it is 'a persuing and a conquering thing' that 'obligeth a Christian', a 'blessed necessity that compells us to do our Saviour service'.[3] Where the Old Testament commands, the New Testament obliges; where the Mosaic law demands, the Gospel constrains by love. Does this mean then that the Christ abrogated the Mosaic law? Peter Martyr gave this warning against hasty generalization:

> the substance of the olde Testament is not abolished. In dede ceremonies are abolished as touching the outward signes: howbeit the signification of thē abideth the selfe same that it was. Judiciall preceptes also, although in our dayes they be not all had in vse, yet the summe and principall scope of them, is still retained, namely, ẏ sinnes should be punished, and

---

[1] Paul Ramsey, *Basic Christian Ethics* (1953), p. 34. Cf. Hobbes's summary statement (brought to my attention by Professor J. P. Brockbank): 'obedience is sometimes called by the names of *charity* and *love*, because they imply a will to obey; and our Saviour himself maketh our love to God, and to one another, a fulfilling of the whole law' (*Leviathan*, ed. Michael Oakeshott (Oxford, 1946), p. 385).

[2] W. G. MacLennan, *Christian Obedience* (1948), p. 40, and further: James Moffatt, *Love in the NT* (1929), pp. 277 f. See also J. O. F. Murray, *The Obedience of the Cross* (1938).

[3] Seriatim: John Sherman, *White Salt* (1654), p. 97; John Stoughton, *XI. Choice Sermons* (1640), i. 5; Fonseca (above, p. 155, n. 2), p. 31; Samuel Rutherford, *Christ Dying* (1647), p. 442; John Worthington, *Charitas evangelica* (posthumous ed., 1691), p. 9; and William Sclater, *Sermons Experimentall* (1638), p. 9.

iustice preserved in comon wealths. But the sence and obseruation of morall preceptes, remaineth stil perfect & whole.[1]

If we claim that the Christ abrogated the Mosaic law, we must hasten to add that his abrogation did not render it obsolete. The Christ's 'law of love' has indeed reduced 'all *Moises* into a brief summe'[2] and yet, paradoxically, the *entire* law must now be fulfilled —'not because it is demanded', Melanchthon pointed out, 'but because the spiritual man cannot do otherwise'. This apparently absurd situation was even more forcefully put by Ralph Cudworth. 'Love', he declared, 'is at once a Freedome from all Law, a State of purest Liberty, and yet a Law too, of the most constraining and indispensable Necessity.'[3]

In *Paradise Lost* Michael's prophecy of the second Adam includes the assurance that

> The Law of God exact he shall fulfill
> Both by obedience and by love, though love
> Alone fulfill the Law.
>
> (XII. 402–4)

This is the final attempt in the poem to link obedience and love according to tradition. Two others occur earlier. Here is part of Raphael's admonition of Adam and Eve:

> Be strong, live happie, and love, but first of all
> Him whom to love is to obey, and keep
> His great command; take heed least Passion sway
> Thy Judgement to do aught, which else free Will
> Would not admit.   (VIII. 633–7)

'Him whom to love is to obey': it is not reason alone which should inform man that the right choice is obedience to the divine will; of far greater consequence is love, for love naturally, inevitably, yields obedience. Raphael had already said as much when he assured Adam and Eve that in time they would ascend to Heaven, provided they are

---

[1] Pietro Martire Vermigli, *Commentaries . . . upon . . . Romanes*, tr. H. B. (1568), fol. 82. This commonplace is treated fully by William Hinde, *The Office and Vse of the Morall Law* (1622).

[2] Luther, *A Commentarie . . . upon . . . Galatians*, tr. Anon. (1575), fol. 244ᵛ. See also his *Table-Talk*, ch. xii, and the full exposition by Thomas M. McDonough, O.P., *The Law and the Gospel in Luther* (1963). The views of Luther and Calvin are compared in Whale II (chs. iii, xi).

[3] Melanchthon, *LC*, p. 229; Cudworth (below, p. 172, n. 2), p. 76. Milton's views on the abrogated Mosaic law are in *DDC*, Bk. I, ch. xxvii.

> found obedient, and retain
> Unalterably firm his love entire
> Whose progenie you are.
>
> (v. 501–3)

To clarify the meaning of his words Raphael proceeds to acquaint
Adam and Eve with the state of affairs in Heaven. The argument
hinges on the old idea that God is served with 'voluntaries':

> Our voluntarie service he requires,
> Not our necessitated, such with him
> Findes no acceptance . . .
> My self and all th' Angelic Host that stand
> In sight of God enthron'd, our happie state
> Hold, as you yours, while our obedience holds;
> On other surety none; freely we serve,
> Because we freely love, as in our will
> To love or not; in this we stand or fall.
>
> (v. 529–40)

The obedience of the angels is not a coldly calculated act, nor does
it arise from fear of the punishment most certain to follow upon the
heels of disobedience. It springs from love: 'freely we serve, /
Because we freely love'. Milton's claim is the claim of Lancelot
Andrewes ('love breeds obedience'), of Jeremy Taylor ('Love is
obedient'), and of the whole Christian tradition.[1] Adam, not slow to
understand, pledges:

> we never shall forget to love
> Our maker, and obey him whose command
> Single, is yet so just.
>
> (v. 550–2)

'To love', 'to obey': are these echoes of the wedding ceremony
intentional? If so, Adam's pledge is transformed dramatically into
the outward seal of an inward covenant, which is a sacrament.

In *Paradise Lost* obedience is indeed 'the proper order of the
universe in relation to a universal law, the law of self-abnegation
in love'.[2]

---

[1] Taylor, *Holy Living*, 7th ed. (1663), p. 202; Andrewes, *A Pattern of Catechisticall
Doctrine* (1641), p. 143. For an extended treatment of the idea see William Freake, *Love
and Obedience* (1637), a sermon on John xiv. 15 ('If ye love me, keep my commandments'). Cf. Gal. v. 13: 'by love serve one another.'

[2] Charles Williams, 'Introduction', *The English Poems of John Milton* (1940), p. xi.
I must also commend the brilliant exposition of the idea of love in *PL* by Joseph H.

III

One of the most persistent strains in Christian thought has been the condemnation of sexual relations as inherently sinful. This tradition is implicitly manifest in the occasional claim that the *copula carnalis* was a result of the Fall,[1] and explicitly in the Augustinian thesis that Adam's sin was seminally transmitted to posterity. Yet such notions strike us as far less bizarre than attempts to establish that Jesus was born not from Mary's womb but from her navel or even her breast.[2] St. Augustine, haunted always by recollection of the life he led before his conversion, demonstrated his view of sex with the grim reminder that we are all born 'inter fæces et urinam'.[3]

Because such ideas could not be substantiated by the Bible, none was able to survive the Protestant adjustment of *humanae traditiones* to 'the standard of Scripture'. We may demur because that adjustment also involved the rejection of such defensible traditions as sacerdotal celibacy, but we cannot deny that the Reformers in both theory and practice revolutionized ethics. Accordingly the celebration in *Comus* of 'the sage / And serious doctrine of Virginity'[4] must be seen in the light not only of the Christian but of the specifically Protestant tradition. Neither virginity nor her handmaiden chastity —the 'Saintly chastity' of *Comus* (l. 453)—was regarded by the Reformers as a negative or limiting virtue leading to mere abstinence. Chastity is rather 'purity of life', the aggregate of 'the duties that touch the puritie of ones person'. Her proper companions are

Summers, *The Muse's Method* (1962), ch. iv. In *DR*, lxxx (1962), 243–9, James W. Douglas has argued correctly that in *PL* obedience and freedom are not opposed. The freedom championed by Satan is negative; it is also non-existent, since the Council in Hell progresses 'with all possible solemnity from Satan's plan to Satan's plan' (Irene Samuel, *PMLA*, lxxii (1957), 609).

[1] On Jerome's view of Adam and Eve's virginity see *NPNF*, 2nd ser. vi. 29, 398. The views of other Fathers, notably Origen and Gregory of Nyssa, are cited by E. C. Messenger, *The Mystery of Sex and Marriage* [*Two in One Flesh: II*] (1949), ch. ii; cf. Oscar D. Watkins, *Holy Matrimony* (1895), pp. 122 ff. The liberal tradition is best represented by Clement of Alexandria, *Stromata*, III. xvii. 102 (*LCC*, ii. 88).

[2] See G. Rattray Taylor, *Sex in History* (1953), pp. 61–62.

[3] *Apud* T. Clifton Longworth, *The Devil a Monk would be* (1936), p. 60. Yet Augustine did allow sexual relations before the Fall (*De civ.* XIV. 26: a remarkably frank discourse *not* translated in *NPNF*, iii. 281 f.).

[4] *Comus*, ll. 786 f. The parallel reference in *Areopagitica* to the 'sage and serious' Spenser has been noted by Edward S. LeComte, *Yet Once More* (1953), p. 8, and W. B. C. Watkins, *An Anatomy of Milton's Verse* (Baton Rouge, 1955), p. 94. The 'serious doctrine' itself is studied within its Christian context by Madsen, pp. 206 ff.

'modestie and temperance', and if she appears at all as abstinence it is only in the sense of 'abstaining from straggling lusts and al impurity', of 'cutting of all superfluity of naughtiness'. She originates in Heaven ('the seate of Chastitie'), and as the mortal enemy of all disorder she is

> that vertue of the minde,
> Which doth the Furiousnesse of Lust retaine
> In reasons bounds; And our affections binde
> In Royall Links of Vertues golden Chaine.[1]

As chastity extends her jurisdiction over both sexes alike, male chastity was also considered to be 'a pretious Jewel', indeed the 'most precious among the jewels of vertue'. As Milton explained it,

if unchastity in a woman whom Saint *Paul* termes the glory of man, be such a scandall and dishonour, then certainly in a man who is both the image and glory of God, it must, though commonly not so thought, be much more deflouring and dishonourable. In that he sins both against his owne body which is the perfeter sex, and his own glory which is in the woman, and that which is worst, against the image and glory of God which is in himselfe.[2]

Chastity, moreover, is not limited to the pre-marital state. Her nature is in fact double ('one of single life, another in wedlocke'). Hence Donne's characteristic statement that 'Marriage and Chastity consist well together', where chastity means not total abstinence but temperance, 'purity of life'. 'The best chastity of all', according to Owen Feltham, is 'Matrimoniall chastitie: when Paires keepe themselves in a moderate intermutualnesse, each constant to the other'.[3]

Milton's concern with 'purity of life' may seem like a precarious journey between the Scylla of indulgence, represented by his sanc-

---

[1] Seriatim: Nicholas Ling, *Politeuphuia* (1626?), p. 237; Sir Henry Finch, *The Sacred Doctrine of Divinitie* (1599), p. 27; Amandus Polanus, *The Substance of Christian Religion*, tr. Elijah Wilcox, 2nd ed. (1597), p. 250; Taylor (above, p. 164, n. 1), p. 66; Peter Smalle, *Mans May* (1615), sig. C3; and Robert Aylett, *Peace* (1622), p. 13.

[2] Seriatim: Burton (below, p. 170, n. 1), p. 570; Michael Jermin, *Paraphrasticall Meditations* (1638), p. 126; and Milton, *An Apology, Works*, iii. 306. It is possible that in *Comus* 'chastity' corresponds to Ficino's 'temperantia' (see John Arthos, *SR*, vi (1959), 261 ff.).

[3] Seriatim: Perkins, *Works* (Cambridge, 1605), p. 62; Donne, *Sermons*, iii. 131; Ling (as above, note 1); and Feltham, *Resolves*, 5th ed. (1634), p. 263. For a compendium of the standard views on marital chastity, see William Hergest, *The Right Rule of Christian Chastitie* (1580). Cf. Ames, pp. 368 ff. Earlier statements are legion: cf. Augustine, *De bono viduitatis*, XII, and Methodius, *Convivium decem virginum*, IX. 4 (*ANCL*, xiv. 99). Thus also Spenser, *Prothalamion*, l. 103.

tion of polygamy, and the Charybdis of abstinence, represented by his 'retraction' of the amatory verses of greener days.[1] But I think it hardly reasonable to stress either extreme at the expense of ideas Milton upheld with far greater consistency. Certainly the retraction can be dismissed as a harmless reiteration of a popular convention.[2] His approval of polygamy lies among the many strange conclusions reached by Protestants excessively devoted to the Old Testament,[3] or among the natural temptations of us all to cast an enviable glance in the direction of polygamous patriarchs.

The nature of the relations between Adam and Eve in *Paradise Lost* is coloured heavily by standard Protestant views on conjugal love.[4] No Protestant commentator ever denied that Adam and Eve 'knew' each other before the Fall, and neither does Milton. Indeed he insists on their physical love (IV. 488 ff., 741 ff.; VIII. 484 ff.) and refuses even to entertain the possibility that before Eve's creation Adam was 'of himselfe happy'.[5] If anything Adam is so distressed by his loneliness that he complains militantly to God: 'with mee / I see not who partakes' (VIII. 363 f.). This first instance of man's free will in action elicits God's immediate approval. A smile brightens the divine countenance and Adam is told:

> Thus farr to try thee *Adam*, I was pleas'd,
> And finde thee knowing not of Beasts alone,
> Which thou hast rightly nam'd, but of thy self,
> Expressing well the spirit within thee free
> . . . I, ere thou spak'st,

---

[1] The 'retraction' is appended to Elegy VII; polygamy is condoned in *DDC*, Bk. I, ch. i.

[2] See the numerous references supplied by J. S. P. Tatlock, *PMLA*, xxviii (1913), 521–9; Karl Young, *MLN*, xl (1925), 274–5; Aldo D. Scaglione, *Nature and Love in the Late Middle Ages* (Berkeley, 1963), pp. 19, 161; and James D. Gordon in *Studies in Medieval Literature*, ed. MacEdward Leach (Philadelphia, 1961), pp. 81–96. Augustine's celebrated retractions may, however, be only revisions (Meredith F. Eller, *CH*, xviii (1949), 172–83).

[3] Witness the practices of left-wing Protestants, discussed by George H. Williams, *The Radical Reformation* (Philadelphia, 1962), pp. 511 ff. The Catholic charge that Luther was 'dangerously . . . inclyned to Poligamie' is not an exaggeration: cf. James Anderton, *The Protestants Apologie* (St. Omer, 1608), pp. 395 f., with John Dillenberger and Claude Welch, *Protestant Christianity* (1954), p. 60.

[4] The best studies are by William and Malleville Haller, 'The Puritan Art of Love', *HLQ*, v (1942), 234–72, and Roland M. Frye, 'The Teachings of Classical Puritanism on Conjugal Love', *SR*, ii (1955), 148–59.

[5] Thomas Gataker, *Certaine Sermons* (1637), ii. 139. Boehme thought that Adam had been alone in the Garden for forty days (*Mysterium magnum*, tr. John Ellistone and John Sparrow (1654), pp. 80 f.). Milton's Adam, however, gets his Eve within a day.

> Knew it not good for Man to be alone . . .
> What next I bring shall please thee, be assur'd,
> Thy likeness, thy fit help, thy other self,
> Thy wish, exactly to thy hearts desire.
>
> (VIII. 437–51)

Milton's argument is Donne's argument: 'God loves not singularity.'[1]

Adam's relations with Eve develop within the circumference of 'Saintly chastity'. That chastity, we have seen, originates in Heaven and is 'receiued from the spirite of God.' All else is likewise God's gift: whatever beauty may be discerned in the universe is 'borrowed from God'; whatever perfection may be claimed by man is 'a beame of glorie issuing from God'; whatever virtue may be found in human beings is 'fetched from him'; whatever truth is accessible to us is 'a beame or lineament of God'; whatever wisdom we possess is 'his gift'.[2] Love too is 'supernatural', 'a gift from above', 'a Beam of Light, and Heat that comes from *Christ*', 'the only fountaine of our love'. 'God himself is love', wrote Jeremy Taylor, 'and every degree of charity that dwels in us, is the participation of the divine nature.' Milton shared this view and asserted that love is 'as a fire sent from Heaven to be ever kept alive upon the altar of our hearts, be the first principle of all godly and vertuous actions in men'.[3] This is restated in *Paradise Lost* when Adam and Eve confess spontaneously that their happiness and love are Heaven-sent (V. 520; VIII. 227 f.). The pattern that emerges is clear: human love is the counterpart of celestial love and derives its sustenance from Heaven.[4]

Not for long. As soon as Eve enters his life, Adam's attention begins to wander. He himself cites accurately his newfangled

---

[1] *Sermons*, ii. 279; cf. v. 113; vi. 81; viii. 155. On the God–Adam exchanges in Bk. VIII see C. M. Coffin (above, p. 51). The incident's 'humour' is noted by Roy Daniells, *Dalhousie Review*, xxxiii (1953), 159–66.

[2] Seriatim: Bullinger, *Fiftie . . . Sermons*, tr. H. I. (1587), p. 237; Charles Anthony, *Gods Presence* (1646), p. 32; Joseph Fletcher, *The Historie of . . . Man* (1629), sig. C3ᵛ; Francis Rous, *The Diseases of the Time* (1622), p. 27; John Gauden, *The Love of Truth* (1640), p. 10; and Richard Kilby, *Hallelu-iah* (1630), p. 19.

[3] Seriatim: Pascal, *Pensées*, § 829; Pierre du Moulin, *The Love of God*, tr. Richard Goring, 5th ed. (1628), p. 24; Samuel Rutherford, *Christs Napkin* (Edinburgh, 1633), p. 13; Henry Holland, *The Historie of Adam* (1606), sig. F2ᵛ; Taylor, *Holy Dying* (1651), pp. 67 f.; and Milton, *RCG*, *Works*, iii. 260. The *locus classicus* is of course 1 John iv. 11 ('love is of God'). The best discussion of the traditional views is John Burnaby's *Amor Dei* (1938).

[4] 'The harmony of Adam and Eve is the earthly counterpart of the harmony that reigns in Heaven; it is complete and satisfying because it is based on love' (C. M. Bowra, *From Virgil to Milton* (1948), p. 203).

experience: 'here passion first I felt / Commotion strange' (VIII. 530 f.). His account of the effect Eve has upon him is hardly calculated to please Raphael:

> when I approach
> Her loveliness, so absolute she seems
> And in her self compleat, so well to know
> Her own, that what she wills to do or say,
> Seems wisest, vertuousest, discreetest, best;
> All higher knowledge in her presence falls
> Degraded, Wisdom in discourse with her
> Looses discount'nanc't, and like folly shewes;
> Autoritie and Reason on her waite.
>
> (VIII. 546–54)

Adam, once 'in' love, has now 'fallen' in love. Raphael is visibly disturbed. He replies 'with contracted brow':

> Accuse not Nature, she hath don her part;
> Do thou but thine, and be not diffident
> Of Wisdom, she deserts thee not, if thou
> Dismiss not her, when most thou needs her nigh,
> By attributing overmuch to things
> Less excellent . . .
> What higher in [Eve's] societie thou findst
> Attractive, human, rational, love still;
> In loving thou dost well, in passion not,
> Wherein true Love consists not; Love refines
> The thoughts, and heart enlarges, hath his seat
> In Reason, and is judicious, is the scale
> By which to heav'nly Love thou maist ascend,
> Not sunk in carnal pleasure, for which cause
> Among the Beasts no Mate for thee was found.
>
> (561–6, 586–94)

The numerous Renaissance writers on psychology would have censured Adam with a brow as contracted as Raphael's. Nearly all regarded love as passion in the sense that the term comprehends 'every naturall and actuall motion in the soule'.[1] But they also

---

[1] La Primaudaye (below, p. 181, n. 1), p. 30. Love is included among the lists of passions given by Léonard Marandé, *The Judgment of Humane Actions*, tr. John Reynolds (1627), pp. 122–32; John Weemes, *The Pourtraiture of the Image of God* (1627), pp. 189–215; Coeffeteau (below, p. 170, n. 2), pp. 78–174; Edward Reynolds, *The Passions. . . of Man* (1640), pp. 74–110; *et al.* Raphael's 'scale of love' may be related to the Neoplatonic ladder of love in Spenser and others (see Edwin Casady, *PQ*, xx (1941), 284–95; James T. Stewart, *JEGP*, lvi (1957), 225–30; etc.).

thought that if love is cut off from its true source, which is God, it grows irrational and immoderate, becoming not so much a passion as a perturbation: 'if it rage', wrote Burton, 'it is no more love, but burning lust, a disease, Phrensie, Madness, Hell.' 'All Lust is Love degenerated, Love Corrupted', said Peter Sterry, and Bishop Joseph Hall agreed: 'the greatest danger of immoderation is in matter of lust; an impetuous passion, and that which commonly beares downe reason before it.'[1] Adam's statement that authority and reason wait on Eve is thus a flagrant violation of the conventional precept that love 'should follow the motions of reason'.[2] Hence Raphael's warning that sexual gratification bereft of rational love reduces man to the level of animals:

> if the sense of touch whereby mankind
> Is propagated seem such dear delight
> Beyond all other, think the same voutsaf't
> To Cattel and each Beast.
>
> (VIII. 579–82)

In 1607 Thomas Tuke remarked that the alternatives open to men are two: 'the one is of the way of loue, and leadeth vnto life, the other is the way of lust, and leadeth vnto death'. A few years later Bishop Godfrey Goodman likened the passion of lust to 'a burning fever, which with shaking fits, puts man into divers inordinate passions, and gives him the shape of a beast'.[3] From such statements we turn to Milton's description of the way of lust immediately after the Fall. Love that once was peace now is rage:

> As with new Wine intoxicated both
> They swim in mirth, and fansie that they feel
> Divinitie within them breeding wings
> Wherewith to scorn the Earth: but that false Fruit
> Farr other operation first displaid,
> Carnal desire inflaming; hee on *Eve*
> Began to cast lascivious Eyes, shee him
> As wantonly repaid; in Lust they burne.
>
> (IX. 1008–15)

---

[1] Seriatim: Burton, *The Anatomy of Melancholy*, 6th ed. (Oxford, 1651), p. 440; *Peter Sterry*, ed. V. de S. Pinto (Cambridge, 1934), p. 169; and Hall, *Christian Moderation* (1640), i. 73.

[2] Nicolas Coeffeteau, *A Table of Humane Passions*, tr. Edward Grimeston (1621), p. 99.

[3] Tuke, *The True Trial* (1607), p. 100; Goodman, *The Fall of Man* (1616), p. 113.

The student of Milton might well recollect the poet's earlier warning that those who fail to practise chastity 'are cheated with a thick intoxicating potion which a certain Sorceresse the abuser of loves name carries about'.[1] Are we to interpret the Fall as a violation of love no less than of 'degree'? The possibility deserves at least some attention and we may begin with the common opposition between love and pride.

Love is centrifugal, pride centripetal. Love 'seeketh not her own' (1 Cor. xiii. 5), 'delivers him that loves into the possession of that that he loves', 'drives a man out of himselfe, and makes him nothing in himselfe'.[2] Pride is selfishness: 'It hates Superiors, It scornes Inferiors, It ownes no equalls.' It is the state of any creature 'curved inwards upon himself' (*incurvatus in se*), and appears whenever man or angel 'setteth up himselfe instead of God', 'when *our selfe* is the circle, both center and circumference'.[3] It is what Augustine meant in his sharp distinction between *caritas* and *cupiditas*:

I mean by *caritas* that affection of the mind which aims at the enjoyment of God for his own sake, and the enjoyment of one's self and one's neighbour in subordination to God; by *cupiditas* I mean that affection of the mind which aims at enjoying one's self and one's neighbour, and other corporeal things, without reference to God.[4]

Custom has defined the sin of both Lucifer and Adam as pride because both were 'puffed up'.[5] The explanation proffered by Bishop Arthur Lake in 1629 is rightly apposite. The rebellious angels, he wrote, 'fixt their Eyes, and setled their Affection vpon themselues, that modell of Diuine being, which they had in themselues, and so fell in loue with themselues, and ouer-valuing their own worth, deemed themselues to be their own Soueraigne Good'. But Richard

[1] *An Apology, Works*, iii. 305.

[2] Donne, *Sermons*, i. 184, and John Preston, *The Breast-plate of Faith*, 5th ed. (1634), i. 58.

[3] Seriatim: Quarles, *Enchyridion* (1640), sig. F2; Luther, *apud* Whale II, p. 35; Sibbes, *The Christians End* (1639), p. 17; and Rutherford (above, p. 162, n. 3), p. 189.

[4] *De doctrina christiana*, III, x. 16 (*Patr. l.* xxxiv. 72; *NPNF*, ii. 561). The distinction invites us to consider Anders Nygren's classic thesis in *Agape and Eros*, tr. P. S. Watson (1954), which should be studied in the light of numerous corrections (as by Frederick C. Grant in *ATR*, xxxvii (1955), 67–73; A. H. Armstrong in *DR*, lxxix (1961), 105–21) and in relation to the NT view of ἀγάπη (on which see Gottfried Quell and Ethelbert Stauffer, *Love*, tr. J. R. Coates (1949), and esp. C. Spicq, *Agapè dans le Nouveau Testament* (Paris, 1958 f.), 3 vols.). A useful companion volume is C. S. Lewis, *The Four Loves* (1960).

[5] John Preston, *The New Covenant*, 9th ed. (1639), pp. 8 f. This common idea was intended as a contrast to 1 Cor. xiii. 4 ('charity . . . is not puffed up').

Sibbes even more directly anticipates *Paradise Lost* when he tells us that Lucifer and his disciples 'would be Gods by usurpation, and robbery, they were not content in the place they were in, but they would bee Gods, independent of themselues'.¹ The idea of independence from God, so roundly castigated by Milton, was denounced also by John Smith, the Cambridge Platonist:

that which first endeavoured a Divorce between God and his Creation, and to make a Conquest of it, was that Diabolical *Arrogancy* and *Self-will* that crept up and wound it self Serpent-like into apostate Minds and Spirits. This is the true strain of that Hellish nature, to live independently of God, and to derive the *Principles* from *another Beginning*, and carry on the line of all motions and operations to *another End*, then God himself, by whom and to whom and for whom all things subsist.

In Ralph Cudworth's parallel statement,

Happinesse is nothing but that inward sweet delight, that will arise from a Harmonious agreement between our wills and Gods will. There is nothing contrary to God in the whole world, nothing that fights against him but *Self-will*. . . . It was by reason of this *Self-will*, that Adam fell in Paradise; that those glorious Angels, those *Morning-starres*, kept not their first station. . . . Now our onely way to recover God & happines again, is not to soar up with our understandings, but to destroy this *Self-will* of ours.²

Milton's Eve obviously fell 'by reason of this Self-will'. Her Fall itself is forecast by two incidents that alike testify to her centripetal tendencies. The first occurred the moment after she was created. Alone in the Garden she chanced to rest by the green bank of a lake. This is her account of what happened:

> As I bent down to look, just opposite,
> A Shape within the watry gleam appeerd
> Bending to look on me, I started back,
> It started back, but pleasd I soon returnd,
> Pleasd it returnd as soon with answering looks
> Of sympathie and love.
>
> (IV. 460–5)

¹ Lake, *Sermons* (1629), i. 18–19; Sibbes, *The Fountaine Opened* (1638), ii. 7 [cf. his *Beames of Divine Light* (1639), ii. 202]. The angels' sin is also mentioned above, p. 93.
² Smith, *Select Discourses* (1660), pp. 399–400; Cudworth, *A Sermon preached . . . at Westminster* (Cambridge, 1647), pp. 19, 20. The castigation of self-will—'I, Mine, Me'— is also the theme of the *Theologia germanica*, a favourite of Luther's.

But the love affair is interrupted by the ever-present warning Voice.
Eve is led before Adam, takes a look at him, decides that he is

> less faire,
> Less winning soft, less amiablie milde,
> Then that smooth watry image,

—and promptly runs away. As Eve recounts her plight someone
other than Adam is also listening. The Monarch of Hell, now a
peeper, is collecting information needed to create the second important incident, Eve's 'high exaltation' in a dream (v. 30–93). We have
earlier dwelt on the subconscious meaning of that dream,[1] so we here
confine ourselves to Satan's attempt to instil in Eve a 'sense of
injur'd merit' similar to his own (I. 98; IV. 80). He therefore plants
in her mind the idea that she deserves to be 'among the Gods . . . a
Goddess' (IV. 77 f.), cultivates it during the temptation at high noon
(IX. 547 f., 568, 612, 684, 732), and finally sees it come to fruition
when Eve falls appetent after 'God-head' (IX. 790). Now 'curved
inwards' Eve plunges into a soliloquy.[2] Should she permit Adam to
partake of her happiness? Were it not better to retain it all herself so
as to be 'more equal' to him, perhaps even superior? But what if the
'great Forbidder' should render her extinct and give Adam another
Eve? Her final decision is not just immersed in irony; it is drowned
in it:

> I resolve,
> *Adam* shall share with me in bliss or woe:
> So dear I love him, that with him all deaths
> I could endure, without him live no life.
>
> (IX. 830–3)

So she bows before the Tree of Knowledge. The gesture may be
symbolic of her intention to 'live independently of God'. It amounts
to idolatry.

Whether Adam also fell 'by reason of this Self-will' is a matter of
controversy. His decision to share Eve's fate has been termed
variously 'true love', 'half-nobility', 'fullness of passion', and even
'frivolity'.[3] The first of these labels—'true love'—seems to have

---

[1] Above, pp. 105–6.

[2] 'The characters in *PL* do not soliloquise until they have fallen; unfallen speech and
gesture are directed always to another person, on the supreme model of light inter-
reflected by Father and Son' (J. B. Broadbent, *Some Graver Subject* (1960), p. 80).

[3] Seriatim: A. J. A. Waldock, '*PL*' *and its Critics* (Cambridge, 1947), p. 52; C. S.
Lewis, *A Preface to 'PL'* (1942), p. 122; Charles Williams (above, p. 164, n. 2), p. xv;

raised the most objections, yet many Renaissance commentators *did* claim that Adam's motive was 'love'. Adam, it was maintained, fell 'partely by the prouocation of the woman, whome greatlye he loued', 'whom he lov'd so much', 'who beeing his wife, yea his onely companion, was no doubt a great pleasure, joy, and delight vnto him'.[1] Adam's decision about Eve was indeed grounded on love, but when we consider the obligations they shouldered, other than towards each other, his 'true love' turns into 'immoderate love', an irrational 'excesse of loue'[2]—even, in Milton's phrase, into 'compliance bad' (IX. 994). Eve herself naturally does not think so. She greets Adam's decision with the cry,

> O glorious trial of exceeding Love,
> Illustrious evidence, example high!
>
> (IX. 961–2)

Milton rarely hit upon greater irony, for her cry is but a dreadful parody of the Son's 'unexampl'd love' (III. 410).

The Christian tradition postulates also that Adam sought to be 'cheekmate with God', to assume to himself—in the words of St. Ambrose—'that which he had not received, that thus he might become as it were his own maker and creator, and arrogate to himself divine honour'.[3] We may think that this interpretation possesses no relevance to *Paradise Lost*, yet Adam *is* discovered to be 'puffed up'. Fascinated by Eve's argument that she grew 'up to Godhead', he observes explicitly that the possibility of becoming 'Gods, or Angels Demi-gods' is an 'inducement strong' to violate any divine command (IX. 877, 934–7). As the Geneva Bible (1560) asserted in a marginal note to Genesis iii. 6, Adam fell 'Not so muche to please his wife, as moued by ambicion at her persuasion'. Seen thus Adam's 'true love' recedes again into self-love. We might consider that love is not love when it is mingled with regards that stand aloof from the entire point.

Once the golden chain of Adam and Eve's love has snapped, they

---

and Rajan, pp. 72, 156. For a valid exposition of the role of self-love in the Fall, see Arnold Stein, *Answerable Style* (Minneapolis, 1953), pp. 97 ff.

[1] Seriatim: John Udall, *Certaine Sermons* (1596), sig. B8ᵛ; Donne, *Sermons*, vii. 78 [following St. Jerome]; and Thomas Morton, *The Three-Fold State* (1629), p. 23.

[2] Erasmus, *De lib. arb.*, p. 22, and Thomas Cartwright, *Christian Religion* (1611), p. 42.

[3] Walter Wylshman, *The Sincere Preacher* (1616), p. 85, and Ambrose, *Epistolae*, lxxiii. 5 (*LF* (1881), p. 434). Cf. Baxter, i. 31.

find themselves isolated from God, from each other, and from themselves.[1] When they appear before God for judgement they are

> discount'nanc'd both, and discompos'd;
> Love was not in thir looks, either to God
> Or to each other, but apparent guilt,
> And shame, and perturbation, and despaire,
> Anger, and obstinacie, and hate, and guile.
>
> (x. 110–14)

'Man was never at odds with himself', wrote Glanvill as if commenting on *Paradise Lost*, 'till he was at odds with the commands
of his Maker.' Sibbes was equally emphatic: 'God punisheth our
rebellion to him, with rebellion in our selves.'[2] Milton brilliantly
exemplifies the familiar thesis when he shows us Adam unscrupu-
lously shifting upon the hapless Eve all responsibility for the Fall (x.
125–43). Nor does he fail to castigate her in a shocking speech after
judgement has been pronounced (x. 867–908). The air is thick with
recriminations:

> they in mutual accusation spent
> The fruitless hours, but neither self-condemning,
> And of thir vain contest appeerd no end.
>
> (ix. 1187–9)

As there was 'no end' to Adam and Eve's predicament, so there was
no end to the predicament of the fallen angels, who

> reasond high
> Of Providence, Foreknowledge, Will, and Fate,
> Fixt Fate, free Will, Foreknowledge absolute,
> And found no end, in wandring mazes lost.
>
> (ii. 558–61)

The chorus in *Samson Agonistes* is clear enough that those who sever
themselves from God

> give the rains to wandring thought,
> Regardless of his glories diminution;
> Till by thir own perplexities involv'd
> They ravel more, still less resolv'd,
> But never find self-satisfying solution.
>
> (ll. 302–6)

---

[1] This threefold isolation is discussed by Roland M. Frye, *God, Man, and Satan*
(Princeton, 1960), pp. 59 ff., and *Perspective on Man* (Philadelphia, 1961), pp. 126 ff.
[2] Glanvill, *The Vanity of Dogmatizing* (1661), p. 4; Sibbes, *Beames of Divine Light*
(1639), ii. 8.

'The mind diverted from God, wanders in Darkness and Confusion', said Whichcote,[1] and his observation is yet another 'commentary' on *Paradise Lost*.

Relations between Adam and Eve before the Fall were an extension of celestial love, so they were, after the Fall, patterned on the 'true love' between Satan and his daughter Sin (II. 761 ff.). But Adam does not merely share one of Satan's experiences; he shares also his 'inner Hell' (IV. 18 ff., 73 ff.; X. 842 ff.). The concept has behind it all the weight of tradition. In its duality ('every one begins his heaven, or his hell, even here in this world'), the unfathomable hell within was usually the one to be stressed. As Satan was commonly said to 'carry his hell about him', so every sinner was decreed well within 'the suburbs of Hell', or descending 'into the *hell* of his own *conscience*', or living 'continually vpon the racke'.[2] Nobody elaborated the theme more repeatedly than the Cambridge Platonists. To quote again from Whichcote,

> Men are of dull and stupid Spirits, who think that that State which we call *Hell*, is *an incommodious place*, only; and that God, by his Sovereignty, throws Men therein. For Hell arises *out of a Man's self*: And Hell's Fewel is *the Guilt of a Man's Conscience*. And it is impossible that any should be *so* miserable as Hell makes a Man, and as there a Man is miserable, but by his own condemning himself: And on the other side, when they think that Heaven arises from any *Place*, or any nearness to God, or Angels: This is not principally *so*; but *it* lies in a *refin'd Temper*, in *an internal Reconciliation to the Nature of God, and to the Rule of Righteousness*. So that both Hell, and Heaven, have their Foundation *within* Men.[3]

In *Paradise Lost*, after reading of the 'vain contest' between Adam and Eve, we are shocked by an occurrence both unexpected and

---

[1] *Select Sermons* (1698), p. 71.

[2] Seriatim: Timothy Rogers, *A Faithfull Friend* (1653), p. 33; Joseph Hall, *The Invisible World* (1659), p. 195; Jeremiah Dyke, *Tuuo Treatises*, 6th ed. (1635), i. 213 ff.; John Rawlinson, *Lex talionis* (1620), pp. 1 f.; and John Dod, *Seven . . . Sermons* (1614), p. 85. Here I need only cite one important precedent: Gregory the Great, *Moralia*, IV. 57 (*LF*, xviii. 223 ff.). Numerous other references and a full bibliography are given in my survey, 'Renaissance and Modern Views on Hell', *HTR*, lvii (1964), 227 ff. After the publication of *PL* Nathaniel Vincent compiled a compendium of the traditional views in *A Heaven or Hell upon Earth* (1676). The best discussion of Milton's use of the idea is by Ernest Schanzer, *UTQ*, xxiv (1955), 136–45.

[3] Above (note 1), p. 86, but also pp. 31 f., 95 f., 144, 180, 417, etc. Thus also [in p. 172, n. 2]: Cudworth, pp. 51, 72 f., and Smith, pp. 149, 446 f., 465 ff., etc. Cf. Peter Sterry, *The Teaching of Christ* (1648), p. 16, on 'the hellish fire flaming in our hearts'. Lust was frequently seen as 'a kinde of Hell'; see the references in R. M. Frye, *SR*, ii (1955), 156–8. Cf. M. Y. Hughes, *Ten Perspectives on Milton* (New Haven, 1965), ch. vi.

altogether out of character. No sooner has Adam delivered himself of a most vehement tirade against Eve than she kneels and implores his forgiveness (x. 909 ff.). What brings about this odd event? While the answer must await our discussion of 'prevenient grace',[1] here we may observe that Eve's centrifugal gesture of beseeching forgiveness on her knees 'constrains' Adam to repent. He raises her from the ground and resolves that both should

> strive
> In offices of Love, how we may light'n
> Each others burden in our share of woe.
>
> (x. 959–61)

Once more 'interinanimated' by their love, Eve at last addresses to Adam some of the loveliest lines in the entire poem:

> In mee is no delay; with thee to goe,
> Is to stay here; without thee here to stay,
> Is to go hence unwilling; thou to mee
> Art all things under Heav'n, all places thou. . . .
>
> (XII. 615 ff.)

We are reminded inevitably of her beautiful utterance before the Fall:

> With thee conversing I forget all time,
> All seasons and thir change, all please alike. . . .
>
> (IV. 639 ff.)

Upon this note of love regained they abandon Eden 'hand in hand'. 'If wee be at peace with God', Sibbes had written, 'all other peace will follow.' Even the loss of Paradise no longer matters, since now we possess 'our Soules Paradice', 'now *Paradise* is placed in man', now 'the Kingdom of God [is] within us'. As Richard Holdsworth, the Vice-Chancellor at Cambridge, pointed out in 1642,

Were a man in paradise, were he in heaven it self, and had not God; he could not be happy. Were he on Jobs dunghill, in Daniels den, in the belly of hell with Jonah, nay in the infernall hell with Dives, and yet had God; he could not be miserable: for heaven is wheresoever God is, because his influxive presence maketh heaven.[2]

---

[1] See below, pp. 203 ff.

[2] Seriatim: Sibbes, *Light from Heaven* (1638), ii. 255; Breton (above, p. 155, n. 1), sig. G2; Daniel Price, *The Spring* (1609), sig. B2; Joshua Sprigge, *A Testimony* (1648), p. 84; and Holdsworth, *A Sermon preached in St. Maries* (Cambridge, 1642), p. 34. See also above, pp. 112–3. The common reference here is to Luke xvii. 21 ('the kingdom of God is within you').

The burden of Michael's argument in *Paradise Lost* is the same. Before touching on the 'paradise within' (XII. 597), he counsels Adam never to doubt that

> in Vallie and in Plaine
> God is as here, and will be found alike
> Present, and of his presence many a signe
> Still following thee, still compassing thee round
> With goodness and paternal Love, his Face
> Express, and of his steps the track Divine.
>
> (XI. 349–54)

As the poem draws to its magniloquent close it dwells not merely upon God's 'influxive presence' but upon his 'paternal Love'. In contrast, Milton's contemporaries often conceived of the expulsion from Eden in the terms suggested by Samuel Austin in 1629: '*Adam* and his Mate / Were tumbled out at dores'. Nicholas Billingsley's God also appears impatient to get rid of them ('Be gone: be gone'). Du Bartas's version is not much better:

> Hence (quoth the Lord) hence, hence (accursed race)
> Out of my Garden: quick, auoyd the place,
> This beautious place, pride of the Vniuerse,
> A house vnworthy Masters so peruerse.[1]

For an instant Milton abandons his Protestant legalism, exchanges places with Dante and becomes too the poet of divine love, echoing St. John Chrysostom's sentiment that 'though God punish, though he plague, he doth it not with a wrathful passion, but with vnspeakeable gentlenesse.'[2]

IV

Dr. Samuel Johnson's dictum that Milton had a 'Turkish contempt of females' started a tidal wave that almost drowned Milton and threatened even Chaucer and Shakespeare. Chaucer somehow emerged into our century unscathed, but Milton remains enmeshed in his 'old grudge against the female sex' and Shakespeare is struggling to overcome recent rumours that his tragedies lack intelligent

---

[1] *Austins Urania* (1629), p. 10; Billingsley, Κοσμοβρεφία (1658), p. 68; Du Bartas, p. 252. The tendency among painters is equally 'foreign to the mood of Milton's ending of his poem' (Merritt Y. Hughes, *JEGP*, lx (1961), 670–9).

[2] *An Excellent Treatise touching the Restoration*, etc., tr. Robert Wolcomb (1609), p. 19.

women.[1] The situation is alarming. Can the tradition help us to salvage what is left of Milton?

Let us glance first at *Paradise Lost*. Upon the first appearance of Adam and Eve we are told that 'in thir looks Divine / The image of thir glorious Maker shon' (IV. 291 f.). As much is unhesitatingly conceded by Satan (IV. 363 f.). But in fact Eve is 'less / His image who made both', for she was created in the image or likeness of Adam (IV. 472; V. 95; VIII. 450, 543 f.). Milton laboured to explain the point. After citing Genesis i. 27 ('God created man in his own image, in the image of God created he him'), he observed:

had the Image of God bin equally common to them both, it had no doubt bin said, In the image of God created he them. But St. *Paul* ends the controversie by explaining that the woman is not primarily and immediatly the image of God, but in reference to the man. *The head of the woman*, saith he, 1 Cor. 11. [7.] *is the man: he the image and glory of God, she the glory of the man:* he not for her, but she for him.[2]

This *decretum horribile* was made worse by Milton's undeviating conviction that man's is 'the perfeter sex', that God has granted 'superior rights to the husband'.[3] But we have no cause for astonishment, since Milton's deplorable attitude was shared by the vast majority of his contemporaries. In that unchivalrous age almost everyone agreed that 'the Image of God is seene in man more perfectly', that 'God's image is *peculiar* to man above the woman', that indeed 'the woman is but the Image of man, as the man is the Image of God'.[4] Behind these affirmations loomed the Pauline verse also cited by Milton (1 Cor. xi. 7) and interpreted usually in the fashion indicated by Zacharias Ursinus:

the Apostle meaneth, that man only is the image of god, not in respect of his nature, being partaker of divine wisedome, righteousnes, & ioy; neither in respect of his dominion over other creatures: for these are

[1] Chaucer has been defended by Thomas R. Lounsbury, *Studies in Chaucer* (1892), i. 112–15. Shakespeare, who needs no defence, has been censured by G. M. H. Darroll in a superficial paper in *English Studies in Africa*, v (1962), 49–58. The judgements on Milton I quote are by Johnson, *Lives of the English Poets* (Everyman ed., 1925), i. 93, and E. M. W. Tillyard, *Milton* (1930; repr. 1949), p. 258.

[2] *Works*, iv. 76. Thus also in *DDD*: 'the woman was created for man, and not man for woman' (*Works*, iii. 475). Cf. *PL*, IV. 299.

[3] *Works*, iii. 306; xv. 121. Cf. Calvin on 'the preeminence which God has given to the man' (*Comm.: 1 Corinthians*, p. 232).

[4] Seriatim: Alexander Ross, *An Exposition on ... Genesis* (1626), p. 23; Robert Mossom, *Sion's Prospect* (1653), p. 54; and John Dove, *Of Diuorcement* (1601), pp. 57–58. Divers views are outlined by Corcoran, pp. 66 f.

comon to mã & woman: but in respect of civill, domesticall, & ecclesiastical order, in which, he will have the publike government & administration to belong vnto the man, not to the womã.[1]

On closer inspection, therefore, Milton's 'old grudge against the
female sex' turns out to be a grudge of universal proportions.

We find in Ecclesiasticus its fundamental principle: 'Of the woman
came the beginning of sin, and through her we all die' (xxv. 24). But
the whole Old Testament, as has been said, 'reflects the oriental
view of woman as an inferior creature, and the New Testament does
little to alter that view'.[2] When Christianity came into contact with
Graeco-Roman civilization the Biblical attitude was firmly cemented
with a fast balm. Thereafter the Fathers of the Church were as a
matter of course 'vitriolic in their contempt for women', and the
tradition extending through the Middle Ages caught up the humanists of the Renaissance. The learned Alberti came directly to the
point: 'Tutte sono pazze e piene di pulci, le femmine' ('They are all
crazy and full of fleas, the women').[3] It was the least adverse of comments and rather different from the constant reminders that the very
first woman was 'the Deuils instrument' and 'the cause of our
miserie'. Joseph Hall offers us a typical warning against women:
'*Adam*, the perfectest man, *Samson*, the strongest man, *Salomon*,
the wisest man, were betrayed with the flattery of their helpers.'[4]
Milton's contemporaries accordingly demanded that women should
retain their appointed place in the Scale of Nature. That place was
clearly indicated. Man is the woman's 'head and chiefe', her 'master
and Lord', and she may not aspire to equality with him ('a thing
prodigious and monstrous in nature') but remain always in 'comely
and Christian-like subjection to him'.[5] No compromise was deemed

---

[1] Ursinus, p. 129.

[2] George Whitehead, *Religion and Woman* (1928), p. 32. See also Derrick S. Bailey,
'The NT Doctrine of Subordination', in *The Mystery of Love and Marriage* (1952),
App. II.

[3] *Apud* Maurice Valency, *In Praise of Love* (1961), pp. 3, 287. Valency's fully docu-
mented survey (ch. i) is indispensable. A number of patristic passages are collected by
Whitehead (previous note), pp. 32–35. Cf. John Langdon-Davies, *A Short History of
Women* (1928), ch. iv.

[4] Seriatim: Harim White, *The Ready Way* (1618), p. 15; Thomas Palfreyman, *The
Treatise of Heauenly Philosophie* (1578), p. 598; and Hall, *A Recollection*, etc. (1621),
i. 931. See further T. F. Kinloch, *The Life and Works of Joseph Hall* (1951), pp. 70–72.
Curious notions had also evolved about Adam's 'crooked' rib used to create Eve (see
Svendsen, pp. 183 f.).

[5] Seriatim: John Downame, *The Summe of Sacred Diuinitie* (1630?), p. 71; Charron,
Of Wisdome, tr. Samson Lennard (1640), p. 487; Thomas Gataker, *Certaine Sermons*

possible. 'A wise woman', affirmed Pierre de la Primaudaye, 'ought to thinke that hir husbands maners are the lawes of hir life, which (if they be good) she is wholy to folow: but if they be bad, she must patiently beare with them.'[1]

I must on the other hand correct an erroneous impression that women were reduced to the status of slaves. Two frequently repeated ideas show that an honourable place was assigned to them. The first of these was of rabbinical origin, the second was sanctioned by St. Paul; and William Perkins expressed the first in these words:

the woman, when she was created, was not taken out of the mans head, because she was not made to rule ouer him; nor out of his feet, because God did not make her subiect to him as a seruant; but out of his side, to the end that man should take her as his mate.[2]

The Pauline idea was cited in nearly every treatise on 'domesticall duties'. It is his celebrated statement that the husband's relations with his wife are analogous to the Christ's relations with his Church:

Wives, submit yourselves unto your own husbands, as unto the Lord. For the husband is the head of the wife, even as Christ is the head of the

(1637), ii. 189; and Thomas Hilder, *Conjugall Counsell* (1653), p. 101. Among the standard expositions of the woman's subjection are: Bullinger, *The Christen State of Matrimonye*, tr. Miles Coverdale (1541), fols. 54 ff.; Vives (below, p. 184, n. 5), sigs. M8ᵛ ff.; Perkins (below, n. 2), chs. xi–xii; Matthew Griffith, *Bethel* (1633), pp. 322 ff.; and William Gouge, *Of Domesticall Duties*, 3rd ed. (1634), pt. iii. The subject has been studied fully by Chilton L. Powell, *English Domestic Relations 1487–1653* (1917), ch. v; Allan H. Gilbert, *MLR*, xv (1920), 7–27, 240–64; Louis B. Wright, *Middle-Class Culture in Elizabethan England* (Chapel Hill, 1935), ch. vii; William and Malleville Haller, *HLQ*, v (1942), 247–55; Corcoran, pp. 66–69; Caroll Camden, *The Elizabethan Woman* (1952), ch. v; Edward S. LeComte, *Yet Once More* (1953), pp. 123–36; Paul N. Siegel, *JHI*, xi (1960), 42–50; and Charles H. and Katherine George, *The Protestant Mind of the English Reformation* (Princeton, 1961), pp. 275–89. Inevitably, many writers *did* argue the equality or even superiority of women. Here Italians led the way (see Conor Fahy's list in *Italian Studies*, xi (1956), 30–55); in England David Clapam translated Agrippa's *Treatise of the Nobilitie and Excellencye of Woman Kynde* (1542), though there were some native products as well: Christopher Newstead's *An Apology* (1620); William Austen's *Haec homo* (1637); etc.

[1] *The French Academie*, tr. T. B. [Thomas Bowes?] (1586), p. 513.
[2] *Christian Oeconomie*, tr. Thomas Pickering (1609), p. 125. This popular idea is far more liberal than the original rabbinical notion (reported by Alfred Edersheim, *Sketches of Jewish Social Life* (1876), p. 146, and Ginzberg, i. 66). Renaissance restatements abound. See Bullinger (above, p. 180, n. 5), fol. 1ᵛ; Mossom (p. 179, n. 4), p. 54; Bucanus, p. 89; Nicholas Gibbens, *Questions and Disputations* (1602), p. 97; John Day, *Festivals* (Oxford, 1615), p. 193; Humphrey Everinden, *A Brothers Gift* (1623), § 27; Donne, *Sermons*, ii. 346; Griffith Williams, *The True Church* (1629), p. 418; Anthony Maxey, *Certaine Sermons*, 7th ed. (1634), p. 404; Richard Carpenter, *Experience*, etc. (1642), i. 62; *et al.*

church: and he is the saviour of the body. Therefore as the church is
subject unto Christ, so let the wives be to their own husbands in every
thing. Husbands, love your wives, even as Christ also loved the church,
and gave himself for it.   (Eph. v. 22–25)

Few Protestants, moreover, were prepared to ignore that although
one woman had been 'a chiefe instrument in [man's] fall', another
became 'a maine agent in his restauratiõ'.[1]

Milton's supposed 'contempt of females', Turkish or otherwise,
within the prevailing climate of opinion must be judged as an
impulsive stricture not even accidentally related to facts.[2] In the
Tetrachordon, for example, Milton's view of the wife's subordinate
status is in full accord with the spirit of St. Paul's attitude:

man is not to hold her as a servant, but receives her into a part of that
empire which God proclaims him to, though not equally, yet largely, as
his own image and glory: for it is no small glory to him, that a creature so
like him, should be made subject to him.[3]

But to appreciate the real extent of Milton's liberal views we must
also note his uncommon argument that while a wife must normally
be subject to her husband,

particular exceptions may have place, if she exceed her husband in prudence and dexterity, and he contentedly yeeld, for then a superior and
more natural law comes in, that the wiser should govern the lesse wise,
whether male or female.[4]

These quotations from the *Tetrachordon* invite us to consider all four
of Milton's tracts on divorce both for their own sakes and for the
light they shed on the relations between Adam and Eve in *Paradise
Lost*.[5]

Milton's principal aim in the four tracts was to plead for divorce
by mutual consent on grounds of mental incompatibility. His major

---

[1] Humphrey Sydenham, *Natures Overthrow* (1626), p. 6. On Protestant Mariology
see above, pp. 123–5.
[2] The most recent study of Milton's sympathetic portrayal of Eve is by Dorothy D.
Miller, *JEGP*, lxi (1962), 542–7. Other studies are listed above, p. 180, n. 5. The
reported misogyny of *SA* is equally erroneous, as shown by William R. Parker, *PQ*,
xvi (1937), 139–44.
[3] *Works*, iv. 76.   [4] Ibid. iv. 77.
[5] The first divorce tract was published in late July 1643. Edward Phillips claims that
Milton had married Mary Powell less than two months before (*The Early Lives of
Milton*, ed. Helen Darbishire (1932), pp. 63 ff.), but in fact the marriage had taken place
in 1642 (see Burns Martin, *SP*, xxv (1928), 457–61, and esp. B. A. Wright, *MLR*, xxvi
(1931), 383–400, and xxvii (1932), 6–23).

treatise, *The Doctrine and Discipline of Divorce* (1643), has been described as 'a marvel of eloquence and humanistic feeling', and he himself as Christendom's 'first protagonist' in the fight for divorce by mutual consent.[1] The price Milton paid for this distinction was certainly high. Instantly denounced by a number of his shocked contemporaries, he remained tarnished in reputation until the end of his life.[2] But the heaviest burden imposed upon him resulted from widespread omission to peruse carefully his tracts, and he was therefore grossly misrepresented, as, for example, in 1660 by 'G.S.', who accused Milton of proposing the husband's right to divorce his wife for any reason whatsoever, to 'turn her off, as soone, or as oft as his wayward spirit can find no delight in her'.[3] But here is an even earlier statement, written in 1649 by Bishop Hall, Milton's former antagonist in ecclesiastical affairs:

> I have heard too much of, and once saw a licentious pamphlet throwne abroad in these lawlesse times, in the defence, and incouragement of Divorces (not to be sued out, that solemnity needed not, but) to be arbitrarily given by the disliking husband, to his displeasing and unquiet wife; upon this ground principally, that marriage was instituted for the help and comfort of man; where therefore the match proves such, as that the wife doth but pull downe a side, and by her innate peevishnesse, and either sullen, or pettish and froward disposition brings rather discomfort to her husband, the end of marriage being hereby frustrate, why should it not, saith he, be in the husbands power (after some unprevailing means of reclamation attempted) to procure his own peace, by casting off this clogge, and to provide for his owne peace and contentment in a fitter match?
>
> Wo is me; To what a passe is the world come . . .[4]

However great the violence done to Milton's true views by such statements, they serve as valuable testimony of the aversion his age had for granting divorce on the grounds of mental incompatibility. Hand in hand with that aversion went recognition of fornication as

[1] E. H. Visiak, *The Portent of Milton* (1958), ch. ix, and Edward Westermarck, *Christianity and Morals* (1939), p. 358.

[2] See William Haller, *Tracts on Liberty in the Puritan Revolution* (1934), vol. i, App. B, and the passages collected by Parker (above, p. 160, n. 3), pp. 73–79, 170 ff.

[3] G. S. [Gilbert Sheldon?], *The Dignity of Kingship* (1660), p. 71. Cf. Robert Baillie, *A Dissuasive from the Errours of the Time* (1645), p. 116: 'Mr *Milton* . . . hath pleaded for a full liberty for any man to put away his wife, when ever hee pleaseth, without any fault in her at all, but for any dislike or dyspathy of humour.'

[4] *Resolutions and Decisions* (1649), pp. 389–90. Hall is probably (but not certainly) referring to Milton.

the single valid ground for divorce. As this was taken to be the Christ's own attitude (Matt. xix. 9), its 'flat contradiction' by Milton naturally horrified his contemporaries and obliged them to protest against his defence of divorce 'for many other causes besides that which our Saviour only approveth, namely, in case of Adultery'.[1] Milton's thesis, like that of Martin Bucer, was clearly formulated ages too early.[2]

Milton rested his case in part upon an appeal to the often used (and as often abused) 'fundamental law book of nature'.[3] Here as elsewhere the basic premise was the well-known idea that 'the first and most innocent lesson of nature [is] to turn away peacably from what afflicts and hazards our destruction'. But existing laws of divorce, Milton protested, have managed to 'turn nature upside down', to violate 'the reverend secret of nature' by frequently forcing 'a mixture of minds that cannot unite'. So long as 'what is against nature is against law, if soundest Philosophy abuse us not', the prohibition of divorce sought on grounds of mental incompatibility violates 'the venerable and secret power of natures impression' and must be reconsidered.[4] Surely the spiritual aspect of marriage ought to take precedence over the physical? 'In marriage', Thomas Aquinas had written, 'the union of souls ranks higher than union of bodies.' Humanists agreed. 'There canne be [no] maryage or concorde', said Vives, where man and wife 'agree not in wyll and minde, the whyche twoo are the beginning & seate of all amitie & friendship.'[5] An identical common sense pervades Milton's divorce tracts. As in *Paradise Lost* the happiness of Adam and Eve is conceived in terms of 'mutual help / And mutual love' (iv. 727 f.), so here Milton

---

[1] Ephraim Pagitt, *Heresiography*, 3rd ed. (1647), p. 150, and Daniel Featley, *The Dippers Dipt*, 5th ed. (1647), sig. A4. Cf. *West. Conf.* xxiv. 6. Yet some theologians rightly sensed that something was amiss. Bullinger, after noting that Jesus specified 'whordome' as the only 'ryght occasion of dyuorce', added: 'With the whych no doute he hath not excepted lyke & greater occasions but vnderstod & comprehended them therin' (above [p. 180, n. 5], fol. 77).

[2] Bucer's thesis in *De regno Christi* (1557)—partially translated by Milton in 1644— was denounced as 'lax and licentious', being 'too far advanced in its warm defence of divorce and re-marriage' (Constantin Hopf, *Martin Bucer and the English Reformation* (Oxford, 1946), ch. iii).

[3] *DDD, Works*, iii. 419. See above, pp. 79–88.

[4] *Works*, iii. 383, 417, 458; iv. 89, 117. Milton's appeal to natural law in the divorce tracts is also noted by Svendsen, pp. 216 f., and Ernest Sirluck, 'Introduction' to Milton's *Complete Prose Works* (New Haven, 1959), ii. 155 ff.

[5] St. Thomas, *S. th.* III. lvi. 1; Vives, *The Office and Duetie of an Husband*, tr. Thomas Paynell (1550?), sigs. K8–K8ᵛ. See also Donne's quotation from the Dominican theologian Domingo Bañez (*Sermons*, x. 214).

stipulated that a marriage is not worthy of the name unless it be grounded in mutual consent,

That consent I mean which is a love fitly dispos'd to mutual help and comfort of life; this is that happy Form of mariage naturally arising from the very heart of the divine institution. . . . This gives mariage all her due, all her benefits, all her beeng, all her distinct and proper beeing. This makes a mariage not a bondage, a blessing not a curse, a gift of God not a snare. Unless ther be a love, and that love born of fitnes, how can it last ?

In *Paradise Lost* Raphael insists that where there is no love there can be no happiness but only gratification of the senses, mere bestiality (VIII. 579 ff., 621). Milton's divorce tracts maintain similarly that 'where love cannot be, there can be left of wedlock nothing, but the empty husk of an outside matrimony; as undelightful and unpleasing to God, as any other kind of hypocrisie'. God did not institute marriage 'to remedy a sublunary and bestial burning', to have man and wife 'grind in the mill of an undelightful and servil copulation'. He rather decreed it as 'a sweet and gladsome society' consisting of 'unfained love and peace', 'founded in the sweet and mild familiarity of love and solace and mutual fitness'.

God in the first ordaining of mariage, taught us to what end he did it, in words expresly implying the apt and cheerfull conversation of man with woman, to comfort and refresh him against the evill of solitary life, not mentioning the purposes of generation till afterwards, as being but a secondary end in dignity, though not in necessity.

'The rib of Mariage,' Milton further observed, 'the nerves and sinews thereof are love and meet help.' To think of marriage as 'the union of peace and love' is to define its essence, to focus on its 'inward knot', on the 'blest subsistence of a Christian family' that is alone able to 'give a human qualification to that act of the flesh, and distinguish it from bestial'.[1]

Milton's argument that love is 'the soul of wedloc' is enforced at key intervals by the traditional analogy of the Christ as the soul of the Church. Thus at one point husbands are urged to love their wives 'in such wise . . . as the Church is belov'd of Christ'; at another, conjugal love is said to be 'such a love as Christ loves his Church'; and finally marriage is described as 'the dearest league of love, and

[1] Seriatim: *Works*, iv. 106; iii. 402, 416, 403, 400; iv. 262, 93; iii. 382; iv. 101, 127; iii. 416, 376; iv. 99.

the dearest resemblance of that love which in Christ is dearest to his Church'.[1] The generous compass of Milton's thesis was widened as he went on to comprehend his belief in the potentialities of 'the divine and softening breath of charity'. 'Our Saviours doctrine', he affirmed, 'is, that the end, and the fulfilling of every command is charity; no faith without it, no truth without it, no worship, no workes pleasing to God but as they partake of charity.' 'This', he added, 'is the greatest, the perfectest, the highest commandment', 'a command above all commands', 'the summ of all commands, and the perfection', 'the supreme dictate', 'whose grand commission is to doe and to dispose over all the ordinances of God and man; that love & truth may advance each other to everlasting'. As the concluding sentence of *The Doctrine and Discipline of Divorce* has it, 'God the Son hath put all other things under his own feet; but his commandments he hath left all under the feet of Charity.'[2]

[1] Ibid. iv. 126 f., 79, 192, 253. See also iv. 126 and 244.
[2] Ibid. iv. 96, 135, 172; iii. 511; iv. 186; iii. 396, 496, 511.

7

Prevenient Grace Descending

THE CONCEPT OF GRACE

A Christians strength lies out of himselfe.
RICHARD SIBBES[1]

I

'It is God that justifieth', 'through the redemption that is in Christ Jesus' (Rom. viii. 33, iii. 24). St. Paul's assertion that the salvation of man is exclusively the work of God is a dogma common to the whole Christian family. Equally common is the stipulation that 'the just shall live by faith', that we are indeed 'justified by faith' (Rom. i. 17, iii. 28). The import of Paul's statements is normally explained in these terms:

by justification St. Paul means the gracious action of God in accepting men as righteous in consequence of faith resting upon his redemptive activity in Christ. . . . The ground of the justifying act is God's redemptive work, and the conditioning cause is faith, but it is the interaction of both which brings a man into right relations with God.[2]

Milton's interpretation in *De doctrina christiana* is couched in the forensic terminology characteristic of all Protestant expositions:

justification, in so far as we are concerned, is gratuitous; in so far as Christ is concerned, not gratuitous; inasmuch as Christ paid the ransom of our sins, which he took upon himself by imputation, and thus of his own accord, and at his own cost, effected their expiation; whereas man, paying nothing on his part, but merely believing, receives as a gift the imputed righteousness of Christ.[3]

[1] *Yea and Amen* (1638), p. 92.
[2] Vincent Taylor, *Forgiveness and Reconciliation* (1946), p. 48.
[3] *Works*, xvi. 27–29; cf. *PL*, XII, 294–7. While 'justification' originally meant 'truly to be forgiven' (Oman [below, p. 198, n. 2], p. 230), Protestants have traditionally insisted on the forensic terminology discussed earlier (above, pp. 135 ff.).

'Merely believing': we are face to face with the expressly
Protestant emphasis on justification by faith alone, rightly described
by one of Milton's Catholic contemporaries as 'the soule, hinges,
and summe of Protestancy'.[1]

It was also a doctrine that often scorched the hands that touched
it. Lit by Luther, it raced wildly across Western Europe setting fire
to the territory on which extremists took their stand and threatening
the existence of Christianity as a socially conscious *ecclesia*. Violent
controversies broke out as Protestant turned on Protestant, and all
against the 'triple Tyrant' at their door. Catholics smote back with
a series of accusations, two of which always managed to send Protestants into paroxysms of fury. One was that the Protestant interpretation of 'justification' elevated faith to the utter detriment of works;
the other, that their doctrine was 'vnknowne in the age before
Luther'.[2] Other charges may have been either true or false; these two
were both. It was certainly true that the Lutheran dogma was novel,
for at no other time had faith been given such absolute primacy; and
yet it was a false charge, since Protestants could—and did—invoke
the support of many Fathers, relying, for example, on the statement of 'Ambrosiaster' that whoever believes in the Christ shall be
saved without works, freely receiving forgiveness of sins by faith alone
('qui credit in Christum, salvus sit sine opere: sola fide gratis accipit
remissionem peccatorum').[3] As for the charge that works were subordinated totally to faith, the truth is that Protestants aimed at
nothing less, the falsehood that they insisted on nothing more. The
point deserves a closer look.

Luther's devotion to the letters of St. Paul went hand in hand

---

[1] Richard Smith, *Of the Author and Substance of the Protestant Church*, tr. W. Bas.
(St. Omer, 1621), p. 291. Among the most lucid Protestant expositions of the doctrine
are the *Conf. Aug.*, Art. IV (Tappert, pp. 107–68) and Richard Hooker, *A Learned Discourse of Iustification* (Oxford, 1612), pp. 3 ff. See also the influential statement by
Martin Chemnitz, *Examinis Concilii Tridentini* (Frankfurt, 1596), i. 153 ff.; Heppe,
ch. xxi; and *Angl.*, pp. 296–306. There is a substantial commentary by E. G. Rupp,
Studies in the Making of the English Protestant Tradition (Cambridge, 1947), ch. viii.
The dogma's development in Luther is traced by Preserved Smith, *HTR*, vi (1913),
407–27; but see also the related essays by A. Skevington Wood, *SJT*, iii (1950), 1–18,
113–26, and George W. Forell, *Faith active in Love* (Minneapolis, 1959), pp. 84 ff. The
Tridentine decree (1547) is in Denzinger, §§ 793 ff.

[2] James Anderton, *The Protestants Apologie* (St. Omer, 1608), p. 453.

[3] *Comment. in epist. I ad Corinthios*, I. 4 (*Patr. l.*, xvii. 195). The statement was often
quoted, as in the *Conf. Aug.*, Art. VI (Schaff, iii. 11). Other Fathers (Origen, Hilary, Basil
the Great, John Chrysostom, *et al.*) were cited with less justice. For two lists see Cranmer,
Selected Writings, ed. C. S. Meyer (1961), pp. 15 f., and John Copley, *Observations*
(1612), pp. 57 ff.

with his antipathy toward the Epistle of James. This was inevitable, since James—as Catholics delighted to point out—stands in fundamental opposition to Paul ('by works a man is justified, and not by faith alone').[1] But Luther was not even pleased by Paul's own statements, whereupon in his version of the Bible he amended the Epistle to the Romans by introducing the crucial word 'alone' ('a man is justified by faith [alone] without the deeds of the law').[2] Such peculiar conduct is comprehensible only if we take account of Luther's passionate efforts to uphold faith even—as Catholics charged—at the expense of works. It is hard to believe that he did not foresee the immediate consequences of his doctrine. In 1609 the 'remarkable preacher' Daniel Price reported them in these terms:

The conflict betweene vs and our aduersaries about Faith and fruites hath beene much, they in to much aduancing them, some of vs too much extenuating them, they so earnest for fruites, that little lesse then blasphemously they affirm that they deserue Saluation: We so negligent in fruites, that to doe a good worke, we think it superstition, they so much hanging on the branches, wee so much rooting at the roote, as if wee would sue out a diuorce betweene Faith and Fruites, neither of vs looking to the moisture of the roote or branches.[3]

Both sides had sought the moisture. The Catholics, reputedly confident in the efficacy of their fruits, replied through the Council of Trent with an anathema on any who should claim that 'man may be justified before God by his own works . . . without the grace of God through Jesus Christ'. The Protestants, said to be 'negligent in fruites', asserted through the Formula of Concord that all Christians are 'debtors to do good works'.[4] Individual apologists were equally explicit. From the Protestant side came categorical statements that

---

[1] Jas. ii. 24. In England the first invocation of this verse was by John Cardinal Fisher in *The Sermon . . . agayn . . . Martin Luuther* (1521 ?), sig. C1. On Luther's view see his *Reformation Writings*, tr. B. L. Woolf (1956), ii. 306–8, but also the observations of Willem Jan Kooiman, *Luther and the Bible*, tr. John Schmidt (Philadelphia, 1961), pp. 110–15, and the comprehensive study by Gustav Kamerau, 'Die Schicksale des Jakobusbriefes im 16. Jahrhundert', *Zeitschrift für kirchliche Wissenschaft*, x (1889), 359–70.

[2] Rom. iii. 28 ('der Mensch gerecht werde ohne des Gesetzes Werke [allein] durch den Glauben'). See Luther's 'explanation' of this translation in Whale II, pp. 73 f.

[3] *The Spring* (1609), sig. D1ᵛ.

[4] Schaff, ii. 110; iii. 121–6. Cf. Rondet (below, p. 198, n. 2), ch. xv, and Heppe, pp. 576 ff. For one remarkable moment during the Colloquy of Ratisbon (1541), Cardinal Contarini and Melanchthon managed to agree even on the meaning of 'justification by faith'.

'a true iustifying faith cannot want his fruites', that 'the true faith-full . . . diligentlie and feruentlie exercise & declare their fayth by good workes', that 'The life of a Christian is his faith, the life of his faith, is his good workes'. John Foxe enthusiastically counselled his congregation to attain what he called (not very happily I think) a 'coniũctiõ copulatiue':

> Joyne the lyuely fayth of S. Paul, with the good workes of S. Iames and bryng both these into one lyfe: and thẽ hast thou reconciled them both . . . Fayth without workes, maketh but a carnall Gospeller. Workes without fayth make but a Pharisaicall hypocrite.

Donne commended the same principle by a brilliant reduction of the two controverted terms to the two commandments: 'love God, and love thy Neighbour, that is, faith and works'.[1]

Protestant apologists never compromised their belief in justification as a God-initiated, God-conducted process that subsequently —only subsequently—'constrains' the faithful to perform good works. If occasionally we encounter extreme statements, it is well to remember that their constant aim was to deflate man's presumptuous confidence in his own abilities. As Bishop John Woolton observed in 1576,

> many take offence with this proposition, which wee preache and teache: That men are iustified by faith onelie in Christe: It is because they doo not vnderstande our doctrine in that behalfe. For we meane nothing lesse, then to reiecte, or take awaye good workes, and honest actions: but wee onelye exclude confidence, and trust in mennes workes, which haue no place at all in iustyfication.

Was it possible for any claim to be further removed from the Catholic position? The difference is the difference stated by Nehemiah Rogers, one of Milton's contemporaries, who readily admitted that both Catholics and Protestants assert the importance of works, yet equally readily pointed out that while 'they say good workes are necessary to Iustification as being Causes of it, wee say they are necessary to Iustification as being Effects thereof'. The balance achieved by Protestants was probably well enough set forth in 1632 by John Ball who was not an Anglican but a 'Puritan':

---

[1] Seriatim: Lucas Osiander, A Manuell . . . of Controuersies, tr. Anon. (1606), p. 187; Bullinger, fol. 215; Jerome Phillips, The Fisherman (1623), p. 7; Foxe, A Sermon of Christ Crucified (1570), fols. 67ᵛ, 68; and Donne, Sermons, ii. 256. Luther's thesis is most clearly set forth in De libertate christiana, tr. James Bell, The Libertie of a Christian (1579). See also Zwingli's exposition in LCC, xxiv. 269 ff.

The power to belieue, and will to vse that power, is of God: But the act of the will in resting vpon Christ is mans. It is man that belieueth, but it is God only & altogether that inableth, stirreth vp, putteth forward and inclineth the heart to belieue. By Gods enlightening man seeth, by his teaching he vnderstands: and the Lord inclining his will, he willeth, embraceth, possesseth and keepeth Christ with all blessings promised in him. So that faith is the motion of mans heart wrought in him by the Spirit of God.[1]

Milton achieved the same balance. In *Paradise Lost* the Father's reference to 'Faith and faithful works' is echoed later by Michael when he commends to Adam 'Faith not void of works' (XI. 64; XII. 427). The two observations are based on the general principle that man's justification by faith depends on the imputation of the Son's merit (XII. 295, 409; cf. XI. 35 f.). In Book III, the Protestant Father informs his Protestant Son:

> [Adam's] crime makes guiltie all his Sons, thy merit
> Imputed shall absolve them who renounce
> Thir own both righteous and unrighteous deeds,
> And live in thee transplanted, and from thee
> Receive new life.
>
> (III. 290–4)

De doctrina christiana also expounds the distinctly Protestant thesis that 'it is faith alone that justifieth'. Yet man's justification, Milton added, must be through 'a faith not destitute of works', 'by a living, not a dead faith; and that faith alone which acts is counted living'.[2]

II

According to St. Augustine's celebrated distinctions, man's journey from the Garden of Eden to the Kingdom of God is divisible into three merging states. The first extended from the moment of creation to the moment of the Fall, and its characteristic was man's ability to avoid sin (*posse non peccare*). The second state already existed before the Fall though it properly encompassed the period from the Fall to the end of history. In it man became capable of

---

[1] Seriatim: Woolton, *The Christian Manuell* (1576), sig. C3ᵛ [echoing Calvin, *Inst.* III. xiv. 18]; Rogers, *The Penitent Sinner* (1640), p. 267; and Ball, *A Treatise of Faith*, with a preface by Sibbes (1632), p. 12.

[2] *Works*, xiv. 123; xv. 339; xvi. 39. The concept of justification is discussed fully in DDC, Bk. I, ch. xxii, which should be read together with Bk. II, ch. i, 'De bonis operibus'.

sinning (*posse peccare*). The third state is the one in which the angels presently find themselves. Man can hope to attain it in the world to come, yet were he by grace reborn, he could even attain it now. In this state he would be incapable of sinning (*non posse peccare*).[1]

The creation of man 'chaungeably good', 'fall-able'—the Augustinian *posse peccare*—has not always elicited the approval of Christian apologists. Their objection rested on the unhappy premise that 'free-will overthrew us', that 'we were no sooner Made, then Fallen; because we stood vpon the tottering Sands of our owne Freedom'. Bishop Henry King smiled as he contemplated the alternative. Presumably, he wrote, God should have created Adam a mere marionette, 'He should haue lockt him vp against all attempts by making him impregnable, and deafe to the tongue of the Charmer'. King's opponents were not amused. Overwhelmed by their belief in the disastrous consequences of the Fall, they were much more prepared to sympathize with the anguished cry of François Lambert, one of the earlier French Reformers: 'O Lorde God what a pestilente doctrine is this in the churche of Christ, of free wyl. . . .' But as lamentations were hardly theology, every conscientious apologist sped in pursuit of authoritative evidence to bolster his convictions. Inevitably each found what he wanted to find. In the triumphant declaration of François de Croi, 'the holy Scripture, and the Councels that are of sound iudgement, haue ouerthrowne the doctrine of free will'.[2]

Actually the overthrow was largely the work of Luther and Calvin. Calvin did not hesitate to implicate God directly in the Fall of Man. 'In the hidden counsel of God', he wrote, 'it was determined that Adam should fall from the unimpaired condition of his nature, and by his defection should involve all his posterity in sentence of eternal death.' Luther was just as brutal, for he thought of man's will as manipulated in accordance with the wishes of God or Satan:

man's will is like a beast standing between two riders. If God rides, it wills and goes where God wills . . . If Satan rides, it wills and goes where

---

[1] *Enchiridion*, cv (*LCC*, vii. 403), and esp. *De correptione et gratia*, xxxiii (*Patr. l.* xliv. 936; Kelly, p. 362).

[2] Seriatim: Beza, *Christian Questions*, tr. Arthur Golding (1574), fol. 66; Bullinger, *Fiftie . . . Sermons*, tr. H. I. (1587), p. 487; William Struther, *True Happines* (Edinburgh, 1633), p. 14; John Gaule, *Practique Theories* (1629), p. 17; King, *An Exposition upon the Lords Prayer* (1634), p. 285; Lambert, *The minde and Iudgement*, tr. N. L. (1548), fol. 16; and Croi, *The Three Conformities*, tr. W. Hart (1620), p. 99.

Satan wills. Nor may it choose to which rider it will run, or which it will seek; but the riders themselves fight to decide who shall have and hold it.[1]

Luther and Calvin may stand accused of divers odd notions, but not of any attempt unduly to compliment and flatter fallen man. Their view was assured and exaggerated by countless other Protestants. John Prime, for example, in 1583 proclaimed with fervour that

In the plenarie view of man both within & without, in body & soule, in whole and in part, appeareth nothing since his fal, but misery, bondage, pollutiõ, vncleannes, darknes, confusiõ, frowardnes, obstinacy, rebellion, and (in a worde) perfit sinne & corruption.[2]

Catholics were certainly scandalized. Edmund Campion, the Jesuit martyr, was horrified that anyone could believe man to be 'so vtterly ouerthrowne, as that not euen anie *Regenerate and holie man* is intrinsecally anie other thing then *meare Corruption, and contagion*, as being in league with all vice'.[3] On the other hand a growing number of Protestants also wondered whether man's depravity was as wholesale as Calvin and especially his extremist disciples claimed. It was, after all, plain to all save these partisan zealots that the Christian tradition does not support any theory of man's total depravity. Indeed, it is at one with Tertullian, who declared that man is 'master of his own will and power', and with Irenaeus, who declared likewise that he is 'a free agent from the beginning, possessing his own power, even as he does his own soul, to obey the behests of God voluntarily, and not by compulsion of God'.[4] Augustine may often have been extreme ('it was in the evil use of his free will that man destroyed himself and his will at the same time'), yet he never denied that man has at least 'a little spark left him of that reason whereby he was like the image of God'.[5] The

---

[1] Calvin, *Articles concerning Predestination*, in *LCC*, XXII. 179 [cf. *Inst.* III. xxiii. 8]; Luther, *De serv. arb.*, pp. 103 f. [cf. *A Commentary on . . . Galatians*, tr. P. S. Watson (1953), pp. 223 f.]. See also *West. Conf.* ix. 3.

[2] *A Frutefull and Briefe Discourse* (1583), pp. 39–40. This entire work is a sweeping attack on 'freewillmen'. See further above, pp. 98 ff.

[3] *Campian Englished. Or . . . the Ten Reasons*, tr. Anon. (Douai? 1632), pp. 133–4.

[4] Tertullian, *Adversus Marcionem*, II. 5 (*ANCL*, vii. 70); Irenaeus, *Adversus haereses*, IV. xxxvii. 1 (*ANCL*, ix. 36). See also Origen, *De pr.* I. v. 5. The most decisive Catholic assertion of free will is by Thomas Aquinas, *S. th.* I. lxxxiii. The classic statement in poetry is by Dante (*Par.* v. 19–24). For the Tridentine formulation see Schaff, ii. 111.

[5] *Enchiridion*, xxx (*LCC*, vii. 356); *De civ.* XXII. 24. The latter is the source for the common affirmation of the 'sparkes' or 'reliques' still possessed by man (Milton, *DDC*, *Works*, xv. 208, and xvi. 100; John Woolton, *Anatomie of Whole Man* (1576), sig. A1; John Downame, *The Summe of Sacred Divinitie* (1630?), sig. 2ᵛ; William Whitaker in

qualification was necessary if only to save appearances; for as Jeremy Taylor pointed out in *Deus justificatus* (1656),

> If by the fall of *Adam*, we are so wholly ruined in our faculties, that we cannot do any good, but must do evill; how shall any man take care of his wayes? or how can it be supposed he should strive against all vice, when he can excuse so much upon his Nature? or indeed how shall he strive at all? for if all actual sins are derived from the Originall, . . . then no man can take care to avoid any actuall sinne, whose cause is naturall, and not to be declined.

Calvinists like Anthony Burgess may anxiously have objected that Jeremy Taylor is 'not meerly Pelagian, Arminian, Papist, or Socinian, but an hotchpotch of all', yet Taylor's statement is backed by the Christian tradition; and, moreover, a majority of Protestants agreed with Arthur Dent, the popular Puritan divine, that '*Adams* will was neither forced, nor by any violence of Gods purpose compelled to consent: but he of a free will and ready mind left God, and joyned with the Divell'.[1]

The same classic principle is voiced by Milton in both *Paradise Lost* and *De doctrina christiana*. In his treatise he proposes according to terms valid in tradition that 'God of his wisdom determined to create men and angels reasonable beings, and therefore free agents'. He follows his theological argument with this philosophical justification:

> for the purposes of vindicating the justice of God, especially in his calling of mankind, it is much better to allow man (whether as a remnant of his primitive state, or as restored through the operation of the grace whereby he is called) some portion of free will in respect of good works, or at least of good endeavours.[2]

But in *Paradise Lost*, if we may judge by the opinion of one reader, Milton was Arminian in his exposition of free will even while presenting 'essentially the God of Calvinism'.[3] This, if true, was an

---

his *Answere* to Campion, tr. Richard Stocke (1606), pp. 216 f.; Dent [next note], p. 7; et al.).

[1] Seriatim: Taylor, *Deus justificatus* (1656), p. 95; Burgess, *The Doctrine of Original Sin* (1658), p. 30; and Dent, *The Plaine-mans Path-way to Heaven*, 25th ed. (1640), pp. 304–5.

[2] *Works*, xiv. 83; xv. 213. The equation 'reasonable *hence* free' is traditional. Cf. John of Damascus, *De fide orthodoxa*, II. 7: ὅθεν πᾶν λογικόν, καὶ αὐτεξούσιον. Variations occur in *Areopagitica*, *Works*, iv. 319 ('reason is but choosing') and *PL*, III. 108 ('Reason . . . is choice').

[3] These opposites are yoked together in a juvenile work by Earle E. Cairns, 'The Theology of *PL*', *Bibliotheca Sacra*, cv (1948), 478–91; cvi (1949), 106–18, 211–15. But

incredible feat; but it is not true. The relevant passages in the epic[1] keep entirely within the Christian tradition; none, I think, can reasonably be located on its periphery. Sufficiently typical is Raphael's categorical denial that the earth is overshadowed by the high overleaped mountains of necessity. As he informs Adam,

> God made thee perfet, not immutable;
> And good he made thee, but to persevere
> He left it in thy power, ordaind thy will
> By nature free, not over-rul'd by Fate
> Inextricable, or strict necessity.
>
> (v. 524-8)

Milton was never so naïve as to miss the grave problems bedevilling the concept of free will. In *De doctrina christiana* he touched upon one of them. 'The liberty of man', he said, 'must be considered entirely independent of necessity, nor can any admission be made in favour of that modification of the principle which is founded on the doctrine of God's immutability and prescience.'[2] His intention here as in *Paradise Lost* was to bid good-night to Calvin. Yet in his epic 'the doctrine of God's immutability and prescience' was pushed to the forefront in an ambitious effort to assess it from the divine standpoint. The result was not felicitous. The Father militantly claims that neither angels nor men

>   can justly accuse
> Thir maker, or thir making, or thir Fate;
> As if Predestination over-rul'd
> Thir will, dispos'd by absolute Decree
> Or high foreknowledge; they themselves decreed
> Thir own revolt, not I: if I foreknew,
> Foreknowledge had no influence on thir fault,
> Which had no less prov'd certain unforeknown.
> So without least impulse or shadow of Fate,
> Or aught by mee immutablie foreseen,
> They trespass, Authors to themselves in all
> Both what they judge and what they choose.
>
> (III. 112-23)

even better critics have sinned: Sir Herbert Grierson thought Milton 'at least a semi-Pelagian' or just 'Pelagian' (*Cross Currents* (1951), pp. 253, 267), and others still invoke whatever terms happen to be on hand.

[1] The major discourses are six: three by the Father (III. 98-128; v. 233-45; x. 43-47), two by Raphael (v. 520-42; VIII. 635-43), and one by Adam on the day of the Fall (IX. 343-56). Satan also acknowledges his free will (IV. 66 f.).

[2] *Works*, xiv. 77.

Perhaps Milton could have steered clear of this problem or settled upon a better-recognized approach. He could have presented, like Dante, the silent eloquence of God; he could have put in the mouth of God words such as we find in the Book of Job; and, as a last resort, he might have reduced the philosophizing of his own garrulous deity and permitted him to expound some version of Boethius's theory of the Eternal Present with which he must have been familiar, as he must have been familiar with Valla who said that 'all give the palm' to Boethius for 'explaining' the problem. Boethius's Eternal Present was a theory often adapted, for example by Duns Scotus, and it remained well-enough known in Milton's day. Walter Charleton in 1652 gave his rendering of it:

> what we (whose imperfect reason cannot compute the durations of things, but by the successive instances, or concatenated moments of time) call *Prædestination*, is really no prædetermination of what's to come, in respect of God, but an act of his will already accomplisht, and as soon fulfilled as decreed; and so we may truely say, that in relation to himself, there is no *Foreknowledge* in God, all things which to our inferior Capacities seem either past, or to come, being actually præsent to him, whose whole duration is altogether or but one constant and permanent part, one *Tò vῦv*, entire in unity, and uncapable of division into successive minutes.[1]

Milton fails to convince us, yet his failure is repeated throughout the Christian tradition, for no definitive solution is possible; the problem outlasts all who undertake its resolution. St. Augustine, who expended more time on it than any other major theologian, could only offer this 'classic' thesis:

> though God has foreknowledge of your happiness in the future, and though nothing can happen otherwise than as he has foreknown it (for that would mean that there is no foreknowledge) we are not thereby compelled to think that you will not be happy voluntarily ... God's foreknowledge, which is even to-day quite certain that you are to be happy at a future date, does not rob you of your will to happiness when you actually attain happiness. Similarly if ever in the future you have a culpable will, it will be none the less your will because God has foreknowledge of it.[2]

Milton's argument in *De doctrina christiana* is equally unsatisfactory:

---

[1] *The Darknes of Atheism* (1652), p. 118. See Boethius, *De consolatione philosophiae*, Bk. v, prose iv et seq. Valla's commendation appears in *De libero arbitrio* (*RPM*, p. 160).

[2] *De libero arbitrio*, III. 3 (*LCC*, vi. 175). Besides this entire treatise, see the statements by Tertullian, *Adversus Marcionem*, II. 5–6, and John of Damascus, *De fide orthodoxa*, II. 25–26.

'to God', he wrote, 'the issue of events is not uncertain, but fore-known with the utmost certainty, though they be not decreed necessarily.' He later 'explains' himself thus:

I allow that future events which God has foreseen, will happen certainly, but not of necessity. They will happen certainly, because the divine prescience cannot be deceived, but they will not happen necessarily, because prescience can have no influence on the object foreknown, inasmuch as it is only an intransitive action. What therefore is to happen according to contingency and the free will of man, is not the effect of God's prescience, but is produced by the free agency of its own natural causes, the future spontaneous inclination of which is perfectly known to God. Thus God foreknew that Adam would fall of his own free will; his fall was therefore certain but not necessary, since it proceedeth from his own free will, which is incompatible with necessity.[1]

Christian apologists, it seems, have made little headway since Rabbi Akiba in the first century A.D. paradoxically observed: 'All is foreseen, and free will is given.'[2]

Another major problem facing 'freewillmen' concerns their common belief in predestination. I say 'common' belief because all Christians share it, being 'a truth which none questions'.[3] This truth is, alas, highly elusive, and in seeking it Protestants fathered a multitude of interpretations, among them Calvin's 'double predestination', exact but morally offensive, and the Anglican tenet, inoffensive but also inexact.[4] Moreover, the Christian ideal that God is love was all too often trampled underfoot. On one hand it was maintained that the Christ's sacrifice applied solely to the 'elect'; on another God was said to have foreordained the greater

[1] *Works*, xiv. 75, 85–87. Other Renaissance statements are just as inconclusive. Three examples: Pierre Viret, *A Christian Instruction*, tr. John Shute (1573), pp. 469 ff.; Ralegh, p. 17; Donne, *Sermons*, ii. 151 f.

[2] *Pirke Aboth*, III. 19; in *The Ethics of the Talmud*, ed. R. Travers Herford (repr. 1962), p. 88.

[3] Richard Maden, *Christs Love* (1637), p. 93. Cf. the decree of the Third Council of Valence (A.D. 855): 'we confess the predestination of the elect to life, and the predestination of the impious to death' (Denzinger, § 322). Thomas Aquinas's lengthy exposition is in *S. th.* I. xxiii.

[4] The differences are set forth in Richard Montagu's controversial *Appello Cæsarem* (1625), pt. i, ch. vii. See esp. Calvin, *De aeterna praedestinatione Dei*, tr. J. K. S. Reid (1961); Heppe, ch. viii; and the exposition by François Wendel, *Calvin*, tr. Philip Mairet (1965), ch. iv [iv]. On the Anglican position consult XXXIX Art. (xvii), and cf. Arminius, iii. 249–519. The soundest study of the Biblical background is by H. H. Rowley, *The Biblical Doctrine of Election* (1950); but see also Krister Stendahl, 'The Called and the Chosen', in *The Root of the Vine*, ed. Anton Fridrichsen (Westminster, Md., 1953), pp. 63–80.

part of creation to perdition so that in effect 'heaven is empty, and hell is full'.[1] Fortunately Milton did not commit himself to these absurdities and trod the safer road of Protestant tradition, whose essence he finally expressed in the Father's statement in *Paradise Lost*:

> Some I have chosen of peculiar grace
> Elect above the rest; so is my will . . .
>
> (III. 183 f.)

We are facing the Christian concept of grace.

III

The concept of grace, always far larger than any conciliar anvil, could not be hammered into any narrow confining dogma. Indeed, grace is so all-encompassing that its frame of reference is that of the Christian faith itself. Its manifestation is a mystery which defies analysis, yet more than half of Christian literature deals with it. Treatises relevant to it were, however, composed in the West, none in the East. Eastern Christians were reluctant to discuss it, while Western Christians, from Augustine to Luther and after him, broke it open, dissected it, and debated it. None doubted its existence, all lived it, for grace is an experience.[2]

The term *agape* ('love') is a specifically Christian contribution; the term *charis* ('grace') is not. 'Grace' belongs to pre-Christian terminology; it was used in classical literature mostly in the sense of beauty, charm, and perfection, or favour, affection, and kindness. The Biblical term 'grace' possesses a related meaning even though it points decisively towards God's activities in history. To the writers of the Old Testament grace (*ḥen*) meant not so much favour and affection as the unmerited love of God toward mankind. The

---

[1] Trelcatius, p .87, and Dent (above, p. 194, n. 1), p. 287. This notion is reputedly based on Matt. xxii. 14 ('few are chosen'). On Milton's view of the all-sufficiency of the Christ's sacrifice, see *DDC*, *Works*, xv. 349.

[2] Introductions to the subject include Oscar Hardman, *The Christian Doctrine of Grace* (1937), and esp. Robert W. Gleason, S.J., *Grace* (1962). Further study should include James Moffatt, *Grace in the NT* (1931); N. P. Williams, *The Grace of God* (1930); T. F. Torrance, *The Doctrine of Grace in the Apostolic Fathers* (Edinburgh, 1948); and the surveys by Henri Rondet, S.J., *Gratia Christi* (Paris, 1948), and the various contributors to *The Doctrine of Grace*, ed. W. T. Whitley (1932). John Oman's *Grace and Personality*, 3rd ed. (Cambridge, 1925), is difficult but rewarding. Further references in Karl Rahner, *Nature and Grace*, tr. Dinah Wharton (1963), pp. 11–13. On the attitude of the Eastern Church see Gleason, App. III; Whitley, chs. ii, viii; and Frank Gavin, *Some Aspects of Contemporary Greek Orthodox Thought* (Milwaukee, 1923), ch. iv [i].

divine love for Israel (Deut. vii. 7 f.) involved no merit on the part of the Israelites; it sprang rather from God's will to elect whomsoever he pleased according to his inscrutable love and wisdom: 'I will be gracious to whom I will be gracious, and will shew mercy to whom I will shew mercy' (Exod. xxxiii. 19; cf. Rom. ix. 15). The attitude of the New Testament is no different. In the letters of St. Paul, who uses the term *charis* more often than anyone else, emphasis falls on grace as 'the gift of God' (Eph. ii. 8). But grace is not simply 'given' (Gal. ii. 9, Rom. xii. 3, xv. 15, etc.); it is specifically 'given you by Jesus Christ' (1 Cor. i. 4), it is offered 'by one man, Jesus Christ' alone (Rom. v. 15), it is indeed 'the grace of our Lord Jesus Christ' (Rom. xii. 20, Gal. vi. 8, 1 Cor. xvi. 23, 2 Cor. xiii. 14, etc.). For Paul the grace of God is meaningless except as it is incarnated in the God-man.

Early Christian thought on the whole tallied steadfastly with Pauline charitology. Yet already a number of theologians were at work laying the groundwork for subsequent developments, and Tertullian anticipated the later distinction between grace and nature, the reduction of grace to an impersonal force not necessarily connected with the Christ's work, and the possible obliteration of man's free will under the impact of grace. According to Tertullian,

Even stones will become children of Abraham, if they are shaped into conformity with Abraham's faith; and even the offspring of vipers will bring forth fruits of repentance, if they first spew forth the venom of wickedness. Such will be the power of divine grace, which is assuredly mightier than nature, having in subjection to itself within us the faculty of free will.[1]

Thereafter the concept of grace in the West developed in unison with controversies concerning free will. Pelagius felt obliged to speak out against Augustine's celebrated prayer 'da quod iubes et iube quod vis' ('Give what thou commandest and command what thou wilt'), as many centuries later Catholics and rebellious Protestants spoke out against Luther's declaration that 'the promises of God give what the commandments of God demand and fulfil what the law prescribes. . . . He alone commands, he alone fulfils'.[2] Yet

---

[1] *De anima*, xxi (*apud* N. P. Williams [previous note], p. 16). See also E. W. Watson, 'Grace in the Latin Fathers to Augustine', in Whitley [as before], ch. iii.

[2] Augustine, *Conf.* x. 29; Luther, *Works*, xxxi. 349. On Augustine's conception of grace, see Gotthard Nygren, *Das Prädestinationsproblem in der Theologie Augustins* (Lund, 1956), esp. ch. ii, and *Studia patristica*, ed. Kurt Aland and F. L. Cross (Berlin, 1957), ii. 258–69. On Luther's view consult Heinrich Hermelink, in Whitley (above, p. 198, n. 2), ch. vi.

Luther's thesis, like Augustine's before him, was not nearly so un-reasonable as we might at first glance think. Both concerned them-selves with arresting any emphasis on man's free will at the expense of God's grace. Augustine saw the danger all too clearly. 'The Pelagians are a new brand of heretics', he warned, 'who assert that human wills are capable of withstanding the Will of God in such a way as to prevent him from doing what he wishes to do.' Much later Bullinger, on behalf of classical Protestantism, remarked that the outcry against free will must not be seen in isolation but in its relationship to 'that proud and arrogant doctrine concerning the merites of man';[1] and Bullinger's comment does not deserve burial under an avalanche of extremist views.

It is tempting to deride Luther for saying that the will of man is a beast led now by God and now by Satan. His metaphor is as ill chosen as that of John Gaule, who in 1629 said that 'God leades his Children oft-times euen hood-winkt to doe his Will'.[2] But here, as elsewhere, the chief aim was to assign initiative to God, to be at one with Jesus's dictum that no man can be saved 'except the Father which hath sent me draw him' (John vi. 44). Hence the Father's sweeping statement in *Paradise Lost* [my italics]:

> Man shall not quite be lost, but sav'd who will,
> Yet not of will in him, but Grace in *mee*
> Freely voutsaf't; once more *I* will renew
> His lapsed powers, though forfeit and enthralld
> By sin to foul exorbitant desires;
> Upheld by *mee*, yet once more he shall stand
> On even ground against his mortal foe,
> By *mee* upheld, that he may know how frail
> His fall'n condition is, and to *mee* ow
> *All* his deliv'rance, and to none but *mee*.
> Some *I* have chosen of peculiar grace
> Elect above the rest; so is *my* will:
> The rest shall hear *me* call, and oft be warnd
> Thir sinful state, and to appease betimes
> Th' incensed Deitie, while offerd Grace
> Invites; for *I* will cleer their senses dark,
> What may suffice, and soft'n stonie hearts
> To pray, repent, and bring obedience due.
>
> (III. 173–90)

---

[1] Augustine, *Retractationes*, I. ix. 3; Bullinger, *Questions of Religion*, tr. John Coxe (1572), fols. 43ᵛ–44.
[2] *Practique Theories* (1629), p. 106.

We ask ourselves, if this is a promise that God is to lead us 'euen hood-winkt to doe his Will', what has happened to free will? Milton's contemporaries preferred to answer the question with a reminder:

That will, which we call Free will, is so far from being ours, as that not only that Freedome, but that Will it self is from another, from God. Not only the rectitude of the faculty, but the faculty it self is his.

Here is the voice not of an extreme Protestant but of the Dean of St. Paul's himself, John Donne.[1]

We stand warned against hasty generalizations not in Christian theology alone but in all great literature. The classical concept of *moira* is instructive, for we could mistake it for 'fate': the Delphic oracle spoke, *therefore* Oedipus acted as he did. But a man fore-warned of his destiny who nevertheless thoughtlessly kills an elderly man and foolishly marries a woman twice his age without ever pausing to reflect the past, is surely 'fated' so long as we take 'fate' to mean the destiny of man as it has been predicted by the gods but is enforced by the individual himself. Christian thinkers arrived at an identical balance. St. Paul exhorted the faithful to 'work out *your own* salvation with fear and trembling; for *it is* God which worketh in you both to will and to do of his good pleasure' (Phil. ii. 12 f.). In the Johannine Apocalypse the Lamb is reported as saying, 'Behold, I stand at the door, and knock: *if* any man hear my voice, *and* open the door, I *will* come in to him, and will sup with him, and he with me' (Rev. iii. 20). Finally, the same balance controls Augustine's brilliant 'inconsistency' in upholding man's free will at one moment and denying it the next, no sooner asserting that our salvation is both 'from the will of man and from the mercy of God' than adding that 'the whole process is credited to God, who both prepareth the will to receive divine aid and aideth the will which has been thus pre-pared'.[2] During the controversies ushered in by the Reformation the balance was upset, as Protestants charged that Catholics made free will 'the absolute Lord of its own actions', and Catholics charged that Protestants 'leaue vs as a stone or blocke to be moued by God

---

[1] *Sermons*, vii. 446; cf. x. 89: 'to will, as well as to doe, to beleeue, as well as to work, is all from God.' I have cited other 'extreme' statements by Donne, Bishop Hall, *et al.*, in *MLN*, lxxiii (1958), 257–60.

[2] *Enchiridion*, xxxii (*LCC*, vii. 358). On Augustine's 'inconsistency' see also T. A. Lacey, *Nature, Miracle and Sin* (1916), pp. 61 ff., and Kenneth E. Kirk, *The Vision of God* (1931), pp. 341 f. The same balance appears in the Greek Fathers (Kelly, p. 352); cf. Origen, *De pr.* iii. i. 19.

onely'.[1] But the substantial spirits of that turbulent era never really abandoned the traditional 'inconsistency' of the Bible and of St. Augustine. There was Luther, beguiled into dazzling contradictions as he defended the folly of his God against the wisdom of Erasmus. There was even Arminius, widely maligned as *Pelagius redivivus*, yet unhesitatingly asserting that God's grace 'goes before, accompanies, and follows', 'excites, assists, operates' whatever we do. There was Hugo Grotius, never in doubt that man possesses free will ('not an errour of *Pelagius*, but Catholick sense'), yet as convinced that grace does not 'depend on Free-will, because Grace worketh how far, and how much it pleaseth'. Similarly, Donne was assured not only that the will of man is 'but Gods agent', but also that 'neither God nor man determine mans will . . . but they condetermine it.' The same 'inconsistency' appears in Shakespeare's plays, manifesting itself at one end of the pendulum's swing in Cassius's statement that the fault is not in our stars but in ourselves, and in the other in Florizel's words in *The Winter's Tale* that we are 'the slaves of chance'.[2] Yet occasionally the pendulum stands still over statements such as Hamlet's:

> There's a divinity that shapes our ends,
> Rough-hew them how we will.
>
> (v. ii. 10–11)

Hamlet's 'fate' is the universal concept of *moira*, which attributes primacy to God yet senses that somehow man's faculties and godlike reason must hew—perhaps only rough-hew—his own destiny. Human experience may confirm that God 'prepareth the will to receive the divine aid', but it confirms also the belief that we were created, in Milton's words, 'reasonable beings, and *therefore* free agents'.

On its way from Augustine to the Reformation the concept of

---

[1] George Downame, *Papa Antichristus* (1620), tr. Richard Baxter in *The Safe Religion* (1657), p. 389; and Parsons (below, p. 218, n. 1), p. 13. Neither side evidently read what the other had to say: Downame's charge does violence to the Tridentine decrees (on which see Harnack, vii. 58 ff., and the discussion by Hubert Jedin, *A History of the Council of Trent*, tr. Dom Ernest Graf (1961), ii. 307 ff.); Parsons's charge is unfair to the common Protestant theme that 'God doth not worke vpon vs, as vpon blockes and stones' (Thomas Adams, *Workes* (1629), p. 1033; but see further *Conf. Aug.* XVIII [Schaff, iii. 18 f.], and Heppe, pp. 268 ff.).

[2] On Luther see esp. B. A. Gerrish, *Grace and Reason* (Oxford, 1962). My quotations are, seriatim, from Arminius, ii. 700 (cf. ii. 189 ff.); Grotius, *Choice Discourses*, tr. Clement Barksdale (1658), Appendix: p. 105; and Donne, *Sermons*, ix. 75, and *Essays*, p. 80. Shakespeare's 'inconsistent' passages on free will are in Frye, pp. 157–65.

grace was divided into several kinds: sufficient and efficient, sanctifying or infused, prevenient or antecedent or operant, subsequent
or assisting or co-operant, and so forth.[1] Protestantism retained only
the most basic terms, and William Perkins was able to reduce these
to three:

In the worke of our regeneration, three graces be required, the preuenting grace, the working grace, and the co-working grace. The *preuenting
grace* is, when God of his mercie sets and imprints in the minde a new
light, in the will a new qualitie or inclination, in the heart new affections.
The *working grace* is, when God giues to the will the acte of well-willing,
namely, the will to beleeue, the will to repent, the will to obey God in his
worde. The *co-working grace is*, when God giueth the deede to the wil,
that is, the exercise & practise of faith and repentaunce. The first giues
the power of doing good; the second the will; the third the deede: and all
three together make the worke of regeneration.[2]

More common even was the thesis that only two kinds of grace
existed. Melanchthon did not go to the trouble of naming them ('the
one precedes, the other follows our repentance'). However, other
apologists were ready to specify them: 'the first is *Gratia præueniens*,
a preuenting grace, to prepare our wils and hearts to workes of
pietie. The second is *Gratia subsequens*, a subsequent grace, to assist
and helpe vs forward in well doing.'[3] Protestant apologists stipulated
repeatedly that neither of these terms should be considered in
isolation, and Thomas Sutton observed in 1632 that 'prevenient
and subsequent . . . are but one, and by the same grace hee prevents
us that wee may will, hee followes us by making us to doe; he
prevents us by moving us to good workes, hee followes us by giving
perseverance'. Donne stood out in his predilection for a variety of
terms, yet in the end even he set forth the recognized Protestant
thesis:

---

[1] Augustine's terms are cited by Kelly, p. 367. St. Thomas's influential analysis is in
S. th. II (i), cxi. For a typical Protestant censure of such excessive terminology see [above,
p. 202, n. 1] Downame, pp. 208 ff., in Baxter, pp. 420 ff.

[2] *Works* (Cambridge, 1605), p. 889. Professor T. F. Torrance reminds me that these
subdivisions of grace are peculiar to later, 'scholastic' Protestantism; they are not in line
with the 'total' terms of Luther and Calvin, who insisted on *tota gratia* because sin, being
sin against grace, is itself total. By Milton's time such totality appears only infrequently
(cf. Wall, below, p. 212).

[3] Melanchthon, p. 104, and Immanuel Bourne, *The Anatomie of Conscience* (1623),
p. 38. The two kinds of grace (more fully expounded by Musculus, fol. 126ᵛ) are also
traditional; cf. their discussion by F. Homes Dudden, *Gregory the Great* (1905), ii.
395 ff.

we call Gods Grace by other names then Preventing, whether *Assisting* Grace, that it stand by us and sustain us, or *Concomitant* Grace, that it work with us, and inanimate our action, when it is doing, or his *Subsequent* Grace, that rectifies or corrects an action, when it is done; when all is done, still it is the *Preventing Power*, and quality of that Grace, that did all that in me . . . all my co-operation is but a post-operation, a working by the Power of that All-preventing Grace.[1]

The statements of Donne and others of his day are so many 'commentaries' on the claim of *Paradise Lost* that the repentance of Adam and Eve was a 'post-operation' anticipated (prevented) by God's grace:

> Thus they in lowliest plight repentant stood
> Praying, for from the Mercie-seat above
> Prevenient Grace descending had remov'd
> The stonie from thir hearts, and made new flesh
> Regenerat grow instead, that sighs now breath'd
> Unutterable, which the Spirit of prayer
> Inspir'd, and wingd for Heav'n with speedier flight
> Then loudest Oratorie.
>
> (XI. 1–8)

We should refrain from close analysis of this passage, if indeed it is capable of analysis, since, apart from asserting the primacy of grace, it remains imprecise, for example, about the role of prayer. Yet its very imprecision is highly appropriate, for grace is no philosophical tenet to be dissected but an experience to be lived. Henry More was quite right: 'These things are safelier felt than spoken.'[2] If spoken they must be, we would be better advised to deal not so much with broken fragments but with the total conception. Such was the method of the Christian tradition, and such also was the method of Milton in *Paradise Lost* and elsewhere.

Milton in his treatise *Of Civil Power in Ecclesiastical Causes* said that man's faculties were 'once indeed naturally free, but now only

---

[1] Sutton, *Lectures* (1632), p. 125, and Donne, *Sermons*, vii. 353 (cf. i. 293; ii. 305; v. 281, 367; etc.). Other statements include those by Luther (in Gordon Rupp, *The Righteousness of God* (1953), p. 207); XXXIX Art. (x); the Council of Trent (in *Documents of the Christian Church*, ed. Henry Bettenson (1954), p. 367); Hooker (in Frye, p. 253); Robert Sanderson, *XXXV. Sermons*, 7th ed. (1681), i. 277; and a host of minor writers (Gabriel Price, *The Laver of the Heart* (1616), p. 12; William Fuller, *A Sermon . . . at Dover Castle* (1625), sig. B1; *et al.*). Cf. Augustine, *Enarrationes in Psalmos*, V. 17 (*Patr. l.* xxxvi. 89): 'bona enim voluntas Dei præcedit bonam voluntatem nostram, ut peccatores vocet in pœnitentiam.'

Discourses (1692), p. 141.

as they are regenerat and wrought on by divine grace'. The treatise
was published in 1659, but he might well have written his comment
at any stage of his life. *De doctrina christiana* in this respect is within
the Pauline–Augustinian tradition, since it asserts that grace is
God's gift, and man's restoration the work 'purely of grace'. Even
more interesting are those statements least resembling theological
dicta, like the exquisite affirmation in *The Reason of Church Government* (1642) that 'when God commands to take the trumpet and blow
a dolorous or a jarring blast, it lies not in mans will what he shall say
or what he shall conceal'.[1] The pronouncement reverberates through
Milton's poetry. It touches the situation in Sonnet XIX involving
'that one Talent which is death to hide', and includes finally the
self-abnegating heroes of *Paradise Regained* and *Samson Agonistes*,
the one obediently led into the wilderness 'by some strong motion'
(1. 290), the other as willingly guided to the arena by 'Some rouzing
motions' (l. 1382). If we may claim justifiably that for Jesus and
Samson 'the readiness is all', we may claim it as much for the Lady
in *Comus*. Discerning students of her predicament have already told
us that the action in *Comus* progresses under the shadow of grace.[2]
It is an acceptable verdict provided we are at pains to leave inviolate
Milton's premeditated inexactness. *Comus* is not simply a collection
of such phrases as 'high mystery' or 'Heaven lends us grace' (ll. 785,
938), still less is it a treatise focusing on 'hæmony', the mysterious
plant 'of divine effect' that reputedly grows best 'in another Countrey' (629 ff.). It is a total dramatic situation in which the experience
that is grace appears subordinate to the lovely dance that is life (974).
I say 'appears' as a precaution against any unilateral reading of
Comus either as the dance apart from grace, or as grace apart from
the dance. We should be wrong in thinking the Lady's temptation
to be unreal, excessively attached though we are to the commonplace
notion that 'Vertue consists in Action', that 'Where there is no Conflict, there can be no Conquest; where there is no Conquest, there is
no Crowne.' Milton had said as much, of course, in a memorable
passage in the *Areopagitica*:

---

[1] Seriatim: *Works*, vi. 21; xv. 325 and 339; iii. 231. The last statement may be
reminiscent of Amos iii. 8 ('the Lord God hath spoken, who can but prophesy?'), but
its sense is not only Biblical; it is universal.

[2] The most relevant essay is that by Cleanth Brooks and John E. Hardy, *Poems of
Mr. John Milton* (1951), pp. 187–237. See also below, p. 214, n. 1. On the traditional
significance of 'hæmony' consult Edward S. LeComte, *PQ*, xxi (1942), 283–98, and John
M. Steadman, *History of Ideas News Letter*, iv (1958), 59–60.

I cannot praise a fugitive and cloister'd virtue, unexercis'd & unbreath'd, that never sallies out and sees her adversary, but slinks out of the race, where the immortall garland is to be run for, not without dust and heat. Assuredly we bring not innocence into the world, we bring impurity much rather: that which purifies us is triall, and triall is by what is contrary.[1]

Judged by this universally valid yardstick we find the Lady wanting, but only because we consider the dance alone, not even the entire dance at that. Are we to deny that they also serve who only stand and wait? Are we to disclaim the reality of the 'rouzing motions' within us all, the total range of things 'safelier felt than spoken'? While we persist in regarding situations torn out of context, Milton saw them whole, saw them 'inconsistently'.

In *Comus* the interpenetration of the visible and the invisible, of the natural and the supernatural, is most plainly set out by the Attendant Spirit. He tells us at the outset that his mansion is

> where those immortal shapes
> Of bright aërial Spirits live insphear'd
> In Regions milde of calm and serene Ayr,
> Above the smoak and stirr of this dim spot,
> Which men call Earth.
>   (2–6)

He is later joined by Sabrina ('''tis my office best / To help insnared chastity' (909 f.)). Her arrival may or may not catch us unawares, but the Lady expects it, already persuaded that

> he, the Supreme good, t' whom all things ill
> Are but as slavish officers of vengeance,
> Would send a glistring Guardian if need were
> To keep my life and honour unassail'd.
>   (217–20)

Milton created the cheerful atmosphere of *Comus* by drawing upon *Romeo and Juliet* and *The Tempest*,[2] but he formulated the Lady's doctrinaire statement by turning chiefly to *The Faerie Queene*. Dealing with Florimel's like predicament Spenser had exclaimed,

> See how the heauens of voluntary grace,
> And soueraine fauour towards chastity,

---

[1] Seriatim: John Davies of Hereford, *The Holy Roode* (1609), sig. K3ᵛ; Quarles, *Enchyridion* (1640), sig. E2ᵛ; and Milton, *Works*, iv. 311. Parallel statements reach back to the Fathers. Cf. Origen: 'Non probata vero nec examinata virtus, nec virtus est' (*Homiliæ in Numeros*, XIV. 2, in *Patr. g.* xii. 678).

[2] So argue Ethel Seaton, *ESEA*, xxxi (1945), 68–80, and John M. Major, *SQ*, x (1959), 177–83.

Doe succour send to her distressed cace:
So much high God doth innocence embrace.
(III. viii. 29)

This belief Spenser had earlier framed within the doctrine of guardian angels:

How oft do they, their siluer bowers leaue,
To come to succour vs, that succour want?
How oft do they with golden pineons, cleaue
The flitting skyes, like flying Pursuiuant,
Against foule feends to aide vs millitant?
They for vs fight, they watch and dewly ward,
And their bright Squadrons round about vs plant,
And all for love, and nothing for reward:
O why should heauenly God to men haue such regard?
(II. viii. 2)

To ask whether Milton shared this belief is to obtain two answers. One scholar informs us that Milton was 'evidently fascinated' by guardian angels; another, that he thought their existence 'a papist superstition'.[1] The first theory may be an exaggeration; the second is merely untrue. The Epistle to the Hebrews, of which St. Paul was believed to have been the author, clearly asserts that angels are 'all ministering spirits, sent forth to minister for them who shall be heirs of salvation' (i. 14). Protestants took such 'evidence' seriously; I have never found one reputable theologian of the time who questioned the 'papist superstition'. The way was led by Luther: 'euery christen mã hathe hys good Angelles assined vnto hym, for to saue hym and to preserue him.' The same belief pervaded English Protestantism, which freely allotted angels to everyone from old men to innocent babes ('yea, euen the little ones haue their Angels').[2] In *Paradise Lost*, where Milton reflects a statement he made in *De doctrina christiana*,[3] the celestial choir maintains that

[1] James H. Hanford, *UTQ*, viii (1938–9), 407, and Denis Saurat, *Gods of the People* (1947), p. 27, respectively.
[2] Seriatim: Luther, *A Fruitfull Sermon . . . of the Angelles*, tr. John Foxe (1560?), sig. C4; Daniel Dyke, *Tuuo Treatises*, 5th impr. (1631), p. 294. For more detailed statements see John Bayly, *Two Sermons* (Oxford, 1630), i. 7 ff.; Henry Lawrence, *Of our Communion and Warre with Angels* (Amsterdam, 1646), pp. 19 ff.; Robert Gell, Ἀγγελοκρατία Θεοῦ (1650); Heppe, pp. 212 f.; *et al.*
[3] *Works*, xv. 101. Milton thought it only probable that angels preside over nations, districts, etc. (ibid., p. 103). His caution is itself traditional. See *The Teaching of the Catholic Church*, ed. George D. Smith (1948), i. 269.

God will deigne
To visit oft the dwellings of just Men
Delighted, and with frequent intercourse
Thither will send his winged Messengers
On errands of supernal Grace.

(VII. 569–73)

The deployment of the Attendant Spirit and Sabrina in *Comus* but especially of the ministering spirits in *Paradise Lost*—Raphael, Michael, Gabriel, Uriel, Ithuriel, and Zephon—offers us part of the evidence showing Milton's belief that man is one world but that he has another to attend him.

The outpouring of God's grace described in *Paradise Lost* is analogous to the act of creation when the divine goodness was 'put forth' over chaos (VII. 171). The analogy is not particularly original. The phrase 'put forth' was variously employed during the Renaissance, negatively in connexion with the 'retirement' of the Christ's divinity on the Cross ('the Deitie did as it were rest it selfe: that is, did not put forth [its] owne operation and working'), and positively in statements to the effect that God 'putteth forth' his wisdom and power, or that the Christ graciously 'puts forth him selfe, and scatters his beams upon a mourning cloudy soule', or that 'he puts forth himselfe in our Persons to become the Fountaine, the Glasse of *truth*, *love*, *life*, *joy* within us'.[1] But man's 'calling' by God was even more commonly set forth, as Milton himself said, 'under the metaphor of hearing or hearkening'.[2] *Paradise Lost* alludes frequently to God's 'ear'. The repentant Adam appears convinced that the divine 'ear' is open always to man's prayer (X. 1060 f.), and he adds later that this experience is to be grasped 'by faith alone' [my italics throughout]:

easily may Faith admit, that all
The good which we enjoy, from Heav'n descends;
But that from us aught should ascend to Heav'n
So prevalent as to concerne the mind
Of God high-blest, or to incline his will,
Hard to belief may seem; yet this will Prayer,
Or one short sigh of human breath, up-borne
Ev'n to the Seat of God. For since I saught

---

[1] Seriatim: Robert Allen, *The Doctrine of the Gospel* (1606), ii. 199; Thomas Taylor, *Christs Victorie* (1633), p. 438; Peter Sterry, *The Spirit convincing of Sinne* (1645), p. 20, and *The Teachings of Christ* (1648), p. 34.
[2] *DDC, Works*, xv. 355.

By Prayer th' offended Deitie to appease,
Kneeld and before him humbl'd all my heart,
Methought I saw him placable and mild,
Bending his *eare*; perswasion in me grew
That I was heard with favour; peace returnd
Home to my breast.

(XI. 141–54)

However, the Father had already anticipated (prevented) the prayers
of Adam and Eve, and even the Son's plea that he should bend his
ear to supplication (XI. 30 f.). As he had promised before the Fall,

I will cleer thir senses dark,
What may suffice, and soft'n stonie hearts
To pray, repent, and bring obedience due.
To prayer, repentance, and obedience due,
Though but endevord with sincere intent,
Mine *eare* shall not be slow, mine eye not shut.

(III. 188–93)

Milton's account of the Father's promise derives from a theological
tenet which Bishop Henry King restated in 1634: ''Tis his grace that
we Pray, and againe 'tis his grace which answers our Prayers.'[1] In
Paradise Lost Adam avoids theological formulas only because, like
Samson, he simply lives them:

these evils I deserve and more,
Acknowledge them from God inflicted on me
Justly, yet despair not of his final pardon
Whose *ear* is ever op'n; and his eye
Gracious to re-admit the suppliant.

(*SA*, ll. 1169–73)

The idea is Biblical. It is also Augustinian: 'the ears of God are
ready to listen.'[2]

Yet God does not only 'put forth' his grace; he sometimes elects to
retract it. Such is God's 'withdrawal', and Jeremiah Burroughs
described its effect as tradition understood it: 'God need do nothing
to destroy a creature; if hee doth but withdraw himself from it, it

---

[1] *An Exposition upon the Lords Prayer* (1634), pp. 9–10. A common symbol for prayer
was Jacob's ladder (Thomas Dekker, *Foure Birds* (1609), sig. A6; Joseph Henshaw,
Horae succisivae, 2nd ed. (1631), p. 157; Alexander Ross, *Three Decads* (1630), p. 8;
et al.). Cf. below, p. 227, n. 2.

[2] *Tractatus in epistolam Johannis decem*, VI. 8 (*LCC*, viii. 307). William Laud also
quoted from Augustine: 'The eares of God are in the heart of him that prayes' (*A Sermon
. . . at White-Hall* (1626), p. 14).

falls to nothing presently.' Donne appealed to another familiar idea. When God 'withdraws his Grace', he averred, 'then, as upon the departing of the Sun, darkness follows'. We appreciate the remark upon remembering how Milton in *Paradise Lost* emphasizes the total darkness of Hell and the partial darkness surrounding Adam and Eve after the Fall. But Milton also drew upon a kindred idea expressed by Bullinger: 'the withdrawing of Gods grace is the hardening of mannes heart: and when wee are left vnto our selues, then we are hardened.'[1] In the Father's words,

> my day of Grace
> They who neglect and scorn, shall never taste;
> But hard be hard'nd, blind be blinded more,
> That they may stumble on, and deeper fall.
>
> (III. 198–201)

Accepted literally we find the statement revolting. But of course the Father speaks metaphorically. We should, moreover, pay heed to the reminder of that 'good disputant and preacher' Samuel Hoard, who wrote in 1636 that

we must understand these speeches *negativè*, in a negative, or privative sense, of the restraint of such gracious operations in sinfull soules, as being present, would hinder their obstinate hardening of themselves . . .; and not *positivè*, in a positive construction, as if God did by *positive acts* either impresse wicked qualities in the hearts of men, or deliver them up into the hands of the devill, to be hurried *quò illi placet*, into what impieties soever hee thinks good to bring them. God forbid. . . . [2]

Not long ago we were told[3] that the crisis of *Paradise Lost* is attained the moment Eve falls on her knees and implores Adam's forgiveness (X. 909 ff.). This theory may appeal to those who maintain that epic poems normally have one 'crisis' only; I myself welcome it because it has focused attention on one of the most important though least understood incidents in *Paradise Lost*. We are tempted, I think, to consider Eve's conduct as a demonstration of her 'true love'. That it assuredly is, but it is far more. I have already drawn attention to the unexpectedness and uncharacteristic nature of this incident. From the moment Eve plucked the fruit until the moment

---

[1] Seriatim: Burroughs, *Gospel-Revelation* (1660), p. 20; Donne, *Sermons*, iv. 115; and Bullinger, *Fiftie . . . Sermons*, tr. H. I. (1587), p. 492. For representative doctrinal statements see *Conf. Aug.*, Art. xix, and *West. Conf.* v. 6; xvii. 3.

[2] *The Soules Miserie* (1636), p. 282.

[3] By E. M. W. Tillyard, *Studies in Milton* (1951), pp. 8–52.

of 'crisis', more than 1,300 lines later, Milton portrays a woman in
centripetal pursuit of her own interests and a man ridiculously ab-
sorbed in how best he can shed responsibility on to her. Then Adam
denounces his wife in the most vicious tirade yet, and turns abruptly
away. We might now expect that Eve, only recently hailed by Satan
as 'Queen of this Universe', would show resentment that Adam has
reduced her to a mere 'Rib, Crooked by nature' (IX. 684; X. 884 f.).
Yet far from replying in kind, or making any protest, or even reminding him that he had asked for her creation, she does the one unexpected thing:

> with Tears that ceas'd not flowing,
> And tresses all disorderd, at his feet
> Fell humble, and imbracing them, besaught
> His peace.
>
> (X. 910–13)

It is certainly odd as well as unnatural, though how 'unnatural' we
discover when we reach Milton's explanation of the episode:

> Prevenient Grace descending had remov'd
> The stonie from thir hearts.

Donne would have agreed. 'Such a renewing', he said—and he might
have been commenting on *Paradise Lost*—'could not be done without
God; no man can prepare that worke, no man can begin it, no man
can proceed in it of himselfe. The desire and the actuall beginning
is from the preventing grace of God.'[1] Loath as we may be to accept
this theological explanation of Eve's conduct, we have little choice.
The issue was well stated by one of Milton's better critics. 'We are
forced to acquiesce', he wrote, because we are aware of 'no reason,
no set of natural circumstances whereby we could predict or expect
that love could be again rekindled after such abusive lust and such
hatred, that life could be again welcomed after such despair.'[2] As
Herbert might have said, who would have thought their shrivelled
hearts could have recovered greenness?

In spite of Milton's supposed 'Turkish contempt of females', it
is not Adam but Eve to whom God's grace is initially 'put forth'. It
is also Eve's love and not Adam's that is patterned most closely after

---

[1] *Sermons*, ii. 305. Cf. Calvin: 'the Father dothe wyth hys loue preuent and goe
before' (*Inst.* II. xvi. 3). See also Heppe, p. 571.

[2] Joseph H. Summers, *The Muse's Method* (1962), p. 108. The 'realistic psychological
complexity' of Eve's regeneration is argued by Mary Radzinowicz in *Reason and the
Imagination*, ed. J. A. Mazzeo (1962), pp. 155–81.

the 'unexampl'd love' of the Son (III. 410). The pronoun 'mee' recurs in two of the Son's most centrifugal statements (III. 236 ff.; XI. 32 ff.), and we find it in Eve's humble confession to Adam that

> both have sinnd, but thou
> Against God onely, I against God and thee,
> And to the place of judgement will return,
> There with my cries to importune Heav'n, that all
> The sentence from thy head remov'd may light
> On mee, sole cause to thee of all this woe,
> Mee mee onely just object of his ire.
>
> (X. 930–6)

Eve's proposal is accepted by Adam:

> What better can we do, then to the place
> Repairing where he judg'd us, prostrate fall
> Before him reverent, and there confess
> Humbly our faults, and pardon beg, with tears
> Watering the ground, and with our sighs the Air
> Frequenting, sent from hearts contrite, in sign
> Of sorrow unfeignd, and humiliation meek.
>
> (X. 1086–92)

The ritualistic repetition, almost word for word, of these very lines (1098–1104) offers us the single example in the whole of *Paradise Lost* of such re-emphasis, and its object is to underline for us that, as Sir John Hayward wrote in 1623, a 'contrite heart is so necessarie for the remission of sinnes, that without it, no man hath euer beene saued; no sinnes haue beene euer remitted'. We need qualify this idea, authenticated in Christian tradition and approved by Milton, only by reminding ourselves that the creation of a contrite heart out of a hardened one is itself the work of God. Peter Martyr was categorical enough: 'that we of our owne accord, wythout the Grace of God penetrating and changing ỹ mind, can open our harte vnto God, we vtterly deny.' John Wall expressed himself even more comprehensively in 1658: 'the Worke is his, the power is his, the merit is his, the performance is his'.[1]

If John Wall was comprehensive and Peter Martyr categorical, Milton was both, yet he managed to maintain the traditional 'inconsistency' we have earlier noted. To perceive this we have only to view

---

[1] Seriatim: Hayward, *Davids Teares* (1623), p. 136; Pietro Martire Vermigli, *Commentaries ... upon ... Romanes*, tr. H. B. (1568), fol. 384; and Wall, *Christian Reconcilement* (Oxford, 1658), p. 20. Cf. Milton: 'Repentance ... is the gift of God', etc. (*DDC*, *Works*, xv. 279). Zanchius (p. 212) has an identical statement.

in its entirety the Father's address, which we have so far quoted piecemeal (pp. 200, 209, 210), emphasizing now the marginal role allotted to man [my italics]:

> Man shall not quite be lost, but sav'd who will,
> Yet not of will in him, but Grace in mee
> Freely voutsaf't; once more I will renew
> His lapsed powers, though forfeit and enthralld
> By sin to foul exorbitant desires;
> Upheld by mee, yet once more he shall stand
> On even ground against his mortal foe,
> By mee upheld, that he may know how frail
> His fall'n condition is, and to mee ow
> All his deliv'rance, and to none but mee.
> Some I have chosen of peculiar grace
> Elect above the rest; so is my will:
> The rest *shall* hear me call, and oft *be* warnd
> Thir sinful state, and to appease betimes
> Th' incensed Deitie, while *offerd* Grace
> *Invites*; for I will cleer thir senses dark,
> What may suffice, and soft'n stonie hearts
> To pray, repent, and bring obedience due.
> To prayer, repentance, and obedience due,
> *Though but endevord* with sincere intent,
> Mine eare shall *not* be slow, mine eye *not* shut.
> And I will place within them as a guide
> My Umpire Conscience, whom *if* they will hear,
> Light after light well us'd *they* shall attain,
> And to the end *persisting*, safe arrive.
> This my long sufferance and my day of Grace
> *They who neglect and scorn*, shall never taste;
> But hard be hard'nd, blind be blinded more,
> That they *may* stumble on, and deeper fall;
> And *none but such* from mercy I exclude.

(III. 173–202)

Once again the pendulum stands still over a remarkable achievement. The absolute primacy of grace is established absolutely, yet once that is done Milton ensures the proper balance through strategically placed words. Grace may constrain but does not necessarily command. It is 'offerd', it 'invites', it can even be 'neglected'. If neglected, it deprives man of mercy; but if 'endevord' with sincere intent, it enables 'persisting' man safely to reach the end. Milton's balanced view is the balanced view of St. Paul, of St.

Augustine, of the Christian tradition: 'work out *your own* salvation with fear and trembling; for *it is* God which worketh in you both to will and to do.'

The exposition of prevenient grace in the opening lines of Book XI of *Paradise Lost* is reconfirmed in many other places and we shall now take note of some of them. At XI. 22, we have the Biblical–Pauline idea that grace is 'implanted' in man, conjuring up the divine gardener's constant efforts to replace withered roots by fresh ones. At XI. 91, we have the Father's description of grace bestowed upon man as 'My motions in him', reminding us at once of the 'rouzing motions' sensed by Samson and the 'strong motion' felt by Jesus. At XI. 139, we have Milton's own comment that Adam and Eve obtained 'strength added from above', which we might identify as the operation of 'subsequent' grace were we not hesitant to multiply theological terms without the poet's explicit approval. But then we have seen already how the various kinds of grace are ultimately but one, and that one 'the Power of that All-preventing Grace'. In *Paradise Lost* this concentration upon fundamentals occurs not only at the outset of Book XI but also in the Son's affirmation during the Council in Heaven that grace—the speediest of God's winged messengers—descends on man 'unprevented, unimplor'd, unsought' (III. 229–31). The chronology of this declaration is significant. It tells us that the era of grace was promulgated in timeless eternity before it was promised in the Old Testament or proclaimed upon the Incarnation, before indeed man had fallen and was in any need of grace. God's grace thus overflows the bounds of history even while coursing through it to involve us all in the mighty effort that is 'supernal Grace contending / With sinfulness of Men' (XI. 359 f.). Adam, like St. Paul, sees 'by faith alone' where the turbulent journey will end. Overjoyed he confesses that 'over wrauth Grace shall abound' (XII. 478).

IV

Readers of Milton have often speculated about his attitude toward all that lies within the provinces of grace and 'nature',[1] and

---

[1] See esp. A. S. P. Woodhouse's inquiry into the two 'orders' of *Comus* (*UTQ*, xi (1941), 46–71, and xix (1949), 218–23) but also its just criticism by A. E. Dyson, *ESEA*, viii (1955), 89–114, and Madsen, pp. 213–18. Woodhouse's similar thesis in connexion with *The Faerie Queene* (*ELH*, xvi (1949), 194–228) was severely criticized by Theodore Gang and intemperately defended by its author (*ELH*, xxvi (1959), 1–22; xxvii (1960),

confusion abounds because opinions are formed upon interpretation of one or other of the innumerable traditions within Christianity. Thus, Eastern Orthodox theologians have denied consistently the addition of any supererogatory grace to nature, since they believe grace was extended to man not after the Fall but at his creation.[1] In sharp contrast, the Reformers upheld a complete divorce between grace and nature resulting in urgent appeals to 'turne' or 'translate' nature into grace, even to prayers that Christians might advance from 'the possibilities of Nature, to the grace of God', or at last to denunciations of all who 'distinguish not betwixt *Nature* and *Grace*'.[2] In this issue the West's traditional centre of gravity lies somewhere within the formidable range of views expressed by St. Augustine, by his successors until after St. Thomas Aquinas, and by Protestant thinkers in Milton's own age. These views, however different from each other in themselves, combine nevertheless to form a protest against the severance of the two 'orders' by all 'contentious spirits' who (in Donne's words) 'have cast such clouds upon both these lights, that some have said, *Nature* doth *all* alone, and others, that Nature hath *nothing* to do at all, but all is *Grace*'. Donne also set a balanced picture for us. 'Consider we alwaies', he affirmed, 'the grace of God, to be the Sun it selfe, but the nature of man, and his naturall faculties to be the Sphear, in which that Sun, that Grace moves.'[3]

St. Augustine would surely have sided with Donne and arrayed himself against Tertullian, who, as we have seen, was inclined to separate nature from grace. At no time did Augustine surrender his belief in the fundamental goodness of nature. He did not think, as Calvin's successors later thought, that evil is 'natural' to man; for him only good was natural, and evil merely the absence of good and in itself 'nothing'. In effect nature cannot be distinguished from grace, since both are good and both are natural, differing from each other not in kind but in degree. Grace *is* needed to remedy the deviation

1–15). I care even less for Michael Macklem's 'Love, Nature and Grace in Milton', *QQ*, lvi (1949–50), 534–47.

[1] See Vladimir Lossky, *The Mystical Theology of the Eastern Church* (1957), pp. 101, 131 f.

[2] Seriatim: Sibbes, *A Glance of Heaven* (1638), ii. 8; John Rawlinson, *Fishermen* (1609), p. 6; Christopher Hampton, *A Sermon preached in . . . Glasco* (1611), p. 31; and Thomas Scott, *The High-waies of God* (1623), p. 61. See also the statements quoted by T. F. Torrance, *Calvin's Doctrine of Man* (1949), p. 107, and Franz Hildebrandt, *Melanchthon* (Cambridge, 1946), p. 24.

[3] *Sermons*, iii. 365, and vii. 305.

of man's will from good, but it works within and through, not beyond or against nature. Thomas Aquinas agreed, stating that

to love God above all things is natural to man. . . . But in the state of corrupt nature man falls short of this in the appetite of his rational will, which, unless it is cured by God's grace, follows its private good, on account of the corruption of nature. And hence we must say that in the state of perfect nature man did not need the gift of grace added to his natural endowments, in order to love God above all things naturally, although he needed God's help to move him to it; but in the state of corrupt nature man needs, even for this, the help of grace to heal his nature.[1]

Thomas Aquinas did not accept Augustine's doctrine without quali-fication, for while Augustine thought that 'grace is the mending of nature,' Thomas thought grace to be 'added to nature'.[2] Even so St. Thomas did not altogether sever grace from nature, and he observed in a celebrated dictum, 'gratia non tollit naturam sed perficit' ('grace does not destroy nature but perfects it'), whose popularity had sur-vived into the age of Milton, which regarded it as a 'worne axiom of Divinity'. It may not always have been quoted word for word, but it lurks implicit in a host of statements down to Herbert's brief 'grace fills up uneven nature'.[3] We seek in vain for its explicit utterance in Milton's *De doctrina christiana*. We are even less likely to meet it in *Comus* or *Paradise Lost*, which are poems and not theological treatises. We are none the less aware that Milton never considered evil to be 'natural' and believed all things to be derived directly from God,[4] so we may justifiably maintain that his attitude toward grace and nature, though post-Augustinian, is largely Augustinian in emphasis. We run the danger of oversimplifying complex issues, but Milton would doubtless have been prepared to endorse Pascal's suitable imprecision in saying that 'grace is in some sense natural', and certainly St. Jerome's ultimate argument that '*Nature* it selfe in the last resolution is of *Grace*; for God gave [us] that'.[5]

---

[1] *S. th.* II. cix. 3. The *locus classicus* of Augustine's belief in nature's goodness is *De civ.* XII. 5; Calvin's contrary view is in *Inst.* II. ii. 11. On evil as 'nothing' see the referen-ces in *LCC*, vii. 343 n., and *HTR*, lvii (1964), 235 n. Consult also Lacey, p. 129, and Kirk, p. 345 (both above, p. 201, n. 2).

[2] Augustine, *De spiritu et littera*, XLVII (*LCC*, viii. 230); Thomas, *S.th.* II. cix. 1.

[3] The 'worne axiome' (the phrase is from Richard Carpenter's *Experience*, etc. (1642), ii. 47) occurs in *S.th.* I. i. 8 (2). The Herbert quotation is from *Faith*, l. 32. Other relevant statements are cited by Allan Holaday, *JEGP*, liv (1955), 580 f.

[4] On the theory of creation *ex Deo*, see above, p. 33.

[5] Pascal, *Pensées*, § 674. Jerome is cited from Robert Sanderson's paraphrase in *Ten*

I should like to terminate these prolegomena to the concept of grace with a glance at the sacraments, the means of grace to all Christians but Protestants. Milton's attitude is militantly partisan. In *Paradise Lost* Michael's vision of the future makes allusion to baptism only (XII. 442 f.), while in *De doctrina christiana*, appropriately enough, we are told that sacraments are 'not absolutely indispensable',[1] since nearly all Protestants look on sacraments as 'optional appendages'. 'The sacraments', we are assured by a student of theology, 'occupy a central and dominating position in the spiritual life of the Catholic Christian which the specifically Protestant type of devotion does not concede to them'.[2] Few of Milton's predecessors and contemporaries could have stated the issue so calmly. For them it was the subject of harsh debate involving not only clamorous exchanges between Protestants and Catholics but thunderous attacks of Protestant upon Protestant as controversy spread to take in the Eucharist. 'Wee all know', lamented Donne, 'what differences have beene raysed in the *Church*, in that one poynt of the *Sacrament*, by these three Prepositions, *Trans*, *Con*, and *Sub*.' We cannot consider all these differences here but select one only for mention because it is fundamental. Robert Parsons, S.J., adequately if polemically summed up the Catholic view:

Sacraments, which according to our doctrine, are heauenly conduites and most excellent instruments, appointed by God, for deriuing of grace vnto vs in euery state and condition of Christian men; these fellowes [Protestants of course] doe first cut off fiue of the seuen, and the other two they doe so weaken and debase, as they are scarce worthy the receiuing.

Sermons (1627), p. 116. One must endorse all cautious remarks on Milton (e.g. Madsen, pp. 275–81) as on Shakespeare (e.g. Robert Speaight, 'Nature and Grace in *Macbeth*', *Essays by Divers Hands*, N.S. xxvii (1955), 89–108, and G. R. Elliott, *Dramatic Providence in 'Macbeth'* (Princeton, 1960)).

[1] *Works*, xiv. 201, being Bk. I, ch. xxviii, 'De obsegnatione fœderis gratiæ externa'. Like all Protestants, Milton accepted only two sacraments, baptism and the Lord's Supper. There are studies of each by Darwell Stone (1899, 1909), and of baptism by G. W. H. Lampe, *The Seal of the Spirit* (1951); an excellent general discussion by Oliver C. Quick, *The Christian Sacraments* (1927); and an historical study of transubstantiation by Charles Gore, *Dissertations* (1895), pp. 230–68. On the Catholic position see esp. St. Thomas, *S. th.* III. lxv. 1; the ecclesiastical formulations in *The Church Teaches*, ed. J. F. Clarkson *et al.* (St. Louis, 1955), pp. 257 ff.; and the discussion by M. M. Philipon, *The Sacraments*, tr. J. A. Otto (1954).

[2] N. P. Williams, in *Essays Catholic and Critical*, ed. E. G. Selwyn, 3rd ed. (1950), p. 369, who also quotes A. E. J. Rawlinson's comment on 'optional appendages'. Cf. *West. Conf.* xxviii. 5, and Andrew Willet, *Synopsis Papismi*, 2nd ed. (1594), p. 565: 'God hath not laid such a necessitie vpon any [sacrament], as that the want of them should cause hazard of saluation.'

Protestants were in no position to deny that they had weakened the sacraments, for they had done just that. Rudolf Gwalter put his finger on the real bone of contention when he attacked 'the error of the Papistes' in attempting 'to tye the grace of God vnto Sacramentes' and in holding that grace is 'poured into vs as by a Pype or Conduite, forasmuch as if we receyue the Sacramentes without fayth, they be vtterlye superfluous'. Gwalter's thesis is aimed specifically at the Catholic claim that grace is conferred by the sacraments *ex opere operato*, through the act performed, irrespective of the attitude either of the minister or of the recipient. As such a claim eliminates any need for faith, Protestants countered that a man may be justified 'even without the sacrament' so long as he 'only believe[s]'. Milton's statement that 'the Papists err when they attribute to the outward sign the power of bestowing salvation or grace by virtue of the mere *opus operatum*, seeing that sacraments can neither impart salvation or grace of themselves, but are given as a pledge or symbol to believers of the actual blessings',[1] is thus illuminated for us.

The Christian tradition supports both Catholic and Protestant views. Catholics may turn to Peter Lombard's definition of a sacrament as 'an efficacious sign of sanctifying grace' (*signum efficax gratiae sanctificantis*), and Protestants may invoke Augustine's statement that a sacrament is 'the visible sign of an invisible grace' (*signum visibile gratiae invisibilis*).[2] Bishop John Jewel did not distort the truth when he claimed that

these Sacraments, together with Tertullian, Origene, Ambrose, Augustine, Hierome, Chrisostome, Basile, Dionisius, and other Catholique Fathers, wee doe call *Figures, Signes, Markes, Badges, Printes, Coppies, Fourmes, Seales, Signets, Similitudes, Patternes, Representations, Remembrances, and Memories*. And wee make no doubt, together with the same Doctors, to say, that these bee certaine *Visible Wordes, Seales of Righteousnesse, and Tokens of Grace.*

Protestant apologists kept reiterating that a sacrament is 'strictly taken to be a seal of grace', 'a seale of sauing graces', 'a visible signe

---

[1] Seriatim: Donne, *Sermons*, vi. 247; Parsons, *A Little Treatise concerning Trial of Spirits* (Douai? 1620), p. 17; Gwalter, *Homelyes . . . uppon the Actes*, tr. John Bridges (1572), p. 463; Melanchthon, *apud* Whale II, p. 58; and Milton, *DDC*, *Works*, xvi. 201.

[2] *Apud* Joseph Pohle, *The Sacraments*, tr. Arthur Preuss (St. Louis, 1915), p. 9, and John M. Shaw, *Christian Doctrine* (1953), p. 294, respectively. On the background to the Protestant view consult Kelly, ch. xvi.

and seale of an inuisible grace' ('a signe, because it setteth forth Christ & his benefits to the outward senses of all: and a seale, because it doth effectually apply the same to the faithfull Receiuer'), and their choice of words is characteristic. Milton, who conceived of a sacrament as 'a seal of the covenant of grace', defined it formally as 'a visible sign ordained by God, whereby he sets his seal on believers in token of his saving grace, or of the satisfaction of Christ; and whereby we on our part testify our faith and obedience to God with a sincere heart and a grateful remembrance'.[1]

[1] Seriatim: Jewel, *The Apologie of the Church of England*, tr. Anne Lady Bacon (1600)' pp. 59–60; Donne, *Sermons*, ii. 255; John Mayer, *The English Catechisme Explained*, 4th ed. (1630), p. 495; Thomas Wilson, *Christian Dictionarie* (1612), p. 418; Stephen Egerton, *A Brief Method of Catechizing*, 29th ed. (1620), pp. 14 f.; and Milton, *DDC*, *Works*, xvi. 201 and 165. Most influential was Calvin's formulation (*Inst.* iv. xiv. 1), restated in England by William Perkins, *The Foundation of Christian Religion* (1591), sig. C1, and *A Golden Chaine* (1591), sig. O4ᵛ. See also *West. Conf.* xxvii. 1, and the statements collected by John Day, *Day's Festivals* (Oxford, 1615), pp. 164–88, and Heppe, chs. xxiv–xxvi.

8

Ascending by Degrees Magnificent

THE CHRISTIAN VIEW OF HISTORY

> In this light of eternity alone, is the Work of God seen
> aright, in the entire piece, in the whole design, from the
> beginning to the end.
>
> PETER STERRY[1]

I

A WELL-KNOWN passage in *The Iliad* avers that

> Like leaves on trees the race of men is found,
> Now green in youth, now withering on the ground;
> Another race the following spring supplies,
> They fall successive, and successive rise;
> So generations in their course decay,
> So flourish these, when those are passed away.[2]

The idea of recurrence underlying these lines is one of the great
commonplaces of ancient Greek thought. Throughout the millennium
after Homer, the Greeks generally viewed temporality as a cyclical
movement. From Greece the idea passed to Rome, where it was
summarily asserted by Seneca when he wrote that 'all things are
connected in a sort of circle; they flee and they are pursued. Night
is close at the heels of day, day at the heels of night; summer ends in
autumn, winter rushes after autumn, and winter softens into spring;
all nature in this way passes, only to return'.[3] This view is encountered almost everywhere we turn, whether it is to Polybius's affirmation of the cycle of periodical revolution, or to Virgil's commemoration

---

[1] *A Discourse of the Freedom of the Will* (1675), p. 166. The present chapter is an
abridged version of *The Phoenix and the Ladder: The Rise and Decline of the Christian
View of History* (Berkeley and Los Angeles, 1964); its supporting evidence of over
1,200 references is reduced here to essentials.

[2] *The Iliad*, VI. 146–9; tr. Alexander Pope.

[3] *Ad Lucilium epistulae morales*, XXIV. 26; tr. R. M. Gummere (1917).

of the circling centuries, or to Marcus Aurelius's conviction of the periodical renovation of all things—nor is it necessary to insist on its explicitness in both Plato and Aristotle. Yet this widespread persuasion that events occur in a series of cycles did not constitute, either for the Greeks or for the Romans, an interpretation of history, much less a philosophy of history. Such a possibility was not even entertained by them, not because they were unconcerned with history but because the very nature of the cycles deprived history of any ultimate meaning. Even Polybius, who regarded Rome's conquest of the world as history's apex, still viewed the Roman era as the crest of one of numberless waves endlessly crashing against the shores of the eternal world. This is not to say, of course, that the Greeks and the Romans deemed history useless; we are well aware of their reiterated conviction that history is a teacher of the first importance: a logical enough deduction when events are said to occur in an interminable series of flux and reflux. But our predecessors in Greece and Rome also realized that the generally inevitable and predictable is not necessarily so in particular, a realization which, when accepted with their belief that 'only what is unchanging can be known', contributed towards a decisive antihistorical tendency, particularly among the Greeks.[1] Hence the absence of any surprise in the Aristotelian thesis that history is inferior to poetry; hence indeed the justice in claiming that, on the whole, the Greeks and the Romans, while vitally concerned with history, were not interested in propagating a philosophy of history, much less any precise and rigid philosophy grafted to metaphysics. Their concern was capitally with the past and the present, and with the future only in so far as the notion of recurrence afforded—within the limitations suggested—opportunities for didacticism.

The Graeco-Roman cycles have their counterpart in nearly all other civilizations, even those as far apart from each other as Aztec and Hindu. However, in Israel we find a distinct exception to the rule, for in the Judaeo-Christian tradition history attains a position of unrivalled prominence and unique importance.

According to the Book of Daniel, 'the Most High ruleth in the kingdom of men, and giveth it to whomsoever he will' (iv. 17). If such a notion was nonsense to the Greeks, to the Jews it stemmed naturally from their conception of God. For the God of Israel is not

[1] R. G. Collingwood, *The Idea of History* (Oxford, 1946), pp. 20-21. I am indebted to Collingwood's thesis throughout this paragraph.

an impersonal abstraction, dwelling beyond the confines of the universe and utterly uncommunicable. On the contrary, as the Bible repeatedly insists, he is a living God,[1] and, because living, concerned actively with the affairs of his creatures, always preoccupied with their fortunes, constantly interfering in the course of human events whether to chastise or to reward, to punish or to commend, to destroy or to save. The psalmist, surveying the past history of Israel, typically saw the hand of God in every event:

We have heard with our ears, O God,
Our fathers have told us,
What work thou didst in their days, in the times of old,
How thou didst drive out the heathen with thy hand, and plantedst
them;
How thou didst afflict the people, and cast them out.
For they got not the land in possession by their own sword,
Neither did their own arm save them:
But thy right hand, and thine arm, and the light of thy countenance.
(Ps. xliv. 1–3)

The psalmist, contemplating the future and the multitude of dangers still encompassing Israel, goes on:

Through thee will we push down our enemies:
Through thy name will we tread them under that rise up against us.

Such an attitude is more a faith than a philosophy; but if we wish to state it in more sophisticated terms, we might concur that history is 'a process determined by the creative act of God vertically from above', or that 'the temporal is inwardly sustained, saturated, pervaded by the untemporal'.[2] In either case we take cognizance of the unique Jewish view that history unfolds under the vigilant eye of God, that it is acted out within a sacred framework. But God, far from being a mere observer of the human drama, is responsible directly for its progress, because, as has been said, history is 'the arena wherein his will expresses itself as action'.[3] The logical

---

[1] Deut. v. 26, Joshua iii. 10, 1 Sam. xvii. 26, Hos. i. 10, Jer. x. 10, etc. —as well as in the NT (Matt. xvi. 16, 1 Thess. i. 19, 1 Tim. vi. 17). On the Jewish and early Christian view of history, see esp. Oscar Cullmann, *Christ and Time*, tr. F. V. Filson (1951); John Marsh, *The Fulness of Time* (1952); Karl Löwith, *Meaning in History* (Chicago, 1949); R. L. P. Milburn, *Early Christian Interpretations of History* (1954); William Temple, *Christianity as an Interpretation of History* (1945); Jean Daniélou, *The Lord of History*, tr. Nigel Abercrombie (1958); and M. C. D'Arcy, *The Sense of History* (1959).

[2] C. H. Dodd, *History and the Gospel* (1938), p. 181, and Josef Pieper, *The End of Time*, tr. Michael Bullock (1954), p. 67.   [3] Whale I, p. 56.

inference, which the Jews did not hesitate to draw, is that God manipulates every aspect of the created order according to his eternal plan for mankind. Jewish historians and the great prophets manifest strikingly this outlook by asserting that God, in dispensing judgement, normally elects certain nations as instruments of his justice. Thus the tribes of Israel were repeatedly delivered, sold to the Philistines,[1] while Babylon later became 'a golden cup in the Lord's hand', Nebuchadrezzar was appointed the sword of God, and Cyrus the Great was crowned the anointed of the Supreme Judge.[2] God's own words, transmitted through Isaiah, are explicit enough:

> O Assyrian, the rod of mine anger,
> And the staff in their hand is mine indignation.
> I will send him against an hypocritical nation,
> And against the people of my wrath will I give him a charge,
> To take the spoil, and to take the prey,
> And to tread them down like the mire of the streets.
>
> (Isa. x. 5–6)

Yet once Israel was punished, God diverted his wrath against his former instruments, punishing the 'high looks' of the Assyrians and reducing Babylon to a 'desolation among the nations' (Isa. x. 12, Jer. l. 23). This view of the Divine Purpose might seem uncomfortably close to Thomas Hardy's President of the Immortals, whose hobby was to sport with his creatures. To the Jews, however, God was anything but unjust; even when they staggered under the burden of divine wrath, they were still persuaded of his justice. Moreover, despite Hardy and similar eccentrics, the emphasis in the Old Testament falls not so much on the winters of God's anger as upon the eternal spring of his infinite mercies. Jewish writers chose invariably as their theme God's covenant with Israel. That covenant is an explanation—'the shadow of the future thrown back on to the past'[3]—of God's constant efforts to safeguard Israel. And those efforts, the Old Testament maintains, are historically demonstrable; indeed, they *are* history.

We often think of the God of Israel as preoccupied exclusively with the affairs of the chosen race, yet the Old Testament presents him not merely as ruling a part of humanity but as 'the God of the

---

[1] Judges, *passim*. The cyclical theory of punishment and redemption is outlined in Judges ii. 11–23.
[2] Jer. li. 7; Ezek. xxx. 24; Isa. xlv. 1.
[3] Alfred North Whitehead, *Adventures in Ideas* (Cambridge, 1933), p. 82.

whole earth' (Isa. liv. 5). In the chapters following the account of creation in Genesis, we are given in outline the Jewish theory of how, out of the first man, arose the various nations of the world. The seemingly endless lists of names, so tedious to us, were of fundamental importance to the compilers themselves. As we pass from the generations of Adam to those of Noah and his three sons, and on through Abraham and Isaac and Jacob to Joseph, we realize that the roll-call of names is included to stress the essential unity of mankind, that under the one Lord of the universe there exists but a single family of nations, divided at various points in history, yet retaining still their unity under God. Though subsequent historians of Israel went on proclaiming their belief in God's particular interest in their nation, they continued to regard him as the Lord of all nations. None couched this belief more explicitly or more forcefully than the great prophets. The very first, Amos, clearly asserted that, before God, all nations are equally deserving of his punishments and his mercies—especially his mercies. Did not God bring Israel out of Egypt, delivering also the Philistines from Caphtor and the Syrians from Kir (Amos ix. 7)? God, speaking to Isaiah, used far more striking words:

> Blessed be Egypt my people,
> And Assyria the work of my hands,
> And Israel mine inheritance.
>
> (Isa. xix. 25)

Yet the most important difference between the Jewish and extra-Biblical views of history is the Old Testament conviction, often repeated, about the 'Day of the Lord'. Belief in the end of the world, involving universal judgement and the advent of 'new heavens and a new earth', was a late development in Jewish thought, its most notable proponents being the prophets—particularly Amos, Isaiah, and Zephaniah—and the author of the apocalypse in the Book of Daniel.[1] This belief, once widespread, completed the Jewish view of history, seen now to be linear, proceeding in a straight line from the six days of creation to the single Day of Judgement. During this progress from one end-point of history to the other, God manifests his purposes in and through everyday events, until at last all rivers of temporal history tumble into the vast ocean of eternity.

Only the author of Ecclesiastes among Hebrew writers took exception to this view. His prolonged meditation upon the nature of

---

[1] On eschatology consult the next Chapter.

things had directed him not to the traditional straight line leading to the Day of the Lord, but to interminable cycles:

One generation passeth away, and another generation cometh: but the earth abideth for ever. The sun also ariseth, and the sun goeth down, and hasteth to his place where he arose. The wind goeth toward the south, and turneth about unto the north: it whirleth about continually, and the wind returneth again according to his circuits. All the rivers run into the sea; yet the sea is not full: unto the place whence the rivers come, thither they return again. (Eccles. i. 4–7)

The original work, obviously the labour of a 'schismatic', was considerably revised by later writers and defended heroically as orthodox by a host of commentators. Even so, the extent to which the book departs from the predominating tenor of the Bible is inescapable. As Biblical scholars now agree, the Book of Ecclesiastes is the work of a sceptic, an early representative of a movement we shall again encounter as we near the later Renaissance.

But the mainstream of ideas moved on, disregarding imperiously such backwaters as Ecclesiastes. It bore along in its flow a fundamental idea emerging slowly out of a group of prophecies concerning the advent of the Messiah. The salvation thereby envisaged was not expected to take place outside but inside history, in conformity with God's normal method of 'working salvation in the midst of the earth' (Ps. lxxiv. 12). Hence Luke's elaborate care in recording that Jesus began his ministry 'in the fifteenth year of the reign of Tiberius Caesar, Pontius Pilate being governor of Judea, and Herod being tetrarch of Galilee, and his brother Philip tetrarch of Iturea and of the region of Trachonitis, and Lysanias the tetrarch of Abilene, Annas and Caiaphas being the high priests' (Luke iii. 1–2).

Jesus the Christ of God constitutes for Christianity history's 'constant uniqueness' because his advent marks the direct entrance of God into the historical process. Moreover, the God-man in executing the divine purpose lends significance to the entire range of human events, past as well as future. Jesus, it must be insisted, did not establish a new religion; indeed, as the New Testament constantly maintains, his birth was not the commencement but the climax of God's gradual revelation of himself to Israel. As the opening words of the Epistle to the Hebrews declare, 'God, who at sundry times and in divers manners spake in time past unto the fathers by the prophets, hath in these last days spoken to us by his Son, whom he hath appointed heir of all things.' The historical continuity claimed from Adam himself by Old Testament writers thus assumed even greater importance to the writers of the New. The very first chapter of Matthew's Gospel traces appropriately the ancestry of Jesus back to Abraham, beyond whom, of course, stood Adam. St. Paul made explicit the extension by stating that as through Adam all men were condemned, so through Jesus all were saved (Rom. v. 18). Using the traditional terms employed by Renaissance expositors, we may state that there is a 'streight and perfect line from *Adam* vnto *Christ*', 'a golden vaine, a golden chaine, consisting of many linkes, from the first *Adam* to the *second*'.[1] In this respect, we recall how extensive the historical typology of the New Testament is, how enthusiastic its reception by the early apologists, and how elaborate its further consideration by subsequent generations.[2] That impressive concern with types had the single purpose of confirming that all events before the Incarnation have meaning only in so far as they are seen to prepare for the advent of the Messiah. John Gaule's statement in 1629 is adequate: 'As doe Lines in their Point and Period; Circumferences in their Center; Riuers in the Sea: So doe both the Law, and the Prophets meet in Christ Iesus.'[3]

The New Testament does not relate the Christ Jesus merely to the past history of Israel, but maintains his relevance not only to the future history of Israel but to that of the whole universe. For the God-man is both historical and supra-historical, transcending the two end-points of history. On the one hand, he existed 'before the foundation of the world', and 'by him were all things created' (1 Pet. i. 20, Col. i. 16); on the other hand, the Last Judgement is also his personal task, although, 'when all things shall be subdued unto him, then shall the Son also himself be subject unto him that put all things under him, that God may be all in all' (1 Cor. xv. 28). Thus the significance of the Christ is more than local or national, it is cosmic, for he 'was, and is, and is to come', 'the same yesterday, and today, and for ever' (Rev. iv. 8, Heb. xiii. 8). The affirmation of the Old Testament that the God of Israel is also the God of the entire universe is thus further expanded in the New Testament. All barriers are now shattered: 'there is neither Greek nor Jew, circum-

---

[1] Lodowick Lloyd, *The Consent of Time* (1590), 'To the Reader', and John Stoughton, *XI. Choice Sermons* (1640), ii. 69. On the Messianic background of such statements see Aage Bentzen, *King and Messiah* (1955); Joseph Klausner, *The Messianic Idea in Israel*, tr. W. F. Stinespring (1956); and Sigmund Mowinckel, *He that Cometh*, tr. G. W. Anderson (Oxford, 1959).

[2] See above, pp. 128–30.   [3] *Practique Theories* (1629), p. 23.

cision nor uncircumcision, Barbarian, Scythian, bond nor free', 'no more strangers and foreigners, but fellow citizens with the saints, and of the household of God'—a cosmic brotherhood marching inevitably along the straight line leading to the end of the world (Col. iii. 11, Eph. ii. 19).

The Old Testament views history theocentrically, the New Testament Christocentrically. The chronology in present use by Jews and Christians is an eloquent testimony of their different attitudes toward history; for while both compute events from a fixed point, Judaism harks back to the creation of the world by God, but Christianity slices history in two with the designations 'B.C.' and 'A.D.' The Christ Jesus stands for Christianity at the very centre of universal history. Before his advent, all events led up to his birth in Bethlehem. Since his advent, all events are similarly linked to him in retrospection of his Nativity, which is an historical reality. In T. S. Eliot's words,

> Then came, at a predetermined moment, a moment in time and of time,
> A moment not out of time, but in time, in what we call history: transecting, bisecting the world of time, a moment in time but not like a moment of time,
> A moment in time but time was made through that moment: for without the meaning there is no time, and that moment of time gave the meaning.[1]

The meaningless cycles of flux and reflux in the Graeco-Roman attitude toward history are like the legendary phoenix, dying periodically only in order to revive again, while to Christians history is like Jacob's Ladder, 'ascending by degrees magnificent' toward the Eternal City, the Christ's presence not only suffused everywhere in the ladder but, according to Renaissance commentators, the ladder itself.[2]

II

The first apologists and the early Fathers, fully persuaded by the validity of the Christian interpretation of history, condemned the cyclical view of temporal events with impressive unanimity. Long

---

[1] *The Rock*, VII; in *Collected Poems* (1936), p. 199.
[2] Thus the Geneva Bible (1560) in a marginal note on Gen. xxviii. 12. With Milton's account as a starting point (*PL*, III. 501–15), I discussed various Renaissance interpretations of Jacob's Ladder in *TZ*, xviii (1962), 411–18. On the iconography of the figure see Louis Réau, *Iconographie de l'art chrétien* (Paris, 1956), II [i]. 146 ff.

before St. Augustine's decisive attack, St. Justin Martyr had looked askance upon the pagan affirmation 'that things will always remain as they are, and further, that you and I shall live again as we are living now, without having become either better or worse'.[1] Even Origen lashed out against the Graeco-Roman cycles,[2] though it was one thing for him to denounce them and another to extricate himself from their mazes.

Another aspect of early Christian thought proved even more decisive, providing the corner-stone of an idea that was to be fundamental to all subsequent expositions of the Christian faith. This was the claim that Christianity existed before the beginning of the world —a claim already advanced by the writers of the New Testament, but now the subject of further exposition by such divers commentators as Justin Martyr and Tertullian, Athenagoras and Clement of Alexandria, Origen and Augustine.[3] The shape of things to come began to grow noticeable towards the end of the second century in a treatise by St. Theophilus of Antioch to Autolycus, where we find a partly systematized recital of events since the beginning of the world. Shortly thereafter the *Chronica* of St. Hippolytus and the highly influential *Chronographiae* of Julius Africanus further conventionalized the tendency to hark back to the creation of the universe. From these the road leads to the great synthesis achieved by Eusebius of Caesarea.

Eusebius's celebrated *opus maius* on chronology is divided into two parts: the *Chronographia*, a narrative account of events since the Chaldeans, and the *Chronici canones*, a tabular compilation of synchronized dates drawn from Assyrian, Hebrew, Egyptian, Greek, and Roman history. Assuredly Eusebius's monumental labours were not entirely original, for he relied extensively on the work of Julius Africanus. Yet he did revise and improve decidedly upon Julius Africanus, notably upon his synchronized tables. He also placed his epoch-making account of the growth of the Church, the *Historia ecclesiastica*, within his comprehensive chronological framework. With the composition of the *Historia* we have at last the clearest divorce between Christian and Graeco-Roman historians. In an attempt to demonstrate that Christianity was not a recent religion,

---

[1] *Dialogus cum Tryphone*, I. 5; tr. A. Lukyn Williams (1930).
[2] *C. Cels.* IV. 67–68; v. 20–21; etc.
[3] Consult Johannes Beumer, 'Die altchristliche Idee einer präexistierenden Kirche und ihre theologische Auswertung', *Wissenschaft und Weisheit*, ix (1942), 13–22.

Eusebius lifted the curtain upon his *Historia* to a stirring vision of the events preceding even the creation of the world, beholding the Christ Jesus 'God by the side of the Father, the first and only offspring of God, before all creation and fabrication, both visible and invisible, the captain of the spiritual and immortal host of heaven'.[1] Thereafter, descending to the realm of history, we are led to witness God's gradual revelation of himself to the people of Israel, until the grand climax is reached in the Incarnation of the pre-existent Word. Here the first book ends. The rest of the work is similar in tenor, at every turn moving further away from the pagan historians with the recurrent affirmation that God marches through history in judgement or in mercy, and always in glory. Even so, Eusebius may not be regarded as the greatest exponent of the Christian view of history, for one fundamental idea, eschatology, is absent from his work. Other apologists had already insisted, and were to insist again, on the teleological aspect of history, notably the resurrection of the dead, for they appreciated that the unity of mankind can be maintained only through an affirmation not merely of a common origin but also of a common *telos* or end. But Eusebius, persuaded as he was that the triumph of Christianity under St. Constantine—ὁ τῷ Θεῷ φίλος[2]—was the terminal point in God's promises to mankind, neglected the ultimate end and thereby limited drastically his vision of history. However, he still occupies an honoured place in Christian historiography for his labours in chronology, for his ecclesiastical history, but most for disseminating still further the tendency to view history from 'the depth of the irreversible Divine Resolve'.[3] Numerous imitations of his *Historia* testify to its just popularity, although only the continuations by three Eastern historians of the earlier fifth century, Socrates, Sozomen, and Theodoret, are worthy of their predecessor. In the West the enthusiasm for Eusebius was greater still. Even before the fourth century had expired, the *Historia* was translated into Latin by Rufinus of Aquileia, with a supplement bringing the Eusebian account up to A.D. 395.

The Christian philosophy of history was most ably formulated by St. Augustine. His major work on the subject, *De civitate Dei contra*

---

[1] *Hist. eccl.* I. ii. 3; tr. Kirsopp Lake and J. E. L. Oulton (1926–32).

[2] Ibid. x. ix. 2: 'the friend of God.'

[3] Anton-Herman Chroust, 'The Relation of Religion to History in Early Christian Thought', *The Thomist*, xviii (1955), 62.

paganos, begun in 413 and completed in 426, was written in the apologetic and polemic vein typical of most of his writings. It was occasioned by Alaric's capture of Rome on 24 August 410, an event that generated pessimism among Christians and pagans alike. The inviolability of the now sacked Rome, containing the hallowed tombs of Peter, Paul, and thousands of martyrs, was to Christians synonymous with the stability of their religion itself. To pagans, the fall of the Mistress of the World could only mean violent disapproval by their gods of Christianity's triumphant rise. To friends and foes alike, therefore, Augustine resolved to address his great *apologia*. He concerned himself chiefly with two among numerous arguments: first, that the world had known far greater disasters in the past than the invasion of Rome; and secondly, that the importance attached to Rome was totally erroneous. What is a mere city in the progress of history from creation to the Last Judgment? Rome, indeed, is but a second Babylon, of the earth, and mortal. All that matters is the Eternal City in the Kingdom of God, of the heavens, and immortal. In the course of his arguments, Augustine dilated upon his sharp division between the two cities, the *civitas Dei* and the *civitas terrena*:

> Two loues therefore, haue giuen originall to these *two Citties*: selfe loue in contempt of God vnto the earthly, loue of God in contempt of ones selfe to the heauenly, the first seeketh the glory of men, and the later desireth God onely as the testimony of the conscience, the greatest glory. That glories in it selfe, and this in God. That exalteth it self in its own glory: this saith to God: *My glory and the lifter up of my head* [Ps. iii. 3]. That boasteth of the ambitious conquerours, led by the lust of souereinty: in this euery one serueth other in charity, both the rulers in counselling and the subiects in obeying. That loueth worldly vertue in the potentates: this saith vnto God, *I will loue thee, O* Lord, *my strength* [Ps. xviii. 1].[1]

The greater part of *De civitate Dei* is devoted to an exposition of, and commentary on, the progress of the world under the shadow of these two cities or states, now inclined toward the one and now toward the other. Augustine, like Eusebius, began his account with the supra-historical era before the creation of the universe; but unlike his great predecessor, he went ahead to affirm the end of the

---

[1] *De civ.* XIV. 28. On Augustine's view of history, see esp. Charles N. Cochrane, *Christianity and Classical Culture* (Oxford, 1940), ch. xii; Christopher Dawson, *The Dynamics of World History*, ed. J. J. Mulloy (1957), pp. 233–50; and Theodor E. Mommsen, *JHI*, xii (1951), 346–74.

world and the consummation of all things in God. Inestimably influential, Augustine, by capping the history of temporal events with the Last Judgement, gave more weight than ever before to the linear nature of history, beginning with Adam, with its 'central datum' in Jesus, and with its 'uni-dimensional movement in time' leading to the end.[1] In his sweeping view of history acted out *sub specie aeternitatis*, Augustine was at one with some of his predecessors in measuring the progress of the world by the Six Ages corresponding to the six days of creation. The first Age extends from Adam to Noah, the second thence to Abraham, the third to David, the fourth to the Babylonian captivity, and the fifth to the Incarnation; the sixth Age is presently unfolding, to be terminated at the Second Coming, with the beginning of the Seventh Age in which we are to rest eternally as God rested on the seventh day of creation.[2] Such a scheme clearly precludes the Graeco-Roman cycles; yet the thorough Augustine lost no opportunity to castigate the notion of the 'continuall rotation of ages past and comming'.[3] At the same time he elaborated further the providential view of history which the prophet Isaiah had long since consolidated, whereby God 'giueth kingdomes to good and bad; not rashly, nor casually, but as the time is appointed, which is well knowne to him, though hidden for vs'.[4] Augustine's contributions did not end here, for he also formulated, if not the traditional, the most widespread Christian view of time and eternity.[5]

St. Augustine is the greatest theologian among the Latin Fathers. His contemporary St. Jerome is beyond doubt the greatest scholar. Considering their contributions to the Christian view of history alone, we can readily see why their successors numbered them both among the four supreme *doctores ecclesiae*. Between them they shaped the course invariably followed by all historians until the Renaissance. All accepted Augustine's philosophy and Jerome's chronology. Jerome's *Chronicon* is, indeed, but a translation of the chronicle of Eusebius, yet it was Jerome's prestige as the translator of the Vulgate that guaranteed general acceptance of Eusebius in the

---

[1] Ernst Hoffmann, in *Philosophy and History*, ed. Raymond Klibansky and H. J. Paton (Oxford, 1936), p. 174.

[2] See esp. *De civ.* XXII. 30, and *De Genesi contra Manichaeos*, I. 23.

[3] *De civ.*, esp. XII. 13–14, 17–20.

[4] Ibid. IV. 33.

[5] I cited over thirty pertinent studies in 'The Renaissance View of Time', *NQ*, x (1963), 408–10.

West. In any event Jerome did more than translate the original into Latin; he carried forward the chronicle to his own day. Jerome's additions to Eusebius's basic structure soon invited further extensions by others, among them Bishop Hydatius of Chaves, followed by Marcellinus Comes and a number of other compilers.

Early in the fifth century Augustine in a letter commended to Jerome 'a religious young man, a brother in the Catholic fold, in age a son, in dignity a fellow priest, alert of mind, ready of speech, burning with eagerness, longing to be a useful vessel in the house of the Lord.'[1] The recipient of this high praise, Paulus Orosius, did not fail to measure up to Augustine's faith in his abilities. He was assigned the important task of elaborating the argument of *De civitate Dei* that the sacking of Rome, far from being the greatest calamity in world history, was only one of numerous similar catastrophes instigated by the Supreme Judge. The result of Orosius's labours, the *Historia adversus paganos*, so far surpassed Augustine's expectations, and had such an immense influence on later writers, that we might justly speak of the Christian philosophy of history as being Orosian rather than Augustinian. For his dates, Orosius made free use of Eusebius's *Chronicon*, by now the standard authority on chronology; for his argument, he summarized the thought of his predecessors, though relying always upon Augustine. Yet Orosius was not a slavish imitator. There is something very moving in his majestic survey of universal history from the creation to A.D. 417, tracing the rise and fall of the four great civilizations of the past, Babylon, Macedon, Carthage, and Rome, discerning in their fortunes the hand of a divinity shaping their ends, now supporting the righteous, and now smashing the proud and the wicked. So earnestly did Orosius try to impose upon history an orderly pattern that we are tempted to forgive his liberal manipulation of dates, as when he claims that since Babylon was conquered by the Medes 1,164 years from her foundation, so Rome was invaded by the Goths 'after an equal number of years'.[2] Ultimately, however, years and even centuries are of no consequence; what matters is that 'one God has directed the course of history'. Before the fifth century ended, Orosius's lucid exposition of the Christian view of history was officially approved by the Bishop of Rome; thereafter he enjoyed a popularity often unrivalled even by Augustine himself. Dante's

---

[1] Letter CLXVI, 2; tr. Wilfrid Parsons (1955).
[2] *Historia*, II. 3; tr. Irving W. Raymond (1936).

verdict that Orosius was 'avvocato dei tempi cristiani'[1] stands as the common view of the entire period until the end of the seventeenth century.

The legacy bequeathed to the future by Eusebius and Jerome on the one hand, and by Augustine and Orosius on the other, was confirmed by two works written before the end of the fifth century. One was St. Prosper of Aquitaine's *Chronicum integrum*, a world chronicle in annalistic form outlining the principal events from Adam to A.D. 455; the other was Salvian of Marseilles's *De gubernatione Dei*, a narrative survey of history since the creation, single-mindedly attempting to establish that God is present throughout history as 'a most anxious watcher, a most tender ruler, and a most just judge'.[2] In other words, we have the stage set, the principal plays already written, and different actors giving essentially similar performances. And so it was to be for more than a thousand years.

The chain of tradition stretching all the way to the Renaissance was strengthened in the sixth century by Cassiodorus and St. Gregory of Tours, and in the seventh by St. Isidore of Seville. Cassiodorus is responsible for a table of events from Adam to A.D. 519, and Gregory for the celebrated *Historia francorum*, which also begins with an account of the creation. Isidore in his *Chronica maiora* compiled yet another table of events from the creation to A.D. 615, and in his *Etymologiae* or *Origines*, the first authoritative encyclopaedia of nearly catholic scope, he included a condensed version of a chronicle in annalistic form.[3] This last version utilizes the division of universal history into Six Ages, already propounded by Augustine and others, but now incorporated for the first time into a formal chronology. But since ideas never remain static, this concept also underwent transformation at the hands of the Venerable Bede.

The major work of St. Bede, the *Historia ecclesiastica gentis anglorum*, demonstrates fully the traditional approach to history which unfolds, as did its prototype, the work of Eusebius, under the eye of Providence. In two other works also, *De temporibus* and *De temporum ratione*, Bede made use of the traditional idea of the Six Ages; but unlike Isidore, who had terminated his account with the Sixth Age, Bede concluded on an eschatological note of 'sublime devotion'[4] by advancing not only to a description of the Last

---

[1] *Par.* X. 119. [2] *De gub. Dei*, II. 1; tr. Eva M. Sanford (1930).
[3] *Et.* V. xxxix.
[4] Wilhelm Levison, 'Bede as Historian', in *Bede*, ed. A. H. Thompson (Oxford, 1935), p. 122.

Judgement but even to the Seventh and Eighth Ages that are to follow the terminating events of temporal history. Earlier exposition of these *eschata* in *De civitate Dei* may hide Bede's originality, yet it is there, in degree if not in kind, for Bede's conception first authoritatively introduces into chronology the Christian philosophy of history. But neither Augustine nor Bede could have foreseen that eschatology, espoused by both in their attempts to demonstrate the linear nature of history, was until the fifteenth century to remain the capital interest of Christian historiography.

The standard expositions of the Christian view of history enjoyed widespread popularity throughout the Middle Ages. According to Einhard, Charlemagne was partial to *De civitate Dei*, and the imperial preference appears to have been shared throughout the Middle Ages. The *apologia* of Paulus Orosius was easily the second most popular work, with Jerome's version of the chronicle of Eusebius, the *Historia ecclesiastica* of Eusebius, the encyclopaedia of Isidore, and the chronological and historical works of Bede coming after. To these must be added the *Antiquitates judaicae* of Josephus, widely respected not only as the universal history that it is, but also as a non-Christian source furnishing 'proof' concerning the divinity of Jesus.[1]

The historians of the Middle Ages, like their predecessors in Israel, were both particular and universal. They were universal because they attempted to be all-encompassing, thereby upholding the total jurisdiction of Providence throughout the created order. They were particular because each believed his nation to be God's ultimate concern. Of the strictly œcumenical works written during the Middle Ages, the most popular universal history was the *Chronica* of Sigebert of Gembloux, evidently concerned only with the period from A.D. 381 to 1111, yet continuing further the chronicle of Eusebius, Jerome, and Prosper of Aquitaine. Similarly, works concerned with 'origins' far outweigh those that were not. Some modest historians were content to hark back only as far as Abraham, while others preferred the Nativity as their starting-point. The majority, however, elected to commence their labours with an account of the creation. Though it is not possible to enumerate all the universal chroniclers, a representative list is called for, if only in order to demonstrate the variety of the writers' nationalities, callings, and stations in life. In the ninth century, soon after Bede's death,

[1] The celebrated and highly controversial *testimonium Flavianum* is in XVIII. iii. 3.

we already find universal chroniclers at work, two of the most noteworthy being Freculph of Lisieux and St. Ado of Vienne. By 1100, it has been estimated, Western Europe possessed nearly sixty universal chronicles.[1] As the dam finally burst, originality struggled for a time to survive but was drowned; by the eleventh century its epitaph was to be read in the world chronicles of Hermann of Reichenau, Marianus Scotus, and Lambert of Hersfeld, all of which propound the scheme of the Six Ages. The most noteworthy of twelfth-century world chronicles were Honorius of Autun's *Summa totius de omnipoda historia*, Peter Comestor's *Historia scholastica*, Gottfried of Viterbo's *Pantheon*, and the *Kaiserchronik*, the oldest metrical world history in the vernacular. In the next century we find Robert of Auxerre's *Chronologia* and Lucas of Tuy's *Chronicon mundi*, both of which elaborate the concept of the Six Ages. Universal histories continued to be written throughout the thirteenth century, mostly in Latin, but occasionally in the vernacular, for example, Brunetto Latini's brief section in his encyclopaedic *Trésor*, the well-known *Primera crónica general* of King Alfonso X surnamed El Sabio, the *Sächsische Weltchronik* usually attributed to Eike of Repgow, and the metrical world chronicles of Jansen Enikel and Rudolf of Ems.

Otto of Freising and Vincent of Beauvais represent in the vast sea of medieval historiography the inclinations of the period. The first, the Bishop of Freising (1114?–58), wrote the *Chronica sive historia de duabus civitatibus*, the most eloquent statement eschatologically of the Christian view of history, often enough proclaimed before but emerging now to the forefront because of contemporary pessimism over this world, which stirred the conviction that the Last Judgement was at hand. Otto shifted the centre of gravity from the Incarnation to the Second Advent. In outline his work is traditional enough. The two opening books review the history of the world from the creation of the first Adam to the birth of the second, with a running commentary interpreting the rise and fall of civilizations as evidence of God's constant presence in history; the next five books carry the narrative, still providentially oriented, from the Nativity to Otto's own time; and the last book sets forth the *eschata* of history, including the Last Judgement, the final conflagration, and the cessation of time in the Eternal Present. Throughout, however, the stress is on the *miseria rerum mutabilium*, constantly

[1] Louis L. Myers, 'Universal History in the Twelfth Century', *HLQ*, v (1942), 162.

accompanied by reminders that Otto and his contemporaries stood witness to 'the closing days' of history, that their times were 'threatening the approaching end of the world in consequence of the enormity of its sinfulness, and indicating that the kingdom of Christ is soon to come'.[1] Such is Otto's pessimism that, through his excessive emphasis on life's vicissitudes, he comes perilously close at times to an affirmation of the cyclical view of history; yet ultimately he did not lose sight of its linear nature, even though his stress was not on the alpha but on the omega.

The other towering figure of medieval historiography is Vincent of Beauvais (c. 1190–1264), the author of the most ambitious project undertaken in Christendom either before or since. His astonishing goal was a compendium of all available knowledge in his time. The wonder is that although Vincent fails to impress us with his critical acumen, he still succeeded in preserving, within the confines of a single work, the chief preoccupations of the period up to the Renaissance. His *Speculum maius* is not merely long; it is colossal. Of its three parts, the one that interests us here, the *Speculum historiale*, itself comprises nearly 4,000 chapters and has been estimated to contain one and a quarter million words. Inevitably, the *Speculum historiale* is a synthesis of traditional views. Beginning with an account of the creation, it progresses to the middle of the thirteenth century; but the *telos* is also kept firmly in view through an epilogue that describes in detail the last events of temporal history. And with this, appropriately enough, Vincent's work concludes.

If I have given the impression that during the Middle Ages original thinking had come to a standstill, we must remember that the medieval historians wrote under outrageously adverse conditions; that they wrote at all is a recognizably significant achievement: for they did not possess the satisfactory chronology that is the backbone of history, nor did they have the opportunities for research we have grown accustomed to accept. Moreover such was the force of tradition—'the gathered force of immemorial tradition'[2]—that minds bent before it naturally. Medieval education itself reflected this servitude to tradition, for instead of attaching any importance to the study of temporal events, it excluded history from its liberal arts altogether. Thus the composition of histories, beyond the compilation of merely derivative annals, marked by discriminating selection of

---

[1] *Chronica*, II. 13, and VII. 9; tr. Charles C. Mierow (1928).
[2] V. H. Galbraith (below, p. 238, n. 1), p. 12.

facts, sound evaluation of the events recounted, and a style commensurate to the argument, remains a considerable achievement. We must allow for the plethora of world chronicles which even the champion of the renaissance of the twelfth century confessed to.[1] Even so, most competent historians sprang up during the Middle Ages, like Adam of Bremen in the eleventh century, Villehardouin and Matthew Paris in the thirteenth, Froissart and Marsilius of Padua in the fourteenth, and at the peak of the period, the twelfth century, we have Eadmer and Ordericus Vitalis, Peter Comestor and William of Tyre, Otto of Freising and William of Malmesbury. This same century saw also multifarious attainments in architecture, in science and jurisprudence, in theology and philosophy. Lastly it stands out as the age of heresy.

In the meantime, developments in Britain were keeping pace with those on the Continent and deriving from the foundations laid by Bede. We must, on the other hand, note the passion of Anglo-Saxon writers for *De civitate Dei*, and note also four early native works that prefigure conspicuously the capital preoccupations of British historians throughout the Middle Ages. One is the *De excidio et conquestu Britanniae* of St. Gildas, which sees history progressing *sub specie aeternitatis*; the other is the chaotic *Historia Britonum* associated with the name of Nennius, which begins with the creation and adopts, among other schemes, the division of universal history into the traditional Six Ages; the third is the translation of Orosius's *Historia* by King Alfred, which confirms the widespread acceptance of the providential view of history; while the fourth is the group of texts constituting the *Anglo-Saxon Chronicle*, according to which events occur precisely 'as God had foreseen' them, the overthrow of enemies is the gift of 'the Lord of Victories', and disasters are the just punishment inflicted by the offended and incensed God ('such things happen because of the people's sins').[2] From world chronicles that are typical and all-inclusive, we may single from the twelfth century Florence of Worcester's encyclopaedic *Chronicon ex chronicis*; from the thirteenth, John of Oxnead's *Speculum chronicae*; from the fourteenth, Thomas of Malmesbury's *Eulogium*, Richard of Cirencester's *Speculum historiale*, and Ranulph Higden's astonishingly popular

[1] Charles H. Haskins, *The Renaissance of the Twelfth Century* (Cambridge, Mass., 1927), p. 237.
[2] *The Anglo-Saxon Chronicle*, ed. Dorothy Whitelock *et al.* (1961), pp. 77, 147, 162.

Polychronicon; and from the earlier fifteenth century, Andrew of Wyntoun's metrical world chronicle of Scotland and its English counterpart by John Capgrave, who glances tenderly back to Adam ('Adam was mad on a Friday, withoute modir, withoute fader'). All these writers commenced their accounts with the creation, but others, who did not, began with Noah or with the times of Brut, as we shall see.

Neither the medieval period in Europe nor the Middle Ages in Britain lend themselves to ready generalizations. In the twelfth century, for example, we come across that phenomenon, William of Malmesbury, whose *Gesta regum anglorum* begins not with the creation but with the year of our Lord 449. It is a work of rare impartiality, wide learning, exceptional style, paying all due attention to characterization and description. As its author self-consciously observes in his preface, he wrote it to extract from posterity 'if not a reputation for eloquence, at least credit for diligence'. Then the early thirteenth century saw established at St. Albans a school of history which began with Roger of Wendover shortly after 1215, continued with his successor Matthew Paris, and terminated with Thomas Walsingham well into the fifteenth century. Until recently the most serious problem confronting students of this period was the relationship between three of its earliest works: the *Flores historiarum* of Roger of Wendover, the *Chronica maiora* of Matthew Paris, and the *Flores historiarum* of 'Matthew of Westminster'. It is now believed that Wendover's work, extending from the creation to 1235, derives in its earliest part from other chronicles and strikes originality only after 1201. The *Chronica maiora*, beginning with the creation and terminating in or about 1259, is a revision of Wendover's work, but after 1235 continues in singularly original vein. The third, again starting from the creation, is largely borrowed from Matthew Paris and was erroneously attributed to the non-existent 'Matthew of Westminster' upon its publication in 1567. Of all English historians of the Middle Ages—our own great respect for William of Malmesbury notwithstanding—Matthew Paris traditionally earns the highest praise. No less discriminating an authority than Milton described Paris as 'the best of our Historians'.[1] We are told Paris was fond of saying that 'laziness is the enemy of the soul'. The massive work he left behind is ample testimony of fidelity to his

[1] *The Tenure of Kings* (1649), *Works*, v. 25. In my account of Paris I am indebted to V. H. Galbraith's brilliant lecture, *Roger Wendover and Matthew Paris* (Glasgow, 1944).

acceptance of this principle. Nevertheless it is assuredly not his prolific tendencies that have exalted him to the rank he occupies, nor his originality of thinking and research into original sources, both of which he avoided like temptations to sin. But he was nevertheless endowed with a personality as strong as that of his Byzantine counterpart, Michael Psellus.[1] Both are picturesque and vivacious writers, both held decidedly personal views, both commend and denounce with equal vehemence, both colour their works with their personalities and decorate them with captivating anecdotes and lively descriptions. The praise bestowed by posterity upon Paris and Psellus was not misplaced.

If we were to pause here, nearly a thousand years after St. Augustine, to seek the finest exposition of the Christian view of history, we would discover it neither in Britain nor in Byzantium, nor even among such impressive chroniclers of Latin Christendom as Otto of Freising and Vincent of Beauvais. It is to be discovered in the work of a poet whose style is answerable to his great argument. Dante does not win this distinction for echoing Augustine and Orosius but because in his *Commedia* he surveys history from the divine standpoint. His is an eloquent testimony that all temporal events, however haphazard they may seem and however tragic they may be, are vital links in the golden chain of history stretching from the creation to the Last Judgement. This truth struck him like a flash of lightning when, from the vantage point of the Eternal Present, he beheld the 'universal form' of all things

> legato con amore in un volume,
> ciò che per l'universo si squaderna;
> sustanzia ed accidenti, e lor costume,
> quasi conflati insieme per tal modo,
> che ciò ch'io dico è un semplice lume.[2]

III

The achievement of Gutenberg (or whoever was responsible for the invention of moveable metal type) offered Renaissance historians the delightful opportunity to prepare world histories that were to be

---

[1] On Byzantine historiography, esp. the universalizing historians, see pp. 26–29 of the study cited above, p. 220, n. 1.

[2] *Par.* XXXIII. 86–90: 'bound by love in one volume, the scattered leaves of all the universe; substance and accidents and their relationships, as though together fused, after such fashion that what I tell of is one simple flame.'

at once more widely read and—if it were possible—even longer than their predecessors. One such massive work was Hartmann Schedel's *Nürnberger Chronik* (1493), which is distinguished less by its formidable size and more by the handsome woodcuts of Michael Wolgemut and Wilhelm Pleydenwurf. The *Nürnberger Chronik* follows the traditional pattern, commencing with the creation and dividing history into Six Ages. There follows a description of the Last Judgement with appropriately terrifying illustrations ingeniously introduced by six folio pages left totally blank.[1] This very blankness constitutes an obvious invitation to readers to take an inventory of their lives before the horrid end. The chronicle ends with a detailed account of the Seventh Age, when, as Spenser was to say in the last extant stanza of *The Faerie Queene*,

> no more *Change* shall be,
> But stedfast rest of all things firmely stayd
> Vpon the pillours of Eternity. . . .

The Renaissance ushered in a series of new ideas which were to pave the way for the ultimate secularization of history. Before turning our attention to those ideas, however, let us consider the attitude of Protestant Reformers. Generally speaking, Protestants adhered to the traditional interpretation of history, for despite their professed lack of interest in the accretions of tradition, their debt to Augustine for numerous aspects of their thought almost necessarily dictated their acceptance of his philosophy of history as well. Protestant historians have no surprises for us. Luther's widely influential annals, the *Supputatio annorum mundi* (1541), typify their efforts, for it commences, predictably, with the creation. The *Chronica* of Sebastian Franck (1531), deriving largely from the *Nürnberger Chronik*, likewise comprehends world history from the creation to the rise of Protestantism.

Protestant historians, without sharing the occasional pessimism of their medieval forerunners, believed fanatically that the end of the world was very near because they were sincerely persuaded that they were themselves accredited to warn mankind of the imminent Judgement. This attitude links nearly all reformers within the Judaeo-Christian tradition, weaving into the pattern the Hebrew prophets, Jesus and the early Christians, the puritans both of the Middle Ages and of the Renaissance, the societies of saints in

---

[1] *Registrum huius operis libri cronicarum* (Nuremberg, 1493), fols. 259–61ᵛ.

England as well as in New England, and finally the evangelists of our own era. Most histories written by early Protestants, coloured by this viewpoint, were thus marked strongly by eschatological tendencies which showed usually in their efforts to interpret world history on the basis of the Book of Daniel, especially according to its vision of the Four Monarchies (vii. 2 ff.). The extremely popular *Chronica* of Johann Carion (1531), edited and subsequently enlarged by Melanchthon, and the more explicit *De quatuor summis imperiis* of Johann Philippson surnamed Sleidanus (1556), constitute two of the most important works written in this mould. Both begin with the creation of the world, and both recount the fortunes of four monarchies: Babylon, Persia, Greece, and Rome. Of them Rome was dealt with in greater detail because of the persistent German view that the Christian empire stemmed from the Roman to form sixteenth-century Europe, now approaching its end in fulfilment of Daniel's prophecy.

Fundamental expositions of the Christian view of history abounded during the Renaissance. *De civitate Dei* was one of the first works to be printed and, in France, one of the first to be translated into the vernacular. Orosius's *apologia* proved just as popular, and by the beginning of the seventeenth century the works of nearly all medieval historians, foremost among them Vincent of Beauvais, had appeared in print. The humanists were directly concerned in all this activity: Scaliger reconstructed Eusebius's chronicle and its continuations, Erasmus introduced the 1522 edition of *De civitate Dei*, and Vives compiled the well-known commentary on the same work. Two other works, produced during the golden age of Italian humanist historiography, demonstrate convincingly the continuity of tradition; both are histories of the universe from the creation. The first was the *Chronica* of Archbishop Pierozzi of Florence, better known as St. Antoninus; the second was the *Enneades* of the famed humanist Marcantonio Coccio surnamed Sabellicus. But other massive universal histories continued to be written until well after the seventeenth century, originating from every corner of Europe.[1]

Such histories of the universe are related to numerous other works of the period, especially the innumerable chronologies I have cited elsewhere.[2] But affinities are even more extensive. In Portugal, for

---

[1] For over sixty-five continental and English titles see pp. 86–88 of the study cited above, p. 220, n. 1.

[2] 'Renaissance Estimates of the Year of Creation', *HLQ*, xxvi (1963), 315–22.

example, when António Galvão, the 'Apostle of the Moluccas', wrote a history of the passage to India, he began his survey with the discoveries since the Flood; in Switzerland, Bullinger's demonstration of the antiquity of Christianity began with the creation; while in France, Gabriel Naudé in his historical study of the occult sciences reverted to Adam.[1] Many histories of the Church also show these universalizing tendencies. Two of them, catholic in scope and staggering in length, offer good examples. The violently partisan *Ecclesiastica historia*, in thirteen folio volumes (1559–74), which was a co-operative labour supervised by the Lutheran theologian Matthias Flacius surnamed Illyricus, traces the development of the Church to the year 1400, century by century (hence the other title of the work, *Centuriae Magdeburgenses*). The *Annales ecclesiastici* of Caesar Cardinal Baronius, in twelve folio volumes (1588–1607), is a year-by-year account completed until 1198 before its author's death, and continued by other great scholars like Henri de Spondee and Odorico Rinaldi.

Although we consider such works in isolation, the Renaissance thinkers did not. The world histories, in fact, lent vital support to the elaborate cosmic structure I discussed in Chapter III: for as the Scale of Nature upheld a vertical unity in the universe, so the world histories affirmed a horizontal unity throughout the created order, from its inception at the act of creation to its termination upon the Last Judgement. The prime aim of both cosmic scheme and world histories was to proclaim the order pervading all existence. They fused into a conception of the universe so magnificent that, even if not quite responsible to demonstrable reality, was at least grandiose enough to offer a poet of the future the necessary background for a major epic.

During the Italian Renaissance the Christian view of history found still another champion in Giovanni Villani. His *Croniche fiorentine*, of universal scope, begins with the period immediately after the Flood; and because it is providentially oriented, it views Totila, for example, as *flagellum Dei*, the destroyer of Florence by divine decree.[2] Villani was in this traditional enough. His novelty is that he concentrated on the fortunes of a single city. Two centuries divide Villani's *Croniche fiorentine* and Machiavelli's *Historie*

---

[1] Galvão, *Tratado . . . dos diuersos & desuayrados caminhos* (Lisbon, 1563); Bullinger, *Der alt gloub* (Zurich, 1539); Naudé, *Apologie*, etc. (Paris, 1625).
[2] *Croniche* (Venice, 1537), Bk. I, chs. i–iii.

fiorentine, yet within this period the broad framework of universal histories broke and other aspects of the Christian view of history were damaged irreparably. Machiavelli did not demolish finally the traditional concepts because no man could single-handed have accomplished that. Nevertheless he affords the extreme example of deviation from traditional methods of historiography. One such deviation was readily noted by Thomas Fuller: 'I know *Machiavel* was wont to say; That *he who undertakes to Write a History, must be of no Religion*: if so, *he* himselfe was the best qualified of any in *his Age* to be a *good Historian*.'[1] Fuller meant, of course, to insult; yet to the brave new wits of the time his statement was, ironically, a compliment.

Deviations from tradition occurred very slowly, and if we may liken their aggregate to a play, then it was a long play featuring a variety of actors, foremost among them Leonardo Bruni surnamed Aretino, whose *Historiae florentini populi* represents current efforts to exclude all fables and legends and to rely only on authenticated fact; Erasmus, whose *Novum instrumentum* practises what he and other humanists so often preached, by paying attention to primary sources; Guicciardini, whose *Storia d'Italia* is the most strictly political history of the era, so half-heartedly oriented to the idea of providential control as to draw criticism; and Bodin, whose *Methodus ad facilem historiarum cognitionem* is in part a violent attack on the concept of the Four Monarchies. The secularization of history became so widespread that it was undertaken even by exponents of other disciplines like the science of international law which Alberico Gentili and Hugo Grotius developed at this time. International law, by uniting the human race under the auspices of an authority other than Providence, ultimately advanced its own view of history, whose secular character was acknowledged, cautiously, by Grotius, who observed that the existence of God was inessential to the validity of his theory. Others proposed new theories of history or revived old ones like the cyclical view which figures in Bodin's numerological mazes in the *Methodus* as in Louis Le Roy's eloquent statement of mutability in his popular treatise *De la vicissitude ou varieté des choses en l'univers* (1576). Such developments signal the abandonment of the providential view of history. Indeed, the scope of histories became ever more limited as the focus of attention gradually shifted from the supernatural to the natural, from the universe to nation, principality, city, and, as

[1] *The Church-History of Britain* (1655), Bk. x, Epistle Dedicatory.

hagiographies were displaced by secular biographies, to individual members of the *civitas terrena*.

During the Renaissance the division of history into Six Ages, together with the concept of the Four Monarchies, was accepted by 'ÿ moste parte of approued Authours'.[1] But the hallmark of the new historiographical temper is to be found in novel schemes of periodization. Their extensive variations are not nearly so important as the concerted effort itself to formulate and to adopt non-traditional schemes. One such scheme was proposed impressively early, had clear-cut implications, and exercised a decisive influence upon later historians. Petrarch, its author, located history's most crucial point in the decline of the Roman Empire, thus neatly disavowing the Christian claim that the Incarnation stands as history's central event. Later humanists, varying Petrarch, concluded that the sum of their activities amounted not to any 'renaissance' chronologically separate from preceding eras but to a revival of the Graeco-Roman civilization which had succumbed with the decline of Rome. The period of Greece and Rome thus became 'classical', the age ushered in by the humanists became 'modern', while the intervening centuries were termed—not always with consistency—'Middle Ages'. All three designations were standardized by the end of the seventeenth century and represented a scheme of periodization in diametric opposition to the Christian division of history into 'B.C.' and 'A.D.'[2]

Across the Channel Sir David Lindsay composed some time in the middle of the sixteenth century his *Dialog betuixt Experience and ane Courteour* (*The Monarche*). This lengthy poem epitomizes the three most important strains in the Christian view of history. First, it is didactic, and includes an account of 'ye miserabyll end off certane tyrane princis'. It is also a metrical version of the typical history of the universe, beginning with the creation and terminating in 'the moste terrabyll day of the extreme iugement'. It expounds,

---

[1] Thomas Fortescue, *The Foreste* (1571), fol. 23ᵛ. This work contains (in pt. i, ch. xi) one of the best summary statements on the Six Ages, translated from Pedro Mexia's *Silua de varia lection* (Valladolid, 1551), pt. i, ch. xxvi. In English poetry the concept appears in Spenser (see Isabel E. Rathbone, *The Meaning of Spenser's Fairyland* (1937), ch. ii) but not in Milton (notwithstanding the claim of George W. Whiting, *Milton and this Pendant World* (Austin, 1958), ch. vi).

[2] See H. Spangenberg, 'Die Perioden der Weltgeschichte', *Historische Zeitschrift*, cxxvii (1923), 1–49; Wallace K. Ferguson, 'Humanist Views of the Renaissance', *American Historical Review*, xlv (1939), 1–28; and Theodor E. Mommsen, 'Petrarch's Conception of the "Dark Ages" ', *Speculum*, xvii (1942), 226–42.

lastly, the providential theory of history, especially the common view that

> God, aye sen the warld began,
> Hes maid of tyrrane Kyngis Instrumentis
> To scurge peple, and to keill mony one man,
> Quhilk*is* to his law wer Inobedientis
> Quhen thay had done perfurneis his ententis,
> In dantyng wrangus peple schamefullye,
> He sufferit thame to be scurgit creuellye.[1]

As Dante Janus-like looks both backward and forward, so Lindsay not only closes the Middle Ages but leads directly into the Renaissance. His threefold formulation of the traditional views, far from expiring with him, survived beyond the Renaissance.

The Renaissance view that history is 'a most clere and perfect myrror' wherein one may behold 'the very lyuely Image and expresse figur of his inward mind enstructyng him how to gwyde and order himself in all things'[2] needs no elaboration here; its reiteration makes it a great commonplace of the age.[3] To Christian writers the capital lesson of history was self-apparent. Richard Brathwait, after glancing swiftly across the centuries, became positively ecstatic:

What ambitious Tyrants proud of their owne strength, and secure of diuine power, are laid flat in the height of their expectancies: so as where they planted the foundation of their hopes, there they were most defeated, to expresse the prouidence, & all-working Maiesty of God, who disposeth of all gouernments, pulling down the tyrannical Empires, and setting wise and discreet Princes in their places.[4]

From here it is only a step to the widely accepted theory that God, as Lindsay observed, 'Hes maid of tyrrane Kyngis Instrumentis/To scurge peple', while George Petter's summary exposition of God's interference in human affairs applies its traditional base:

in the times of the Old Testament, God punished the wicked Jews by the *Chaldeans* or *Assyrians*, and therefore the King of *Assyria* is called the rod of Gods anger, Esay 10. 5. Afterward he punished the *Chaldeans* or

---

[1] *The Monarche*, ll. 4147–53; ed. Douglas Hamer (Edinburgh, 1931).

[2] Arthur Golding, *Thabridgment of the Histories of Trogus Pompeius* (1564), Epistle Dedicatory.

[3] See esp. D. T. Starnes, *MP*, xx (1923), 281–300; Willard Farnham, *MP*, xxix (1932), 395–410; Lily B. Campbell, *HLQ*, i (1937–8), 135–67, and *Shakespeare's 'Histories'* (San Marino, Calif., 1947), pt. i; E. M. W. Tillyard, *Shakespeare's History Plays* (1944), pp. 54 ff.; *et al.*

[4] *The Schollers Medley* (1614), p. 112.

Assyrians, by the *Persians*; the *Persians*, by the *Grecians*, the *Grecians*, by the *Romans*; . . . the *Romans* by other Nations, as by the *Goths* and *Vandalls*. . . . And of later times, how God hath scourged one Nation by another for their sins, and doth at this day, is well known unto all.[1]

The Ottoman Empire was 'at this day', as I have elsewhere pointed out, foremost among the scourges of God.[2] Yet extension of a theory initiated long ago by Isaiah also stirred argument that God uses all aspects of the created order, as 'by shooting out his three *evill arrowes* (so called in regard of their evill effects) *Plague, Famine, Sword*'.[3]

The avalanche of universal chronicles testifies most eloquently to the persistence of the traditional view of history in England. Nor is the metaphor hyperbolic. England managed to produce her own formidable collection of universal chronicles in addition to innumerable translations of continental histories. The first such work of the sixteenth century, *The Cronycle of Fabyan* (1516), did not begin with the creation because, as Robert Fabyan explained, 'in the accomptynge of the yeres of the worlde from ẙ Creacion of Adam vnto the incarnation of Crist been many and sundry oppynyons'; and so, displaying remarkable critical acumen, Fabyan began with a much more reliable event, the Flood. Next we have *The Chronicle of Ihon Hardyng* (1543), which conveyed another aspect of the tradition into the sixteenth century, since it was a metrical version of the usual universal history. Hardyng, less scrupulous than Fabyan, chose to begin with Adam ('in all vertue/Was none him lyke in no place that men knewe'). Shortly after, John Bale, who concerned himself endlessly with 'origins', took matters even further. In *A Tragedye or Enterlude manyfestyng the Chefe Promyses of God unto Man* (1547?), he offered a dramatized panorama of the most significant events from 'before the heavens were create' to John the Baptist. In the meantime a young man, Thomas Lanquet, was composing *An Epitome of Cronicles* which started from the creation and reached out, 'through the thicke mistes and darkenes' of the past, to the Incarnation. Lanquet left his work unfinished, but Bishop Thomas Cooper completed it for him (1549) and Robert Crowley continued

---

[1] *Commentary upon . . . Mark* (1661), p. 1077. The same idea is most lucidly set forth by Guillaume du Vair, *A Buckler against Adversitie*, tr. Andrew Court (1622), pp. 76 ff.

[2] ' "The Bloody and Cruell Turke" ': The Background of a Renaissance Commonplace', *SR*, x (1963), 126–35.

[3] William Gouge, *Gods Three Arrowes* (1631), *passim*.

it to the reign of Elizabeth I (1559). Four years later Richard Grafton published an abridgement of yet another world history, expanded later into *A Chronicle at large and meere History of the Affayres of Englande* (1569), which also commenced with the account of creation by that 'deuine Prophet and Historiographer' Moses. But a far more ambitious project was already being planned as Reginald Wolfe, printer to the Queen, began to think in terms of 'an vniuersall Cosmographie of the whole world'. But Wolfe's death reduced his grandiose plans to a mere collection of *The Chronicles of England, Scotland, and Irelande* (1577), which did not fail to begin 'in the beginning whë God framed the worlde'. The editor of this composite work was Raphael Holinshed, who leads us, of course, directly to Shakespeare.[1]

The traditional attitude again received support from the antiquary John Stow, who in *A Summarie of Englyshe Chronicles* (1565), later renamed *Annales*, started his account with the Flood. It is, moreover, a sign of the times that Stow's work had by 1631 run through more than twenty revised editions. Equally interesting is the attitude of John Speed, for critical-minded though he showed himself to be when commenting on the futility of attempting to discover 'things so farre cast into the mistie darknesse of obscuritie and obliuion', he nevertheless signalled his agreement with Stow by commencing his own narrative with the Flood.[2] Encouraged by such formidable example, greater and lesser writers only too naturally compiled numerous similar chronicles. Most started with the creation, among them Lodowick Lloyd's *The Consent of Time* (1590), John More's *A Table from the Beginning of the World* (1593), Roger Cotton's *A Spirituall Song: containing an Historicall Discourse from the Infancie of the World* (1596), William Perkins's *Specimen digesti* (1598), and Anthony Munday's *A Briefe Chronicle . . . from the Creation* (1611). However, no work attained the popularity either of Sir Walter Ralegh's magniloquent discourse or Joshua Sylvester's translation of the poem by Du Bartas.

Du Bartas's *La Sepmaine ou création du monde* was first published in 1578 and was followed six years later by its sequel, *La Seconde Semaine ou enfance du monde*. By the first decade of the seventeenth

---

[1] On Shakespeare see esp. T. F. Driver, *The Sense of History in Greek and Shakespearean Drama* (1960), pt. iii, but also the studies by Campbell and Tillyard (above, p. 245, n. 3).

[2] *The History of Great Britaine* (1611), pp. 161 ff.

century the work had already been translated, in whole or in part, into Italian, German, Dutch, English, and Latin. Du Bartas, praised with restraint on the Continent, achieved in England phenomenal popularity: Sylvester's translation was a tremendous success, going through countless editions, Du Bartas thereby receiving unmerited recognition as 'a Poet above the ordinary level of the world'.[1] Judged as poetry, his work is found wanting; but judged by its scope and influence, it amounts to a major achievement, for it is easily the most ambitious metrical history of the universe available to Renaissance England until that time. It expounds in strict orthodoxy the providential view of history; and though the narrative is carried only to 586 B.C., history's end is kept firmly in view through the vision of the universal conflagration to be initiated by 'the *Chief-Chief-Iustice*, venging Wrath'.[2]

Ralegh's *History of the World* (1614) is equally orthodox. Fifty years after its publication Thomas Fuller could fault it only because it was left unfinished;[3] but though Ralegh did interrupt his narrative in 168 B.C., his work is as unaffected by its incompleteness as is *The Faerie Queene*. It ran through ten editions before the Restoration, which attests its enormous popularity, and repeated quotations from it throughout the seventeenth century attest equally an approbation verging on hagiolatry. The decision of Alexander Ross to abridge and continue it[4] is the most eloquent testimony to its essential orthodoxy. Nor can we dismiss lightly Ross's undertaking because he was excessively preoccupied with any deviation from the straightest and narrowest of paths: he chastised for their 'unorthodoxy' Sir Thomas Browne, Sir Kenelm Digby, Sir Francis Bacon, William Harvey, Thomas Hobbes, and all the followers of Copernicus and Galileo.

Though Ralegh's universal history is the best, it is far from unique in the seventeenth century. In 1659, introducing Denis Pétau's world chronicle to England, 'R.P.' observed that 'Sir *Walter Rawleigh* and others that have highly deserved by their Atchievements in the Theatre of History, have so voluminously inlarged themselves, that the Reader's patience is too discourteously oppressed'. Such thoughtful concern, once expressed, was soon

---

[1] William Hodson, *The Divine Cosmographer* (Cambridge, 1640), p. 147.
[2] Du Bartas, p. 12. I quoted the pertinent passage in its entirety in *HTR*, li (1958), 174 f.
[3] *The History of the Worthies of England* (1662), 'Devon-shire', p. 262.
[4] *The Marrow of Historie* (1650); *The History of the World: The Second Part* (1652).

forgotten; and universal histories continued to be written: James Gordon's *Opus chronologicum* (1617), Henry Isaacson's *Saturni ephemerides* (1633), William Vaughan's *The Church Militant* (1640), James Ussher's *Annales* (1650–4), Thomas Allen's *Chain of Scripture Chronology* (1659), William Howell's *Institution of General History* (1661). Moreover, a host of other writers, both before and after Ralegh, although preoccupied with enterprises other than the composition of world chronicles, still exemplify in their works certain aspects of the traditional attitude. Heywood's best non-dramatic work, the *Troia britanica* (1609), a comprehensive deposi-tory of myths cast within the framework of 'an Vniuersall Chronicle from the Creation', is a good example; so is Samuel Purchas's *Purchas his Pilgrimage* (1613), representative of the literature of travel, which he expanded into a universal history out of sheer inability to discard any of the consulted 'seuen hundred Authors, of one or other kind' (the kinds: 'Sacred, Prophane, Learned, Vnlear-ned, Ancient, Moderne, Good, and Bad'). Finally we have John Swan's *Speculum mundi* (1635), an encyclopaedic work of such catholic scope that it includes everything conceivable, and many things inconceivable, from the beginning to the end of history.

In order to appreciate the multitude of branches sprouting from the single tree, we should glance also at perhaps the most moving prose work of the English Reformation, the martyrology of John Foxe. Neither the author nor the work has fared well in modern times. The uncompromising verdict is that the work is 'the longest pamphlet ever composed by the hand of man', and its author 'the first great journalist in English history'.[1] Admittedly Foxe was a partisan, but he was writing in an age of profound partisanship. However, the purpose of the work, which transcends its frequent lack of literary merit, is what matters. The capital concern of Foxe was not so much to prove that the Vatican had turned 'truth into heresie', but to celebrate that 'true christian fortitude' which is patience and heroic martyrdom. His labours are for our purposes only too relevant: for in claiming that his work constitutes 'a liuely testimony of Gods mighty workyng in the life of man', he accepted the providential view of history; in harking back to the apostolic times, he clasped hands with all ecclesiastical historians; in record-ing the acts and monuments of the heroes of the faith as 'examples

[1] Charles Whibley, *Literary Studies* (1919), p. 45, and Hugh Massingham, in *Great Tudors*, ed. Katharine Garvin (1935), p. 379.

of great profite', he allied himself with the tradition of the *exempla*; while in his conception of true fortitude he looked not only back to the impressive tradition that had already translated patience from weakness into strength, but also ahead to the exposition of the same ideal at the outset of the ninth book of *Paradise Lost*.[1]

Though the traditional view of history seemed to meet with English approval, opinion in England was already merging with the stream of Italian historiography to become, in the two centuries following, a mighty torrent. The feverish activities of translators in England, more than in Italy, help us in our consideration of shifting viewpoints. Nearly all translators apologized for having stripped so many works of their original garments and dressed them with 'a playne English cote'. However, this signified little, for no translation was a light burden, but, as William Crosse said of his version of Sallust, each 'smelles of the Lampe'. Thus, despite their open disavowal of 'our vulgar toong', the pride they all shared in their native language and its potentialities is all too evident, and their concerted endeavours must be seen as contributing to the severance of the last bond uniting Europe, the Latin language. It is the works selected for translation that tell the real story. Though we are at first glance impressed by the quantity of theological and religious books rendered into English, closer scrutiny reveals that they are predominantly by continental Reformers. Only five of the older traditional texts were made available in English because circumstances of the time subjected them to discrimination. Thomas Lodge, for example, translated Josephus in 1602 probably less for doctrinal reasons than because Josephus was recommended by Scaliger and other humanists as a reliable historian.[2] Meredith Hanmer, in rendering the ecclesiastical histories of Eusebius and others (1577), was motivated by the peculiarly Protestant desire to proclaim what should still be done in order to eliminate 'the difference that is in these our dayes betwene the Church and the Apostolicke times'. Similarly, Thomas Stapleton translated Bede's *Historia ecclesiastica* (1565) in order to demonstrate 'the misse information of a fewe for displacing the auncient and right Christian faith'. Stapleton also pointedly observed that Bede is 'a countreman of oures', sounding a patriotic note which Thomas Habington rang

---

[1] See above, pp. 149–52.
[2] See Scaliger's *Opus de emendatione temporum*, 2nd rev. ed. (Leyden, 1598), Prolegomena, sigs. γ2ᵛ f.

again in 1638 when he published his version of the history of Gildas, who 'above a thousand yeeres ago' proved that England was not 'overwhelmed with Barbarisme' but was in fact the fountain-head of 'wisdome'. John Healey's celebrated translation of *De civitate Dei* (1610), a work only too enthusiastically welcomed by Protestants since Augustine was the guiding light of the Reformation, caps the four traditional works we have mentioned.

These five works excepted, none of the many expositions since Augustine of the Christian view of history was translated into English. The whole array of medieval world chronicles remained imprisoned in the original Latin, and even philosophers of history like Paulus Orosius were unavailable in English, which suggests that English eyes were no longer fixed squarely on the Christian tradition but on the historians of Greece, Rome, and Renaissance Italy, as we may infer from the impressive number of classical and humanist texts rendered into English.[1] Translations of Machiavelli's *Discorsi* and *Il Principe* supply our best evidence of the changing climate of opinion. Though numerous translations in manuscript survive, only those by Edward Dacres were published, the *Discourses* in 1636 and the *Prince* in 1640. Dacres wisely approached his perilous task with caution. In his preface to both translations he denounced Machiavelli's theories as pernicious, although he also had the courage to suggest that perhaps some good might still derive from the evil ('From the same flower the Bee sucks hony, from whence the Spider hath his poyson'). Machiavelli was of course widely known even without Dacres's 'English cote'. George Webbe, who was no enthusiast about 'this incarnate Deuill', nevertheless reported faithfully his claim to fame:

Alas he liueth yet, and is liked too much: his writings are too plentifull in Stationers shops, in Gentlemens studies, in Citizens chambers; yea it is to bee feared, that it is now growne habituall amongst vs, which a French writer complained, was crept in amongst his Countrimen; *They make Tacitus their Gospell, They studie Lucian more than the old Testament, and Machiauel more than the new.*[2]

Translations of classical and humanist historians yielded another villain besides Machiavelli. He was Hobbes, the translator of Thucydides in 1629. He launched a career whose impact on the old order

[1] See Henrietta R. Palmer, *List of English Editions and Translations of Greek and Latin Classics before 1641* (1911).
[2] *The Pathway to Honour* (1612), pp. 26–27.

later caused an alarmed Alexander Ross to answer in exasperation with his tellingly entitled *Leviathan drawn out with a hook* (1653).

The great interest taken in classical and humanist historians was stimulated by a belief that the Greeks and the Romans, as well as their heirs in Renaissance Italy, had drawn closest to the truth. Moses had by no means lost his place as the most accurate historian in the world, but his displacement had begun already in the Renaissance. In 1600 Philemon Holland, though referring to Livy, also accounted for the increasing partiality to classical historians. He said of 'that which most of all commendeth an historie':

an historie, . . . being *lux veritatis*,[1] ought especially to deliver with synceritie the whole truth & nothing but the truth, without respect of face or person: to keep only to the substance & train of the subiect argumēt; the due & orderly regard of the important circumstances thereto belonging, without inserting extravagant & impertinent by-matters, much lesse then, fabulous tales.[2]

Holland failed to specify the 'fabulous tales' he had in mind. Yet any intelligent reader could deduce that he was thinking of such legends as those of Brut and Arthur. By 1600 both were in a decline that was soon to be complete. This decline is attributable to factors that illuminate the historiographical temper of Renaissance England; and since scholars have been more generous in their treatment of Arthur, I propose to give my attention mostly to Brut.

Geoffrey of Monmouth (c. 1100–54) thought it 'curious' that both Gildas and Bede were silent about the noble eras of Brut and Arthur. To fill the omission he translated into Latin 'a certain most ancient book' that is supposed to have come into his possession, the *Historia regum Britanniae*. The book, which was almost certainly his own work, met with such wide and lasting favour that historical writing in England for the next four hundred years largely constitutes a series of footnotes to Geoffrey's imaginative 'history'. English medieval chroniclers inadvertently elevated the *Historia* to the level of the Book of Genesis, for if ever they did not begin with the Mosaic account of creation, they were almost sure to do so with Geoffrey's Brut. Bishop John Lesley's adaptation of the legend of Brut, written in Scots during the middle of the sixteenth century, demonstrates the continuity of tradition:

---

[1] Part of Cicero's celebrated 'definition' of history in *De oratore*, II. 9.
[2] *The Romane Historie written by T. Livius* (1600), 'To the Reader'.

Gif quha walde knawe the name of Britannie monie referris it vnto Brut*us* the sone of Siluí*us* Posthum*us* King of the Latines, and oye of Æneas, and him to be author baith of the name and natione of Britannie. The maist com*m*oune speiking is this, that xl. ʒeirs eftir the seige of Troy, quhill Brutus with grett sollicitude and kair was seiking a resting place with some troiane Iwalis and reliques, eftir sair trauell quhen mony dangeris he escaped had, at last he landet in Albion. Thaireftir the Ile he named Britannie, and his cu*m*panie britanis. Bot quhat vthiris lait writeris speik of this name p*er*chance mair curious than true, I, handeng me content with the opinione of ancient Antiquitie, regarde nocht.[1]

At the time Lesley wrote these lines Geoffrey's reputation was secure, but Lesley was well aware that some 'lait writeris' had begun to wonder whether such stories were 'mair curious than true'. Ranulph Higden had already decided that King Arthur was largely a mythical figure, while Erasmus bluntly dismissed the entire Arthurian matter as 'stupid'.[2] Brut fared no better. In the words of John Rastell, written as early as 1529, 'this story semyth more meruelouse thã trew & though it hath cõtynued here in Englõd & takyn for a trewth amõg vs Englyshmẽ yet other pepull do therfore laugh vs to skorne & so semyth they may ryght well'.[3] Five years later the Italian humanist Polydore Vergil in his *Anglica historia* (Basle, 1534) reconsidered the stories and repudiated them both as un-authentic. Though English historians drew generously on Vergil, his book was never once praised during the Tudor era. Indeed, it served as a rallying point of patriotic outbursts against Vergil ('that most rascall dogge knave').[4]

A single blow cannot kill a tradition, and so the legend of Brut persisted in the face of mounting criticism. In 1547 Arthur Kelton, contemptuously disregarding Vergil, published *A Chronycle with a Genealogie declaryng that the Brittons and Welshemen are lineally descended from Brute*, tracing the line even further back to Osiris ('the first kyng of Egipt'). Such claims, already numerous before Elizabeth's accession, became even more numerous during her reign. Thus in 1565 the antiquary John Stow, despite 'paynfull searche' into primary sources, accepted Brut's existence in agreement

[1] *The Historie of Scotland*, tr. James Dalrymple (1596), ed. E. G. Cody (Edinburgh, 1888), i. 2–3.
[2] *Apud* Myron P. Gilmore, in *Teachers of History*, ed. H. S. Hughes (Ithaca, N.Y., 1954), p. 15. On Higden see J. E. Housman, *RES*, xxiii (1947), 209–17.
[3] *The Pastyme of People* (1529), 'Prologus'.
[4] See the standard account by Denys Hay, *Polydore Vergil* Oxford, 1952).

with 'the most ancient and best approued Authours'; in 1574
John Higgins confidently commenced with Brut his extension of the
Mirror for Magistrates; in 1577 Holinshed dismissed criticism of the
legend firmly ('wee shall not doubte of Brutes hyther comming');
in 1589 William Warner added an appendix to his *Albions England*
to clarify the rather remote times of Aeneas, 'Patriarke of our
Brutones'; while a year later, in the most calculated defiance of that
rascal Vergil, appeared the first three books of *The Faerie Queene*.
But the new critics proved just as resourceful, since they were able
to enlist the cooperation of William Camden, England's 'rare
ornament' 'vniuersally admyred throughout Christendome'.[1] Camden was the most diplomatic of all writers on Brut. He refused in his
Britannia (1586) to start even with such an event as the Flood by
pleading ignorance ('whether there were any Islands at all before the
Deluge, it is not my purpose here to argue'), and going on to speak
of 'those reports of Brutus' as follows:

> For mine owne part, it is not my intent, I assure you, to discredit and
> confute that story which goes of him, for the upholding whereof (I call
> *Truth* to record) I have from time to time streined to the heighth, all that
> little wit of mine. For that were, to strive with the streame and currant of
> time; and to struggle against an opinion commonly and long since
> received. How then may I, a man of so meane parts, and small reckoning,
> be so bold, as to sit in examination of a matter so important, and thereof
> definitively to determine? Well, I referre the matter full and whole to the
> Senate of Antiquaries, for to be decided. Let every man, for me, judge as
> it pleaseth him; and of what opinion soever the Reader shall be of, verily
> I will not make it a point much material.[2]

After Camden the two extremes persisted. We have on the one hand
the enlightened attitude of such writers as John Speed, who paused
long enough to deliver the pun that 'neuer any such *Brute* raigned
in the world';[3] and on the other, the defenders of tradition, still
insisting that 'We are not *Brittons*, we are *Brutans*', and still scorn-
fully dismissing such 'strangers' as Vergil, who 'deserue not to be
laid in ballance to counterprize the authority of so many learned
Authors in our countrey'.[4] The traditionalists were, however,
gradually whittled down to a minority. The cautious mood of the

---

[1] Thomas Nashe, *The Terrors of the Night* (1594), sig. F3ᵛ.
[2] *Britain*, tr. Philemon Holland (1637), p. 6.
[3] *History* (above, p. 247, n. 2), p. 164.
[4] Richard Harvey, *Philadelphus* (1593), p. 2, and Edmund Howes, Preface to his
continuation of Stow's *Annales* (1631).

early seventeenth century is exemplified by Samuel Daniel's attempt to strike the proper balance between reliable sources ('the best approued Monuments domesticall and forraine') and opinions sanctified by time ('we are not . . . so freed, to trafficque, all vppon our owne coniectures, without custome of tradition'); yet even Daniel was compelled to reject the authenticity of Brut completely and of Arthur tentatively.[1] Hesitant criticism then grew into open rebellion, dramatically expedited by the collapse of the monarchy and the break with the past. However, only two years before, in 1647, Thomas May asserted in his *History of the Parliament of England* that it was no longer 'needful to begin the Story from times of any great distance', and by 1658 Francis Osborn, at the outset of his *Historical Memoires*, felt at liberty to denounce the traditional confinement to '*Patterns* and *old Forms*' and to challenge his contemporaries to '*new* and *forbidden Discoveries*'. By the Restoration in 1660 William Winstanley was uncompromisingly rebuking all past historians for confounding 'naked truth' with 'ridiculous falshoods'.[2]

Osborn's grand challenge did not constitute a revolution. As he himself must have known, it was merely the culmination of an evolutionary process to which translators of classical and humanist historians, and the critics of the 'fabulous tales' of Brut and Arthur, had each contributed a share. The rise of secular biographies as opposed to the hagiographies of the past, and the fragmentation of historiography brought about by Bacon's formidable influence, were also developments of importance. The revival of the cyclical view of history on the Continent too played its part, although it appeared in England under the cloak of an idea related with it. 'Mutability' was its most popular name; and the wheel was its most common metaphor, 'the euer-whirling wheele / Of *Change*, the which all mortall things doth sway'.[3] Appearances were saved so long as the gyrations of this wheel were assumed to be under the ultimate control of Providence. But more and more writers would not be so explicit, while certain others thought it was beyond their province to assume the role of a 'diuyne'. Ralph Carr's epistle dedicatory to

---

[1] *The First Part of the Historie of England* (1612), p. 2.

[2] *England's Worthies* (1660), p. 8.

[3] *The Faerie Queene: Mutabilitie*, VI. i. 1–2. On the cyclical view of history during the Renaissance, see Samuel C. Chew, *ELH*, vi (1939), 83–113; Herbert Weisinger, *JHI*, vi (1945), 415–35; Hiram Haydn, *The Counter Renaissance* (1950), pp. 428 ff.; Raymond Chapman, *RES*, i (1950), 1–7; Herschel Baker, *The Wars of Truth* (1952), pp. 65 ff.; and Ernest L. Tuveson, *Millennium and Utopia* (Berkeley, 1949), pp. 56 ff.

The Mahumetane or Turkish Historie (1600) furnishes us with an interesting example of changing attitudes. Acknowledging the Turks to be 'the terror of the West', Carr dutifully asserted that 'God almightie in his secret iudgements doth hasten their proceedings, to chastice the ingratitude of vs Christians for the small thankefulnesse wee show for so many his gratious benefits liberally (though vn-worthely) bestowed on vs.' Suddenly, however, he strikes a new note. 'But my office', he goes on, 'is not of a diuyne, hauing in purpose to make knowẽ onely what they [the Turks] haue euen from the first done, and daylie doe, rather then the reason of the deede.' Then comes the cyclical view of history: 'I am in opinion often a *Platonist*, assigning all mortall affaires necessarelie a periode in theyr perfection, to which hauing attayned, they fall into a retrograde of declining, vntill they be brought to the lowest degree which miseries can alot: nor there long continuing, againe and againe reuiue and arise from foorth the ashes like to the *Arabian Phœnix....*' Yet the ladder whereon Jacob saw angels ascending and descending still did not topple. It held firm, for a while at least, because of Milton.

IV

Milton's *History of Britain*, first published in 1670, was the product of the recent developments in contemporary historiography. Milton, being conscious of the admonitions of the humanists, consulted all the sources at his disposal; and he selected his material in such a diligent and constructive manner that he has been judged 'a judicious and conservative scholar'.[1] In his *History* he retained a number of the portents reported by earlier writers, but lest we are inclined to regard them as an obviously 'medieval' element in his work, we must remember that rarely did the humanists think it wise to forego popular superstitions. Even the critical Polydore Vergil wove into the fabric of his *Anglica historia* an overwhelming series of portents. Vergil, though not necessarily one of Milton's 'sources', constitutes one of his finest precedents. Milton not only resorted to portents but carried further Vergil's break with the annalistic form of history by writing as he did a continuous narrative. Milton's work is clearly an application of Vergil's conclusion that 'ther is nothinge

---

[1] Harry Glicksman, *The Sources of Milton's 'History of Britain'*, Univ. of Wisconsin Studies in Lang. and Lit. xi (1921), 140. The best study of Milton as an historian is by Sir Charles Firth, *Essays Historical and Literary* (Oxford, 1938), pp. 61–102.

misgivings concerning the conception of the Second Advent by 'the literall commentators',[1] and on the Continent, in an earlier and far more sweeping generalization, Calvin decided that nearly all *eschata* are 'images' of the actual truth, 'adapted to our capacities of understanding'.[2] With the notable exception of William Perkins, Calvin's attitude gained few disciples that I have been able to discover. Where nature's 'fearefull alterations' were concerned, commentators agreed in thinking that they were to occur—as Byfield put it—'in the very letter'. Hence this picturesque—and very typical—description by the popular writer Thomas Tymme:

in the dissolution and fall of this whole frame, . . . the sun shall be turned into darknesse, and the moone into bloude, and the starres shall fall from heaven, the ayre shall be full of whirl-windes, stormes, corruscations, flashing meteors, and thunders: the earth with fearfull tremblings, and swallowing gulfes: the flouds of the sea, shall swell so high, as if they would overflow the whole world: and the roaring and raging noise of the fretting billows, and tossing waves, shall greatly terrifie.[3]

Milton's formulation, while hardly identical with Tymme's, reproduces the generally received point of view. On the Day of the Lord, according to the *Nativity Ode*,

> to those ychain'd in sleep,
> The wakefull trump of doom must thunder through the deep,
> With such a horrid clang
> As on mount *Sinai* rang
> While the red fire, and smouldring clouds out brake:
> The aged Earth agast
> With terrour of that blast,
> Shall from the surface to the center shake;
> When at the worlds last session,
> The dreadfull Judge in middle Air shall spread his throne.
> And then at last our bliss
> Full and perfet is.
>
> (ll. 155–66)

For thoroughness, however, we must turn to the maturer account in *Paradise Lost*, where the Father thus magnificently addresses the Filial Similitude:

---

[1] *RM*, i. 45.
[2] *Apud* Heinrich Quistorp, *Calvin's Doctrine of the Last Things*, tr. Harold Knight (1955), pp. 123 f. On the theory of accommodation involved here, see above, pp. 9 ff.
[3] *A Silver Watch-Bell*, 18th impr. (1638), p. 51.

> thou attended gloriously from Heav'n
> Shalt in the Skie appeer, and from thee send
> The summoning Arch-Angels to proclaime
> Thy dread Tribunal: forthwith from all Windes
> The living, and forthwith the cited dead
> Of all past Ages to the general Doom
> Shall hast'n, such a peal shall rouse thir sleep.
> Then all thy Saints assembl'd, thou shalt judge
> Bad men and Angels, they arraignd shall sink
> Beneath thy Sentence; Hell, her numbers full,
> Thenceforth shall be for ever shut. Mean while
> The World shall burn, and from her ashes spring
> New Heav'n and Earth, wherein the just shall dwell,
> And after all thir tribulations long
> See gold'n days, fruitful of gold'n deeds,
> With Joy and Love triumphing, and fair Truth.
> Then thou thy regal Scepter shalt lay by,
> For regal Scepter then no more shall need,
> God shall be All in All.

(III. 323–41)

Milton's evident stress on the dread aspect of the Second Advent is a commonplace deduction from the standard conception of the Lord Christ as the terror-inspiring Supreme Judge. Yet the ultimate tribunal was conceived not only in terms of dread but also in terms of glory. In Arthur Dent's summary of the traditional view, 'the comming of Christ shall not be base and contemptible, as in the first visitation: but it shall be most terrible, princely, and glorious'.[1]

The literal conception of the Last Judgement by Renaissance thinkers is nowhere more clearly evident than in their view of the resurrection of the dead. The orthodox position was lucid in the extreme: 'at the sound of the trumpet, the elect, which were dead, shall arise with their bodies: and those very bodies, which were turned to dust, and one part rent from another, shall by the omnipotent power of God, be restored, and the soules of them shall descend from heauen, and bee brought againe into those bodies.'[2] The strain that this point of view necessarily imposed on man's credulity was appreciated by a number of apologists, among them the Lutheran theologian Otto Werdmüller, who readily confessed that 'at all tymes it hath been a hard thyng for man to beleue, ẏ the

---

[1] *The Plaine-Mans Path-way to Heaven*, 25th ed. (1640), p. 379.
[2] William Perkins, *A Golden Chaine* (1591), sig. S5.

bodyes, which are buryed and resolued to corrupcion, shoulde wholy, wyth oute imperfeccyon or blemysh, be broughte agayne, and restored'; none the less, Werdmüller continued, the Christian faith calls for precisely such an assent, that 'euen the very same body, which at the firste was made of duste, and now into dust is sowen, and thorow the corrupciõ is become dust agayne, yea euen that very body and none other, shalbe raysed vp'.[1]

The extent of the opposition may be gathered partly from the frequent complaints of the orthodox that the attempts 'to euacuate the resurrection of the deade' had multiplied alarmingly, and partly from their violent denunciations of the sceptics, tellingly identified as 'scoffing Athenians, Braine-sicke Philosophers, stupid Stoickes, hoggish Epicures, disputing Peripaticians'.[2] Given this formidable opposition, the spokesmen for Christianity resolved to present a unified front; whereupon we find Protestants no less than Catholics concurring with Cardinal Bellarmine that there is no doubt that the same bodies will be resuscitated ('the men shal be men, and the wemen shall be wemen').[3] Stressing the explicit affirmation of the resurrection of the flesh (*carnis*) by the Apostles' Creed, and leaning heavily on the expositions of the Fathers, Renaissance commentators defended the traditional interpretation by advancing two arguments in particular. On the one hand they insisted that the resurrection of the body is not a subject for discussion, since 'the roote and founda-tion thereof is in Faith'; and on the other, they reminded the sceptics that this article of faith is after all entirely consistent with divine omnipotence, for as St. Ambrose had observed long since, 'it would not be difficult for God to join together what was dispersed,

---

[1] *The Hope of the Faythful*, tr. Miles Coverdale (Antwerp, 1554?), pp. 86, 91. Of the numerous statements of this belief, I may cite Urbanus Rhegius, *The Twelue Articles* (1548), art. xi; John Northbrooke, *Spiritus est vicarius Christi in terra* (1571), ch. xliv; Thomas Burt, *The Glory of the Godlie Graine* (1607); Nicholas Byfield, *The Paterne of Wholsome Words* (1618), ch. xxvi; Alexander Gil, *The Sacred Philosophie* (1635), ch. xxxviii; William Hodson, *Credo resurrectionem carnis* (Cambridge, 1636), esp. ch. xi; and Henry More, *The Apologie* appended to *A Modest Enquiry* (1664), chs. iii–iv. For Donne's reiterated formulations, see *Sermons*, iii. 109; iv. 359; vii. 103, 105; viii. 92, and esp. 98. The NT doctrine has been studied by Robert M. Grant, *JR*, xxviii (1948), 120–30, 188–208; P. Hadfield, *CQR*, clviii (1957), 298–305; and Robert Martin-Achard, *From Death to Life*, tr. J. P. Smith (Edinburgh, 1960).

[2] William Hughe, *The Troubled Mans Medicine* (1546), sig. H5, and Stephen Jerome, *Seaven Helpes to Heaven*, 3rd ed. (1620), ii. 336.

[3] *Christian Doctrin* (above, p. 267, n. 2), pp. 100, 102. This is essentially a reaffirma-tion of the decree of the XIth Council of Toledo in A.D. 675 (Denzinger, § 287); but the Formula of Concord also maintained that 'precisely the substance of this our flesh . . . shall arise' (Tappert, p. 516).

to unite what was scattered'.[1] In retrospect, it seems unfortunate
that attention was so often diverted to irrelevant issues like the age
of human bodies at their resurrection.[2] On such matters, however,
Milton and the more responsible theologians of his age fortunately
retained a discreet silence. To him, as to them, the essential point
was that some day the numberless infinities of souls would arise to
join their scattered bodies—a belief which Milton maintained in the
Nativity Ode and *Paradise Lost* no less than in *De doctrina christiana*.[3]

The literal acceptance of the resurrection of the flesh by the
orthodox thinkers of the Renaissance is paralleled by their belief
in a cosmic conflagration that is to precede what Milton called the
'perfection and consummation' of all things in God.[4] That conception was founded upon the Biblical claim that the heavens and
the earth are 'reserved unto fire against the day of judgement', when
'the elements shall melt with fervent heat, the earth also and the
works therein shall be burned up' (2 Pet. iii. 7, 10; cf. Ps. cii. 26,
Isa. lxv. 17, etc.). The literal interpretations by Renaissance commentators were not without precedent. For instance, St. Thomas
Aquinas, in his lengthy exposition of the subject, concluded that
the nature of the ultimate fire will be identical with our elemental
fire[5]—a view that had become so widely disseminated during the
Renaissance as to justify Nathaniel Holmes's flat statement that there
is 'no Dispute among the Learned, but 'tis agreed on all hands, that
Physical, natural, material fire is here to be understood'.[6] St. Augustine had also emphasized that the final conflagration must be literally
accepted when he declared that the world will lose its form by

---

[1] Donne, *Sermons*, vii. 95, and Ambrose, *De excessu fratris sui Satyri*, ii. 58 (*NPNF*,
2nd ser., x. 183). Sooner or later commentators turned to the classic treatise of Athenagoras, *De resurrectione mortuorum*, though Protestants inevitably preferred the statements
of Augustine (see esp. *De civ.* XII. 20; *Sermones*, CCLXIV. 6; *Enchiridion*, LXXXII ff.; and
the discussion by Hans Eger, *Die Eschatologie Augustins* (Greifswald, 1933)). Cf. Baxter,
i. 55 f. The similar attitude of the Eastern Church had been summed up by John of
Damascus, *De fide orthodoxa*, IV. 27.

[2] The common theory was stated by Bellarmine: 'All shall rise . . . in that stature, and
in that state which they had, or were to haue, at the age of thirtie three yeares, in the
which our Lord rose. Aug. *Li. de. ciu. ca.* 15. So that the children shall rise, so great as
they should haue bene, if they had arriued, vnto thirtie three yeares, and the olde men
shall rise in that flowre of age, which they had, when they were thirtie and three yeares
olde' ([above p. 267, n. 2], pp. 103-4). For a Protestant statement of this same notion,
see Lewis Bayly, *The Practice of Piety*, 35th ed. (1635), p. 105.

[3] *Works*, xvi. 352.

[4] *DDD*, ibid. 367. Thus *PL*, III. 341.

[5] *S. th.* III. lxxiv.3.

[6] *The Resurrection-Revealed* (1661), pp. 26-27.

wordly fire 'as it was erst destroyed by earthly water'.[1] John Harvey's affirmation of this belief in 1588 is typical: 'as we assuredly know that the world had once his extreame κατακλυσμός, or watrie winter, at *Noahes* floud; so do we no lesse stedfastly beleeue that there shall once likewise be πύρωσις κόσμου, whereby it shall feele as extream a fierie sommer with burning flames, and brimstone from heauen, utterly consuming, and wasting euerie part, and parcell thereof.'[2]

But it is Milton who is the most distinguished English expositor of the literalistic belief in the conflagration of the universe. His first formulation of the common view was in an academic exercise,[3] but the detached statement of his greener days was replaced later in life by a stronger conviction. In *Paradise Lost* the concept appears with surprising frequency, first in the magnificent address of the Father quoted earlier (III. 334 ff.), and after the Fall in the promise of the Almighty that 'Heav'n and Earth renewd shall be made pure' (X. 638), in the angels' celebration of the 'New Heav'n and Earth' to be brought forth by the Son (X. 647), in the Father's reaffirmation of the same event (XI. 66), and in Michael's assurance to Adam and Eve that ultimately

> fire [will] purge all things new,
> Both Heav'n and Earth, wherein the just shall dwell.

That these lines conclude Book XI is all the more significant because, in the first edition of the poem (1667), the present Books XI and XII were joined, to be separated in 1674 at this very juncture. Milton, indeed, leaves no doubt about his belief in the termination of history by fire; Michael, interestingly enough, reasserts the concept on two more occasions. As the epic draws to its conclusion, he foretells that the heavens and the earth shall be purified and fused into one realm:

> the Earth
> Shall all be Paradise, farr happier place
> Then this of *Eden*, and farr happier daies.
> (XII. 463–5)

The Son of God, he affirms later on, will finally set fire to the universe,

---

[1] *De civ.* xx. 16. This commonplace is based on 2 Pet. iii. 6–7.

[2] *A Discoursive Problem* (1588), p. 31. For similar statements see Arthur Lake, *Ten Sermons* (1640), pp. 164–71, and Isaac Ambrose, *Ultima* (1650), pp. 94 f. A later discourse on the conflagration—seductively eloquent and imaginative—is Thomas Burnet's, in *Telluris theoria sacra* (1681; revised English version, 1684–90), Bk. III.

[3] *Naturam non pati senium*, ll. 65–69.

then raise
From the conflagrant mass, purg'd and refined,
New Heav'ns, new Earth, Ages of endless date,
Founded in Righteousness and Peace and Love,
To bring forth fruits Joy and eternal Bliss.

(XII. 547–51)

With these words Michael's revelation of the future ends; and
Adam, aware at last of the linear nature of universal history, acknowledges its predetermined progress through time until time itself
stands fixed (XII. 555).

IV

Notwithstanding the attitude of Milton in *Paradise Lost*, Christians
have not always maintained that time will necessarily cease upon
the Second Advent. So long as commentators tended to interpret
the Johannine Apocalypse literally, it was inevitable that at least
some of them would expect time's cessation to be postponed for a
thousand years—for that, according to the Book of Revelation (xx.
1–6), will be the duration of the temporal reign to be established
by the Christ after his return. The resultant theory of chiliasm
or millenarianism, though enthusiastically espoused by a host of
'literall commentators' during the Renaissance, was promptly censured by the greater apologists of the faith as 'a prodigious and a
wonderfull madde errour'.[1] At the same time, it were patently false
to think—as did Stephen Jerome in 1619—that 'the whole streame
of the Auncients haue runne counter' to the millenarian theory; in
point of fact, chiliasm was 'a most antient and Primitive Doctrine'—
'very ancient', as John Hales observed, 'and very general'—that had
enlisted the approval of nearly every theologian prior to the Council
of Nicaea, among them the author of the Epistle of Barnabas, Papias
and Justin Martyr, Irenaeus and Tertullian.[2] If after Augustine

---

[1] Erasmus, *Exposition . . . of the Cōmune Crede* (1533), sigs. L3ᵛ–L4. Of the Protestant
theologians who reacted adversely, see Luther, *apud* Köstlin (above, p. 265, n. 2), II.
575; Calvin, *apud* Quistorp (p. 273, n. 2), pp. 158 ff.; Bullinger (p. 265, n. 6), p. 221;
Rudolf Gwalter, *Homelyes . . . uppon the Actes*, tr. John Bridges (1572), p. 98; *et al*. The
arguments advanced against the Christ's millennial reign on earth often included
absurdities such as this: 'I do not see how the Saints can spare him out of heaven so
long' (William Bridge, *Christs Coming* (1648), p. 6).
[2] Seriatim: Stephen Jerome, *Origens Repentance* (1619), sig. A2; Sir James Harrington, *A Holy Oyl* (1669), p. 217; and Hales, *Sermons preach'd at Eton* (1660), p. 41. On
the chiliasm of the early Church, consult Ernst Wadstein, *Die eschatologische Ideengruppe*
(Leipzig, 1896), pt. ii; Archibald Robertson, *Regnum Dei* (1901), ch. iv; T. Francis

chiliasm continued to decline but for an occasional exception such as 'Ambrosiaster', the tradition had none the less been established and could be invoked, if need were, to justify its revival by Protestants. Hence, no doubt, the marked unwillingness of the opposition to denounce it in the abusive terms characteristic of Renaissance controversies: 'a fond surmize' was the worst description of chiliasm that Augustin Marlorat could think of, while Joseph Hall, who wrote a lengthy treatise to confute it, finally decided that the theory was after all not 'so deadly and pernicious in it selfe, as to make shipwracke of their own or others faith'.[1] I am not quite certain whether Hall would have been as conciliatory toward Milton, his antagonist in the ecclesiastical controversy of the early 1640's, had he known that Milton in *De doctrina christiana* had espoused chiliasm.[2] But if he had known this and objected to it, Milton no doubt would have replied with the reminder that chiliasm, besides being 'very ancient and very general', is securely grounded upon the New Testament. In *Paradise Lost* at any rate, in which Milton possibly enunciated his final conclusions, he silently passed over chiliasm.

Turning from chiliasm to the conception of life in the eternal hereafter, we progress from the fringe of Christian eschatology to its very core. The torments of Hell are at present conceived by the popular mind—if they are conceived at all—as being either physical or mental. If mental, the tendency is to allude to Milton's conception in *Paradise Lost*; if physical, then reference is usually made to the sermons of medieval and Puritan preachers. In part, no doubt, the popular mind is not deceived, for countless preachers had indeed chosen to stress the physical pains of Hell ('nastie smels, mens bodies frying: horrible sights, the damned gnashing: fearefull cries, the diuels roring: fire and brimstone').[3] In 1645 Francis Cheynell stated,

Glasson, *His Appearing and his Kingdom* (1953), ch. xiii; Tixeront, ii. 199 ff.; and Kelly, pp. 466 f., 473, 479.

[1] Marlorat, *Exposition upon the Reuelation*, tr. Arthur Golding (1574), fols. 272ᵛ f., and Hall, *The Revelation Unrevealed* (1650), p. 6. For a defence of chiliasm, see Holmes (above, p. 276, n. 6). Of other relevant works available in English, see the treatises of Thomas Brightman (1615), Johann Alsted [tr. William Burton] (1643), and Thomas Hayne (1645).

[2] *Works*, xvi. 385 ff. Milton was not always a chiliast, but he was certainly apocalyptically inclined most of his life: see Michael Fixler, *Milton and the Kingdoms of God* (1964).

[3] John Hull, *Saint Peters Prophesie* (1611), p. 411. Here I use only five of over two hundred authors invoked in my fuller discussion, 'Renaissance and Modern Views on Hell', *HTR*, lvii (1964), 217–36. A particularly relevant study is D. P. Walker's *The Decline of Hell* (1964).

before launching into an even more terrifying description, the rationale of the common attitude: 'I do so often thunder out damnation, that I might keep you from being damned',[1] which amounts to saying that the intention was to frighten people into Heaven. But this notion only formed a tributary in the long mainstream of Christian ideas, and though the tributary may have flowed turbulently on occasions, the truth is that in the mainstream the physical torments of Hell were subordinated to the mental. As Richard Carpenter summarized the tradition in 1642, 'the Divines say, that whereas there are two much different paines in Hell, *pœna sensus*, the paine of sense, caused by the fire of Hell; and *pœna damni*, the pain of losse, by the losse of God: the paine of losse, is the greatest.'[2] In *Paradise Lost* Hell comprehends both 'a fiery Deluge' and 'a frozen Continent' (I. 68; II. 587), though it is the theme of loss that pervades the poem from its very outset (I. 54 f.). Earlier William Perkins, influenced by Calvin, had affirmed that the torments of Hell are not 'bodily, such as bee inflicted in this world: but rather they are spirituall, being the apprehension and feeling of Gods wrath and vengeance, whose iealousie burnes like fire'.[3] But Milton, well aware of the traditional two aspects of Hell,[4] judged it best to avoid the singular views of Calvin and Perkins, as well as the other extreme position that was the excessively literal conception of Hell in terms of 'nastie smels' and other odoriferous details.

Though the Protestant apologists of the Renaissance were normally unwilling to say precisely where Hell is ('let hell be where it hath pleased God in his secret counsel to place it'),[5] they were none the less militant in their insistence that Hell is an actual place somewhere in the universe. For his part, Milton never doubted that Hell is an actual place as much as it is a state of mind. The Cambridge Platonists, with whom Milton is often allied, were frequently inclined to believe that Hell is '*rather a Nature* then *a Place*',[6] but the poet kept to the traditional notion that Hell is both a state within and an actual place in the 'utter darkness' of Chaos.[7] Milton's

---

[1] *The Man of Honour* (1645), p. 34.

[2] *Experience, Historie, and Divinitie* (1642), i. 88.

[3] *Commentarie upon . . . the Reuelation*, 2nd ed. (1606), p. 67. Calvin's view (*Inst.* III. xxv. 12) was anticipated at least by Nicholas of Cusa (*De docta ignorantia*, III. 10).

[4] See his statement on the *pœna damni* and the *pœna sensus* in DDC, *Works*, xvi. 371.

[5] Tymme (above, p. 273, n. 3), pp. 76–77.

[6] John Smith, *Select Discourses* (1660), p. 446.

[7] *PL*, I, 'Argument'. Hell is regarded as a specific place in *DDC* as well (*Works*, xv. 108; xvi. 372).

adherence to the traditional conception of Hell extended even to details, among them the notion that the fire of Hell sheds no light (1. 62 f.). 'Hell is presented to us by fire, but fire without light', declared Donne—wherein he looked with Milton upon the impressive tradition that in its steady progress included St. John Chrysostom's effort to explain that the fire of Hell 'as it hath not a nature of consuming, so hath it not of illumining, but it is a darke fire, the flame thereof giuing no light'.[1] At the same time, Milton refused to be drawn into the controversy still alive in his own day as to whether the fire of Hell is spiritual or material. This was wise, for had he committed himself in favour of the metaphorical fire of Hell, there would always be the alarming possibility that (as Bishop Thomas Bilson warned, giving his opponents something to think about) 'they that go thither shall find it no metaphore'.[2]

Protestant and Catholic theologians categorically refused to entertain the possibility of redemption for Satan and his disciples. Richard Sibbes spoke on behalf of the Western Christian tradition when he stated that the fallen angels would 'remaine in their cursed condition to all eternity'; indeed, added Sir John Hayward, were forgiveness to be extended to them, which is an impossibility, they could not repent because their wills are 'inflexible, they are immoueable from that which once they apprehend'.[3] Hence in *Paradise Lost* the fallen angels are by divine decree confined to Hell 'without redemption, without end' (v. 615), and this is followed in *Paradise Regained* by Satan's acknowledgement that 'all hope is now lost / Of my reception into grace' (III. 204 f.). Finally, again according to *Paradise Lost*, the fallen angels will be joined after the Second Advent by the reprobate on earth, whereupon 'Hell, her numbers full, / Thenceforth shall be for ever shut' (III. 332 f.). Collectively these statements indicate Milton's awareness of, and express disagreement with, the occasional claim of Eastern theologians that beyond the end of history the damned may be pardoned by Divine Love. This view, normally ascribed to Origen,[4] was denounced by Renaissance theologians with impressive unanimity. Thus Bishop

---

[1] Donne, *Sermons*, vi. 319, and Chrysostom, *An Excellent Treatise touching the Restoration*, etc., tr. Robert Wolcomb (1609), p. 51. For numerous other references see John M. Steadman, *Anglia*, lxxvi (1958), 116–28.

[2] *The Effecte of Certaine Sermons* (1599), p. 52.

[3] Sibbes, *Light from Heaven* (1638), ii. 17, and Hayward, *Davids Teares* (1623), p. 94.

[4] *De pr.* III. vi. 5. Cf. Clement of Alexandria, *Stromata*, VI. vi. 47, and Gregory of Nyssa, *Oratio catechetica*, XXVI.

Henry King, alarmed by Origen's inclination to place a limit 'not onely to the Paines of the Damned, but of the Deuils themselues', gave warning that 'to beleeue this is more dangerous than his Pity was foolish'.[1] George Rust's was the first major English treatise (1661) to argue against the prevalent views in favour of the ultimate restoration of the damned.[2] Milton may or may not have heard of Rust's work; in any case, adamant in his support of the unforgiving Western theologians, he was convinced to the very last that Satan's damnation is 'without end'.

The notion of eternal damnation, however convincingly argued by theologians, is not particularly attractive; but Milton, and Protestants generally, never went so far as some medieval expositors who even claimed that the joy of the blessed in Heaven will be increased by the sight of the torments of the damned in Hell. This view, born and nurtured in the West,[3] was also shared by Thomas Aquinas, who was canonized.

V

John Donne, referring to the many unsatisfactory attempts to describe Heaven, observed that 'the Holy Ghost is figurative, the Fathers wanton, and the School-men wilde'.[4] Yet the wantonness of the Fathers and the wildness of the scholastics are surely understandable, since they faced the very difficulties with which all Christian apologists have to contend in trying to describe the indescribable through a language that is inadequate, an imagination that refuses to soar so high, and a piety that commands restraint at every turn. There were, of course, a number of possibilities always open: one was to invoke the theory of accommodation, to claim with silver-tongued William Bates that all descriptions of Heaven are 'faint

---

[1] *An Exposition upon the Lords Prayer* (1634), pp. 332 f.

[2] *A Letter of Resolution concerning Origen* (1661), facsimile ed. by M. H. Nicolson (1933).

[3] G. G. Coulton, *Medieval Panorama* (repr. Cleveland, 1955), pp. 414–16, cites Thomas Aquinas, Peter Lombard, Vincent of Beauvais, Bonaventura, *et al.* Protestants generally avoided this notion. Two of the rare exceptions were Baxter, i. 96, and Henry Greenwood, *The Great and Generall Daye of Iudgement* (1606), sig. D3.

[4] *Sermons*, vii. 137. On the 'glowing language' used by some of the Fathers, see Kelly, pp. 486 f. The best studies of the traditional views are Ulrich Simon's *Heaven in the Christian Tradition* (1958) and *The Ascent to Heaven* (1961). The finest attempt to explain the Christian idea of Heaven is E. L. Mascall's *Grace and Glory* (1961). On the OT background consult H. H. Rowley, *Congregational Quarterly*, xxxiii (1955), 116–32, and Solomon Schechter, *Aspects of Rabbinic Theology* (1961), pp. 109 ff.

Metaphors' of the reality;[1] and another was to resort to the *theologia negativa*, to state what will *not* be found in Heaven ('no sicknesse, no sorrowes, no disease nor maladie, no crosse, no curse, no vexation, nor calamitie, no defect'—and so on almost endlessly).[2] But the method of accommodation was never really welcomed by the popular mind, which normally preferred such a work as John Vicars's *A Prospective Glasse to Looke into Heaven* (1618), a horrid poem that devotes over 2,500 incredible lines to Heaven's material possessions, notably its substantial collection of jewels. On the other hand, the negative approach was not always successful either, if only because disaster struck during the transition from the negative statement ('there shall be no Cripples, no blind nor diseased ones', etc.) to the triumphant positive conclusion ('Heaven is an healthful Country').[3]

Despite their difficulties Renaissance commentators refused to lapse into silence before the prospect of Heaven. Indeed on one occasion, when they composed their numerous expositions concerning the nature of the glorified bodies, their output increased. Though here speculation had already been excessively rife,[4] Protestant theologians were generally unanimous in their persuasion that the bodies of the blessed will be distinguished by four qualities: agility, subtlety, impassibility, and clarity or brightness.[5] Just as generalized was the standard view set forth by Thomas Burt in 1607, that the glorified body will have 'no slownes, no waightines, no massines, no cumbrance, no grossenes, none vnaptnes, (as it hath now:) But further it shall be made as subtile as ayer, as light as wind, as quick as lightning, as swift as thought, hauing all celeritie, dexteritie, abillitie, actiuitie, placed in the same'.[6] In all, the expectation was that the resurrected body will be 'metamorphiz'd', undergoing—as Milton maintained in *De doctrina christiana*—a distinct mutation.[7]

---

[1] *The Four Last Things* (1691), p. 276. On accommodation see above, pp. 9 ff.

[2] Thomas Tuke, *The High-way to Heauen* (1609), p. 188. On negative theology see above, pp. 9 f.

[3] John Hart, *Christ's Last Sermon* (1679), sig. B7ᵛ.

[4] According to Origen the resuscitated body will be spherical (σφαιροειδῆ); according to Justinian, upright (ὄρθιον). See Wilfred L. Knox, *JTS*, xxxix (1938), 247 f., and cf. above, p. 49.

[5] Thus John Woolton, *A Neuue Anatomie* (1576), fols. 42ᵛ ff.; Richard Sheldon, *Mans Last End* (1634), sect. vi; Joseph Hall, *The Invisible World* (1659), Bk. II, ch. viii; Donne, *Sermons*, vi. 73 f.; *et al.* On the similar Catholic view see Nicolas Caussin, *The Holy Court*, tr. Sir Thomas Hawkins *et al.* (1650), iii. 441 f.

[6] *The Glory of the Godlie Graine* (1607), pp. 33–34.

[7] *Works*, xvi. 352. The quoted word is from Quarles, *Divine Fancies* (1632), p. 20.

Once the subject of the glorified body was exhausted, Renaissance apologists again showed a reluctance to discuss details of the state in Heaven. On occasion, given the ever-present interest in things invisible to mortal sight, intellectuals were assured that once in Heaven they would have their fill of knowledge ('God shall create us all Doctors in a minute'), while men unwilling to forgo their wives even in Eternity were calmed by the guarantee that 'there is no doubt to be made, but that they shall know each other still in Heaven, though . . . after a spiritual and heavenly manner'.[1] In general every commentator, invoking the Pauline statement that 'now we see through a glass, darkly' (1 Cor. xiii. 12), agreed with Calvin that the Kingdom of God is for us all 'moste farre remoued from our sense, and remayne[s] as it were wrapped in darke speaches, vntill that daye come when he himselfe shall geue to vs his glorie to be seene face to face'.[2] Before the Day of the Lord the nature of the life everlasting must necessarily remain 'a mystery which hath no bottome',[3] a palpable obscure which only the faint metaphors of the poet-prophets can perhaps penetrate: in Dante's case, the eternal rose; in Milton's, the radiant centre toward which the angels advance irresistibly, to stand at last—orb within orb—'quaff immortalitie and joy'. The conduct of the angels in *Paradise Lost*, we see readily, is itself 'metaphoric': those in Hell are imagined prostrate before Satan (II. 477 ff.), but these in Heaven stand in dignified humility before God (v. 594 ff.). Both 'move', yet the devils merely to serve themselves, the angels in Heaven freely to serve others—Adam and Eve or, on another occasion, young Lycidas:

> There entertain him all the Saints above,
> In solemn troops, and sweet Societies
> That sing, and singing in their glory move,
> And wipe the tears for ever from his eyes.
>
> (ll. 178–81)

Milton, in common with the Christian tradition, upheld this quality of 'otherness' as the fundamental aspect of life in 'the blest Kingdoms meek of joy and love'.

---

[1] Donne, *Sermons*, iv. 128, and George Petter, *Commentary upon* . . . *Mark* (1661), p. 969.

[2] *Inst*. III. xxv. 10.

[3] Joseph Mede, *A Paraphrase* . . . *of the Prophesie of St Peter*, 3rd ed. (1652), p. 18. Mede was Milton's tutor at Cambridge.

INDEX NOMINUM

The asterisk designates individuals of the sixteenth and seventeenth centuries;
italicized numbers (or '*f.*') refer to quotations from their works. Editors,
translators, and Biblical personalites are not generally included.

INDEX RERUM

'Words, and lesse particles then words have busied the whole Church'
JOHN DONNE

PRINTED IN GREAT BRITAIN
AT THE UNIVERSITY PRESS, OXFORD
BY VIVIAN RIDLER
PRINTER TO THE UNIVERSITY